# Economic Transformations in Population Aging:

## Unlocking the Silver Economy

Zyed Achour
https://orcid.org/0000-0002-1578-9062
*University of Carthage, Tunisia*

Ihsen Abid
https://orcid.org/0000-0003-1358-7536
*Imam Mohammad Ibn Saud Islamic University, Riyadh, Saudi Arabia*

IGI Global
Scientific Publishing
Publishing Tomorrow's Research Today

Vice President of Editorial	Melissa Wagner
Director of Acquisitions	Mikaela Felty
Director of Book Development	Jocelynn Hessler
Production Manager	Mike Brehm
Cover Design	Jose Rosado

Published in the United States of America by
IGI Global Scientific Publishing
701 East Chocolate Avenue
Hershey, PA, 17033, USA
Tel: 717-533-8845 | Fax: 717-533-7115
Website: https://www.igi-global.com E-mail: cust@igi-global.com



Library of Congress Cataloging-in-Publication Data

Names: Achour, Zyed, 1966- editor
Title: Economic transformations in population aging : unlocking the silver economy / edited by Zyed Achour.
Description: Hershey. PA : IGI Global Scientific Publishing, [2026] | Includes bibliographical references and index. | Summary: "This book offers an interdisciplinary analysis of the silver economy, exploring how population aging reshapes markets, policies, and organizations. By integrating insights from economics, management, and sociology, it provides a holistic framework to address the challenges and opportunities of demographic transformation in the 21st century"-- Provided by publisher.
Identifiers: LCCN 2025039414 (print) | LCCN 2025039415 (ebook) | ISBN 9798337361178 hardcover | ISBN 9798337361185 paperback | ISBN 9798337361192 ebook
Subjects: LCSH: Population aging--Economic aspects | Older consumers | Older people--Economic conditions
Classification: LCC HQ1061 .E257 2026 (print) | LCC HQ1061 (ebook)
LC record available at https://lccn.loc.gov/2025039414
LC ebook record available at https://lccn.loc.gov/2025039415
British Cataloguing in Publication Data
A Cataloguing in Publication record for this book is available from the British Library.

# Table of Contents

# Detailed Table of Contents



This introductory chapter provides a systemic analysis of how demographic aging transforms into economic opportunity through the silver economy, a complex ecosystem generating trillions in value. Using an interdisciplinary approach combining economics, sociology, and management, it maps key actors, sectors, and mechanisms of value creation. The chapter identifies drivers and barriers to growth and proposes an integrated theoretical and methodological framework based on demographic, economic, and organizational indicators. Findings reveal the silver economy as a systemic transformation needing holistic strategies. This foundational analysis sets the basis for the volume, emphasizing a forward-looking interdisciplinary vision to harness the demographic revolution's opportunities.



Aging is reshaping economies, labor markets, and social systems worldwide. Far from a demographic crisis, longevity can be a source of innovation and inclusive growth when policy, technology, and institutions adapt to longer lives. This chapter examines the Silver Economy—the network of economic and social activities driven by and for older adults—and its potential as a foundation for sustainable development. Drawing on global policy frameworks such as the United Nations' Madrid International Plan of Action on Ageing and the European Union's Active Ageing Index, it analyzes how demographic change influences employment, innovation, and welfare systems. The chapter advocates an integrated approach that treats aging as a structural driver of transformation, requiring coordinated governance and investment in human capital. It concludes that the Silver Economy offers both an economic opportunity and a social imperative for the twenty-first century.

Social innovation represents a transformative approach to addressing the multifaceted challenges and opportunities presented by population aging. This chapter examines how social innovations—defined as novel solutions that simultaneously meet social needs and create new social relationships—are reshaping the silver economy landscape. Through comprehensive analysis of contemporary initiatives across healthcare, housing, employment, and community engagement, we demonstrate how social innovation catalyzes economic value while enhancing quality of life for older adults. The chapter synthesizes evidence from diverse geographical contexts, highlighting successful models of age-tech startups, intergenerational programs, co-housing initiatives, and platform economies designed for older populations. We present a framework for understanding the ecosystem enabling social innovation for aging populations, analyzing the roles of entrepreneurs, policymakers, civil society, and older adults themselves.



This chapter examines Living Labs as innovation catalysts in the silver economy, addressing global population ageing challenges. Living Labs are participatory environments where older adults co-create solutions with stakeholders in real-world settings, transforming how ageing technologies are developed. Analysis of cases from Europe, Asia-Pacific, Africa, and Latin America reveals how Living Labs address the 70% failure rate of gerontechnology by ensuring user needs drive innovation. Through co-creation, multi-stakeholder collaboration, and real-world testing, Living Labs develop effective ageing-in-place solutions whilst empowering older adults as active partners. Key challenges include digital divides, funding sustainability, and ensuring marginalised populations' participation. The chapter demonstrates that Living Labs provide essential infrastructure for demographic transitions, requiring supportive policy frameworks and sustained investment to maximise their potential for inclusive innovation.



This integrative review examines senior entrepreneurship through a comprehensive analysis of academic and institutional literature, with a particular focus on OECD economies and the silver economy context. It highlights the profound heterogeneity of entrepreneurial trajectories at later stages of life, shaped by individual resources, motivational profiles, and institutional environments. Drawing on the Resource-Based View and lifespan-oriented approaches, the chapter introduces the concept of mature resources, emphasizing the dynamic configuration of human, social, and financial capital among older entrepreneurs. The analysis also explores systemic barriers and enabling factors, including social protection systems, age-related discrimination, and policy frameworks. Finally, the chapter discusses implications for public policy and entrepreneurial support practices, contributing to a more nuanced and integrative understanding of senior entrepreneurship.



This conceptually based chapter draws from the thirty year action research case study, exploring how Carris Reels continuing efforts in 100% employee ownership and employee governance move forward concomitantly in support of its business success goals as a reel manufacturer and how these experiences might be applied to improve the quality of life in the upcoming silvering economy. Addressed in this chapter, is how the Carris Reels' experience provides and incentivizes developmental opportunities within its culture of belonging for its work-life processes at Carris to mature and increase personal capacities. Its employee ownership and governance are aimed toward improvement in quality of life, operations and production planning with safety and outputs as priorities through retirement benefits with the ESOP repurchase of company stock. As employee owners retire, their stock is repurchased by the company and then redistributed to the working employee owners.

The chapter explores the growing significance of the silver economy, the economic ecosystem surrounding aging populations, and its intersection with digital adoption and e-commerce. As global demographics shift toward older age groups, this segment represents an untapped market with increasing purchasing power. It proposes a multidisciplinary strategic framework integrating management, economics, and behavioural science to help businesses and policymakers engage older adults effectively. It identifies key drivers and barriers of digital adoption among seniors, emphasizing that adoption is shaped less by technology itself and more by behavioural, psychological, and social factors. Issues like age-based stereotypes, discriminatory marketing, and a lack of digital literacy hinder engagement. Conversely, social support networks and trust-building through user-friendly interfaces can foster inclusion.



Italy, one of the world's oldest countries, offers a preview of how population ageing will reshape Grocery Retail. For over-65s, grocery shopping is both a functional activity and a social ritual that supports autonomy and well-being. Yet retailers still overlook this segment or rely on outdated stereotypes, despite its size and growth. Grocery stores must serve multiple generations simultaneously, making inclusion a strategic priority. Drawing on 1,005 survey responses collected in 2025 by REM Lab, this chapter analyses how older shoppers behave, what they value, and where gaps emerge across pricing, assortment, services, private labels and communication. The goal is to highlight opportunities for more inclusive, evidence-based strategies that enhance the shopping experience for all ages.



This study aims to analyze the effects of the increasingly visible demographic transformation in the 21st century on Turkey's public finances in terms of the silver economy and uses deterministic dynamic modeling to analyze the dynamic

# Preface

## INTRODUCTION

*"By the late 2070s, the global population aged 65 and older is projected to reach 2.2 billion, exceeding the number of children under 18."*

*— United Nations, World Population Prospects*

We are living through one of the most profound demographic shifts in human history, yet societies remain surprisingly ill-prepared for its implications. By 2050, one in six people worldwide will be over the age of 65—a proportion that stood at just one in eleven in 2019. This transformation is not a distant prospect; it is already unfolding, reshaping economies, communities, and the very fabric of our societies. And yet, public discourse on aging remains largely anchored in outdated narratives of burden, dependency, and decline.

*Economic Transformations in Population Aging: Unlocking the Silver Economy* is published at a pivotal moment. As we move deeper into the 2020s, the silver economy has evolved from an abstract concept confined to academic debate and policy reports into a tangible economic reality. Valued at an estimated 15 trillion US dollars globally, it encompasses healthcare innovation, digital services, tourism, retail, and new models of work and enterprise. The question, therefore, is no longer whether population aging deserves attention, but how this demographic reality can be transformed into a source of innovation, resilience, and shared prosperity.

The urgency of this transformation lies not only in the scale of demographic change, but also in the convergence of multiple structural forces. Technological disruption, climate imperatives, shifting labor markets, and growing inequalities intersect with longer life expectancy in ways that challenge existing economic and institutional models. Today's older adults are healthier, better educated, and more digitally engaged than any previous generation. They are consumers with significant purchasing power, workers with deep expertise, entrepreneurs launching new ventures, and citizens calling for more age-friendly societies. Yet many economic systems, business models, and policy frameworks still operate as though aging were primarily a challenge to be managed rather than a potential to be mobilized.

This volume directly challenges that assumption. Bringing together scholars and practitioners from diverse disciplines and regions, *Economic Transformations in Population Aging: Unlocking the Silver Economy* advances a different vision—one in which population aging acts as a catalyst for economic and social transformation. The chapters that follow do not underestimate the challenges involved, including financial sustainability, social inequalities, digital divides, and market fragmentation. Instead, they approach these issues as opportunities for innovation, highlighting pathways grounded in social innovation, participatory design, inclusive business strategies, and integrated policy approaches.

A defining feature of this book is its ecosystem perspective. Discussions of aging are too often fragmented, with limited dialogue across sectors or disciplines. This volume deliberately crosses such boundaries by linking macro-level demographic trends with micro-level organizational and market strategies. It connects digital transformation with lifelong learning, retail innovation with financial protection, tourism development with employee governance, and environmental sustainability with healthy aging. In doing so, it reflects the interconnected reality of the silver economy, where innovation in one domain inevitably reshapes others.

The timing of this book also reflects a broader sense of urgency. The COVID-19 pandemic exposed the vulnerabilities of older populations while simultaneously accelerating digital adoption and underscoring the essential contributions of experienced workers. In the post-pandemic context, recovery strategies increasingly recognize the silver economy as a potential engine of growth. At the same time, climate commitments demand a rethinking of consumption patterns and resource management, with older adults emerging as both stakeholders and agents of change. As artificial intelligence and automation continue to reshape labor markets, the experience, adaptability, and accumulated knowledge of senior workers may prove more valuable than ever.

## ORGANIZATION OF THE BOOK

### Chapter 1: From Demographics to Market: Mapping the Silver Economy Ecosystem

At the intersection of demographic change and economic restructuring, this opening chapter maps the silver economy as a complex and evolving ecosystem shaped by interactions across macro, meso, and micro levels. It situates population aging within broader institutional, market, and societal dynamics, highlighting the expanding roles of older adults as consumers, workers, and entrepreneurs. Alongside these opportunities, the chapter addresses persistent challenges, including market fragmentation, social inequalities, and digital exclusion. By advocating a systemic and interdisciplinary perspective, it lays the conceptual foundations for understanding aging not as a constraint, but as a driver of innovation, inclusion, and sustainability in contemporary economies.

## Chapter 2: The Silver Economy Measuring and Steering Growth in Aging Societies

Rather than framing population aging as a demographic burden, this chapter conceptualizes the Silver Economy as an integrated economic system that mobilizes the needs, capacities, and productive potential of individuals aged 50 and over. Drawing on demographic, economic, technological, and policy perspectives, it highlights a paradigm shift toward innovation, growth, and social inclusion. Particular attention is devoted to measurement and governance tools, notably the Active Aging Index, as instruments for steering development in a sustainable direction. While acknowledging enduring challenges such as market fragmentation and social inequality, the chapter outlines strategic pathways that strengthen the roles of older adults as consumers, workers, and entrepreneurs, positioning the Silver Economy as a cornerstone of long-term societal resilience.

## Chapter 3: Social Innovation for Aging Population: Catalyzing Economic Opportunities in the Silver Economy

Population aging is examined here as a strategic opportunity for economic and social transformation through the lens of social innovation. Emphasizing participatory design, cross-sector collaboration, and systemic change, the chapter illustrates how socially driven innovations are reshaping domains such as healthcare, housing, employment, digital inclusion, and community engagement. Drawing on international evidence and comparative cases, it demonstrates how these initiatives simultaneously enhance older adults' quality of life and generate economic value. By repositioning older adults as active co-creators rather than passive beneficiaries, the chapter shows how inclusive innovation ecosystems can transform longevity into a sustainable demographic dividend.

## Chapter 4: Living Labs as Innovation Catalysts in the Silver Economy: Co-creating Solutions for Aging in Place

Living Labs are presented as essential innovation infrastructures for developing inclusive aging-in-place solutions within the silver economy. Against the backdrop of rapid global aging, the chapter highlights the value of co-creation approaches that engage older adults as active partners in innovation processes. Comparative insights from Europe, the Asia-Pacific region, Africa, and Latin America illustrate how Living Labs reduce the high failure rates of gerontechnological innovations by grounding them in real user needs. The analysis further addresses equity concerns related to digital divides and the exclusion of marginalized populations, while exploring the integration of emerging technologies such as AI, IoT, and robotics. Policy-oriented conclusions stress the importance of sustainable funding, scalability, and methodological adaptation in positioning Living Labs as pillars of inclusive silver economy development.

## Chapter 5: An Integrative Model of Senior Entrepreneurship in the Silver Economy

This integrative review examines senior entrepreneurship through a comprehensive synthesis of academic and institutional literature, with particular emphasis on OECD economies. Highlighting the heterogeneity of entrepreneurial trajectories later in life, the chapter shows how individual resources, motivational profiles, and institutional contexts shape entrepreneurial outcomes. Drawing on the Resource-Based View and lifespan-oriented approaches, it introduces the concept of mature resources, emphasizing the dynamic configuration of human, social, and financial capital among older entrepreneurs. The discussion also addresses systemic barriers and enabling factors, including social protection systems, age discrimination, and policy frameworks, contributing to a nuanced understanding of entrepreneurship within the silver economy.

## Chapter 6: Employee Ownership and Governance as a Strategy for the Silver Economy: The Carris Reels Case (1995–2025)

Based on three decades of mixed-methods research, this chapter offers a rare longitudinal analysis of Carris Reels' transformation from a family-owned firm into a fully employee-owned and employee-governed organization. The case illustrates how participatory governance, shared ownership, and a developmental organizational culture enhance resilience in the context of demographic aging. Particular attention is given to the benefits for older workers, including income stability, wealth accumulation, job security, and retirement protection. By emphasizing intergenerational learning, inclusive decision-making, and responsible succession planning, the chapter positions employee ownership as a strategic model aligned with the values and objectives of the silver economy.

## Chapter 7: Digital Adoption and E-Commerce in the Silver Economy: A Strategic Framework for Market Entry and Growth

The rapid expansion of the silver economy is profoundly reshaping digital markets, creating both strategic opportunities and new forms of exclusion. This chapter analyzes how demographic aging, rising purchasing power among older adults, and evolving digital practices are transforming e-commerce and service ecosystems. Integrating perspectives from management, behavioral science, and public policy, it explores structural, psychological, and social barriers to digital adoption, while underscoring the importance of trust, usability, and inclusive design. Comparative evidence from advanced and emerging economies illustrates how regulatory environments, digital infrastructures, and business models shape market readiness. Sectoral examples from health, wellness, fintech, and online retail support the development of a holistic framework for sustainable market entry, positioning the digital silver economy as both an economic opportunity and a lever for social inclusion.

## Chapter 8: Retail Grocery and the Silver Economy: Rethinking Strategies and the Retailing Mix for an Inclusive Shopping Experience

Focusing on the Italian grocery sector, this chapter addresses a striking paradox: despite representing a rapidly growing share of the population, consumers aged 65 and over remain largely underserved. Drawing on a mixed-method study combining corporate diversity reports and survey data from more than 1,000 shoppers, the analysis reveals how older consumers navigate inflationary pressures, digital transformation, and evolving store formats. The findings challenge prevailing assumptions, portraying seniors as price-conscious yet quality-oriented shoppers who value trust, fresh products, and in-store cues. The chapter argues for a shift away from age-based segmentation toward life-course events, such as retirement or widowhood, and outlines a forward-looking research agenda for understanding heterogeneity among aging consumers.

## Chapter 9: Exploring the Silver Economy: Public Finance Sustainability Using a Mathematical Model – The Case of Turkey

This chapter develops a deterministic dynamic model to analyze the implications of population aging and the silver economy for public finance sustainability. Combining formal mathematical proof with calibration based on Turkey's fiscal data, the model captures the long-term interaction between demographic pressures and expenditure dynamics. The findings demonstrate how small imbalances between revenue and expenditure growth can gradually undermine fiscal sustainability, even under disciplined budgeting. At the same time, the chapter highlights the potential of targeted policy measures—such as extending working lives or improving spending efficiency—to stabilize public finances in aging societies.

## Chapter 10: Healthy Aging and Resource Sustainability: Integrating Health Economics and Natural Resource Management in the Silver Economy

Healthy aging is explored in this chapter as a strategic nexus linking the silver economy, health economics, and environmental sustainability. Moving beyond narratives that portray aging as a fiscal burden, the analysis shows how preventive and eco-health approaches can transform longevity into a sustainability opportunity. By conceptualizing natural ecosystems as productive health assets, the chapter illustrates how green and blue infrastructures, digital health solutions, and community-based interventions enhance well-being while containing long-term healthcare costs. Drawing on economic modelling and comparative evidence, it argues that aligning fiscal planning, health governance, and resource management can convert demographic aging into a resilient and sustainable growth pathway.

# CONCLUSION

The silver economy is not about preparing for an aging society—we are already living in one. What is now at stake is not anticipation, but choice: whether longevity will deepen inequalities and strain economic systems, or whether longer and healthier lives can be harnessed as a source of innovation, growth, and social cohesion.

*Economic Transformations in Population Aging: Unlocking the Silver Economy* advances a clear proposition. The opportunities associated with population aging are real, but they will not emerge spontaneously. Transforming demographic change into a genuine dividend requires deliberate policy choices, forward-looking business strategies, inclusive innovation ecosystems, and, above all, a fundamental shift in perspective. Older adults must no longer be viewed as passive recipients of support, but as active partners in shaping more resilient, sustainable, and humane economies.

The chapters brought together in this volume offer both analytical insight and practical direction. They demonstrate what becomes possible when aging is no longer treated as a marginal concern, but recognized as a central economic and social challenge of our time. The silver economy is neither a future scenario nor a temporary trend—it is a defining dimension of contemporary transformation. This book invites readers not only to understand it, but to actively engage in shaping its trajectories.

**Zyed Achour**
*University of Carthage, Tunisia*

**Ihsen Abid**
*Imam Mohammad Ibn Saud Islamic University (IMSIU), Riyadh, Saudi Arabia*

# Chapter 1
# From Demographics to Market:
## Mapping the Silver Economy Ecosystem

**Zyed Achour**
https://orcid.org/0000-0002-1578-9062
*National Institute of Labor and Social Studies, University of Carthage, Tunisia*

## ABSTRACT

*This introductory chapter provides a systemic analysis of how demographic aging transforms into economic opportunity through the silver economy, a complex ecosystem generating trillions in value. Using an interdisciplinary approach combining economics, sociology, and management, it maps key actors, sectors, and mechanisms of value creation. The chapter identifies drivers and barriers to growth and proposes an integrated theoretical and methodological framework based on demographic, economic, and organizational indicators. Findings reveal the silver economy as a systemic transformation needing holistic strategies. This foundational analysis sets the basis for the volume, emphasizing a forward-looking interdisciplinary vision to harness the demographic revolution's opportunities.*

## INTRODUCTION: THE PARADOX OF DEMOGRAPHIC AGING

The 21st century is witnessing one of its most profound and accelerated changes: the aging of the global population.This phenomenon is transforming the very foundations of modern societies. According to United Nations projections (2022), the global population aged 65 and older is expected to reach 994 million by 2030, up from 771 million in 2019. By 2050, it could rise to 1.6 billion—more than double

DOI: 10.4018/979-8-3373-6117-8.ch001

the 2019 elderly population. These demographic transformations are not evenly distributed across regions. In 2020, nearly one in four people in Europe was over 60 (Eurostat, 2021). Japan, often seen as the archetype of advanced aging, recorded an old-age dependency ratio exceeding 50% in 2021, with only two people of working age for every elderly person (OECD, 2024). Meanwhile, most sub-Saharan African countries still maintain predominantly young populations, though demographic transition has begun there as well.

This rapid aging trend is especially pronounced in emerging economies, where demographic trajectories diverge sharply from those of Western nations. France, for example, took 115 years to see the proportion of people aged 65+ double from 7% to 14%. China and Singapore are set to undergo the same shift in just 27 and 19 years, respectively (Harper, 2014). This rapid compression creates both new socioeconomic challenges and major opportunities for actors who can adapt their strategies to changing demographic realities. Life expectancy is a major force behind this transformation. In most developed countries, it already averages around 80 years and is projected to reach 85 by 2050 (World Health Organization, 2021). More importantly, healthy life expectancy is rising as well, producing large cohorts of older adults who are active, autonomous, and possess substantial purchasing power. This qualitative shift has begun to reshape how aging is understood—no longer just a medical or social care issue, but an emerging driver of economic activity and innovation.

Where aging was once viewed primarily as a demographic burden threatening social systems and fiscal stability, recent years have seen a real paradigm shift. Empirical studies suggest that older adults no longer fit the outdated image of dependency and decline (Rothermund, 2024; Rasset et al., 2024). While many face negative stereotypes, research increasingly highlights the diversity of aging experiences and the capacity for adaptation—cognitive, social, and even professional (Wang et al., 2024). Some companies and regions have gone further, turning this challenge into an advantage. This is where the concept of the silver economy comes in (IMF, 2025). It refers to the full range of economic activity linked to aging—not just healthcare and eldercare, but shifting consumption patterns, product and service innovation, and even restructured value chains.

The economic footprint of the silver economy varies depending on measurement methods, but estimates are consistently substantial. In the United States, the over-50 population held purchasing power of $8.3 trillion in 2020, accounting for 56% of national consumer spending (AARP, 2020). In Europe, seniors generated roughly €3.7 trillion in annual value and supported 88 million jobs (European Commission, 2018a). In Japan, age-related spending reached 100 trillion yen—about 20% of its GDP (METI, 2019). These figures are not marginal and demonstrate a structural transformation of the global economy.

However, capturing the full potential of the silver economy requires more than tweaking products or services for older consumers. It calls for a systemic approach that moves beyond narrow sectoral thinking. The question is no longer whether aging occurs, but how societies can transform it into genuine economic value through innovation and new institutional mechanisms.

From a scientific standpoint, this question demands contributions from multiple disciplines: demographic economics, life-course sociology, gerontology, public policy, and management science, to name a few. Interdisciplinary thinking is no longer optional here (Foster and Walker, 2015). On the ground, the implications are just as broad, involving businesses, policymakers, local governments, and civil society.

This chapter builds its analysis across three interlocking levels. At the macro level, it maps the broader silver economy ecosystem: key players, dominant sectors, and structural dynamics driving this growing market. The meso level focuses on how organizations and industries are evolving—how business models, institutions, and service systems are adapting to demographic change. At the micro level, the focus shifts to processes of innovation, product and service redesign, and value creation within firms—often in close collaboration with older users themselves.

This multi-layered analysis rests on an original framework combining three dimensions. The demographic dimension examines changing age structures, socioeconomic profiles, and life trajectories of older adults. The economic dimension centers on value creation mechanisms, emerging business models, and sectoral trends. Finally, the organizational and policy dimension examines institutional responses—how firms, governments, and public agencies are shifting to accommodate a transformed demographic landscape.

Constructing this framework required drawing on diverse knowledge sources and analytical approaches. The chapter synthesizes interdisciplinary scholarship published primarily between 2015 and 2024, spanning demographic economics, gerontology, life-course sociology, and management sciences. This academic foundation is enriched by institutional assessments from international organizations—particularly the United Nations, OECD, European Commission, IMF, and WHO—whose data and projections provide empirical grounding for the analysis. The innovative adaptation models examined here were selected not for comprehensiveness but for their documented capacity to illustrate emerging patterns across different national contexts. Where quantitative indicators are presented, they consolidate measurement frameworks that have gained traction in recent aging economics literature, chosen for their international comparability and analytical rigor. This methodological approach allows the chapter to bridge conceptual depth with practical relevance, connecting abstract frameworks to concrete organizational and policy realities.

The goal is twofold. First, to offer a robust, interdisciplinary conceptual framework for understanding the silver economy in all its complexity. Second, to present a methodology adaptable to more detailed sector-specific studies. The approach is deliberately forward-looking: not only describing the current state of affairs but also anticipating future developments, emerging trends, and potential disruptions in an environment shaped by rapid demographic, technological, and social changes (Harper & Hamblin, 2014).

By weaving together these threads, this chapter aims to move beyond fragmented or siloed perspectives. The objective is to make sense of a structural, systemic transformation—and to support informed, strategic decision-making for the years ahead.

## THEORETICAL FOUNDATIONS OF THE SILVER ECONOMY

### A Multidisciplinary Conceptual Grounding

The silver economy has emerged as a truly interdisciplinary field. Understanding it requires moving beyond traditional academic silos and drawing simultaneously on economics, sociology, gerontology, and management sciences. This is not a stylistic choice but a structural necessity. Population aging is inherently multidimensional—shaping economies, social structures, and individual behaviors all at once.

In economics, the classical life-cycle hypothesis developed by Modigliani and Brumberg (1954) remains a foundational framework, suggesting that individuals accumulate wealth during their working years and draw it down in retirement through a predictable savings-dissaving path. Yet this linear view is increasingly challenged by contemporary demographic and socioeconomic dynamics. Instead of the traditional "hump-shaped" trajectory of rising assets in midlife followed by their gradual depletion, recent evidence points to older adults maintaining—or even expanding—their wealth well into retirement, a trend supported by advances in health and longevity highlighted by Brown and Finkelstein (2009) as well as recent IMF analyses (2025). Several factors contribute to this shift, including longer life expectancy, higher post-retirement quality of life, evolving patterns of intergenerational transfers, and new forms of consumption associated with more active and diversified lifestyles. As a result, seniors today no longer appear as passive dependents but as economic actors with substantial, and often growing, financial capacities. Consistent with this evolution, studies by Davies et al. (2016) and reports from Rothschild & Co (2024) show that older cohorts—particularly individuals between 45 and 64—now command an expanding share of global wealth.

In sociology, the contributions of Martin Kohli (2007) on the institutionalization of life courses and Anne-Marie Guillemard (2000) on active aging have significantly reshaped how aging is understood. These frameworks emphasize that aging is not just a biological process but a socially constructed experience, shaped by norms, institutions, and public policies that frame individual life paths. Economic gerontology, an emerging cross-field discipline, builds on this foundation by exploring how demographic change interacts with individual economic behavior and collective transformations.

## Demographic-Economic Transformation Models

Aging takes place within the longer trajectory of demographic transition, a framework first outlined by Warren Thompson in 1929 and later broadened to include economic considerations. Changes in the age structure affect macroeconomic dynamics in several ways. One of the most direct channels is the link between the size of the working-age population and national savings rates, a relationship examined by Bloom et al. (2003). Although aging is often associated with slower growth in GDP per capita, more recent work—particularly that of Kotschy and Bloom (2023)—suggests that this effect becomes far less pronounced when functional abilities, rather than age alone, are taken into account.

The idea of a demographic dividend helps clarify these dynamics. It describes a period during which economies benefit from the sheer weight of a large working-age cohort, whose productivity and savings can drive growth. Mason (2005) emphasizes that this is only a temporary advantage. Once these cohorts reach retirement, the balance shifts, bringing higher pressure on public finances and a more constrained growth outlook. These shifts make policy choices especially important. Ensuring healthier aging, reducing gender gaps in labor market participation and retirement, and encouraging targeted migration to address skill shortages are among the measures frequently cited in policy reports, including those of the European Commission (2018b) and the IMF (2025). Without such efforts, the slowdown linked to aging risks becoming more permanent.

Another lens comes from Norman Ryder's (1985) work on cohort effects. Each generation carries the imprint of the conditions it experienced growing up—from economic cycles to technological change. These experiences shape how people save, spend, and form expectations about the future. This generational imprint is central to understanding the silver economy: today's older adults do not behave like earlier cohorts, and the next generations of seniors are likely to differ even more.

## The Emergence of a New Economic Paradigm

The silver economy reflects a new economic paradigm—one that disrupts the industrial-age assumptions on which many models still rest. The familiar phrase "60 is the new 40" captures this shift in social perception: aging is no longer synonymous with withdrawal from economic and social life. Older people are more active, and their consumption behaviors reflect this fundamental change. The senior market has become increasingly diverse, featuring wide variations in health, autonomy, income, and personal aspirations. This diversity challenges traditional market segmentation approaches based primarily on chronological age. At the same time, seniors' purchasing power has sharply increased, driven by decades of asset accumulation and sustained savings patterns that differ markedly from previous generations. Most importantly, seniors demonstrate a restructured relationship with time, showing stronger demand for leisure activities, lifelong learning opportunities, and civic engagement (Alves Martins et al., 2022).

These structural characteristics set the silver economy apart from traditional market segmentations based solely on income or occupation. Its scale is expanding quickly: the global number of older consumers is expected to grow by about 66% in the coming years, rising from 459 million to 760 million (United Nations, 2022; Dataintelo, 2024). At the same time, their expectations are shifting, with a growing emphasis on personalization and innovation that genuinely reflects user needs.

The idea of the longevity economy, developed by Lynda Gratton and Andrew Scott (2021), offers a useful lens for interpreting these profound shifts in the life course. Rather than progressing through education, work, and retirement in strict succession, individuals now move through overlapping phases of learning, employment, leisure, and caregiving. Longer lives make these cycles more frequent and more interdependent, pushing social policies, workforce strategies, and lifelong learning systems to evolve in fundamental ways.

In this new context, organizations and governments must adjust to career paths that are no longer linear. Lifelong learning, later-life entrepreneurship, and portfolio careers are becoming increasingly common. These trajectories not only extend working lives but also create space for richer intergenerational exchange, sustained social participation, and greater opportunities for personal fulfillment across the life span. Such transformations challenge several long-standing economic models. The classic life-cycle model proposed by Modigliani and Brumberg (1954) requires significant revision, as contemporary patterns of asset accumulation are shaped less by peak earnings and more by steady income flows over longer careers. Extended retirement periods also alter long-term financial planning, making the traditional notion of smooth consumption across life stages increasingly difficult to apply.

Human capital theories, originally advanced by Theodore Schultz (1961) and Gary Becker (1964), gain renewed relevance in this environment. Their core insight—that investing in education and skills enhances productivity and earnings—now applies over a much longer horizon. Rapid technological change reinforces this trend: education can no longer be concentrated in youth but must continue throughout adulthood to maintain employability. This shift reshapes how individuals and organizations conceive of training and skill development.

The evolution of the silver economy also echoes Schumpeter's concept of creative destruction (1942). Demographic change is pushing outdated business models aside and spurring new forms of innovation aimed at older adults. Digital technologies, expanding connectivity, and rising expectations for autonomy further accelerate this process, as highlighted in recent analyses such as Butt et al. (2021).

Finally, institutionalist perspectives—particularly those developed by Douglass North (1990)—underscore the need for new policy and organizational arrangements. North's emphasis on the role of institutions, both formal and informal, in shaping economic behavior takes on heightened relevance in a context where demographic, economic, and social forces increasingly intersect. Effective responses to longevity will require closer coordination between public and private actors, along with institutional mechanisms capable of integrating these different policy areas.

Taken together, these theoretical perspectives show that demographic change cannot be addressed through isolated adjustments. A holistic approach—one that brings demographic, economic, social, and organizational dimensions into alignment—is essential for understanding the dynamics of the silver economy and for developing strategies suited to a society shaped more and more by longevity.

## MAPPING THE SILVER ECONOMY ECOSYSTEM

The silver economy is best understood as a dynamic and multifaceted ecosystem, shaped by a wide range of actors, ongoing transformations across sectors, and emerging forms of value creation. To clarify its structure and functioning, this section outlines the ecosystem along three complementary dimensions: the key actors who drive it, the major economic sectors that contribute to its expansion, and the mechanisms through which value is produced and circulated.

### Key Actors in the Ecosystem

Figure 1 highlights the diverse categories of actors that collectively shape the dynamics of the silver economy ecosystem.

*Figure 1. Silver Economy Ecosystem*

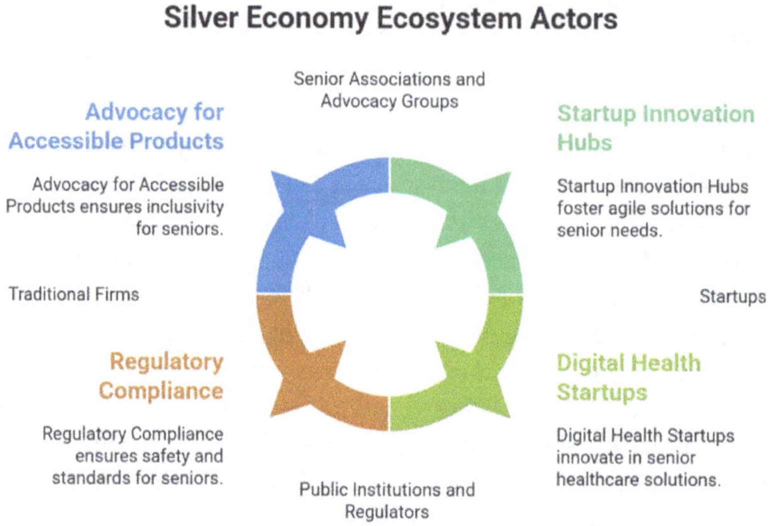


*Source: Author*

Traditional firms, from pharmaceutical leaders like Pfizer and Sanofi to medical equipment providers such as Philips Healthcare and telecom companies like Orange, face increasing pressure to respond to the evolving needs of older consumers. Meeting these demands requires not only product innovation and service diversification but also a rethinking of entire business models. As the United Nations (2019) and Wang & Zhao (2024) note, integrating aging populations into strategic planning has become essential for maintaining relevance. Digital transformation is central to this adaptation: connected health services and digitized offerings must account for seniors' cognitive and ergonomic preferences, as emphasized by Charness and Boot (2016) and exemplified in initiatives such as the Senior Eco-Nect Project (2024).

Startups, by contrast, occupy a more agile space within the ecosystem, targeting gaps left by traditional markets. These companies drive innovation in areas such as digital health, smart home technologies, and mobility solutions that directly address the daily needs of older adults. This emerging sector, often referred to as AgeTech or silver tech, leverages AI, robotics, and connected devices to support independence and enhance quality of life (Sixsmith & Sixsmith, 2008; Peine et al., 2021). Crucially, these startups do not operate in isolation; partnerships with established industry players, accelerators, and policymakers allow them to influence market development and redefine how aging is addressed economically and socially (Golant, 2017; Vines et al., 2015). Their strength lies in designing with older adults rather than for them, incorporating lived experiences into innovation processes, which naturally embeds them within broader silver economy ecosystems (Peine et al., 2021; Schulz et al., 2015).

Public institutions and regulatory bodies play a pivotal role in shaping this ecosystem. Governments, at national, regional, and international levels, establish the frameworks that enable innovation and promote active engagement of older adults in society and the workforce (Walker, 2002; OECD, 2018). European initiatives like Senior Eco-Nect illustrate how coordinated policies and cross-border partnerships can amplify the silver economy's impact (Senior Eco-Nect Project, 2024). Regulatory agencies such as the FDA in the United States or ANSM in France ensure product safety, while countries like Japan are investing heavily in infrastructure adapted to aging populations. As Klimczuk (2021) emphasizes, these institutions are not merely gatekeepers; they actively construct and guide the silver economy by shaping regulations, fostering innovation, and encouraging collaboration across sectors.

Senior associations and advocacy groups occupy a complementary role. By connecting older adults with companies and policymakers, they ensure that products and services meet real needs rather than assumptions. Their involvement in co-design processes grounds innovation in the everyday experiences of seniors, keeping initiatives both practical and socially relevant (Phillipson, 2013; Buffel & Phillipson, 2016).

## Economic Sectors in Transition

Healthcare stands out as the sector most visibly transformed by population aging, undergoing deep structural changes in service delivery and market organization. Rising demand for long-term care, chronic disease management, and home-based services is driving innovation in care models, as evidenced by recent initiatives such as the Senior Eco-Nect Project and studies by Barber et al. (2021). Telemedicine, personalized medical devices, and remote monitoring systems are reshaping how care is provided, emphasizing continuity and proximity over traditional hospital-centered approaches, a shift highlighted by Topol (2015). At the same time, the personal services sector—aimed at preserving autonomy and enhancing quality of life—is expanding, reflecting a broader move toward prevention, wellness, and life-course health management (Liu et al., 2022; Schulz et al., 2015).

Beyond healthcare, numerous other sectors are adapting to better serve aging populations. Financial services are increasingly offering tailored products such as retirement-focused asset management, long-term care insurance, and senior-friendly digital banking platforms designed for accessibility and security (Bosworth et al., 2004; Financial Conduct Authority, 2016). In housing, innovations such as adapted living spaces, senior service residences, and co-living models respond to evolving expectations around independence and social integration (Sixsmith & Sixsmith,

2008; Oswald & Kaspar, 2012). Similarly, the tourism and leisure sectors are shifting to provide safer, more accessible, and meaningful experiences for older adults, prompting destinations to tailor offerings to different levels of mobility and comfort and thereby fostering more inclusive environments.

Emerging sectors, particularly silver tech and adapted housing, have become central to the silver economy's innovation and growth. Silver tech combines artificial intelligence, robotics, smart home systems, and integrated health platforms, with both nimble startups and major tech companies driving rapid expansion to capture this growing market. Adapted housing goes beyond simple accessibility improvements to integrate safety, prevention, and universal design principles, requiring close coordination among architecture, healthcare, public policy, and design disciplines to support aging in place successfully (Sixsmith & Sixsmith, 2008).

Network effects further reinforce this evolving ecosystem through specialized clusters, public-private partnerships, and integrated supply chains, which facilitate knowledge transfer, scalability, and responsiveness to changing senior needs. In this context, organizational agility and cross-sector collaboration are no longer optional—they have become essential prerequisites for success, as noted by the Senior Eco-Nect Project (2024) and the OECD (2020).

## Mechanisms of Value Creation

The silver economy has fostered the development of innovative hybrid business models that depart from traditional approaches. These models emphasize deep personalization, subscription-based service delivery, and functional value propositions rather than one-off product sales. By focusing on long-term engagement, they generate recurring revenue streams, particularly in health support platforms and integrated care services, as observed by Bocken et al. (2014). Value creation in this context also involves intergenerational networks that connect seniors, working-age adults, and younger generations in mutually beneficial ways. Albertini and Kohli (2013) demonstrate that caregiving arrangements exemplify this dynamic, with family members co-producing services, sharing responsibilities, and creating value across generational boundaries.

Albertini and Kohli (2013) further show that innovation in the silver economy increasingly relies on open and collaborative approaches. Participatory methods such as living labs, co-creation workshops, and human-centered design integrate the experience and expertise of older adults from the earliest stages of product and service development. Rather than being treated as a constraint or afterthought, older adults actively shape the design, functionality, and implementation of solutions. Principles drawn from collaborative and circular economies provide a sustainable foundation for long-term value creation, addressing both economic and social objectives. Intergenerational exchange programs, product reuse initiatives, extended maintenance services, and adaptive product modifications reinforce environmental sustainability while promoting social inclusion and community cohesion. These practices anchor the silver economy in responsibility and solidarity, aligning profit generation with broader social aims, as highlighted by Moulaert et al. (2013) and Geissdoerfer et al. (2017).

Moreover, digital platforms have become central to this ecosystem, coordinating complex service networks and connecting older adults directly with providers. By reducing transaction costs, mitigating information asymmetries, and employing advanced matching algorithms and user feedback systems, these platforms continuously improve service quality and enhance user satisfaction over time. For instance, platforms like Papa or Honor in the United States match seniors with vetted caregivers for in-home assistance, combining real-time scheduling, reviews, and personalized service options to ensure both safety and convenience, demonstrating how digital infrastructure can transform traditional care delivery.

## Typologies of Corporate Response

Companies display widely varying levels of engagement with the silver economy, reflecting differences in strategic orientation, resource availability, and understanding of senior markets. Their responses can be broadly categorized into three types, based on the timing and depth of their market involvement.

Pioneers and early adopters anticipate the implications of demographic aging and develop comprehensive products and services tailored specifically to older populations. This group includes specialized silver tech firms, forward-looking insurance companies, and innovative home care providers, whose strategies prioritize continuous innovation and deep personalization. AI-driven solutions for home medical care exemplify the approaches these companies take, as highlighted by Rogers (2003) and Peek et al. (2014).

Followers and adapters, by contrast, engage more cautiously. They typically enter the market after industry standards have begun to stabilize and successful business models have emerged. Many small and medium-sized enterprises adopt this approach, diversifying existing product lines or forming strategic partnerships with innovation hubs and specialized providers. For instance, some retailers have launched age-friendly product ranges through collaborations with research centers and incubators, demonstrating how adaptation can occur through incremental and networked strategies (Lee & Trimi, 2018).

Latecomers and resistors remain hesitant to seize opportunities in the silver economy. Often tied to rigid traditional models, they cite high perceived adaptation costs or limited internal capabilities as barriers. Small businesses in rural areas or conventional industries frequently fall into this category, remaining unprepared for the growing demands and opportunities presented by aging populations.

These differences in corporate response are shaped by structural factors such as company size, sector characteristics, digital maturity, organizational culture of innovation, access to knowledge networks, and the intensity of competitive pressures. Large technology and pharmaceutical firms tend to lead adoption, while many SMEs struggle to pivot toward senior-focused strategies (Chesbrough, 2003; Klimczuk, 2021).

Such diversity in corporate engagement underscores the need for differentiated policy tools and support mechanisms. Accelerating ecosystem-wide participation requires tailored strategies that address the specific barriers and opportunities facing each type of organization—from innovation grants for pioneers to capability-building programs for latecomers.

Mapping the silver economy in this way reveals a dynamic and multi-layered landscape, where traditional sectoral boundaries are increasingly blurred and novel forms of collaboration are emerging. Success in this environment depends not only on understanding individual actors but also on grasping the complex interdependencies that drive innovation and value creation across the entire ecosystem.

## INDICATORS AND METRICS OF THE SILVER ECONOMY ECOSYSTEM

The silver economy is inherently complex and cannot be fully understood through a single analytical perspective. Its dynamics and potential for growth require a structured, multidimensional framework that draws on a wide range of indicators across demographic, economic, and social domains. These metrics capture not only the structural transformations driven by population aging but also their broader economic and societal implications. As illustrated in Figure 1, the analytical ecosystem of the silver economy is organized around three main families of metrics: demographic indicators, economic metrics, and social & territorial impact.

*Figure 2. Main Families of Silver Economy Metrics*

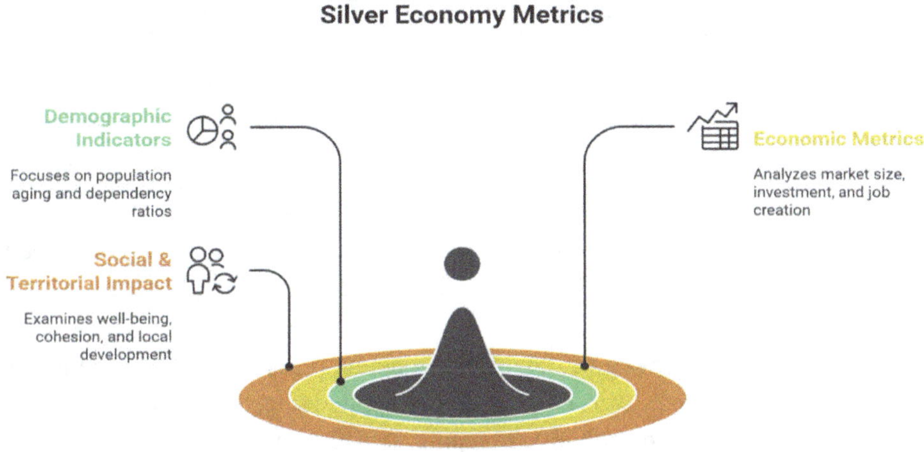


*Source: Author*

Table 1 synthesizes these key indicators, providing a concise overview of the elements that shape the silver economy. Beyond serving as a measurement tool, this framework offers strategic guidance for public authorities, businesses, and other stakeholders seeking to navigate a rapidly evolving landscape.

*Table 1. Key Multidimensional Indicators and Metrics for Analyzing the Silver Economy Ecosystem*

| Category | Sub-Metric | Key Information |
|---|---|---|
| Demographic Indicators | Dependency ratios & aging indexes | Ratio of population aged 65+ relative to working-age adults (20–64); aging index (65+ vs <15) |
| | Healthy Life Expectancy (HALE) | Expected remaining years of healthy life at age 65, highlighting regional disparities |
| | Senior income & wealth projections | Median income levels and distribution of wealth among older adults |
| Economic Metrics | Market size & growth rate | Global market estimated at $5.5 trillion in 2023, with projected growth through 2032 |
| | Investment & financing activity | Venture capital flows in silver tech remain robust despite slight fluctuations |
| | Job creation & labor transformation | Increases in both the quantity and quality of age-related employment |
| | Productivity & innovation | Adoption of robotics, telemedicine, and hybrid service models |

continued on following page

*Table 1. Continued*

| Category | Sub-Metric | Key Information |
|---|---|---|
| Social & Territorial Impact | Well-being indexes & quality of life | Measures of subjective well-being, social participation, and autonomy |
| | Intergenerational cohesion & solidarity | Patterns of family interactions, wealth transfers, and mentoring policies |
| | Territorial development & local economies | Emergence of tech clusters, proximity services, and demographic attractiveness |
| | Sustainability & social responsibility | Low-impact housing, circular economy initiatives, and corporate responsibility programs |

In sum, this matrix provides a flexible yet coherent framework for exploring the multifaceted nature of the silver economy. When applied selectively, it enables more than just demographic and economic mapping; it also opens avenues for engaging with social, territorial, and sustainability challenges associated with aging. For policymakers and economic actors alike, this framework functions not merely as a dashboard, but as a strategic tool to guide policy design, inform innovation agendas, and support informed decision-making in an ecosystem that is continually evolving.

## TRANSFORMATIONAL DYNAMICS: FROM DEMOGRAPHY TO MARKET

The silver economy is increasingly viewed as a space for both social and economic innovation. It illustrates how societies can turn demographic challenges into dynamic, high-potential markets. This transformation doesn't happen spontaneously—it depends on a set of mechanisms, accelerators, and constraints that shape the transition from demographic facts to economic value creation.

### Mechanisms Linking Demography and Economy

Turning demographic aging into market opportunities requires moving beyond broad assumptions about older adults and actively uncovering their often invisible, evolving needs. This approach pushes analysts to examine life trajectories, major transitions—retirement, shifts in autonomy, family reorganization—and the cohort-specific aspirations that shape them. Guido, Ugolini, and Sestino (2022) show that this level of granularity allows firms to break away from age-based stereotypes and build market segmentations grounded in health status, financial capacity, lifestyles, and social networks.

Several mechanisms actively drive this transformation. Demographic pressure increases demand by concentrating purchasing power among older cohorts and revealing persistent gaps in areas such as health management, social connection, and independent living. Technological convergence then amplifies this effect by turning previously costly or complex solutions into accessible and intuitive tools for seniors. At the same time, institutions respond by developing new capabilities, forging cross-sector partnerships, and redesigning service models to better align with the realities of aging populations.

The challenge is therefore not simply to launch new products; it involves fundamentally reimagining how organizations create and deliver value. Firms increasingly adopt active strategies centered on personalization, inclusive design, universal accessibility, and continuous user involvement through living labs or co-design workshops. Business models evolve accordingly, placing more emphasis on niche positioning, modular products, and integrated service pathways that reflect the multidimensional nature of senior needs. Vimarlund et al. (2021) argue, in this regard, that this shift marks a wider transition toward adaptive, user-responsive systems capable of supporting innovation in aging societies.

## Acceleration Drivers

Several forces are driving the emergence of the senior market as a structured and dynamic economic sector. A major catalyst is the evolving socioeconomic profile of older adults, as newer cohorts exhibit more diverse life trajectories, higher levels of education, and stronger purchasing power, trends widely documented in the literature (Formosa, 2019). This shift is producing a more sophisticated consumer base and reinforces the notion of active aging, which underscores autonomy and sustained social participation.

Digitalization and technological innovation further accelerate this transformation. The expansion of internet access and the rapid growth of "Silver Tech" solutions—ranging from IoT devices to e-health platforms and smart home systems—are reshaping how older adults live, interact with institutions, and engage with markets, as highlighted by recent analyses (Peine et al., 2021). These technologies enable new forms of connectivity and support aging in place in ways not previously possible.

Public policy initiatives also contribute to this acceleration. Programs such as the European Innovation Partnership on Active and Healthy Ageing promote cross-sector collaboration, stimulate innovation, and help economic actors adapt to demographic change, a role emphasized by the European Commission (2021). These initiatives simultaneously foster job creation within age-friendly industries.

Cultural perceptions of aging are evolving as well. Contemporary narratives increasingly portray older adults as active contributors rather than societal burdens, a shift that strengthens social acceptance of senior-oriented innovations and supports the expansion of the sector, as noted by Chang et al. (2020). This normative evolution complements socioeconomic, technological, and policy developments, collectively shaping a more favorable environment for the growth of the senior market.

## Structural Barriers

Despite these acceleration dynamics, the silver economy continues to encounter several structural obstacles that constrain its development. Organizational and cultural resistance remains particularly persistent, as many institutions still operate with limited specialized training and rely on outdated structures and routines that are poorly suited to the realities of aging populations, a limitation emphasized by Wilckens et al. (2021). These rigid frameworks slow adaptation and hinder the creation of age-responsive services.

Technological barriers also endure, even with recent improvements in accessibility. Unequal access to digital tools and significant disparities in digital literacy among older adults continue to generate inclusion challenges; the literature notes that such inequalities weaken both the reach and effectiveness of technology-based solutions, as Friemel (2016) observes. These gaps reduce the transformative potential of digital innovation for certain segments of the senior population.

Economic model limitations further complicate market development, especially when considering low-income or dependent households. These groups often attract limited private investment, and conventional economies of scale rarely accommodate the multidimensional needs they present, a point highlighted by Stjernberg et al. (2021). As a result, significant gaps persist in service provision and market coverage.

The inherent complexity and diversity of senior demand also present major challenges. Cultural preferences, degrees of autonomy, and regional conditions vary widely, making it difficult to design scalable and standardized solutions. Such heterogeneity contributes to a fragmented market in which generalized, one-size-fits-all approaches repeatedly fail to address the full spectrum of senior needs.

## Managing the Transformation

The transformation from demography to market in the silver economy involves a delicate balance between leveraging acceleration drivers while systematically addressing structural barriers. Success requires coordinated efforts across multiple levels: individual organizations must develop senior-focused capabilities, industry sectors need supportive ecosystems and standards, and policy frameworks must facilitate innovation while ensuring inclusive access.

This transformational dynamic suggests that the silver economy's full potential will only be realized through integrated approaches that combine technological innovation, organizational adaptation, and policy support—all grounded in deep understanding of senior diversity and needs. The challenge lies not in recognizing the opportunity, but in orchestrating the complex institutional and market changes necessary to capture it effectively.

## INNOVATIVE ADAPTATION MODELS: FROM THEORY TO PRACTICE

The silver economy has sparked a wave of innovative adaptation models that go beyond traditional approaches to serving aging populations. Rather than simply modifying existing products or services, leading organizations are developing entirely new paradigms that reimagine how value is created, delivered, and sustained in aging-focused markets. This section examines six distinctive models that illustrate the transformative potential of strategic innovation in the silver economy.

### Integrated Ecosystem Models

The most comprehensive adaptation approach involves creating integrated ecosystems that address multiple senior needs within a unified environment. The Netherlands' Villages Alzheimer represent a pioneering example of this model, where entire residential communities are designed to replicate normal life while providing specialized care.

These villages integrate retail spaces, cafes, gardens, and residential areas within a secure perimeter, allowing residents with dementia to maintain familiar routines while receiving appropriate support. Staff members, trained in dementia care, and are embedded naturally throughout the environment— working in shops, restaurants, and common areas rather than in traditional clinical settings. This approach has demonstrated significant improvements in resident quality of life while reducing care costs through environmental design rather than intensive staffing.

The model's success lies in its holistic integration of housing, healthcare, retail, and social services within a coherent spatial and operational framework. Similar concepts are now being adapted in other countries, including the United States and Australia, showing the international scalability of integrated ecosystem approaches.

## Intergenerational Co-innovation Models

A second innovative approach leverages intergenerational collaboration to create mutual value while addressing senior needs. The Humanitas program in the Netherlands exemplifies this model by housing university students in senior care facilities rent-free in exchange for spending time with elderly residents.

Students commit to at least 30 hours monthly of social interaction—from simple conversations to teaching technology skills or organizing activities. This arrangement provides affordable housing for students while combating social isolation among seniors. The program has expanded across multiple Dutch cities and has been replicated in Spain, Germany, and other European countries.

The model demonstrates how demographic challenges can become opportunities for innovative social contracts that benefit multiple generations simultaneously. Beyond immediate benefits, participants report enhanced intercultural understanding, reduced ageism, and stronger community bonds that extend beyond the program duration.

## Technology-Enabled Service Platforms

Digital platforms specifically designed for senior populations represent another significant adaptation model. Papa, often described as "Uber for Seniors," connects older adults with vetted young people ("Papa Pals") for companionship and assistance services ranging from technology support to transportation and light household tasks.

The platform's innovation lies in its simplicity and human-centered approach. Rather than complex interfaces, Papa emphasizes easy booking through phone calls and provides extensive training for service providers on senior-specific communication and assistance techniques. The model has scaled rapidly across multiple U.S. states and has attracted significant healthcare partnership investments.

Similar platforms like GrandPad have revolutionized senior technology adoption by offering ultra-simplified tablets with integrated support services, family connectivity features, and curated content designed specifically for older users. These examples show how technology platforms can succeed in senior markets by prioritizing accessibility and human connection over technical sophistication.

## Frugal Innovation Models

Frugal innovation approaches focus on creating maximum value through simplified, accessible solutions rather than feature-rich offerings. The Jitterbug Smart3 smartphone exemplifies this model with its deliberately simplified interface, large buttons, emergency features, and integrated customer support designed specifically for seniors who may be intimidated by mainstream smartphones.

This approach extends beyond products to services. Organizations like AARP have developed streamlined insurance, financial services, and advocacy programs that strip away complexity while maintaining essential functionality. The success of these models demonstrates that innovation in senior markets often involves thoughtful subtraction rather than addition of features.

Frugal innovation proves particularly relevant in addressing economic diversity within senior populations, offering high-value solutions accessible to middle and lower-income segments often underserved by premium-focused strategies.

## Professional Transition and Encore Career Models

Innovative models for leveraging senior professional expertise represent another significant adaptation strategy. Encore Fellowships place experienced professionals in nonprofit organizations for structured, paid assignments that utilize their corporate expertise while providing meaningful post-retirement engagement.

The program creates value for all participants: nonprofits gain access to high-level expertise they couldn't otherwise afford, corporations support community engagement while maintaining connections with retired talent, and participants find purposeful work that leverages their skills. The model has expanded across multiple industries and geographic regions, demonstrating scalable approaches to senior workforce engagement.

These models recognize that many seniors possess valuable expertise and desire continued engagement, challenging traditional retirement assumptions while creating new economic value streams.

## Collaborative Housing and Community Models

Innovative housing approaches address seniors' evolving preferences for independence combined with community connection. Abbeyfield International has developed a distinctive model featuring small-scale residential communities where seniors maintain private apartments while sharing common spaces and optional services.

Residents participate in community governance while accessing flexible support services ranging from meal preparation to social activities. The model emphasizes resident agency and choice while providing security and community connection. Abbeyfield has successfully adapted this approach across diverse cultural contexts in over 15 countries.

Similar innovations include co-housing communities where seniors actively participate in design and governance, and university-affiliated senior housing that provides access to educational and cultural resources while maintaining independent living arrangements.

### Principles of Successful Innovation

These diverse adaptation models share several common principles that distinguish them from conventional approaches to serving aging populations. First, they prioritize user agency and choice rather than dependency relationships. Second, they create multiple value streams that benefit various stakeholders simultaneously rather than extracting value from seniors alone.

Third, successful models typically integrate rather than isolate seniors, fostering connections across generations and communities. Fourth, they emphasize simplicity and accessibility in design, recognizing that complexity often creates barriers rather than value for aging populations.

Finally, these models demonstrate that innovation in the silver economy requires reimagining fundamental assumptions about aging, dependency, and value creation rather than simply adapting existing approaches. The most successful adaptations create entirely new paradigms that transform how society understands and responds to demographic aging.

These innovative models illustrate that the silver economy's greatest potential lies not in serving older adults as a separate market segment, but in creating integrated approaches that benefit entire communities while addressing the specific needs and contributions of aging populations.

## PROSPECTIVE CHALLENGES AND FUTURE ISSUES

The innovative adaptation models explored in the previous section represent current responses to silver economy opportunities. However, the field continues to evolve rapidly, shaped by converging demographic trends, technological transformations, shifting social norms, and emerging sustainability imperatives. This section provides a forward-looking analysis of how these forces will reshape the silver economy landscape, examining both the challenges and opportunities that lie ahead.

### Emerging Scenarios and Transformative Forces

The future trajectory of the silver economy will depend on several interconnected transformative forces building on the dynamics and innovations previously outlined. Demographic change remains a central driver, although its pace differs across regions. In Europe and East Asia, advanced population aging has already reshaped market structures by increasing dependency ratios and altering housing, healthcare, and consumption patterns—developments documented extensively by Klimczuk (2016) and the European Commission (2018a). In emerging economies such as China and Brazil, demographic transitions are unfolding more rapidly but among populations that remain highly heterogeneous in terms of income and access to the innovations discussed earlier.

Technology continues to act as a decisive enabler, reinforcing platform-based models and expanding emerging innovation ecosystems. Advances in artificial intelligence, robotics, and biotechnology are transforming elder care by improving prevention, diagnostics, and personalized treatment strategies. Assistive robotics are beginning to mitigate labor shortages in healthcare environments, while AI systems enhance diagnostic precision and optimize care pathways, trends highlighted by Song (2019) and recent IMF analyses (2025). As automation scales and predictive medicine becomes embedded in routine practice, entire professional fields and care delivery models are being reconfigured, extending the principles already observed in current adaptation frameworks.

At the same time, evolving social and family structures are reshaping the support systems available to older adults. The decline of traditional nuclear family arrangements, combined with rising longevity and prolonged periods of autonomy, is challenging conventional care norms. New forms of digital and community-based solidarity are emerging, supporting older adults who live alone or without close relatives and expanding intergenerational co-innovation into broader social infrastructures, as illustrated in recent work by Gonyea (2013) and the Silver Economy Innovation initiative (2024).

Environmental sustainability is also becoming a core dimension of silver economy development. What once appeared as optional or peripheral—such as frugal innovation models—is now integrated into systemic transformations. Sustainable housing design, low-emission mobility options, reduced energy use within elder services, and investments in circular economy principles increasingly constitute essential pillars for creating resilient and durable senior-oriented markets.

## Strategic Challenges and Adaptive Responses

While the silver economy offers substantial opportunities, several strategic challenges demand careful and proactive management to ensure its development remains inclusive and sustainable. The accelerating pace of population aging is deepening both intergenerational and spatial inequalities, in ways that could weaken the collaborative models currently taking shape. Persistent disparities in access to healthcare, employment, and essential services continue to affect seniors, working-age adults, and younger generations alike, with these gaps shaped by intersecting social factors such as class, gender, geographic location, and ethnicity, as shown in analyses by Eurofound (2023) and Abramson (2016).

Geographical inequalities present a particularly complex barrier to scaling the innovative models discussed earlier. Urban areas, supported by agglomeration effects, tend to attract investment and infrastructure that facilitate the growth of silver economy ecosystems. In contrast, many rural regions remain underserved, lacking the necessary resources to adopt or implement innovations effectively—an imbalance repeatedly emphasized by Klimczuk (2016). This uneven distribution raises the risk that the benefits of silver economy development will cluster in already-privileged territories.

The long-term sustainability of social protection systems is also under increasing strain as demographic transformations accelerate. Aging populations are placing unprecedented pressure on public budgets and pension schemes, prompting calls for deep structural reforms in collective funding models. According to recent OECD assessments (2024), these financial pressures may ultimately limit the public investment and policy support that have been instrumental in enabling many successful adaptation strategies.

A further and perhaps more fundamental concern involves the risk of over-commercialization. When aging is framed predominantly as a market opportunity, vulnerable seniors risk being excluded from essential services and technological advances. Klimczuk (2016) cautions that a system dominated by profit-driven actors may prioritize easily accessible and lucrative segments while neglecting equity, affordability, and long-term innovation designed to meet the diverse needs of older populations. Such tendencies could erode the inclusive foundations required for a truly sustainable silver economy.

## Strategic Opportunities and Innovation Pathways

Despite these challenges, the evolution of the silver economy continues to generate significant opportunities for sustained innovation and inclusive development, building directly upon the successful models observed in recent years. The sector's potential for job creation is considerable, spanning healthcare, digital technology, construction, and localized support services. Demographic projections indicate that the steady increase in the senior population could generate millions of new jobs in developed economies over the coming decade, while simultaneously stimulating the expansion of silver-tech startups and personalized service ecosystems, a trend already noted by Schultz et al. (2015).

At the societal level, emerging forms of solidarity extend the collaborative principles that have underpinned many current innovation models. Intergenerational, associative, and digital networks are strengthening social resilience by promoting co-housing arrangements, mentoring initiatives, volunteer programs, and knowledge-sharing platforms—all of which reinforce community cohesion and offer promising avenues for scaling community-driven solutions. These initiatives demonstrate how local cooperation can evolve into robust social infrastructures that address both care needs and social inclusion.

The silver economy is also increasingly aligned with broader environmental and ecological objectives. Innovations in age-friendly housing, low-emission mobility, and circular production systems tailored to older adults contribute to more sustainable modes of living and caring. This convergence between demographic adaptation and green transition strategies opens new possibilities for integrated policy frameworks capable of addressing multiple societal challenges simultaneously.

International cooperation and knowledge exchange represent a further strategic frontier. Several countries are gaining global influence by exporting expertise and best practices from their silver economy strategies, thereby reinforcing their soft power in international arenas and accelerating cross-border innovation. Japan's collaboration with Scandinavian countries on robotics-assisted eldercare, for example, illustrates how joint initiatives can fast-track technology diffusion while fostering shared learning and capacity building across continents.

## Toward Integrated Future Scenarios

Looking ahead, the silver economy's development will likely follow multiple pathways that combine elements of the challenges and opportunities outlined above. Success in realizing the sector's positive potential will depend on society's ability to manage the inherent tensions between market development and inclusive access, technological innovation and human-centered care, and local adaptation and global knowledge sharing.

The innovative models currently emerging provide valuable blueprints for addressing these tensions, but their scaling and evolution will require continued attention to the systemic integration principles that have made them successful. The future silver economy will likely be characterized by hybrid approaches that combine market mechanisms with social innovation, technological solutions with community-based care, and global knowledge networks with locally-adapted implementations.

This evolutionary trajectory suggests that the silver economy's ultimate impact will be determined not only by technological capabilities or market dynamics, but by society's capacity to maintain the collaborative, inclusive, and innovative approaches that distinguish the most successful current models from conventional market responses to aging.

# CONCLUSION: TOWARD A SYSTEMIC APPROACH TO THE SILVER ECONOMY

## Summary of Key Insights

The silver economy is increasingly understood as a complex, multidimensional phenomenon that extends far beyond a discrete economic sector or a set of products designed solely for older adults. Rather, it functions within an interconnected ecosystem shaped simultaneously by demographic transitions, evolving social dynamics, technological innovation, organizational transformations, and public policy decisions, as emphasized by Klimczuk (2016) and Peine et al. (2021).

The analysis developed above underscores the need for an integrated and interdisciplinary perspective—one that brings together demographic, economic, sociological, and institutional considerations. It is precisely at this intersection that value creation occurs and where both the opportunities and vulnerabilities of the silver economy become visible, a point highlighted by Harper (2006).

Another key insight concerns the growing importance of foresight and long-term strategic planning. The combination of rapid demographic shifts and the accelerating diffusion of new technologies makes reactive approaches increasingly inadequate. As Kasai (2021) notes, policymakers and stakeholders must identify demographic trajectories, anticipate multiple plausible futures, and systematically assess emerging risks in order to design policies that are not only responsive but genuinely forward-looking.

## Implications for Future Research

This analytical framework offers a solid methodological foundation for guiding thematic and sectoral inquiries in future research directions. First, it underlines the need to consistently interweave three complementary dimensions: forward-looking demographic indicators, targeted economic metrics, and organizational or policy-level factors. This triangulated methodology helps produce a nuanced and grounded understanding of the silver economy—one that resists oversimplification.

Second, several cross-cutting questions require deeper exploration. How are technological innovations fundamentally reshaping the relationship between older adults and markets? To what extent are public policies shaping the territorial structuring of senior-focused industries? How do patterns of inclusion and exclusion manifest and evolve in these contexts? Addressing such questions calls for tight articulation between micro-level analyses and macro-strategic perspectives (Peine et al., 2021; European Commission, 2018b).

The methodologies employed should emphasize mixed-methods approaches that combine quantitative data sources (demographics, economics) with qualitative investigations including fieldwork and direct senior engagement. Co-design practices, living labs, and collaborative research models are especially well-suited to capturing innovation as it unfolds, along with documenting the actual uses of technologies and services by older adults themselves.

## Research and Policy Agenda

The landscape described throughout this analysis reveals several research and policy priorities that require sustained attention. From a scientific perspective, deepening our understanding of how demographic aging can generate sustainable economic value remains essential, as highlighted by Albertini and Kohli (2013). Achieving this goal demands greater investment in longitudinal data collection and closer examination of the substantial intra-group disparities that characterize older populations. Addressing the social, territorial, and generational inequalities documented by Aburto et al. (2022) is therefore a central challenge for future research and policy design.

For practitioners—whether businesses, municipalities, or nonprofit organizations—the key priority is to implement agile and collaborative strategies grounded in a nuanced reading of older adults' diverse needs and expectations. User-centered innovation approaches, in which seniors participate as co-creators rather than passive recipients, should play a central role. Long-term success will also depend on strengthening human resource training and cultivating ecosystem-based partnerships that support continuous collaborative development.

In the policy sphere, the emphasis should fall on integrated initiatives that connect health promotion, autonomy support, digital inclusion, employment facilitation, and territorial planning. Building such coherence requires regulatory frameworks that remain flexible enough to encourage experimentation and innovation, yet sufficiently protective to ensure the wider diffusion of successful practices. The European Commission (2021) underscores the importance of these multi-level, cross-sectoral approaches.

More broadly, adopting a systemic perspective implies rethinking the silver economy not as a simple market niche but as a fundamental component of a sustainable and inclusive societal model. Moulaert et al. (2013) stress the value of reinforcing social and environmental impact assessments, developing novel intergenerational alliance models, and expanding international cooperation to foster cross-national learning and knowledge transfer across diverse cultural contexts.

Ultimately, the silver economy serves both as a response to accelerating demographic shifts and as an opportunity to redesign how societies organize economic activity, social support, and intergenerational solidarity in an era of extended longevity. Its successful development depends on the integrated, collaborative, and forward-looking approach articulated throughout this analysis.

## REFERENCES


AARP. (2020). *The longevity economy outlook: How people age 50 and older are fueling economic growth, stimulating jobs, and creating opportunities for all.* AARP. https://www.aarp.org/pri/topics/work-finances-retirement/economics-aging/longevity-economy-outlook/

Abramson, C. M. (2016). Unequal aging: Lessons from inequality's end game. *The Public Policy and Aging Report*, *26*(2), 68–72. DOI: 10.1093/ppar/prw006

Aburto, J. M., Schöley, J., Kashnitsky, I., Zhang, L., Rahal, C., Missov, T. I., & Kashyap, R. (2022). Quantifying impacts of the COVID-19 pandemic through life-expectancy losses: A population-level study of 29 countries. *International Journal of Epidemiology*, *51*(1), 63–74. DOI: 10.1093/ije/dyab207 PMID: 34564730

Albertini, M., & Kohli, M. (2013). The generational contract in the family: An analysis of transfer regimes in Europe. *European Sociological Review*, *29*(4), 828–840. DOI: 10.1093/esr/jcs061

Alves Martins, T., Arriscado Nunes, J., Dias, I., & Menezes, I. (2022). Learning and the Experience of Social, Civic, and Political Participation in Old Age. *Adult Education Quarterly*, *72*(4), 401–421. DOI: 10.1177/07417136221080432

Barber, S. L., Ong, P., & Han, Z. A. (2021). Long-term care in ageing populations. In *Handbook of Global Health* (pp. 1–34). Springer International Publishing.

Becker, G. S. (1964). *Human Capital: A Theoretical and Empirical Analysis, with Special Reference to Education*. Columbia University Press for the National Bureau of Economic Research.

Bloom, D., Canning, D., & Sevilla, J. (2003). *The demographic dividend: A new perspective on the economic consequences ofpopulation change*. Rand Corporation.

Bocken, N. M., Short, S. W., Rana, P., & Evans, S. (2014). A literature and practice review to develop sustainable business model archetypes. *Journal of Cleaner Production*, *65*, 42–56. DOI: 10.1016/j.jclepro.2013.11.039

Bosworth, B., Bryant, R., & Burtless, G. T. The Impact of Aging on Financial Markets and the Economy: A Survey (July 1, 2004). Available at *SSRN*: https://ssrn.com/abstract=1147668 or http://dx.doi.org/DOI: 10.2139/ssrn.1147668

Brown, J. R., & Finkelstein, A. (2009). The private market for long-term care insurance in the United States: A review of the evidence. *The Journal of Risk and Insurance*, *76*(1), 5–29. DOI: 10.1111/j.1539-6975.2009.01286.x PMID: 20046809

Buffel, T., & Phillipson, C. (2016). Can global cities be 'age-friendly cities'? Urban development and ageing populations. *Cities (London, England)*, *55*, 94–100. DOI: 10.1016/j.cities.2016.03.016

Butt, S. A., Elhadjamor, E. A., Pappel, I., Õunapuu, E., & Draheim, D. (2021). A knowledge map for ICT integration in the silver economy. *Procedia Computer Science*, *181*, 693–701. DOI: 10.1016/j.procs.2021.01.220

Camargo, C. M. L., et al. (2020). Exploring sources of uncertainty in steric sea-level change estimates. *Journal of Geophysical Research: Oceans*, 125, e2020JC016551. https://doi.org/DOI: 10.1029/2020JC016551

Chang, E. S., Kannoth, S., Levy, S., Wang, S. Y., Lee, J. E., & Levy, B. R. (2020). Global reach of ageism on older persons' health: A systematic review. *PLoS One*, *15*(1), e0220857. DOI: 10.1371/journal.pone.0220857 PMID: 31940338

Charness, N., & Boot, W. R. (2016). Technology, gaming, and social networking. In *Handbook of the psychology of aging* (pp. 389–407). Academic Press., DOI: 10.1016/B978-0-12-411469-2.00020-0

Chesbrough, H. W. (2003). *Open innovation: The new imperative for creating and profiting from technology*. Harvard Business Press.

Dataintelo. (2024). *Silver economy market report: Global forecast from 2024 to 2032*. https://dataintelo.com/report/global-silver-economy-market

Davies, J. B., Sandström, S., Shorrocks, A., & Wolff, E. N. (2016). The level and distribution of global household wealth. *Economic Journal (London)*, *126*(593), 296–334. DOI: 10.1111/j.1468-0297.2010.02391.x

Eurofound. (2023). *Intergenerational inequalities: How to close the gaps?* Publications Office of the European Union. https://www.eurofound.europa.eu/en/publications/all/intergenerational-inequalities-how-close-gaps

European Commission. (2018a). *The 2018 ageing report: Economic and budgetary projections for the EU member states (2016–2070)*. Institutional Paper 079. https://economy-finance.ec.europa.eu/system/files/2018-05/ip079_en.pdf

European Commission. (2018b). *The Silver Economy: Final report*. Publications Office of the European Union. https://vanuseioletakistuseks.ee/sites/default/files/imce/ee/The%20Silver%20Economy.%20Final%20Report.%20European%20Union%202018.pdf

European Commission. (2021). European Innovation Partnership on Active and Healthy Ageing (EIP-AHA). https://digital-strategy.ec.europa.eu/en/policies/eip-aha

Eurostat. (2021). *Ageing Europe — 2021 interactive edition.* Publications Office of the European Union. https://ec.europa.eu/eurostat/web/products-interactive-publications/-/ks-08-21-259

Financial Conduct Authority. (2016). The ageing population and financial services. Future Horizons Research. https://www.fca.org.uk/publication/research/future-horizons-ageing-population-financial-services.pdf

Formosa, M. (2019). Active Ageing Through Lifelong Learning: The University of the Third Age. In Formosa, M. (Ed.), *The University of the Third Age and Active Ageing. International Perspectives on Aging* (Vol. 23). Springer., DOI: 10.1007/978-3-030-21515-6_1

Foster, L., & Walker, A. (2015). Active and successful aging: A European policy perspective. *The Gerontologist, 55*(1), 83–90. DOI: 10.1093/geront/gnu028 PMID: 24846882

Friemel, T. N. (2016). The digital divide has grown old: Determinants of a digital divide among seniors. *New Media & Society, 18*(2), 313–331. DOI: 10.1177/1461444814538648

Geissdoerfer, M., Savaget, P., Bocken, N. M., & Hultink, E. J. (2017). The Circular Economy–A new sustainability paradigm? *Journal of Cleaner Production, 143*, 757–768. DOI: 10.1016/j.jclepro.2016.12.048

Golant, S. M. (2017). A theoretical model to explain the smart technology adoption behaviors of elder consumers (Elderadopt). *Journal of Aging Studies, 42*, 56–73. DOI: 10.1016/j.jaging.2017.07.003 PMID: 28918822

Gonyea, J. G. (2013). Changing family demographics, multigenerational bonds, and care for the oldest old. *The Public Policy and Aging Report, 23*(2), 11–15.

Gratton, L., & Scott, A. J. (2021). *The 100-year life: Living and working in an age of longevity.* Bloomsbury Publishing.

Guido, G., Ugolini, M. M., & Sestino, A. (2022). Active ageing of elderly consumers: Insights and opportunities for future business strategies. *International Journal of Consumer Studies, 46*(1), 146–162. PMID: 35018351

Guillemard, A. M. (2000). *Aging and the welfare-state crisis.* University of Delaware Press.

Harper, S. (2014). Economic and social implications of aging societies. *Science, 346*(6209), 587–591. DOI: 10.1126/science.1254405 PMID: 25359967

Harper, S. (2006). *Ageing societies: Myths, challenges and opportunities*. Hodder Arnold.

Harper, S., & Hamblin, K. (Eds.). (2014). *International handbook on ageing and public policy*. Edward Elgar Publishing.

IMF. (2025). The rise of the silver economy: Global implications of population aging. *World Economic Outlook*, April 2025, Chapter 2. https://www.imf.org/-/media/Files/Publications/WEO/2025/April/English/ch2.ashx

Kasai, T. (2021). Preparing for population ageing in the Western Pacific Region. *The Lancet Regional Health. Western Pacific*, *6*, 100069. DOI: 10.1016/j.lanwpc.2020.100069

Klimczuk, A. (2016). Comparative analysis of national and regional models of the silver economy in the European Union. *International Journal of Ageing and Later Life*, *11*, 1–29. DOI: 10.3384/ijal.1652-8670.15286

Klimczuk, A. (2021). The silver economy as a constructive response in public policy on aging. In *Strategic approach to aging population: Experiences and challenges* (pp. 19-35). Sveučilište Josipa Jurja Strossmayera u Osijeku, Ekonomski fakultet u Osijeku.

Kohli, M. (2007). The institutionalization of the life course: Looking back to look ahead. *Research in Human Development*, *4*(3-4), 253–271. DOI: 10.1080/15427600701663122

Kotschy, R., & Bloom, D. E. (2023). Economic growth prospects in the face of population ageing. *VOX, CEPR Policy Portal*. https://cepr.org/voxeu/columns/economic-growth-prospects-face-population-ageing

Lee, S. M., & Trimi, S. (2018). Innovation for creating a smart future. *Journal of Innovation & Knowledge*, *3*(1), 1–8. DOI: 10.1016/j.jik.2016.11.001

Liu, L., Daum, C., Miguel Cruz, A., Neubauer, N., Perez, H., & Ríos Rincón, A. (2022, September). Ageing, technology, and health: Advancing the concepts of autonomy and independence. In *Healthcare Management Forum* (Vol. 35, No. 5, pp. 296-300). Sage CA: Los Angeles, CA: SAGE Publications. https://doi.org/DOI: 10.1177/08404704221110734

Mason, A. (2005, August). Demographic transition and demographic dividends in developed and developing countries. In *United Nations expert group meeting on social and economic implications of changing population age structures* (Vol. 31, No. 5). New York: United Nations, Population Division.

METI. (Ministry of Economy, Trade and Industry, Japan). (2019). *Annual report on the ageing society [Summary]* FY 2019. Government of Japan. https://www8.cao.go.jp/kourei/english/annualreport/2019/pdf/2019.pdf

Modigliani, F., & Brumberg, R. (1954). Utility analysis and the consumption function: An Interpretation of cross-section data. In *Post-Keynesian Economics* (pp. 388–436). Rutgers University Press., https://www.princeton.edu/~deaton/downloads/Deaton_Franco_Modigliani.pdf

Moulaert, F., MacCallum, D., Mehmood, A., & Hamdouch, A. (Eds.). (2013). *The International Handbook on Social Innovation: Collective Action, Social Learning and Transdisciplinary Research.* Edward Elgar Publishing.

North, D. C. (1990). *Institutions, institutional change and economic performance.* Cambridge university press.

OECD. (2018). *Working Better with Age.* OECD Publishing., DOI: 10.1787/9789264201996-

OECD. (2020). Who cares? Attracting and retaining care workers for the elderly. OECD Health Policy Studies. https://www.oecd.org/content/dam/oecd/en/publications/reports/2020/05/who-cares-attracting-and-retaining-care-workers-for-the-elderly_735ab920/92c0ef68-en.pdf

OECD. (2024). Addressing demographic headwinds in Japan: A long-term perspective. OECD Publishing. https://www.oecd.org/content/dam/oecd/en/publications/reports/2024/04/addressing-demographic-headwinds-in-japan-a-long-term-perspective_85b9a67f/96648955-en.pdf

Oswald, F., & Kaspar, R. (2012). On the quantitative assessment of perceived housing in later life. *Journal of Housing for the Elderly, 26*(1-3), 72–93. https://doi.org/10.1080/02763893.2012.673391

Peek, S. T., Wouters, E. J., Van Hoof, J., Luijkx, K. G., Boeije, H. R., & Vrijhoef, H. J. (2014). Factors influencing acceptance of technology for aging in place: A systematic review. *International Journal of Medical Informatics, 83*(4), 235–248. DOI: 10.1016/j.ijmedinf.2014.01.004 PMID: 24529817

Peine, A., Marshall, B. L., Martin, W., & Neven, L. (2021). *Socio-gerontechnology: Interdisciplinary critical studies of ageing and technology.* Routledge.

Phillipson, C. (2013). *Ageing.* John Wiley & Sons.

Rasset, P., Mange, J., & Augustinova, M. (2024). What do we really know about age-related stereotypes and well-being of older adults? A commentary on the state of the art. *Frontiers in Psychology*, *15*, 1358403. DOI: 10.3389/fpsyg.2024.1358403 PMID: 38807961

Rogers, E. M. (2003). *Diffusion of innovations* (5th ed.). Free Press.

Rothermund, K. (2024). Age stereotypes: Dimensions, origins, and consequences. *Current Opinion in Psychology*, *53*, 101577. DOI: 10.1016/j.copsyc.2023.101747 PMID: 38035656

Rothschild & Co. (2024). Silver economy: The age of opportunity. https://www.rothschildandco.com/en/newsroom/insights/2024/12/thematic-insights-silver-economy-the-age-of-opportunity/

Ryder, N. B. (1985). The Cohort as a Concept in the Study of Social Change. In Mason, W. M., & Fienberg, S. E. (Eds.), *Cohort Analysis in Social Research*. Springer., DOI: 10.1007/978-1-4613-8536-3_2

Schultz, T. W. (1961). Investment in human capital. *The American Economic Review*, *51*(1), 1–17. http://links.jstor.org/sici?sici=0002-8282%28196103%2951%3A1%3C1%3AIIHC%3E2.0.CO%3B2-4

Schulz, R., Wahl, H. W., Matthews, J. T., De Vito Dabbs, A., Beach, S. R., & Czaja, S. J. (2015). Advancing the aging and technology agenda in gerontology. *The Gerontologist*, *55*(5), 724–734. DOI: 10.1093/geront/gnu071 PMID: 25165042

Schumpeter, J. A. (1942). *Capitalism, socialism and democracy*. Harper & Brothers.

Senior Eco-Nect Project. (2024). Horizon Europe project. https://www.senior-eco-nect.com

Silver Economy Innovation. (2024). *Silver Economy meets Innovation: Aging Better, Together*. https://silvereconomyinnovation.com/

Sixsmith, A., & Sixsmith, J. (2008). Ageing in Place in the United Kingdom. *Ageing International*, *32*, 219–235. DOI: 10.1007/s12126-008-9019-y

Song, S. (2019). Challenges in Technology, Aging, and Market Transparency. *Chinese Economy*, *52*(6), 423–426. DOI: 10.1080/10971475.2019.1617942

Stjernberg, M., Sigurjónsdóttir, H. R., & Wøien Meijer, M. (2021). *Unlocking the potential of silver economy in the Nordic Region*. Nordregio.

Thompson, W. (1929). Population. *American Journal of Sociology*, *34*, 959–975. DOI: 10.1086/214874

Topol, E. J. (2015). *The patient will see you now: the future of medicine is in your hands* (Vol. 130). Basic Books.

United Nations, Department of Economic and Social Affairs, Population Division. (2019). *World Population Ageing 2019 Highlights.* UN. https://digitallibrary.un.org/record/3846855

United Nations, Department of Economic and Social Affairs, Population Division. (2022). *World Population Prospects 2022: Summary of Results.* UN DESA/POP/2022/TR/NO. 3. Available at: https://www.un.org/development/desa/pd/sites/www.un.org.development.desa.pd/files/wpp2022_summary_of_results.pdf

Vimarlund, V., Nikula, N., & Nøhr, C. (2021). Business models and eHealth social innovations for social care services: Serving the two sides of the market. *Health Policy and Technology, 10*(4), 100555.

Vines, J., Pritchard, G., Wright, P., Olivier, P., & Brittain, K. (2015). An age-old problem: Examining the discourses of ageing in HCI and strategies for future research. [TOCHI]. *ACM Transactions on Computer-Human Interaction, 22*(1), 1–27. DOI: 10.1145/2696867

Walker, A. (2002). A strategy for active ageing. *International Social Security Review, 55*(1), 121–139. DOI: 10.1111/1468-246X.00118

Wang, X., Li, Y., & Zhang, S. (2024). Association of social integration with cognitive function trajectories among older adults. *Frontiers in Aging Neuroscience, 16*, 1322974. Advance online publication. DOI: 10.3389/fnagi.2023.1322974 PMID: 38274988

Wang, P., & Zhao, T. (2024). Impact of population aging on corporate digital transformation strategies: An empirical investigation based on population census data from various provinces in China. *Finance Research Letters, 67*, 105838. DOI: 10.1016/j.frl.2024.105838

Wilckens, M. R., Wöhrmann, A. M., Deller, J., & Wang, M. (2021). Organizational practices for the aging workforce: Development and validation of the Later Life Workplace Index. *Work, Aging and Retirement*, *7*(4), 352–386. https://doi.org/10.1093/workar/waaa012

World Health Organization [WHO]. (2021). Ageing and health. https://www.who.int/news-room/fact-sheets/detail/ageing-and-health

# Chapter 2
# The Silver Economy Measuring and Steering Growth in Ageing Societies

**Ihsen Abid**
https://orcid.org/0000-0003-1358-7536
*Imam Mohammad Ibn Saud Islamic University (IMSIU), Riyadh, Saudi Arabia*

## ABSTRACT

*Aging is reshaping economies, labor markets, and social systems worldwide. Far from a demographic crisis, longevity can be a source of innovation and inclusive growth when policy, technology, and institutions adapt to longer lives. This chapter examines the Silver Economy—the network of economic and social activities driven by and for older adults—and its potential as a foundation for sustainable development. Drawing on global policy frameworks such as the United Nations' Madrid International Plan of Action on Ageing and the European Union's Active Ageing Index, it analyzes how demographic change influences employment, innovation, and welfare systems. The chapter advocates an integrated approach that treats aging as a structural driver of transformation, requiring coordinated governance and investment in human capital. It concludes that the Silver Economy offers both an economic opportunity and a social imperative for the twenty-first century.*

## INTRODUCTION

The term "Silver Economy" broadly refers to the system of production, distribution, and consumption of goods and services associated with population ageing.

DOI: 10.4018/979-8-3373-6117-8.ch002

Throughout the world, and especially in industrialized countries, governments and international organizations seek to develop a systematic approach whereby the Silver Economy unlocks new sources of growth and employment while improving the quality of life of older people (Pauhofova & Dovalova, 2015). The growing interest in the Silver Economy reflects a paradigm shift in understanding aging not as a burden but as an opportunity for innovation, productivity, and social inclusion. Clearly, achieving such an objective would require the development of measurement tools. In the European Union, several initiatives have emerged to operationalize this vision, most notably through the Active Ageing Framework, which integrates policy areas such as employment, social participation, and independent living.

The EU's active ageing framework emerged as a comprehensive policy approach to address labour market participation, social inclusion, and independent living among older adults. To move beyond descriptive perspectives, recent research emphasizes the need for quantifiable indicators to evaluate progress in active ageing and its economic implications. To analyse the emerging models of the Silver Economy in the EU, the Active Ageing Index (AAI) is used given its capability to quantify relevant active-ageing outcomes (Abid, 2025a). This chapter extends previous studies by offering a multidimensional and comparative perspective that integrates demographic, economic, technological, and policy dimensions of the Silver Economy. The analysis aims to identify strategic pathways through which ageing societies can transform demographic challenges into opportunities for inclusive and sustainable growth.

Specifically, this chapter contributes to the literature in three ways:

- ✓ It synthesizes demographic and economic evidence to contextualize the emergence of the Silver Economy within broader sustainability and innovation agendas.
- ✓ It compares national and regional policy frameworks, highlighting the role of the Active Ageing Index in shaping strategic responses.
- ✓ It outlines actionable pathways for policymakers to integrate longevity, productivity, and social innovation into long-term economic planning.

By adopting this approach, the chapter underscores the central role of the Silver Economy as a catalyst for redefining growth in ageing societies, linking well-being, employment, and innovation with sustainable economic transformation.

## UNDERSTANDING POPULATION AGING

Aging denotes a process characterized by a rise in life expectancy that stimulates the production of goods and services for older consumers and aging societies.

The Silver Economy comprises all types of goods and services for older adults and an aging population, including extending working life, volunteerism, and active citizenship or, more narrowly, a combination of adequate supply of goods and services and the growing purchasing power of older consumers. In this sense, aging represents not only a demographic phenomenon but also an economic and social transformation that reshapes labor markets, consumption patterns, and welfare systems. Age-friendly products and services connected with gerontechnology, and social innovations constitute central elements of the Silver Economy (Klimczuk, 2016). The United Nations' Madrid International Plan of Action on Ageing (MIPAA), adopted in 2002, sets forth guidelines for social policy toward old age. It emphasizes mainstreaming aging into all policy domains and encourages countries to develop integrated strategies that promote dignity, participation, and economic independence among older adults.

Aging lies at the core of public policies aimed at innovation, job creation, and economic growth in developed and emerging countries. Rather than being viewed solely as a fiscal challenge, aging can act as a driver of economic transformation if properly leveraged through human capital development, lifelong learning, and technological adaptation. Technological advances provide means to mitigate labor shortages induced by demographic shifts through enhanced productivity and automation. These advances, ranging from robotics to digital health, also enable the redesign of workplaces, healthcare systems, and urban environments to better accommodate aging populations.

## Demographic Trends

Aging in the world continues to grow. It is estimated that the number of individuals aged 65 years or above worldwide will increase from 727 million in 2020 to more than 1.5 billion in 2050. The number of older people in China, as well as the USA, India, Indonesia, Pakistan, Brazil, Bangladesh, Nigeria, Russia, and Mexico, will increase by more than 45 million between 2020 and 2050. By 2050, China's older population of 65+ is expected to be 366 million individuals. In 2019, 48.2 percent of the population lived in urban areas, a ratio predicted to grow to 68.4 percent by 2050 (Klimczuk, 2016). These demographic dynamics illustrate a global transition from youth-dominated societies to longevity-driven societies, where aging becomes a defining feature of development. Major regions such as Africa, Asia, Europe, Latin America, and the Caribbean have experienced large increases in the international migrant stock, with Europe having the greatest concentration of migrants. Africa,

Europe, Latin America and the Caribbean are projected to experience particularly large increases.

A broad definition of the Silver Economy includes the range of economic opportunities arising from public and consumer expenditure related to population ageing and the specific needs of the population over 50, as well as the economic activity of the 50+ age group. This perspective captures both the demand side (older consumers' purchasing power and preferences) and the supply side (firms and institutions adapting goods, services, and employment opportunities to aging demographics). International organizations such as the UN, OECD, WHO, and the European Commission recognize the significance of developing the Silver Economy. Consequently, it has become a priority at the regional, national, and local levels. This growing policy alignment signals the emergence of a global consensus that aging, when properly managed, can serve as an engine for sustainable and inclusive growth.

## Global Perspectives on Aging

Several worldwide demographic and economic efforts examine implications for accounting and policy design. The global nature of aging is addressed in associative attempts to develop a generic Silver Economy definition (Klimczuk, 2016). These definitions advocate the creation of a balanced yet diverse economic ecosystem, together with an appropriate science and technology policy, to accommodate increased demand from an aging worldwide population. Such an approach requires recognizing the heterogeneity of aging experiences across countries, where differing income levels, institutional capacities, and cultural norms shape how societies respond to demographic change.

Future aging must be managed through flexible individualized public policies, encompassing voluntary work, family provision, or continued employment. A spatial perspective recognizes the heterogeneous reality of aging, which entails sociodemographic diversity of older citizens, as well as possible territorial singularities in the production of aging goods and services. For example, urban regions may prioritize smart housing and mobility, while rural areas may focus on healthcare access and intergenerational solidarity. Such perspectives point to the European Union as a transnational laboratory for aging. Current demographic transition forecasts an unprecedented aging pace, requiring new economic, social, and political paradigms. Integrating territorial and demographic considerations into policy design ensures that responses to aging are context-sensitive and equitable.

Aging within a region's own territory encourages novel knowledge production regarding the sociology and economics of contemporary aging. Therefore, understanding aging from global and regional viewpoints is essential for identifying the drivers, challenges, and opportunities that define the emerging Silver Economy.

## THE CONCEPT OF THE SILVER ECONOMY

Older adults have become a significant stimulus for economic growth, an opportunity that requires policies promoting extended years of good health and additional working lives. The growth of the Silver Economy has been supported by stronger demand for health-related technologies and the willingness of older adults to self-care, embrace new technologies, and remain productive. The Silver Economy can be defined as the "system of production, distribution and consumption of goods and services aimed at satisfying the specific needs of the population aged 50+" (Klimczuk, 2016). Beyond this definition, the concept also embodies a transformative vision of aging societies, wherein longevity becomes a driver of innovation, entrepreneurship, and inclusive growth.

Two drivers stand out as a defining characteristic: the age structure (a larger cohort, aging from one age group to another) of the population, and the economic configuration (how economically empowered older adults are). Together, these drivers determine both the potential demand for age-related goods and services and the capacity of older individuals to contribute economically through labor participation, savings, and consumption.

Aging presents one of the greatest challenges of the 21st century, influencing economies across a wide array of dimensions. The transition from an age structure where dominant age groups as well as the focusing-and-purchasing-age groups are between 25 and 54, to one in which these dominant age groups grow older, alters the flow and volume of economic activity including consumption, saving, financial markets, and government expenditure long before one's 65th birthday. This shift has far-reaching implications for macroeconomic stability, labor supply, fiscal sustainability, and intergenerational equity.

Change in a few years can result in aggregate variables being "large" affected and transform key economic relationships. In advanced economies, the demographic shift is for the first time in history coupled with the ongoing pressure of technological revolution, a new industrial revolution that will reshape the world economy and eradicate some of the socio-demographic consequences of ageing such as labour shortages. Consequently, the Silver Economy emerges as a cross-sectoral framework that links demographic dynamics with innovation, digital transformation, and social policy. When well-managed, population ageing represents an opportunity for economic transformation and a factor of disinflation, framing autonomy, interdependence, continuity, security, and relations between generations. Thus, the Silver Economy does not only address the needs of older adults but also contributes to societal resilience and long-term sustainability.

## Defining the Silver Economy

The Silver Economy designates the economic potential of the population aged 50 and over as consumers and workers. Key drivers include demographic changes, prolonged life expectancy, limitations on older adults' participation in the labour market, and the increased economic opportunities associated with flexible work organization and the emergence of platforms and services tailored primarily to the needs and expectations of the older generation. It also encompasses the development of markets, technologies, and institutions that enable older individuals to maintain autonomy, productivity, and social engagement.

The challenge is to make demographic shifts an opportunity, rather than a break, for economic and social progress. In this context, effective policy design must reconcile three goals: (1) extending labor market participation, (2) fostering innovation and business development in age-related sectors, and (3) ensuring equitable access to goods and services for diverse older populations. The concept is closely related to the economic consequences of population ageing and the ageing economy. However, the Silver Economy adopts a more proactive stance, emphasizing opportunity creation rather than cost containment.

## Key Drivers of the Silver Economy

The concept of the Silver Economy rests on the identification of two key drivers. In the first place there is a demographic shift towards a larger proportion of older people in the total population. Such a shift relates not only to the visible phenomenon of demographic aging in Europe, but also part of a more pervasive, worldwide trend that has only very recently been tackled as a policy agenda. The various underlying causes of this development were analysed in detail above in "Understanding Population Ageing" and are therefore not repeated here. Nevertheless, it is important to recognize that demographic change operates differently across regions, influenced by fertility rates, migration flows, and life expectancy.

It is important only to keep in mind the message accompanying that snapshot of the demographic situation: that population ageing is occurring on a global scale, albeit on differing times scales across countries and regions. "The concept of the 'Silver Economy' attempts to capture the broad range and various dimensions of opportunities based on the commercial and consumer opportunities arising from the economic activities of the silver market as well as employment opportunities for (or provided by) older adults." (Klimczuk, 2016).

A parallel driver pertains therefore to the age segment itself, capturing the sphere of economic and social activities of older people, particularly as consumers of the 'silver market' and as both the providers and beneficiaries of the emerging silver labour market. In addition to their direct economic roles, older adults also contribute indirectly through intergenerational transfers, volunteering, and civic engagement, which have measurable economic and social value. Various forms of labour market involvement are common among (older) people, ranging from paid work on a full-time or part-time basis to vocational guidance, self-employment, job search or any type of internship and apprenticeships just to name a few. In line with the underlying paradigm of active aging and extended working lives, it is therefore rather appropriate to portrait most of these activities as a basis to assess the Silver Economy, rather than confining to 'paid employment' only.

It is likewise important to keep in mind that both these drivers continue to be crucial: extending the working lives of older workers and leveraging the economic and entrepreneurial 'silver market' power to foster economic growth or to secure the long-term financial sustainability of any given country on a global scale (Klimczuk, 2016). Thus, policies and business strategies should jointly address both supply-side factors (labor participation, entrepreneurship, skills) and demand-side factors (consumption, service design, accessibility) to fully realize the potential of the Silver Economy.

## ECONOMIC IMPACTS OF AGING POPULATIONS

Current demographic changes have encouraged a global debate on economic transformations due to aging. Several economic and social benefits of increased longevity and longer life expectancy have emerged. The Silver Economy offers new opportunities for innovation, growth, and a better response to societal challenges. Although no unified definition exists, the Silver Economy typically refers to all economic and social activities relevant to the needs of people aged 50 and over, connected to their expenditure, consumption, use of resources, or via their economic and social impact on society. This broad conceptualization highlights aging not merely as a fiscal challenge, but as a driver of new demand, market expansion, and structural transformation across sectors.

European Union statistics models use the Active Ageing Index (AAI) as a synthetic indicator to measure active and healthy aging more systematically. Analysis of the AAI, country typologies, and coping strategies underlines the strategic relevance of the Silver Economy in the European context. By quantifying active-aging outcomes across multiple domains, employment, social participation, independent living, and enabling environment, the AAI provides policymakers with a multidimensional tool to guide interventions and assess progress. Aging defines a new social and economic paradigm, considered an opportunity to develop and stimulate economic growth through innovation and the implementation of new technical, cultural, and technological models (Abid, Goaied & Ben Ammar, 2019). This paradigm emphasizes human capital retention, lifelong learning, and labor market adaptability as mechanisms to sustain productivity in aging societies.

Promotion of a new cultural approach to aging, fully integrated into all societal sectors, allows for better understanding of system dynamics and acknowledgment that the elderly are not a burden on society. In fact, reframing older adults as active contributors, through paid work, caregiving, volunteering, and entrepreneurship, enhances social cohesion and economic resilience. Exploration of the link between the Active Aging Index, country typologies, and coping strategies across countries and regions highlights the strategic role of the Silver Economy, emphasizing its transversal dimensions, culture, gender, health, social, behavior, personal, environmental, and economic factors, and its capacity to embrace diverse fields, contexts, resources, and objectives in a dynamic and evolving manner (Klimczuk, 2016). Therefore, understanding the economic impacts of aging requires an integrated approach that links demographic dynamics with institutional responses, labor market structures, and welfare system reforms.

## Labor Market Dynamics

There is no dissense that the amply discussed age-determined increase in contribution and tax rates will have eminently important effects on future labor markets. While we have little precisely quantifiable evidence, what evidence we do have is qualitatively compelling and suggests that the growing wedge between gross and net earnings will reduce the labor force participation of the younger generation. This implies that intergenerational equity and fiscal sustainability are closely intertwined with labor market incentives and social contribution systems.

If the government wants to reduce this wedge, it should strengthen the equivalence principle as much as possible by introducing "notional defined contribution" system for the pay-as-you-go social insurance system. The impact of fiscal and social policy on the labor force participation of the older generation is easier to quantify. Simply increasing the retirement-age-specific adjustment factors to about 7 percent per year of earlier retirement would correct the average retirement age upwards by about 2 years. This would also remove the subsidization of early retirees by later retirees, which is also difficult for voters to accept, and would, at the same time, reduce the contribution and tax burden of the pay-as-you-go system. These policy adjustments could simultaneously enhance the sustainability of pension schemes and expand the effective labor supply.

Alongside the reform of social security systems there are, however, two further important areas of policy which, to date, have attracted very little attention in the political discussion about aging. First, the decrease in the relative size of the economically active population cannot be offset by higher capital intensity. Labor productivity will in fact need to increase over and above this mechanism to compensate for the effects of the shift in the age structure on domestic production. The strengthening of human capital formation through education and training thus assumes central importance particularly in the face of aging. Policies should therefore promote lifelong learning and skill upgrading, ensuring that older workers remain employable and competitive in changing labor markets.

Second, the change in the structure of consumer goods and services' demand will trigger additional sectoral mobility. If the government wants to accommodate these structural changes, an important task of labor market policy must be to remove current constraints on mobility. Moreover, tax and social policy also must accommodate increased mobility (Boersch-Supan, 2001; Abid, 2025b). Facilitating occupational mobility and regional flexibility is essential for matching labor supply with evolving patterns of demand in Silver Economy sectors, such as healthcare, social services, and digital technologies.

## Healthcare Costs and Implications

The ageing of the population in the medium and long term generates concerns regarding the likely increase in health care expenditure (Cristea et al., 2020). The trend in expenditures related to health care and long-term care exceeds the population over 65 years of age, which suggests that the relationship is not merely a matter of maturation (Wildman & McMeekin, 2016). Rather, health expenditure growth reflects complex interactions between longevity, technological change, lifestyle patterns, and institutional arrangements.

The coordination of support policies for dependent adults and long-term services remains limited, often creating additional risks and inefficiencies. The evolution of health-care needs depends on multiple factors, including cohort effects, increases in longevity, changes in medical practice and innovation, and public perception and regulation through insurance models. A precise discussion of expenditure dynamics must take these parameters into account. Moreover, policymakers must distinguish between healthy life expectancy gains and morbidity expansion to design effective financing strategies.

In financial terms, the transition of the Social Security fund from surplus to deficit is projected to occur in 2023, with exhaustion expected by 2036. Medicare's home health-care scheme faces depletion of funds by 2024. Health-care costs are rising rapidly, from 4% of GDP in 2000 to over 30% by mid-century, which necessitates the identification of equitable and efficient funding methods. Many predictions fail to consider changes in epidemiology. The optimal approach to funding is subject to scrutiny, with options and challenges delineated in various studies. The debate encompasses health care, social care, and pension costs. In the United States, discussions focus on market provision of long-term care, with social insurance perceived as politically less viable. Future systems must balance public solidarity and private responsibility while leveraging technological innovation to control costs and enhance care quality.

### Pension Systems and Sustainability

The pension systems existing in almost all countries exhibit a coupling between the contribution timeframe and the circulation timeframe, which presents a significant challenge for long-term sustainability amid demographic aging (Klimczuk, 2016). As society ages, the demographic support ratio declines, leaving fewer contributors to support a growing base of recipients. Although the impact of this imbalanced dependence is partly mitigated through successive utopian expansions of the retirement age, governments are now being confronted with the impending severity of this challenge. This imbalance underscores the urgency of structural reforms aimed at diversifying funding sources and strengthening intergenerational equity.

Long-distance, intergenerational, or governmental transfer mechanisms have yet to be sufficiently implemented, and the property distribution in most countries is not heavily tilted toward a younger generation that could offset this imbalance. Responding to these challenges has become a pivotal concern for governments and social institutions. While theoretical and experimental economic models exploring these issues are a growing research domain, presently the pension system remains the area most acutely affected under the prevailing demographic trends. Sustainable pension reform strategies may include the gradual increase of contribution periods, partial capitalization, occupational pension diversification, and incentive mechanisms to extend working lives. Such measures, when coordinated with active aging and labor market policies, can strengthen fiscal resilience while maintaining adequacy and fairness.

## OPPORTUNITIES IN THE SILVER ECONOMY

The Silver Economy is an emerging economic sector that addresses the social, economic, and environmental challenges and opportunities of aging and encourages the development of the silver market. It is understood as a cross-cutting market that many industrial sectors engage with (Klimczuk, 2012). This integrative nature means that the Silver Economy does not operate as a single industry but rather as a multidimensional ecosystem spanning healthcare, housing, technology, finance, and leisure. The silver market is divided into fourteen segments, encompassing products and services designed for the 50+ and 60+ consumer groups by organizations aiming to meet the expectations of older consumers. Consequently, competitive advantage in the Silver Economy depends on enhanced responsiveness to the needs of these demographic groups. Firms that successfully adapt business models, product design, and marketing strategies to age-diverse populations can capture significant market share and contribute to inclusive economic growth.

The silver industries cover a broad range of fields, including healthcare, smart living, housing adaptations, supported living services, education, culture, information and communication technologies, media, service robotics, mobility, recreation, travel, fitness, wellness, clothing, fashion, care services, insurance, and financial services. These industries together represent a powerful engine for job creation, innovation, and local development, particularly when linked with public policy initiatives and regional development strategies. Gerontechnologies and social innovations are also key components of the Silver Economy. The latter involve new strategies, concepts, products, services, and organisational forms designed to satisfy needs that arise at the intersections of various sectors of the social system. Social innovations embody social goals, means, and generate new social relations and cooperative ties, exemplified by the creative application of new technologies for and by older people; novel models of care combining formal and informal support; age-friendly environments; and the mobilisation of trusted networks. Such innovations not only enhance quality of life but also stimulate social capital formation, contributing to community resilience and cohesion.

The development of the Silver Economy should begin with an analysis of different production spheres and the distribution of goods and services. It is vital to integrate and stimulate the activity of entities from diverse sectors, while accounting for the characteristics of each country and region. A context-sensitive approach is essential, as demographic structures, institutional capacities, and cultural expectations differ widely across nations. Key issues include addressing the internal diversity of the elderly, devising effective marketing strategies, catering to the needs of less affluent older adults, empowering senior consumers, and promoting consumer rights. Coordination among the public sector, commercial enterprises, and non-governmental organisations is crucial for effective technology transfer. Public–private partnerships (PPPs) and multi-stakeholder collaborations can accelerate the scaling up of innovative solutions and ensure equitable access.

Four barriers to building regional silver economies have also been identified. At both national and regional levels, obstacles to the expansion of the Silver Economy include limited interest from market participants, the perception of the Silver Economy as targeting only wealthy seniors, unfavourable consumption patterns among older consumers, and the low attractiveness of certain areas to older migrants and travellers. Addressing these challenges requires policy frameworks that encourage inclusive innovation, reduce affordability gaps, and promote age-diverse consumer engagement. Focusing exclusively on goods and services for affluent seniors may further impede development. Therefore, a successful Silver Economy strategy must embrace socioeconomic diversity and foster universal design principles to reach a broad spectrum of older adults.

## Consumer Behavior of Older Adults

The older population is growing rapidly and is purchasing an increasing share of goods and services. The expanding number of older consumers raises the potential of the Silver Economy, which is shaped by opportunities arising from aging populations (Klimczuk, 2016). Older adults represent a heterogeneous group with diverse needs, preferences, and purchasing capacities, making consumer segmentation and behavioral analysis essential for effective market targeting. The demand for products and services that cater for the requirements of the older population, and for technologies and innovations specific to this age group, offers new economic prospects.

Older consumers represent a clearly defined market segment with specific needs and requirements, while also exhibiting distinct patterns of purchasing behaviour. Therefore, it is especially important to analyse their food purchasing habits (Alhammadi et al., 2021). Beyond food, other areas such as healthcare, housing, mobility, and leisure also show age-related consumption patterns shaped by lifestyle, health status, and social participation.

The consumption of goods and services by older consumers has a positive effect on economic development, as the varying demand stimulates supply. There is a growing interest in the Silver Economy in different parts of the world, including in developed nations, where the expanding older population are becoming a key driving force for the economy. This virtuous cycle, where increased longevity generates demand, which in turn spurs innovation and job creation, illustrates the macroeconomic potential of the Silver Economy.

The accumulation of experience over a long lifetime influences the values and expectations of older consumers and thus the demand for products and financial security. Having amassed sufficient capital, older consumers remain a valuable market: products and services tailored solely to younger consumers may underestimate the potential of those in the older age group (Pauhofova & Dovalova, 2015). In addition, older consumers often prioritize quality, safety, reliability, and ease of use, favoring brands that offer trust and long-term value.

Older consumers therefore embody a clearly identifiable market segment with distinct tendencies and requirements, potentially representing an enormous market that may yield valuable perspectives for businesses. Pension holders also tend to be less emotionally involved in spending than their younger counterparts, being less susceptible to impulse buying. Due to more extensive life experience, older consumers tend to focus on the long term; this approach influences their attitudes to debt and commitment and moderates their spending on convenience. Having strong relationships with retailers, they are less attracted by loyalty cards and points schemes. Businesses seeking to engage this demographic should therefore emphasize trust, service quality, and personalization over short-term incentives.

In the wake of population ageing, ageing workers represent a vital, but frequently overlooked, issue. Supranational organisations such as the International Labour Organization and the Organisation for Economic Co-operation and Development, and others, have broadened their focus on the Silver Economy, and sustainable economic development, to encompass workers. This intersection between consumption and production highlights the dual role of older adults, as consumers driving demand as workers sustaining supply, in the evolution of the Silver Economy.

## Innovations in Products and Services

Technological progress enables the broader application of solutions that partially counter labour shortages stemming from demographic shifts such as ageing and population decline. This is achieved by enhancing labour productivity and substituting physical activities. The Silver Economy, therefore, encompasses a diverse array of sectors. Beyond goods and services tailored for older adults, it also covers the education, research, development, and career prospects linked to silver industries (Klimczuk, 2016). These innovations, ranging from assistive devices and smart homes to e-health and digital learning platforms, reflect the integration of gerontechnology into mainstream markets. Silver industries include health care; smart living, housing adaptations and supported living services based on information and communication technologies (ICTs); education and culture; ICTs and media; service robotics; mobility; recreation; travel; fitness and wellness; clothing and fashion; care services; insurance; and financial services. The convergence of these sectors fosters new business ecosystems centered on healthy aging and inclusive design.

Gerontechnologies constitute crucial components of the Silver Economy. These refer to technologies, products and services designed to support older individuals in their health, housing, mobility, communication, work and leisure. Examples include electronic aids and assistive devices. Social innovation denotes new strategies, concepts, products and organisational configurations aimed at satisfying emergent social requirements. These are often developed at sector boundaries. Instances comprise the deployment of new technologies designed for and adopted by older people; care models that integrate formal and informal support; age-friendly environments; and the mobilisation of trusted networks. Together, gerontechnology and social innovation create synergies that enhance independence, reduce costs, and promote well-being among aging populations.

## Entrepreneurship and Older Adults

Entrepreneurship offers promising avenues to foster active and healthy aging, social inclusion, engagement, and participation among older adults, an expansion of the Silver Economy still insufficiently explored. Older entrepreneurs bring valuable experience, networks, and financial stability that can be leveraged to create social and economic value. Perspectives for senior entrepreneurship contain two approaches from the social entrepreneurship and active aging literatures. Social entrepreneurs seek to address social and business challenges with explicit attention to the pursuit of social value and sustainability, yet the importance of senior entrepreneurship within these broad trends remains underestimated (Stypińska et al., 2019).

In the active aging domain, the production of social value and the creation of social impact have been linked to seniors acting as social entrepreneurs in local communities. Nineteen European initiatives by senior social entrepreneurs addressed social problems such as food waste, social isolation, multicultural integration, and other social needs, generating social value and positive impacts, thereby supporting the idea that senior social entrepreneurism could help alleviate societal issues. Policymakers have been urged to encourage social-entrepreneurial practices among older adults to benefit local communities at large (Socci et al., 2020). Encouraging senior entrepreneurship through mentoring, microfinance, and incubation programs can unlock untapped potential and promote intergenerational knowledge transfer.

Economic silver industries represent the core of the Silver Economy, encompassing goods and services consumed by older adults and work opportunities available to the burgeoning population of aging workers. Gerontechnology stands out by developing innovative solutions designed to assist older individuals in critical life areas including health, housing, mobility, communication, and leisure. Social innovation plays a transformative role in silver industries by fostering a distinct set of goods and services or pioneering organizational arrangements and regulatory support. Though significant barriers persist, not least limited business commitment attributable to a perception of older adults as a distinct group of wealthy consumers, largely disregarding less affluent subgroups, the Silver Economy increasingly blends public and private actors, alongside research and education. These complementarities set the foundations for a more dynamic outlook in the ensuing decades (Klimczuk, 2016). Consequently, promoting entrepreneurship and innovation among older adults can serve as a cornerstone for sustainable growth and inclusive development within aging societies.

## POLICY RESPONSES TO POPULATION AGING

Aging is a global process affecting all countries because of declining fertility rates and growing life expectancy (Klimczuk, 2016). Policies aimed at these challenges include boosting fertility and immigration, increasing labor market participation and the retirement age, and fostering autonomous living and social innovation for aging populations. Effective policy responses require a holistic and long-term perspective that integrates economic, social, and technological dimensions while promoting intergenerational solidarity. A significant problem in care services is the black labor market, which often fails to meet legal standards for personnel training. Regions tend to focus on fostering independent living, home care services, support services at home, and the use of ICTs. Job profiles in the care field frequently blend traditional, systematic, and professional tasks. Thus, workforce planning and training systems must be adapted to ensure adequate supply of qualified care professionals while safeguarding labor rights. Emphasis is placed on social networks, informal care, and dividing help tasks into distinct job profiles. Such diversification of care models helps balance formal and informal mechanisms, improving accessibility and quality of care for older people.

### Social Security Reforms

The changes in societies and families have essential social, political and economic consequences, such as increasing demand on welfare state and social security system. Governments are currently encouraged to promote a Silver Economy that stimulates consumption and creates employment opportunities, which in turn enhances economic growth and welfare for all generations. This requires rethinking traditional welfare systems to ensure financial sustainability, equity, and adequacy in the context of demographic transitions. In connection with its plan for the Silver Economy, the European Union has funded several projects and initiatives to promote opportunities for a sustainable and inclusive economy and society for all ages. Although people have generally longer and healthier lives with the improvement of medicine, many geriatric health problems yet need to be considered. Among the existing health and social infrastructures, the current care-services system is unable to satisfy the projected potential demand for Silver Economy services. Therefore, policy innovations should align social protection systems with demographic realities, promoting active and healthy aging rather than passive dependency.

The first problem concerns social security systems. It is vital to note that not everyone benefits from pension systems as many elderly people consider that their pensions are insufficient. Disabilities and chronic health problems can induce additional sources of expenditures on care, while long-term residencies in healthcare services are generally not covered by insurance. Finally, with population ageing and a shrinking support ratio, new welfare models need to be designed and implemented so that the increase of social expenditure can be limited and remain affordable. Potential solutions include diversifying revenue sources (e.g., through occupational schemes and partial capitalization), incentivizing delayed retirement, and integrating preventive health policies to reduce long-term costs. Countries such as France and Japan that have traditionally implemented pay-as-you-go systems are now moving toward systems in which the pension benefits will be reduced and the retirement age increased. Such reforms, though politically sensitive, are essential to maintain fiscal balance and intergenerational fairness.

The second problem concerns long-term care services, which remain for the moment primarily supported by informal familial networks and voluntary commitments. As the household structure evolves and becomes less supportive with a shrinking familial network, the workload of caregivers is becoming unsustainable. Consequently, governments should formalize and support informal care through allowances, respite services, and training, recognizing the social and economic value of unpaid caregiving. Many studies have tried to model the dynamics on the supply of informal carers, which is generally a declining function of time and based on the household structure and the working activity. Various regions addressed the issue of the well-being of older people by formulating the concept of a (Regional) model of the Silver Economy, an initiative of collaboration between governments, private companies and civil society. These regional models, which integrate social innovation and public-private partnerships, exemplify how tailored approaches can address local demographic realities. In liberal, social-democratic and corporative regimes, the focus is on fostering independent living, home care services, support services at home and the use of ICTs. Job profiles in the care field in these countries tend to mix traditional, systematic and professional tasks. Familistic and transition regimes focus on social networks, informal care and dividing the help and care tasks into different job profiles (Curl & Hokenstad, 2006). This typology underscores that welfare regime design strongly shapes the capacity of societies to adapt to aging populations and sustain intergenerational cohesion.

## Workforce Participation Initiatives

Ireland has responded legislatively to an anomaly concerning the age of eligibility for the State Pension, broadly extending opportunities for work until age 70, with specific arrangements for certain cohorts such as Gardaí or Prison Officers. Workers aged 25 and above must receive access to information regarding their potential contribution records. The doubling of the State Pension between 2012 and 2020 further facilitates continued workforce participation by reducing reliance on supplementary income. Longer work is also promoted and supported on European and international levels. Such measures exemplify how pension reforms can be coupled with incentives for extended working lives, thus alleviating fiscal pressure while maintaining individual autonomy.

The European Union's Strategic Framework on Health and Safety at Work 2014-20 emphasizes improvement of occupational safety and health conditions for all workers while addressing challenges related to an ageing workforce. The European Agency for Safety and Health at Work gathers and analyses case studies of practical solutions to workforce ageing and annually recognizes innovative workplace safety practices through its Healthy Workplaces Awards. Ensuring safe, age-friendly workplaces is central to retaining older workers and preventing premature exit from the labor force. EU-wide research efforts via Horizon 2020 primarily focus on health and demographic change rather than socio-economic perspectives. However, future programs should better integrate economic, social, and technological dimensions to create comprehensive active aging strategies.

Promoting active labor market engagement involves establishing flexible retirement arrangements, creating inclusive work environments, and fostering positive perceptions accompanied by anti-discrimination policies supporting the continued engagement and engagement of older employees (Slowey & Zubrzycki, 2018). To remove barriers for older workers, policies improve awareness of age discrimination legislation, prevent social security incentives for early retirement, and strengthen employability. Raising the Age Pension eligibility threshold and allowing continued work while receiving pensions have effectively increased labour-force participation among Australians aged 65-74. Concerns persist regarding early lump-sum superannuation benefits, disability pensions, and reduced pension income, which continue to discourage workforce participation. Current initiatives address this situation through enhanced education and training, promotion of flexible working arrangements, incentives for hiring individuals aged 50 and above, and further increases to the superannuation preservation age and Age Pension eligibility. These strategies illustrate how structural and behavioral interventions can jointly support later-life employment.

Maintaining extended workforce participation necessitates policies focused on health, employability, flexibility, and secure transitions to retirement. Preventing or managing chronic diseases and disability among workers aged 50-60 is critical to averting long-term unemployment, calling for a health-centered approach alongside strategies to mitigate lifelong disadvantage (Gong & He, 2019). Integrating occupational health, adult education, and career transition services will be essential to build age-inclusive labor markets that sustain productivity in aging economies.

## Healthcare Policy Adjustments

There is a need to accompany the economic shift triggered by aging with adjustments in political and healthcare policies, differentiating between overarching issues that demand concerted action across all countries and more specific themes where the nature of public interventions should consider variations in economic development, institutional structures and social and cultural factors. Such differentiation enables tailored approaches that respect local capacities while ensuring global policy coherence. Simultaneously, older individuals retain a significant role in economic growth after retirement, indicating the importance of integrating them properly into the labour market to foster productivity and sustainability. Those who have left the workforce continue to support public expenditures through taxation and income redistribution, while accumulated assets contribute to broader economic welfare (Cristea et al., 2020). Hence, healthcare policy should not only address cost containment but also leverage older adults' productive capacities and preventive health potential.

Because aging is inevitably associated with surges in healthcare expenses, especially for age-related procedures and long-term care, adapting healthcare systems to the epidemiological challenges and diversifying risk-sharing mechanisms constitute essential policy priorities. Key reforms include expanding community-based care, promoting healthy aging through prevention and lifestyle interventions, integrating digital health tools, and aligning funding mechanisms with value-based care models. Ultimately, sustainable healthcare systems for aging populations must balance efficiency, equity, and quality, ensure universal access while support innovation and workforce development.

# CASE STUDIES IN THE SILVER ECONOMY

To explore how the Silver Economy operates across different policy contexts, it is essential to examine specific country examples. These case studies illustrate how national strategies integrate demographic realities, institutional capacities, and socio-economic priorities. By comparing diverse approaches, one can identify common success factors, policy innovations, and contextual challenges shaping the Silver Economy's evolution. Below are examples from selected countries, each representing a unique model of Silver Economy development.

## Japan

Japan is one of the most rapidly ageing countries in the world, with more than 28% of its population aged 65 and over. This demographic shift has transformed Japan into a global laboratory for aging-related policy innovation. The Japanese government has proactively implemented various measures to adapt to this change, focusing on healthcare, labor participation, and community-based welfare systems. Japan's approach is guided by the concept of "Society 5.0," which integrates technological advancement, human well-being, and demographic adaptation.

The Comprehensive Strategy on an Aging Society promotes active aging through extended working lives, lifelong learning, and participation in local communities. The government encourages firms to employ older workers beyond retirement age and invests heavily in assistive technologies, robotics, and smart housing solutions. Japan's "Long-Term Care Insurance" (LTCI) system, established in 2000, represents a landmark policy combining universal access, community-based services, and co-payment mechanisms to balance equity and fiscal sustainability.

The silver market in Japan encompasses health technologies, home care, telemedicine, and leisure services. Companies have introduced "universal design" principles to meet the needs of all age groups. Furthermore, Japan's innovation ecosystem, linking universities, firms, and municipalities, has accelerated the development of gerontechnologies and age-friendly urban planning. However, challenges remain, including regional disparities, labor shortages in caregiving, and intergenerational inequality. Japan's experience underscores the importance of integrated strategies combining labor, health, and technology policies to transform aging into a source of economic dynamism.

## Germany

Germany faces demographic aging due to low fertility rates and increased longevity. The proportion of the population aged 65 and above is projected to reach 30% by 2050. Recognizing the economic and social implications, Germany has developed targeted policies focusing on active labor participation, vocational training, and digital inclusion for older adults. The federal strategy on "Demographic Change" (Demografiestrategie) integrates policy domains such as family support, lifelong learning, regional development, and health promotion.

The German Silver Economy framework is driven by collaboration between government, private sector, and civil society. Labor market reforms encourage flexible retirement, part-time work, and phased exit programs. Germany's "Initiative New Quality of Work" (INQA) promotes age-diverse workplaces, ergonomic adjustments, and intergenerational knowledge transfer. In addition, the government supports innovation in healthcare and social services through programs such as "Smart Living" and "Ageing in Place." These initiatives strengthen autonomy, reduce institutional care dependency, and foster technological adoption among seniors.

Germany's insurance-based social care system ensures comprehensive coverage for long-term care while promoting preventive and rehabilitative measures. Integration of digital solutions, such as e-health platforms and telecare, further enhances accessibility and efficiency. Despite these advances, Germany faces persistent challenges, including regional workforce disparities, financial sustainability concerns, and adaptation to migration-driven diversity. Nonetheless, Germany's model exemplifies a balanced approach that links demographic foresight, social partnership, and technological innovation to sustain economic competitiveness in an aging society.

## France

France's population is aging steadily, with nearly 21% aged 65 and above. French policy emphasizes solidarity, social protection, and inclusivity, viewing older citizens as integral contributors to society. The French Silver Economy model, launched in 2013 under the "Silver Economy Plan," seeks to position aging as a vector of growth, innovation, and job creation. This plan unites public institutions, businesses, and research organizations to promote age-friendly products and services.

France's strategy operates under three main pillars:

✓ Innovation and Industry Development – fostering the growth of age-related sectors, including healthcare, home automation, and e-health.
✓ Employment and Skills – promoting lifelong learning and the employment of older adults.
✓ Social Cohesion and Territorial Equity – addressing regional disparities and ensuring universal access to services.

The "Silver Valley" cluster near Paris functions as an innovation hub linking start-ups, research institutions, and investors to develop age-friendly technologies. Public funding mechanisms and tax incentives encourage private investment in the silver market. Moreover, France's comprehensive pension and healthcare systems provide a foundation for security and consumption among older citizens. However, fiscal constraints, bureaucratic complexity, and uneven local implementation present ongoing challenges. Overall, France's model demonstrates how state-led industrial policy can catalyze a Silver Economy through coordinated innovation, regulation, and welfare support.

## United States

The United States exhibits unique features in its approach to the Silver Economy, shaped by market-oriented policies and decentralized governance. The country's aging population, expected to reach 80 million by 2040, creates expanding demand across healthcare, housing, and financial services. Unlike many European countries, the U.S. relies heavily on private-sector initiatives and consumer-driven solutions to address aging-related needs.

Healthcare innovation represents a central pillar of the U.S. Silver Economy, with rapid growth in telehealth, precision medicine, and assistive technology markets. Programs such as Medicare Advantage encourage private insurers to offer integrated care options, while initiatives like Aging in Place promote home-based support and community living. Tech companies have developed AI-driven health monitoring tools, fall detection devices, and digital platforms facilitating independent living.

Senior entrepreneurship and employment flexibility are additional hallmarks of the American model. Older workers increasingly engage in part-time, freelance, and remote work facilitated by the gig economy. Government-backed schemes, such as the "Senior Community Service Employment Program" (SCSEP), support training and job placement for low-income seniors. The United States also demonstrates leadership in age-friendly city networks, intergenerational housing projects, and volunteerism. Nevertheless, disparities in healthcare access, income inequality, and long-term care coverage remain significant barriers. The U.S. experience reveals both the strengths of market dynamism and the risks of insufficient public coordination in addressing aging.

## Sweden

Sweden has one of the most advanced welfare states, offering a model of comprehensive, universal support for older citizens. Its approach combines generous social protection with proactive labor market and innovation policies. The Swedish government emphasizes active aging, gender equality, and technological adaptation, integrating these priorities into national and regional planning. Policies such as the "Vision Zero for Age Discrimination" ensure inclusivity across employment, healthcare, and social participation.

Sweden's eldercare system, primarily funded through taxes, provides universal access to high-quality services, with a strong emphasis on autonomy and community care. Municipalities are central actors in delivering age-friendly infrastructure, home care, and preventive health programs. In addition, Sweden promotes digital literacy among seniors through nationwide education initiatives, enabling participation in e-services and reducing social isolation. The integration of smart technologies, such as remote monitoring and assistive robotics, strengthens efficiency and safety in eldercare.

Sweden's model reflects a comprehensive welfare approach, where economic growth, social equity, and technological progress reinforce one another. Challenges include maintaining fiscal sustainability amid rising demand and addressing regional disparities in service provision. Nonetheless, Sweden demonstrates how cohesive, rights-based welfare frameworks can align with innovation to sustain an inclusive and resilient Silver Economy.

In summary, these country experiences illustrate the diversity of Silver Economy pathways, ranging from Japan's technology-driven model and France's state-led industrial strategy to the United States' market orientation and Sweden's universal welfare approach. Despite contextual variations, successful strategies share common elements: cross-sectoral coordination, investment in innovation, support for active aging, and inclusive social protection systems.

## CHALLENGES IN IMPLEMENTING THE SILVER ECONOMY

While the Silver Economy presents significant opportunities for innovation, employment, and social cohesion, its implementation faces numerous structural, institutional, and cultural challenges. Translating demographic potential into economic performance requires coordinated action across multiple policy domains and stakeholders. Many countries struggle to move from conceptual frameworks to operational strategies that are both inclusive and sustainable. These challenges often stem from fragmented governance, limited awareness, and inadequate alignment between social policy, market incentives, and demographic trends.

The first major challenge is insufficient policy integration. In many contexts, Silver Economy initiatives remain isolated within specific sectors, such as health or social care, without broader coordination with labor, education, housing, and innovation policies. This siloed approach limits the capacity to harness synergies between demographic change, technological progress, and economic development. For example, innovative policies may promote assistive technologies without concurrent investments in digital literacy or workforce training for older adults. A comprehensive Silver Economy strategy must therefore adopt a whole-of-government approach, linking social inclusion, employment, and competitiveness agendas.

The second challenge relates to market perception and segmentation. Businesses often perceive the Silver Economy as targeting a narrow group of affluent seniors, neglecting the heterogeneity of older populations. Such misconceptions constrain market expansion, excluding middle- and low-income older adults whose needs are equally significant. Moreover, limited consumer research and stereotypes about older adults as risk-averse or technologically resistant hinder product innovation and marketing strategies. Addressing these biases requires evidence-based segmentation, participatory design processes, and promotion of age-diverse consumer insights.

A third obstacle is the digital divide and technological accessibility. As digital transformation accelerates, older adults risk exclusion due to limited skills, affordability barriers, or inadequate infrastructure. Ensuring digital inclusion is essential not only for social participation but also for equitable access to e-health, online banking, and digital public services. Policies must therefore integrate digital education, subsidized access, and user-friendly design standards across sectors. Without such measures, the Silver Economy may inadvertently exacerbate inequality rather than promote inclusion.

A further challenge concerns labor market adaptation. Despite growing recognition of the value of older workers, age discrimination, rigid retirement norms, and limited flexible work options persist. Organizations often overlook the productivity and experience advantages of senior employees, focusing instead on youth-centric recruitment and training models. This not only reduces labor force participation among older adults but also constrains intergenerational knowledge transfer. Reforming employment practices, promoting lifelong learning, and offering phased retirement schemes are key to unlocking the productive potential of aging workforces.

Another critical issue involves financing and investment mechanisms. Developing the Silver Economy requires substantial public and private investment in infrastructure, innovation, and human capital. However, budgetary constraints and short-term fiscal pressures frequently undermine long-term commitments to aging-related programs. In many regions, insufficient venture capital and risk-averse financial markets further limit the growth of age-focused enterprises. Public–private partnerships, impact investing, and dedicated funding instruments (e.g., silver bonds) could help mobilize resources for sustainable development in this field.

Institutional capacity is also a limiting factor. Implementing Silver Economy strategies demands coordination among ministries, regional authorities, and non-state actors, which is often hampered by overlapping responsibilities or weak governance frameworks. Monitoring and evaluation systems remain underdeveloped, reducing accountability and the ability to measure progress. Building robust institutional architecture with clear mandates, performance indicators, and stakeholder engagement mechanisms is vital for effective implementation.

Cultural attitudes toward aging constitute an additional barrier. Ageism and negative stereotypes can discourage policy innovation, reduce investment, and marginalize older citizens. Public narratives that portray aging solely as a burden impede the recognition of older adults as active contributors to society. Combating ageism through education, media representation, and intergenerational dialogue is therefore essential for fostering a positive vision of longevity.

Finally, territorial disparities present a persistent challenge. Urban areas often benefit from greater access to services, technology, and investment, while rural or peripheral regions lag behind. This spatial inequality undermines inclusive growth and limits the reach of Silver Economy benefits. Tailored regional strategies that leverage local assets and address specific demographic patterns are necessary to ensure balanced development. Integrating place-based approaches, such as age-friendly cities and rural revitalization programs, can enhance territorial cohesion.

In sum, the successful implementation of the Silver Economy hinges on overcoming these interrelated challenges through integrated policy design, stakeholder collaboration, inclusive innovation, and sustained investment. Only by addressing structural, institutional, and attitudinal barriers can societies transform demographic aging into an engine of sustainable prosperity and social well-being.

## MEASURING THE SILVER ECONOMY

The measurement of the Silver Economy remains a central challenge for policymakers, researchers, and practitioners. Despite the growing policy relevance of the concept, there is still no standardized methodology or comprehensive framework for quantifying its size, dynamics, and socioeconomic impacts. Developing robust indicators is essential for understanding how demographic aging translates into economic activity, innovation, and well-being. Without reliable metrics, it is difficult to evaluate policy effectiveness, compare national strategies, or identify best practices.

The Active Ageing Index (AAI), developed through collaboration between the European Commission and the United Nations Economic Commission for Europe (UNECE), is one of the most widely used tools to assess progress in active and healthy aging (Zaidi et al., 2017). The AAI provides a multidimensional framework that captures the extent to which older people contribute to society and the economy through employment, social participation, and independent living. It includes four main domains: employment, participation in society, independent, healthy, and secure living, and capacity and enabling environment for active aging.

By combining outcome-based and capacity-based indicators, the AAI offers an integrated approach to measuring both the realized and potential contributions of older adults.

The index facilitates benchmarking across countries and supports evidence-based policymaking. Its composite nature allows for cross-national comparisons while highlighting areas of policy strength and weakness. However, the AAI primarily focuses on social outcomes and individual well-being rather than the broader economic dimensions of the Silver Economy. As such, it does not fully capture market activities, business innovation, or fiscal implications associated with aging. To address this gap, researchers and institutions are increasingly exploring complementary frameworks that integrate economic, demographic, and technological indicators.

One promising direction involves constructing "Silver Economy Satellite Accounts" (SESA), extensions of national accounts designed to identify and quantify economic activities linked to aging populations. These accounts can help estimate the contribution of age-related sectors (e.g., healthcare, long-term care, assistive technologies, housing, and leisure) to GDP, employment, and value added. Several pilot studies, notably in France and Japan, have demonstrated the feasibility of such approaches (OECD, 2025). However, challenges remain concerning data availability, definitional boundaries, and consistency across statistical systems.

Another approach focuses on input–output analysis to trace intersectoral linkages within the Silver Economy. By mapping production and consumption flows associated with older adults, policymakers can better understand multiplier effects and identify strategic sectors for investment. Similarly, micro-level surveys and longitudinal studies, such as the SHARE (Survey of Health, Ageing and Retirement in Europe) and HRS (Health and Retirement Study) in the United States, provide valuable data on income, consumption, labor participation, and health among aging populations. Integrating these datasets into macroeconomic models can enhance the precision of policy simulations and scenario planning.

The development of composite indices tailored to the Silver Economy is also gaining attention. Such indices could combine indicators related to demographic structure, market performance, innovation, employment, and social inclusion. For example, the Silver Economy Development Index (SEDI) might include metrics such as share of GDP from age-related industries, labor participation rate of older workers, expenditure on lifelong learning and upskilling, R&D investment in age-friendly technologies, digital inclusion rates among older adults, and social protection adequacy.

A multidimensional index would allow policymakers to monitor progress toward inclusive and sustainable Silver Economy development, akin to how the Human Development Index (HDI) measures overall well-being.

However, constructing such an index entails methodological complexities. Selecting appropriate indicators, ensuring data comparability, and balancing comprehensiveness with simplicity are persistent challenges. Moreover, the heterogeneity of aging experiences across regions, driven by cultural, institutional, and socioeconomic factors, necessitates context-sensitive measurement frameworks. Therefore, international cooperation among statistical agencies, academic institutions, and policy networks is crucial for developing harmonized tools.

Ultimately, measuring the Silver Economy requires a combination of quantitative and qualitative methods. Quantitative indicators capture economic outputs, labor trends, and spending patterns, while qualitative assessments evaluate policy coherence, innovation ecosystems, and social inclusion. Mixed-method approaches can thus provide a holistic understanding of how aging shapes economic and social transformations.

In summary, while progress has been made through tools like the Active Ageing Index, there remains an urgent need for integrated and standardized measurement frameworks that reflect the multidimensional nature of the Silver Economy. Developing such tools will enable governments to design evidence-based strategies, allocate resources efficiently, and harness the full potential of demographic change as a driver of sustainable development.

## THE FUTURE OF THE SILVER ECONOMY

The future of the Silver Economy is shaped by the interplay between demographic change, technological progress, policy innovation, and evolving societal values. As populations age worldwide, the challenge will be to transform longevity from a fiscal and social burden into an engine of inclusive growth and sustainable development. The next decades will require comprehensive strategies that harness the capabilities of older adults, promote intergenerational solidarity, and ensure equitable access to opportunities across age groups. This transformation calls for adaptive institutions, responsive markets, and forward-looking policies that align demographic realities with economic and social objectives.

Demographically, ageing will continue to accelerate, especially in Asia, Europe, and Latin America. By 2050, one in six people globally will be aged 65 or older, significantly altering labor markets, consumption patterns, and fiscal systems. These shifts will increase demand for healthcare, housing, and long-term care while also generating opportunities in education, leisure, and digital services. Countries that proactively plan for this transition, investing in health promotion, lifelong learning, and digital infrastructure, will be better positioned to capture the benefits of longevity.

Technological innovation will be a defining driver of the Silver Economy's evolution. Advances in artificial intelligence (AI), robotics, and digital health can enhance autonomy, safety, and quality of life for older adults. The proliferation of smart homes, wearable health devices, and telemedicine platforms will enable aging in place and reduce pressure on institutional care systems. At the same time, digital transformation will reshape labor markets, requiring continuous skill development and inclusive design. Bridging the digital divide will thus become a central priority to ensure that all older individuals can benefit from technology-enabled solutions.

Economic restructuring will accompany demographic transitions. The growth of age-related industries, healthcare, wellness, financial planning, and silver tourism, will create new markets and employment opportunities. Firms that embrace universal design and age diversity in their workforce will gain a competitive advantage in aging societies. Moreover, longevity-driven demand will stimulate innovation in business models, such as subscription-based care services, social enterprises, and platform cooperatives. The Silver Economy will increasingly intersect with the green economy, as sustainable technologies and age-friendly infrastructure converge to meet environmental and social goals simultaneously.

Policy innovation will be indispensable to navigate these transformations. Governments must design coherent frameworks that integrate aging into all policy areas, employment, education, housing, transport, and health. Mainstreaming aging considerations into economic planning, fiscal policy, and research agendas will ensure that demographic change is treated as a cross-cutting issue rather than a specialized niche. Pension and healthcare reforms must balance adequacy with sustainability, while active labor market policies encourage lifelong participation and re-skilling. Adopting a life-course perspective in policymaking will help anticipate aging-related needs and promote preventive action.

Intergenerational solidarity will also define the future trajectory of the Silver Economy. As societies become more age-diverse, fostering cooperation between generations is crucial for social cohesion and equitable resource distribution. Policies that encourage mentoring, volunteering, and knowledge transfer can leverage the experience of older adults for community and economic benefit. Educational systems should integrate intergenerational learning, while workplaces adopt inclusive practices that value age diversity. Such initiatives strengthen mutual understanding, reduce ageism, and create shared value across age groups.

Global cooperation will be essential. Aging is a universal phenomenon, but its pace and consequences vary by region. International collaboration, through the United Nations, OECD, WHO, and regional bodies like the EU, can promote policy convergence, share best practices, and coordinate data collection and research. Developing countries can benefit from knowledge transfer and capacity-building support to anticipate demographic transitions before they become acute. A global framework for the Silver Economy, aligned with the Sustainable Development Goals (SDGs), could serve as a roadmap for equitable and resilient aging societies.

However, the realization of the Silver Economy's potential will depend on overcoming persistent challenges, ageism, inequality, digital exclusion, and institutional inertia. Shifting societal narratives about aging from dependency to empowerment will be key to unlocking both individual and collective capacities. Governments, businesses, and civil society must collaborate to create ecosystems that value longevity as a public good. Ethical considerations, including privacy, accessibility, and social justice, must guide innovation and investment decisions.

In the coming decades, success will hinge on integrating demographic foresight with inclusive innovation. Countries that invest in people throughout their lives, embrace technological adaptation, and cultivate intergenerational equity will turn aging into an asset rather than a liability. Ultimately, the Silver Economy's future rests on our collective ability to design societies where longer lives are not only lived but lived well marked by dignity, participation, and shared prosperity.

## CONCLUSION AND POLICY IMPLICATIONS

The emergence of the Silver Economy marks a profound transformation in how societies conceptualize and respond to demographic aging. Rather than framing longevity as a fiscal burden, the Silver Economy recognizes it as a catalyst for innovation, growth, and social inclusion. By integrating older adults as active participants in labor markets, consumers in expanding sectors, and contributors to community well-being, the Silver Economy offers a multidimensional response to twenty-first-century demographic realities. Harnessing its full potential requires coordinated efforts across policy domains, economic sectors, and levels of governance.

This chapter has demonstrated that the Silver Economy is not a single industry but a cross-cutting system encompassing healthcare, technology, housing, finance, and education. Its scope extends beyond products and services for older adults to include broader institutional and societal adaptations that enable participation, independence, and intergenerational solidarity. The evidence reviewed highlights that successful Silver Economy strategies rely on three interdependent pillars: (1) proactive public policy frameworks, (2) inclusive and innovative markets, and (3) supportive social and cultural environments.

From a policy perspective, several implications emerge:

Mainstream Aging Across Sectors – Policymakers must integrate aging considerations into employment, education, housing, transport, and fiscal policy. This "aging mainstreaming" approach ensures coherence across domains and prevents duplication or fragmentation of initiatives.

Promote Active and Healthy Aging – Investments in health promotion, lifelong learning, and age-friendly workplaces are essential to maintain productivity and well-being across the life course. Preventive health measures and flexible employment arrangements can reduce dependency and sustain economic participation.

Reform Welfare Systems for Sustainability and Equity – Pension and healthcare systems must adapt to demographic realities through balanced reforms that secure both adequacy and fiscal stability. Diversified funding, delayed retirement incentives, and social innovation can enhance resilience and fairness.

Foster Innovation and Digital Inclusion – Technological adaptation is central to meeting the needs of aging societies. Governments should support R&D in gerontechnology, expand digital literacy programs, and promote universal design to ensure accessibility for all.

Encourage Public–Private Collaboration – Effective Silver Economy strategies require partnerships between government, industry, academia, and civil society. Such collaborations can mobilize investment, facilitate technology transfer, and scale innovative solutions.

Combat Ageism and Foster Intergenerational Solidarity – Overcoming negative stereotypes and building mutual understanding among age groups are vital for cohesive societies. Education, awareness campaigns, and intergenerational programs can reshape cultural attitudes toward aging.

Strengthen Measurement and Evaluation – Developing standardized metrics, such as satellite accounts or composite indices, will improve evidence-based policymaking and allow benchmarking of progress. Data-driven approaches are key to refining interventions and demonstrating socioeconomic returns.

For businesses, the Silver Economy opens vast opportunities for product diversification, market expansion, and corporate social responsibility. Firms that adopt age-friendly design, flexible employment practices, and inclusive marketing can gain competitive advantages while contributing to societal well-being. The integration of older adults as both consumers and producers enriches innovation ecosystems and enhances brand trust.

For researchers, advancing the theoretical and empirical foundations of the Silver Economy remains a priority. Future studies should explore its macroeconomic impacts, regional variations, and intersections with sustainability, gender, and technology. Developing interdisciplinary frameworks will deepen understanding and guide policy experimentation.

Internationally, knowledge sharing and policy coordination are crucial. Global institutions, such as the UN, OECD, WHO, and EU, should promote capacity-building, data harmonization, and best-practice exchange to support both developed and emerging economies in navigating demographic transitions. Cooperation can help ensure that aging is managed equitably across diverse socioeconomic contexts.

In conclusion, the Silver Economy represents a transformative paradigm for aging societies, one that redefines growth, inclusion, and well-being in the twenty-first century. By aligning demographic foresight with economic and social innovation, governments and stakeholders can transform longer lives into a foundation for shared prosperity. The challenge now lies not in recognizing the potential of the Silver Economy, but in building the institutional, financial, and cultural conditions necessary to realize it.

## REFERENCES


Abid, I. (2025a). *Drivers of Labor Force Participation and Economic Growth in Gulf Cooperation Countries Region: A Dynamic Panel Analysis.* International Journal of Sustainable Development and Planning, 20(5), 2065–2077. https://doi .org/ IIETA+1DOI: 10.18280/ijsdp.200523

Abid, I. (2025b). *Balancing Growth and Sustainability: The Role of Economic Factors in Adjusted Net Savings in South Asia.* International Journal of Sustainable Development and Planning, 20(4), 1487–1497. https://doi.org/ IIETA+1DOI: 10.18280/ijsdp.200412

Abid, I., Goaied, M., & Ben Ammar, M. (2019). *Conventional and Islamic Banks' Performance in the Gulf Cooperation Council Countries; Efficiency and Determinants.* Journal of Quantitative Economics, 17(3), 623–665. https://doi.org/ IDEAS/ RePEc+1DOI: 10.1007/s40953-018-0139-2

Alhammadi, K., Santos-Roldán, L., & Cabeza-Ramírez, L. J. (2021). *A Theoretical Framework on the Determinants of Food Purchasing Behavior of the Elderly: A Bibliometric Review with Scientific Mapping in Web of Science.* Foods, 10(3), 688. https://doi.org/ MDPI+1DOI: 10.3390/foods10030688

Boersch-Supan, A. (2001). *Labor Market Effects of Population Aging.* National Bureau of Economic Research., DOI: 10.3386/w8640

Cristea, M., Noja, G. G., Stefea, P., & Sala, A. L. (2020). The Impact of Population Aging and Public Health Support on EU Labor Markets. *International Journal of Environmental Research and Public Health, 17*(4), 1439. DOI: 10.3390/ijerph17041439 PMID: 32102277

Curl, A. L., & Hokenstad, M. C. "Terry. (2006). Reshaping Retirement Policies in Post-Industrial Nations: The Need for Flexibility. The Journal of Sociology &amp. *Social Welfare, 33*(2). Advance online publication. DOI: 10.15453/0191-5096.3162

Gong, C. H., & He, X. (2019). Factors Predicting Voluntary and Involuntary Workforce Transitions at Mature Ages: Evidence from HILDA in Australia. *International Journal of Environmental Research and Public Health, 16*(19), 3769. DOI: 10.3390/ ijerph16193769 PMID: 31597239

Klimczuk, A. (2012). Supporting the development of gerontechnology as part of silver economy building. *Ad Alta: J Interdisciplinary Res, 2*(2), 52–56.

Klimczuk, A. (2016). Comparative analysis of national and regional models of the silver economy in the European Union. *International Journal of Ageing and Later Life, 10*(2), 31–59. DOI: 10.3384/ijal.1652-8670.15286

OECD. (2025), The Economic Benefit of Promoting Healthy Ageing and Community Care, OECD Health Policy Studies, OECD Publishing, Paris, https://doi.org/ DOI: 10.1787/0f7bc62b-en

Pauhofova, I., & Dovalova, G. (2015). POTENTIAL OF SILVER ECONOMY IN THE EUROPEAN UNION (SELECTED VIEWS). *European Scientific Journal, ESJ, 11*(10). Retrieved from https://eujournal.org/index.php/esj/article/view/6149

Slowey, M., & Zubrzycki, T. (2018). *Living longer, learning longer – working longer? Implications for new workforce dynamics*. Dublin City University., https://www.dcu.ie/sites/default/files/staff/2022-02/Living%20longer%2C%20learning%20longer%20-%20working%20longer%3F%20Implications%20for%20new%20workforce%20dynamics_final%20report_0.pdf

Socci, M., Clarke, D., & Principi, A. (2020). Active Aging: Social Entrepreneuring in Local Communities of Five European Countries. *International Journal of Environmental Research and Public Health, 17*(7), 2440. DOI: 10.3390/ijerph17072440 PMID: 32260209

Stypińska, J., Franke, A., & Myrczik, J. (2019). Senior Entrepreneurship: The Unrevealed Driver for Social Innovation. *Frontiers in Sociology, 4*. Advance online publication. DOI: 10.3389/fsoc.2019.00030 PMID: 33869354

Wildman, J., McMeekin, P., Grieve, E., & Briggs, A. (2016). Economic evaluation of integrated new technologies for health and social care: Suggestions for policy makers, users and evaluators. Social Science &amp. *Medicine, 169*, 141–148. DOI: 10.1016/j.socscimed.2016.09.033 PMID: 27721138

Zaidi, A., Gasior, K., Zolyomi, E., Schmidt, A., Rodrigues, R., & Marin, B. (2017). Measuring active and healthy ageing in Europe. *Journal of European Social Policy, 27*(2), 138–157. DOI: 10.1177/0958928716676550

# Chapter 3
# Social Innovation for Aging Population:
## Catalyzing Economic Opportunities in the Silver Economy

**Deepak Gupta**
https://orcid.org/0000-0003-3929-1362
*Institute of Technology and Management, Gwalior, India*

**S. Murugesan**
https://orcid.org/0000-0002-8347-5516
*Saveetha Engineering College, Thandalam, India*

**Y. Dasaratha Rami Reddy**
*CBIT Proddatur, India*

**Binoy Mathew**
https://orcid.org/0000-0002-9365-4374
*Centre for Post Graduate Studies, Muddenahalli, India*

**Vijaya Babu Panthagani**
https://orcid.org/0000-0002-6872-6911
*Vignan's Foundation for Science Technology and Research, Vadlamudi, India*

**Pratish Rawat**
https://orcid.org/0000-0003-3230-7464
*Poornima University, Jaipur, India*

**Subhash Atmaram Nalawade**
*Dr. D.Y. Patil Institute of Technology, Pimpri, India*

## ABSTRACT

*Social innovation represents a transformative approach to addressing the multi-faceted challenges and opportunities presented by population aging. This chapter examines how social innovations—defined as novel solutions that simultaneously meet social needs and create new social relationships—are reshaping the silver*

DOI: 10.4018/979-8-3373-6117-8.ch003

*economy landscape. Through comprehensive analysis of contemporary initiatives across healthcare, housing, employment, and community engagement, we demonstrate how social innovation catalyzes economic value while enhancing quality of life for older adults. The chapter synthesizes evidence from diverse geographical contexts, highlighting successful models of age-tech startups, intergenerational programs, co-housing initiatives, and platform economies designed for older populations. We present a framework for understanding the ecosystem enabling social innovation for aging populations, analyzing the roles of entrepreneurs, policymakers, civil society, and older adults themselves.*

## INTRODUCTION

The world stands at a demographic inflection point unprecedented in human history. Between 1974 and 2024, the global share of people aged 65 and older nearly doubled from 5.5% to 10.3%, and projections indicate this proportion will double again to 20.7% by 2074. By the late 2070s, persons aged 65 and older will outnumber children under 18 globally, reaching approximately 2.2 billion individuals. These demographic shifts, driven by declining fertility rates—now at 2.25 births per woman globally compared to 3.31 in 1990—and increasing life expectancy of 73.3 years at birth, represent what the United Nations describes as one of the most significant social transformations of the twenty-first century.

Regional variations in aging intensity demand particular attention. Japan leads globally with 29.4% of its population aged 65 or older as of 2025, followed by the European Union at 21.6%, and the United States at 18.0%. China's rapid aging acceleration—from 15.4% aged 65+ currently to a projected 26% by 2050—represents the most dramatic demographic transition in history, with 310 million people already aged 60 and older. These demographic realities translate into shifting dependency ratios: the OECD average old-age dependency ratio stood at 31% in 2023 but is projected to reach 52% by 2060, with Korea potentially reaching 96% and Japan 80.7%.

The silver economy—defined as economic activities serving the needs of people aged 50 and above—has emerged as a significant economic force. The European Commission's comprehensive study valued the EU silver economy at €3.7 trillion in 2015, projected to reach €5.7 trillion by 2025, representing approximately 32% of EU GDP and supporting 88 million jobs. If measured as a sovereign nation, the European silver economy would rank as the third-largest economy globally, behind only the United States and China. Global AgeTech investment has surged dramatically, reaching $8.49 billion in the longevity sector in 2024—a 220% increase from the previous year—signaling growing market recognition of aging-related opportunities.

This chapter argues that social innovation provides the essential framework for addressing the complex, multidimensional challenges of population aging while simultaneously unlocking the economic potential of the longevity dividend. Social innovations—defined as novel solutions to social problems that are more effective, efficient, sustainable, or just than existing solutions—offer pathways beyond traditional market mechanisms and government interventions that have proven insufficient for meeting aging-related needs. The analysis proceeds through seven sections: theoretical foundations establishing conceptual frameworks; the social innovation ecosystem mapping key actors and relationships; domains of social innovation identifying intervention areas; business models and economic impacts analyzing sustainable approaches; challenges and enabling factors assessing barriers and facilitators; comparative case studies examining successful implementations; and policy recommendations offering actionable guidance for policymakers and practitioners.

## THEORETICAL FOUNDATIONS

The theoretical architecture for understanding social innovation in aging contexts rests upon four interconnected pillars: social innovation theory, aging-specific frameworks, innovation ecosystem models, and participatory design approaches. Each contributes essential conceptual tools for analyzing how novel solutions emerge, diffuse, and transform systems serving older populations.

### Social Innovation Theory

Social innovation as a distinct field of study has crystallized around several foundational definitions. Phills, Deiglmeier, and Miller (2008) articulated the concept as "a novel solution to a social problem that is more effective, efficient, sustainable, or just than existing solutions and for which the value created accrues primarily to society as a whole rather than private individuals." Mulgan and colleagues at the Young Foundation similarly defined social innovations as "innovative activities and services that are motivated by the goal of meeting a social need and that are predominantly developed and diffused through organizations whose primary purposes are social." These definitions emphasize three distinguishing characteristics: novelty in approach, orientation toward social rather than private value creation, and organizational structures prioritizing social mission.

The process of social innovation follows identifiable stages. Mulgan's six-stage model traces innovations from prompts and inspirations through proposals and ideas, prototyping and pilots, sustaining, scaling and diffusion, and ultimately systemic change. This trajectory underscores that social innovation is not merely invention but encompasses the entire journey from conception to societal transformation. A comprehensive historical analysis by Satalkina and Steiner (2022) identified seven core characteristics: the nature of innovation as new combinations, creation of new social organizations, system-level adaptations, transformation of social mindsets, orientation toward positive impacts, potential for disruption, and reliance on cooperation and exchange across sectors.

## Aging-Specific Theoretical Frameworks

The WHO Active Ageing Framework (2002) established the dominant policy paradigm, defining active aging as "the process of optimizing opportunities for health, participation and security in order to enhance quality of life as people age." The framework identifies four pillars—health, lifelong learning, participation, and security—shaped by determinants including personal factors, behavioral characteristics, physical and social environments, economic conditions, and health service systems. Research has confirmed strong associations between active aging pillars and survival outcomes among older adults.

The Successful Aging Model developed by Rowe and Kahn (1987, 1997) posited three components: low probability of disease and disease-related disability, high cognitive and physical functioning, and active engagement with life. While influential, subsequent scholarship has expanded this framework to include positive spirituality (Crowther et al., 2002) and structural factors beyond individual control. Rowe and Kahn themselves updated their model for the twenty-first century, acknowledging societal-level determinants and the role of social structures in enabling or constraining successful aging.

The Age-Friendly Cities and Communities Framework operationalizes aging theory into eight actionable domains: outdoor spaces and buildings, transportation, housing, social participation, respect and social inclusion, civic participation and employment, communication and information, and community support and health services. Recent scholarship has developed validated measurement instruments including the Age-Friendly Community Survey and the Age-Friendly Cities and Communities Questionnaire.

## Innovation Ecosystem Theories

The Triple Helix Model provides essential understanding of how innovation emerges through interactions among academia, industry, and government. Etzkowitz and Leydesdorff (2000) demonstrated that knowledge-based economic development depends on trilateral networks and hybrid organizations bridging institutional spheres. For aging innovation, this framework explains how universities generate gerontological knowledge, firms commercialize products and services, and governments create enabling regulatory environments.

The Quadruple and Quintuple Helix Models extend this framework by incorporating civil society as a fourth helix and the natural environment as a fifth. Carayannis and Campbell (2010) argued that meaningful innovation increasingly requires active citizen engagement—particularly relevant for aging innovations where older adults themselves must be co-creators rather than passive recipients. Recent analysis confirms the applicability of quadruple helix approaches for empirical studies of social innovation.

## Participatory Design Approaches

Co-creation and participatory design principles are essential for aging innovations given the heterogeneity of older adult populations and the risk of technological solutions designed without input from intended users. Sanders and Stappers (2008) established theoretical foundations for co-creation in design, while Voorberg, Bekkers, and Tummers (2015) systematically reviewed co-creation in social innovation contexts. Research specifically examining co-design with older adults has identified best practices including involvement across all stages from empathizing through prototyping and testing to evaluation.

The emerging field of socio-gerontechnology integrates these theoretical streams, examining how technologies and aging mutually constitute one another through social practices, power relations, and cultural meanings. This interdisciplinary perspective emphasizes that technologies are never neutral tools but embody assumptions about aging that can either reinforce or challenge ageist stereotypes.

## Social Innovation Ecosystem for Aging Population

The social innovation ecosystem as shown in figure 1, for aging comprises eight interconnected actor categories operating across multiple levels from micro (individual) to macro (societal). At the center stand Older Adults themselves—not merely as beneficiaries but as active co-creators, experts by experience, and increasingly as investors and entrepreneurs. Surrounding them, Social Entrepreneurs develop novel organizational models and business approaches addressing unmet needs through mission-driven enterprises. Civil Society Organizations including foundations, nonprofits, and advocacy groups provide funding, convening capacity, and political voice. Government at local, regional, national, and supranational levels establishes regulatory frameworks, provides funding, and coordinates policy responses through initiatives like the WHO Global Network for Age-Friendly Cities and Communities.

*Figure 1. Social Innovation Ecosystem for Aging Population*

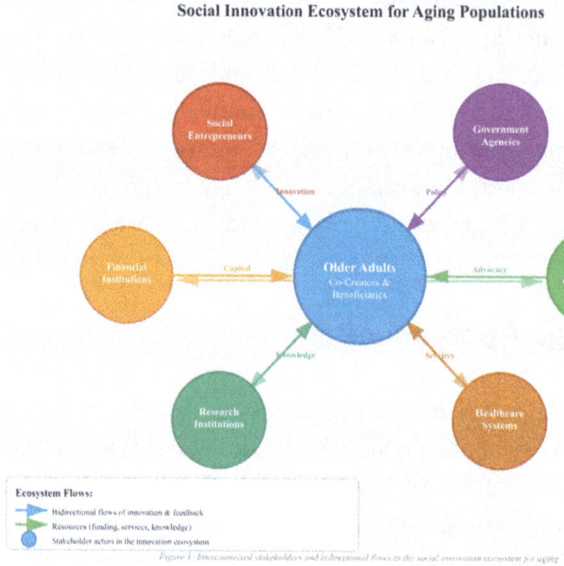


Healthcare Systems including hospitals, primary care, long-term care, and insurance institutions serve as both innovation adopters and sources of demand for new solutions. Research Institutions generate evidence, evaluate interventions, and train the next generation of gerontologists, social innovators, and healthcare professionals. Financial Institutions including venture capital, impact investors, foundations, and public funding bodies provide capital across the innovation lifecycle from early-stage grants through growth equity. Finally, Technology Companies from global platforms to specialized AgeTech startups develop digital tools, assistive devices, and data infrastructure enabling new care models.

These actors interact through multiple channels: formal collaborations and partnerships; market transactions; knowledge exchange and diffusion; policy advocacy and influence; and funding relationships. Critical enabling infrastructure includes regulatory sandboxes permitting experimentation, innovation hubs and accelerators fostering development, standards bodies ensuring interoperability, and evaluation frameworks demonstrating effectiveness. The ecosystem perspective emphasizes that no single actor can address aging challenges alone; rather, transformative change requires coordinated action across institutional boundaries through what innovation scholars term "systemic innovation."

## DOMAINS OF SOCIAL INNOVATION FOR AGING

Social innovations addressing population aging span seven interconnected domains, each presenting distinct challenges and opportunities for novel solutions.

### Healthcare and Long-Term Care

Healthcare innovation represents the most active domain, driven by rising costs, workforce shortages, and quality imperatives. The Netherlands' Buurtzorg model exemplifies how organizational innovation can transform care delivery through self-managed nursing teams operating without middle management, achieving 30% higher patient satisfaction and 50-67% fewer care hours while maintaining quality. AI-powered health monitoring systems are proliferating, with Japan's smart healthcare market projected to reach $34.5 billion by 2035. Digital therapeutics have gained regulatory approval—Japan's CureApp became the first approved digital therapeutic in 2020—while telehealth has become permanent following pandemic-accelerated adoption.

### Housing and Living Arrangements

Housing innovations address the overwhelming preference of older adults to age in place—90% in AARP surveys—while providing appropriate support. Senior cohousing communities, originating in 1980s Denmark, now number approximately 250 communities in Denmark alone with 80,000 on waiting lists, demonstrating strong demand for community-oriented alternatives. The Dutch Dementia Village model pioneered purpose-built environments enabling people with severe dementia to live relatively normal lives while reducing antipsychotic medication use from 50% to under 10%. Smart home technologies integrate sensors, voice assistants, and monitoring systems enabling independence with appropriate oversight.

### Social Participation and Connection

Social isolation affects 10-46% of older adults living alone and carries health risks comparable to smoking 15 cigarettes daily. The US Village Model, launched in Boston's Beacon Hill in 2001, has expanded to over 375 villages enabling neighbor-to-neighbor support through member-driven nonprofits. Japan's Fureai Kippu time banking system allows volunteers to earn care credits transferable to relatives in distant locations, with approximately 374 organizations and 70,000 active participants. Digital platforms increasingly facilitate virtual social connection, though the digital divide remains a persistent barrier.

## Mobility and Transportation

Transportation barriers significantly constrain older adults' independence and social participation. Autonomous vehicles promise future solutions, with Japan testing self-driving mobility in Smart Wellness Cities. Current innovations include ride-sharing services adapted for older adults, volunteer driver programs coordinated through villages and NORCs, and accessible public transit improvements under age-friendly city initiatives. Mobility assistance technologies including exoskeletons like Cyberdyne's HAL demonstrate how wearable devices can extend physical capabilities.

## Financial Security and Employment

Longer lifespans require innovations in retirement financing, with AgeTech increasingly targeting “longevity fintech” solutions for wealth management, retirement planning, and insurance products. Employment opportunities for older workers have expanded dramatically—Japan now has 9.3 million employed workers aged 65+, representing 13.7% of the workforce. Social enterprises increasingly focus on senior employment, recognizing both economic necessity and the contributions older workers bring through experience and reliability.

## Cognitive Health and Dementia Care

With dementia affecting approximately 55 million people globally, innovations in cognitive health represent urgent priorities. Japan's Basic Act on Dementia (2024) established a comprehensive legal framework for support. Technology applications include AI-based cognitive assessment (FOVE's Virtual Reality Checker, Sanda City's Touch de Brain), facial recognition systems preventing unauthorized exits (LYKAON), and therapeutic robots like PARO demonstrating measurable benefits for people with dementia. Brain health apps for prevention (Eisai's NOU-KNOW) reflect growing emphasis on early intervention.

## Intergenerational Solidarity

Innovations fostering intergenerational connection address age segregation while generating mutual benefits. Shared housing arrangements pair older adults with younger people in exchange for assistance. Intergenerational learning centers combine senior services with childcare and education, as exemplified by Fujisawa Sustainable Smart Town's Wellness SQUARE. Technology training programs pairing students with seniors demonstrate effectiveness in improving digital literacy while building cross-generational understanding.

## BUSINESS MODELS AND ECONOMIC IMPACTS

Sustainable social innovation requires viable business models generating sufficient resources to maintain and scale operations while achieving social objectives. Analysis of successful aging innovations reveals diverse approaches to value creation, capture, and distribution.

### Value Creation and Capture Mechanisms

Successful aging innovations employ three primary value creation strategies. Efficiency innovations reduce costs while maintaining or improving quality—Buurtzorg's minimal overhead demonstrates this approach, achieving 8% administrative costs compared to the industry average of 25%. Access innovations extend services to underserved populations—the Village Model and NORC programs exemplify community-based approaches reaching people who might otherwise fall through service gaps. Quality innovations improve outcomes and experiences—Dementia Villages' dramatic reduction in antipsychotic medication use illustrates how organizational redesign can achieve superior clinical results.

Value capture mechanisms vary significantly across models. Healthcare innovations like Buurtzorg operate within existing payment systems, billing insurance while achieving efficiency gains. Membership-based models like Villages generate revenue directly from beneficiaries, creating accountability but potentially excluding lower-income populations. Time banking systems like Fureai Kippu create non-monetary value exchange, though hybrid approaches incorporating modest payments prove more sustainable. Policy-based approaches like WHO Age-Friendly Cities rely on public investment and in-kind contributions from municipal partners.

### Economic Impact Assessment

The economic impact of social innovations for aging operates through multiple channels. Direct cost savings accrue when innovations deliver services more efficiently—Ernst & Young estimated that universal adoption of the Buurtzorg model could save 40% of Dutch home care costs. Indirect benefits include reduced hospitalizations, delayed institutional placement, improved health outcomes, and enhanced productivity of family caregivers freed from intensive care responsibilities. Broader economic effects include job creation in the silver economy, increased consumer spending by healthier older adults, and extended workforce participation.

AgeTech investment trends signal growing market recognition of these opportunities. Global longevity sector investment reached $8.49 billion in 2024, a 220% increase from $3.82 billion in 2023. The United States dominates with 57-58% of global funding across 1,130+ startups, followed by the United Kingdom and broader Europe. Subsector analysis reveals concentration in health/longevity therapeutics (Altos Labs' $3 billion raise), aging-in-place technologies, and caregiver support platforms. The elder care services and devices market is projected to grow from $868 billion in 2024 to $1.1 trillion by 2029.

## CHALLENGES AND ENABLING FACTORS

Scaling social innovations for aging populations confronts persistent challenges while benefiting from emerging enablers that can accelerate diffusion and impact.

### Structural Barriers

Regulatory fragmentation poses significant obstacles, as aging-related services span health, social care, housing, and transportation sectors governed by distinct regulatory frameworks. Innovations requiring cross-sectoral integration—such as Buurtzorg's holistic approach or NORC programs bridging health and housing—must navigate multiple oversight bodies with potentially conflicting requirements. Payment system misalignment compounds these difficulties; fee-for-service reimbursement rewards volume over value, disadvantaging innovations achieving better outcomes with fewer interventions.

Workforce constraints represent perhaps the most binding limitation. Japan faces projected shortages of 570,000 care workers by 2040 despite aggressive robotics investment. The Netherlands struggles with nursing shortages threatening Buurtzorg's expansion. Across OECD countries, care work remains undervalued and underpaid, creating recruitment and retention challenges that no amount of organizational innovation can fully overcome without policy attention to compensation and working conditions.

Capital gaps affect innovations at different lifecycle stages. Early-stage social innovations struggle to attract investment given uncertain returns and limited collateral. Growth-stage ventures face the "missing middle"—too large for grants, too risky for traditional debt, insufficiently profitable for commercial equity. The AgeTech investment surge remains concentrated in therapeutics and technology platforms rather than service innovations with lower financial returns but potentially greater social impact.

## The Digital Divide

Technology-enabled innovations confront the persistent digital divide affecting older adults. While this gap is narrowing—US internet use among those 65+ grew from 12% in 2000 to 88-90% in 2024—significant disparities remain. Only 61% of US adults 65+ own smartphones compared to 96% of those 18-29. The 65-74 age group in the EU achieved 76% individual internet access in 2024, up from 41% in 2015, but the oldest-old remain largely disconnected. In China, only 50% of adults 60+ have yet joined the internet.

Barriers extend beyond access to encompass physical limitations (28% of US adults 65+ report health problems affecting activities), cognitive considerations, privacy concerns (the biggest barrier for one-third of older Americans), cost constraints (16% cite cost barriers), and design failures—64% of adults 50+ do not feel technology is designed with their age group in mind. Effective digital inclusion requires intergenerational training programs, simplified interfaces, and co-design approaches ensuring technologies meet actual user needs.

## Ageism as a Systemic Barrier

The WHO Global Report on Ageism (2021) documented that one in two people globally hold ageist attitudes against older people, with profound implications for innovation. Ageism in technology design results from workforces skewing young—the average tech worker is 38 versus 43 for non-tech, and less than 11% of professional developers are over 45. Technologies designed without older adult input embed assumptions that may inadvertently exclude or stigmatize intended users. Research has documented various forms of exclusion including age caps in user testing, sampling biases, and low involvement across design stages.

## Enabling Factors

Several emerging enablers create favorable conditions for scaling aging innovations. Policy momentum has accelerated through initiatives including the UN Decade of Healthy Ageing (2021-2030), which has catalyzed over 20% increases in countries reporting legislation against ageism and national age-friendly programs. The WHO Global Network for Age-Friendly Cities now encompasses 1,739 cities in 57 countries covering over 370 million people, creating infrastructure for innovation diffusion.

Technological maturation enables new possibilities as AI, IoT, and robotics advance. Japan's approval of AI diagnostics (nodoca influenza detector), digital therapeutics, and care robots demonstrates growing regulatory pathways for novel technologies. Voice interfaces, smart home integration, and wearable health monitors have achieved usability levels appropriate for older adult adoption.

Demographic awareness has shifted from viewing aging as burden to recognizing opportunity. The framing of "silver economy" and "longevity economy" positions older adults as consumers, contributors, and assets rather than costs. Dedicated AgeTech investment funds including Primetime Partners, 1843 Capital, and Third Act Ventures reflect growing sophistication about market opportunities.

COVID-19 acceleration significantly advanced digital adoption among older adults, with 44% viewing technology more positively post-pandemic and four in five relying on technology to stay connected during lockdowns. The pandemic also demonstrated the vulnerability of congregate care settings, strengthening the case for home and community-based alternatives that many social innovations provide.

## COMPARATIVE CASE STUDIES

### Case Study 1: Buurtzorg Netherlands — Reinventing Home Care Through Self-Management

**Background and Origins:** Founded in 2006 by Jos de Blok, a former nurse and healthcare executive frustrated with the fragmentation and bureaucratization of Dutch home care, Buurtzorg ("neighborhood care" in Dutch) began with a single team of four nurses. De Blok's vision centered on returning nursing to its relationship-centered roots while eliminating management layers that had proliferated as home care industrialized during the 1990s and 2000s.

**Innovation Model:** Buurtzorg's core innovation is organizational rather than technological. Self-managed teams of 10-12 nurses operate without middle managers, handling all aspects of care including patient assessment, care planning, scheduling, hiring, and administrative tasks. The "Onion Model" begins from client needs at the center, working outward through self-management capacity, family and informal networks, formal professional networks, and finally Buurtzorg nurses as the outer layer—inverting traditional care models that start from professional services.

A purpose-built IT platform, BuurtzorgWeb, enables coordination without hierarchy, incorporating the Omaha System for standardized assessment across 42 problem areas. Approximately 15-20 regional coaches each support 40-50 teams, providing advice rather than direction and intervening more actively with newer teams while stepping back as teams mature. Central administrative staff number only 49 people supporting over 14,000 employees—a span of control unthinkable in traditional organizations.

**Outcomes and Evidence:** The 2015 KPMG study commissioned by the Dutch Ministry of Health found Buurtzorg uses 50-67% fewer care hours per patient than comparable organizations while achieving the highest client satisfaction scores nationally. Overhead costs of 8% compare to industry averages of 25%. Employee satisfaction has earned "Best Employer in Netherlands" recognition multiple years, with absenteeism two-thirds lower and turnover significantly reduced compared to industry norms. Ernst & Young estimated potential system savings of 40% if all Dutch care adopted the model.

However, KPMG also found that total per-patient costs including hospital and physician services were approximately average rather than lower, suggesting that Buurtzorg's impact may be on quality and efficiency rather than total healthcare spending. The organization experienced a €7 million loss in 2022 due to post-COVID absenteeism peaking at 9.7%, demonstrating vulnerability to external shocks despite organizational resilience.

**Global Expansion:** Buurtzorg now operates in approximately **25 countries** including Japan (Orange Cross Foundation with 40+ nurse stations), China (1,000+ clients across multiple cities), the United Kingdom (pilots in multiple NHS areas), the United States (Minnesota), and European adaptations in Germany, France, Sweden, and Switzerland. A 2022 scoping review found that implementation requires significant adaptation at team, organizational, and system levels—upskilling networking competencies, leadership commitment, IT infrastructure, and supportive policy environments.

## Case Study 2: Japan's Smart Aging Innovation Ecosystem — Society 5.0 in Action

Background and Context: Japan's demographic extremity—29.4% of the population aged 65+ with projections reaching 38.4% by 2065—has catalyzed comprehensive policy responses positioning aging as a national priority requiring transformative innovation. Society 5.0, proposed in the 5th Science and Technology Basic Plan (2016) and expanded in the 6th Plan (2021), envisions a "human-centered society in which economic development and the resolution of social issues are compatible with each other through a highly integrated system of cyberspace and physical space."

**Innovation Ecosystem Components:** Japan's approach combines substantial public investment with coordinated private sector engagement. The Moonshot Research and Development Program has allocated $440 million through 2050 for ambitious goals including extending healthy lifespan. The Robot Revolution Initiative (2023) targets approximately $300 million for healthcare robotics. The Ministry of Health, Labour and Welfare allocated $400 million (¥61.7 billion) for digital health transformation.

Specific innovations demonstrate ecosystem productivity. PARO, the therapeutic seal robot developed by AIST with approximately $20 million government R&D investment, has demonstrated measurable benefits for people with dementia. HAL (Hybrid Assistive Limb) by Cyberdyne provides wearable exoskeletons magnifying strength tenfold. AIREC, a 150kg humanoid robot from Waseda University capable of repositioning patients and preventing bedsores, represents next-generation care robotics targeted for 2030 deployment. Digital therapeutics including CureApp have gained regulatory approval, while AI diagnostics like nodoca for influenza demonstrate healthcare AI maturation.

**Living Lab Implementation:** The Kashiwa City Living Lab exemplifies place-based innovation, partnering the University of Tokyo Institute of Gerontology, municipal government, and UR housing corporation at the Toyoshikidai Housing Complex (4,666 rental units, 45% elderly households). The Kashiwa Cohort Study has tracked 2,044 older adults since 2012 for biological, psychosocial, and functional aging research. Projects include the "Work Places for Second Life" program employing retirees in agriculture and childcare, and the Future Elderly Model demographic simulator predicting chronic disease patterns.

**Smart Wellness Cities** (62 member municipalities) pursue "walkability" as a core theme, implementing connected health monitoring, autonomous mobility testing, and age-friendly urban design. Fujisawa Sustainable Smart Town (opened 2014) integrates energy, security, mobility, wellness, and community in a purpose-built development including the Wellness SQUARE combining assisted living with intergenerational facilities.

**Challenges and Limitations:** Despite substantial investment, robot adoption in care facilities remains limited—only 10% of 9,000+ elder care institutions had introduced any care robot as of 2019, though 63% now use monitoring robots and 26.4% mobility robots. Costs exceeding ¥5-10 million ($35,000-70,000) per unit create adoption barriers. Research suggests robots may create additional work for caregivers rather than reducing burden. The projected shortage of 570,000 care workers by 2040 remains unaddressed by technology alone.

## Case Study 3: Senior Cohousing — From Danish Bofællesskab to Global Movement

**Origins and Development:** Modern cohousing emerged from 1960s Danish activism, with Bodil Graae's influential 1967 article "Children Should Have One Hundred Parents" inspiring early communities and Jan Gudmand Høyer's architectural writings providing design principles. The first modern cohousing community, Sættedammen near Copenhagen, opened in 1972. Senior-specific cohousing (seniorbofællesskaber) developed in Denmark from 1987, adapting the model for aging populations seeking community-oriented alternatives to both isolated living and institutional care.

American architects Charles Durrett and Kathryn McCamant introduced cohousing to North America following their 1984-1985 study of Danish communities, coining the English term and publishing foundational texts that inspired US development beginning with Muir Commons. Silver Sage Village in Boulder, Colorado (2006) became the first US senior cohousing community. The UK's New Ground in High Barnet, London (2016)—the first UK senior women's cohousing—required 18 years from conception to completion, illustrating development challenges.

**Model Characteristics:** Senior cohousing combines private homes with shared facilities (common house, gardens, workshops) in self-governing communities of typically 20-50 households. The participatory design process, often spanning years, builds social capital before construction. Governance operates through consensus-based decision-making and committee structures. Senior-specific adaptations include age restrictions (typically 50+/55+), universal design features, and health buddy systems.

Mutual support mechanisms distinguish cohousing from conventional housing: shared meals (typically 2-4 weekly), informal caregiving networks, resource sharing, and "co-care" approaches to supporting members through health challenges. Research on the "communal coping" model demonstrates how collective stress management produces positive health outcomes (Glass, 2013).

**Global Spread and Evidence:** Denmark hosts approximately 250 senior cohousing communities housing some 5,500 units with 80,000 on waiting lists, suggesting substantial unmet demand. The Netherlands has approximately 300 groepswonen van ouderen (senior group housing). The United States counts 17 established senior cohousing communities with 28 forming and broader cohousing totaling 160+ in 25 states. The UK has 11 new-build communities with 65+ groups developing. Canada, Australia, Germany, and Sweden all have active movements.

Outcome evidence consistently demonstrates benefits. A Realdania study found 91% of Danish senior cohousing residents report better quality of life and 75% report improved social relationships. Research across five US elder cohousing communities found loneliness prevalence of 24%, lower than national averages. A scoping review concluded that "cohousing model can be positively associated with health outcomes through psychosocial determinants of health, such as increased social support, sense of community and physical, emotional and economic security" (Carrere et al.,2020).

**Challenges:** Development timelines of 3-10+ years, regulatory barriers including zoning restrictions and parking minimums, financing difficulties with unfamiliar banks, and the intensive time commitment required from founding members all constrain expansion. The model remains most accessible to relatively affluent, highly educated populations with capacity for extended participatory processes.

## POLICY RECOMMENDATIONS

Drawing on theoretical frameworks, empirical evidence, and case study insights, the following ten recommendations offer actionable guidance for policymakers seeking to foster social innovation ecosystems that address population aging while catalyzing silver economy opportunities.

### 1. Establish Innovation-Enabling Regulatory Environments

Create regulatory sandboxes specifically designed for aging-related innovations, permitting controlled experimentation with novel service models, technologies, and organizational forms while maintaining essential consumer protections. Japan's Society 5.0 regulatory sandbox approach and the UK's Care Quality Commission sandbox provide models. Streamline approval pathways for digital therapeutics, AI diagnostics, and assistive technologies following Japan's PMDA example. Harmonize regulations across health, social care, and housing sectors to enable integrated innovations.

### 2. Reform Payment Models to Reward Outcomes Over Volume

Transition from fee-for-service reimbursement toward value-based payment models that reward quality, outcomes, and efficiency improvements. Buurtzorg's success within Dutch insurance frameworks demonstrates compatibility between innovation and existing payment systems when properly structured. Develop specific payment codes and reimbursement pathways for evidence-based social innovations including technology-enabled remote monitoring, self-management support, and community-based interventions. Pilot global capitation or bundled payment arrangements that give providers flexibility to innovate while maintaining accountability for outcomes.

### 3. Build Innovation Infrastructure and Intermediary Organizations

Invest in infrastructure supporting social innovation development including incubators and accelerators focused on aging, living labs enabling real-world testing (following Kashiwa City and Kamakura examples), and evaluation centers generating evidence about what works. Support intermediary organizations that facilitate innovation diffusion—the Village to Village Network, UK Cohousing Network, and Buurtzorg's consulting arm demonstrate how knowledge transfer accelerates replication. Fund training programs for professionals in participatory design, gerontechnology, and social entrepreneurship.

## 4. Mandate and Resource Cross-Sector Collaboration

Establish formal requirements and funding mechanisms for collaboration across health, social care, housing, transportation, and technology sectors at local and regional levels. NORC programs' mandatory partnership models and age-friendly cities' cross-domain frameworks provide templates. Create joint budget pools allowing flexible resource deployment across traditional sector boundaries. Support quadruple helix arrangements formally incorporating older adults and civil society alongside government, academia, and industry in innovation governance.

## 5. Institutionalize Participatory Processes with Older Adults

Require meaningful involvement of older adults in all stages of innovation design, implementation, and evaluation—not merely as subjects but as co-creators with decision-making power. Establish panels, advisory bodies, and review processes ensuring older adult voice in public procurement, research funding, and regulatory decisions. Fund training to build older adults' capacity for effective participation. Address accessibility barriers including transportation, technology, and scheduling that may limit participation.

## 6. Develop Rigorous Evaluation Frameworks and Evidence Infrastructure

Invest in robust evaluation methodologies appropriate for complex social innovations that cannot be assessed through randomized controlled trials alone. Adopt standardized measurement instruments (Age-Friendly Community Survey, 4Ms Framework) enabling comparison across contexts. Support longitudinal research following innovations through development, implementation, and scaling phases. Create publicly accessible databases of evaluated innovations with transparent reporting of both successes and failures to enable learning.

## 7. Address Digital Divide Through Multi-Pronged Strategies

Implement comprehensive digital inclusion initiatives combining infrastructure investment (broadband expansion), affordability programs (subsidized access for low-income older adults), device provision, and skills training. Scale effective intergenerational programs pairing younger mentors with older learners. Mandate accessibility requirements in publicly funded technology development. Invest in co-design approaches ensuring technologies genuinely serve older adult needs rather than imposing youth-oriented assumptions.

## 8. Combat Ageism in Innovation Systems

Implement WHO Global Report on Ageism recommendations including policy/law interventions, educational activities, and intergenerational contact programs. Require age diversity in technology development teams receiving public funding. Monitor and report workforce demographics in AgeTech sectors. Challenge ageist assumptions in design through awareness campaigns and training. Ensure older adults are portrayed accurately and positively in innovation narratives, emphasizing contributions and agency rather than deficits.

## 9. Transform Public Procurement as Innovation Driver

Leverage public purchasing power to accelerate innovation adoption by establishing pre-commercial procurement programs for aging-related innovations, streamlining procurement processes for small and social enterprises, and incorporating innovation criteria alongside cost in evaluation. Create challenge prizes and competitions stimulating innovation in priority areas. Develop procurement frameworks that permit pilots and scaling pathways rather than requiring proven solutions from inception.

## 10. Foster International Exchange and Learning Networks

Support systematic cross-national learning about what works in different contexts through researcher exchanges, practice networks, and policy dialogues. Fund comparative research examining how innovations adapt across cultural, regulatory, and economic contexts. Participate actively in international frameworks including WHO Age-Friendly Cities network, OECD aging policy community, and EU innovation partnerships. Translate and disseminate evidence across languages to enable broader learning.

# CONCLUSION

The demographic transformation reshaping societies worldwide demands innovation responses commensurate with the scale and complexity of population aging. This chapter has demonstrated that social innovation—novel solutions creating value for society through new organizational models, technologies, relationships, and collaborative arrangements—offers essential pathways for addressing aging-related challenges while catalyzing economic opportunities within the burgeoning silver economy.

Theoretical foundations from social innovation studies, gerontology, and innovation ecosystem research converge on key insights: effective aging innovations require cross-sector collaboration transcending traditional boundaries; older adults must be positioned as co-creators rather than passive recipients; and systemic change demands coordinated action across multiple levels from micro interventions through macro policy reforms. The cases examined—Buurtzorg's transformation of home care through self-management, Japan's comprehensive Society 5.0 ecosystem mobilizing robotics and AI, and senior cohousing's community-based alternative to isolation—demonstrate diverse pathways toward these objectives while revealing persistent challenges in scaling and sustaining innovations.

The economic case for social innovation in aging has strengthened considerably. The silver economy now represents a multi-trillion-dollar global market with demonstrated growth trajectories. AgeTech investment has surged to record levels, signaling market recognition of opportunities. Evidence from implemented innovations documents significant impacts including cost savings, quality improvements, and enhanced outcomes. Yet market mechanisms alone cannot address aging-related needs given pervasive market failures, information asymmetries, and the non-market dimensions of care and community.

Three novel insights emerge from this analysis. First, the most impactful innovations are often organizational rather than technological—Buurtzorg's transformation required no new technology, only radical reorganization of existing capabilities. Policy and investment attention should balance technology enthusiasm with support for organizational and social innovations. Second, the digital divide remains a binding constraint on technology-enabled aging innovations, requiring dedicated and sustained attention to inclusion rather than assumptions that adoption will naturally diffuse. Third, ageism functions as a systemic barrier embedded in innovation systems themselves, requiring deliberate countermeasures rather than passive assumptions of neutrality.

Future trajectories will be shaped by choices made today. The policy recommendations offered here provide actionable guidance for fostering innovation ecosystems capable of transforming how societies age. Success will require sustained commitment, cross-sector coordination, and genuine partnership with older adults themselves as experts on their own lives and needs. The demographic dividend of longevity—longer, healthier, more productive lives—represents enormous potential, but realizing that potential demands innovation equal to the challenge.

## REFERENCES


Cai, Y., & Lattu, A. (2022). Triple helix or quadruple helix: Which model of innovation to choose for empirical studies? *Minerva, 60*, 257–280. DOI: 10.1007/s11024-021-09453-6

Carayannis, E. G., & Campbell, D. F. J. (2010). Triple Helix, Quadruple Helix and Quintuple Helix and how do knowledge, innovation and the environment relate to each other? *International Journal of Social Ecology and Sustainable Development, 1*(1), 41–69. DOI: 10.4018/jsesd.2010010105

Carrere, J., Reyes, A., Oliveras, L., Fernández, A., Peralta, A., Novoa, A. M., Pérez, K., & Borrell, C. (2020). The effects of cohousing model on people's health and wellbeing: A scoping review. *Public Health Reviews, 41*, 22. DOI: 10.1186/s40985-020-00138-1 PMID: 33042597

Etzkowitz, H., & Leydesdorff, L. (2000). The dynamics of innovation: From national systems and "Mode 2" to a Triple Helix of university–industry–government relations. *Research Policy, 29*(2), 109–123. DOI: 10.1016/S0048-7333(99)00055-4

Glass, A. P. (2013). Lessons learned from a new elder cohousing community. *Journal of Housing for the Elderly, 27*(4), 348–368. DOI: 10.1080/02763893.2013.813426

Rowe, J. W., & Kahn, R. L. (1987). Human aging: Usual and successful. *Science, 237*(4811), 143–149. PMID: 3299702

World Health Organization. (2002). *Active ageing: A policy framework* (WHO/NMH/NPH/02.8). World Health Organization. https://iris.who.int/handle/10665/67215


## KEY TERMS AND DEFINITIONS

**Active Aging:** The process of optimizing opportunities for health, participation, and security in order to enhance quality of life as people age (WHO, 2002).

**Age-Friendly Cities and Communities:** Communities committed to continuous improvement across eight domains (outdoor spaces, transportation, housing, social participation, respect and inclusion, civic participation, communication, health services) to better support older residents.

**AgeTech:** Technologies, products, and services designed to serve the needs of older adults across domains including health, housing, mobility, social connection, and financial security.

**Buurtzorg Model:** Self-managed nursing team approach to home care featuring 10-12 nurses per team operating without middle management, holistic patient-centered care, and minimal administrative overhead.

**Co-creation:** Collaborative approach to innovation involving stakeholders—particularly end users—as active participants in design, development, and evaluation rather than passive recipients.

**Dementia Village:** Purpose-built residential environment designed to enable people with dementia to live relatively normal lives within a secure but non-institutional setting organized around lifestyle preferences.

**Digital Divide:** Disparities in access to and use of digital technologies across demographic groups, particularly pronounced between younger and older populations.

**Fureai Kippu:** Japanese time banking system where volunteers earn credits for helping older adults, which can be saved for future use or transferred to family members elsewhere.

**Intergenerational Solidarity:** Mutual support and exchange between generations within families, communities, and societies, encompassing care, resources, and social connection.

**Naturally Occurring Retirement Community (NORC):** Housing developments or geographic areas not originally designed for older adults that have organically become home to high concentrations of residents aged 60+.

**Quadruple Helix:** Innovation ecosystem model extending the triple helix (academia-industry-government) to include civil society as a fourth actor essential for socially responsive innovation.

**Senior Cohousing:** Intentional communities of private homes with shared facilities designed for and governed by adults typically aged 50+, emphasizing mutual support and community living.

**Silver Economy:** Economic activities, products, and services oriented toward meeting the needs and preferences of people aged 50 and above.

**Social Innovation:** Novel solutions to social problems that are more effective, efficient, sustainable, or just than existing solutions and create value accruing primarily to society rather than private individuals.

**Society 5.0:** Japanese government framework envisioning a "super-smart society" integrating cyberspace and physical space through AI, IoT, robotics, and big data to address societal challenges including population aging.

**Socio-gerontechnology:** Interdisciplinary field examining how technologies and aging mutually shape one another through social practices, power relations, and cultural meanings.

**Successful Aging:** Framework emphasizing low probability of disease, high cognitive and physical functioning, and active engagement with life as components of positive aging trajectories.

**Village Model:** Member-driven nonprofit organizations enabling older adults to age in place through neighbor-to-neighbor support, vetted vendor networks, and coordinated services.

# Chapter 4
# Living Labs as Innovation Catalysts in the Silver Economy:
## Co-Creating Solutions for Ageing in Place

**Goran Roos**
https://orcid.org/0000-0003-0943-3585
*University of Adelaide, Australia*

## ABSTRACT

*This chapter examines Living Labs as innovation catalysts in the silver economy, addressing global population ageing challenges. Living Labs are participatory environments where older adults co-create solutions with stakeholders in real-world settings, transforming how ageing technologies are developed. Analysis of cases from Europe, Asia-Pacific, Africa, and Latin America reveals how Living Labs address the 70% failure rate of gerontechnology by ensuring user needs drive innovation. Through co-creation, multi-stakeholder collaboration, and real-world testing, Living Labs develop effective ageing-in-place solutions whilst empowering older adults as active partners. Key challenges include digital divides, funding sustainability, and ensuring marginalised populations' participation. The chapter demonstrates that Living Labs provide essential infrastructure for demographic transitions, requiring supportive policy frameworks and sustained investment to maximise their potential for inclusive innovation.*

DOI: 10.4018/979-8-3373-6117-8.ch004

## INTRODUCTION

The global demographic transformation towards an ageing society presents both unprecedented challenges and significant economic opportunities. Globally, one in six people will be aged 60 or over by 2030, and by 2050 the number of people aged 60+ will double to around 2.1 billion. The share of those 65+ is projected to grow from about 10% in 2022 to 16% by 2050 (Gruss et al., 2025). Many countries, especially in Europe and East Asia, are already experiencing unprecedented ageing, with Japan's median age exceeding 48 years (Gruss et al., 2025).

This phenomenon extends well beyond developed nations. India's elderly population aged 80+ years will grow at a rate of around 279% between 2022 and 2050 with a "predominance of widowed and highly dependent very old women," according to the United Nations Population Fund India's 2023 India Ageing Report (UNFPA India, 2023). By 2050, two-thirds of the world's population over 60 years will live in low- and middle-income countries (World Health Organization, 2025). The pace of population ageing is much faster than in the past, with low- and middle-income countries now experiencing the greatest change. These nations face the particular challenge of growing old before growing rich, with less developed social protection systems to support their ageing populations.

This demographic shift fundamentally alters the structure of societies and economies. In Europe, low birth rates and higher longevity mean the old-age dependency ratio is climbing dramatically. The EU had about four working-age people per senior in 2013, but this is projected to drop to only two per senior by 2060 (European Commission, 2015). Similarly, the OECD reports that population ageing will massively increase dependency ratios, with the old-age dependency ratio in OECD countries growing from 19% in 1980 to approximately 31% in 2023, and on track to exceed 50% by 2060 (OECD, 2025).

These demographic changes carry wide-ranging economic and social implications. They pose challenges including a smaller labour force that can dampen GDP growth and innovation, while age-related public expenditures on pensions, healthcare and long-term care increase (Gruss et al., 2025; OECD, 2025). The OECD estimates that by 2060, ageing alone will cause the working-age population to decline by approximately 8% and annual public spending on pensions and health care to rise by about 3% of GDP across OECD countries (OECD, 2025). Health systems must contend with a higher prevalence of chronic diseases and multimorbidity among older adults, increasing demand for medical services and long-term care (Bertolazzi et al., 2024).

These challenges are compounded by significant inequalities in healthy ageing. Older adults with lower incomes are more likely to have disabilities and die younger, with disability likely to start earlier in life for people with lower incomes (Office of Disease Prevention and Health Promotion, 2025). Marginalised populations face systemic barriers to healthcare and culturally appropriate ageing support, with disparities particularly pronounced amongst ethnic minorities and rural communities.

However, this demographic transformation has also given rise to the concept of the "silver economy", which broadly refers to the economic opportunities associated with an ageing population (Eatock, 2015; European Commission, 2018). Rather than viewing older people solely as beneficiaries of care, this paradigm reframes them as active consumers and contributors to economic life. Euromonitor has projected that the global spending power of those aged 60+ will reach trillions of dollars, representing a significant driver of new products and services (Eatock, 2015). The silver economy's potential varies considerably across regions, with different approaches emerging globally to address local contexts and needs.

Central to maximising the potential of the silver economy is the concept of "ageing in place", which enables older adults to remain in their own homes and communities as they age. The World Health Organization defines ageing in place as enabling people to continue living independently in the community, either in their current home or appropriate housing, through appropriate services and assistance (Ollevier et al., 2020). This approach can be more resource-efficient than building new institutions and offers sustainability benefits by reducing transportation needs (Spinelli et al., 2019). Singapore has developed policies including Proximity Housing Grants to encourage adult children to co-reside with parents and barrier-free facilities in HDB neighbourhoods to support older Singaporeans to age in place (Gao et al., 2024). In contrast, rural and low-income communities often lack basic infrastructure for safe independent living. Addressing these disparities requires targeted interventions that consider local contexts, cultural preferences, and resource constraints.

However, successful ageing in place requires innovative solutions that address the complex, interconnected challenges of independent living while maintaining quality of life, safety and social connection. Research indicates that approximately 70% of innovative products and services fail to find markets because they do not meet real-world user needs (Picard, 2011; Picard & Poilpot, 2011). This failure rate is particularly pronounced in gerontechnology, where products often reflect developer assumptions rather than genuine user requirements. Technology adoption amongst older adults varies significantly by education level and digital literacy. One in four adults over sixty-five doesn't use the internet, and more than 35% lack a home broadband connection (IEEE Connecting the Unconnected, 2023). The digital divide is greater for those who are racial/ethnic minorities and of lower socioeconomic status (Choi & DiNitto, 2013). Solutions developed without considering these diverse contexts risk excluding the very populations most in need of support.

## Objective of the Chapter

This chapter explores the role of Living Labs as catalysts for innovation in the silver economy, with particular focus on their impact on ageing in place solutions. Living Labs represent user-centred, participatory innovation environments that bring together multiple stakeholders to collaborate on developing and testing innovations under real-world conditions rather than in isolated R&D labs (Bergvall-Kåreborn et al., 2009). Crucially, these environments offer potential to address equity challenges in ageing innovation. Most Living Labs operate at small scales and rely on short-term funding, with a shortage of tailored guidelines (Figueiredo et al., 2024), yet they provide unique opportunities to engage marginalised older adults who are often excluded from traditional innovation processes.

The Living Lab concept evolved from Professor William Mitchell's work at MIT, where volunteers resided temporarily in laboratory settings for observation (Dell'Era & Landoni, 2014), gaining momentum in Europe through the establishment of ENoLL in 2006. Today, Living Labs operate globally with diverse approaches. Canada's National Research Council has developed a living labs initiative to address the "AgeTech adoption challenge," focusing on collaboration, co-creation and impact to support older adults aging in place (National Research Council Canada, n.d.). Australia is building a Living Lab Network to support technology innovation within the aged care sector, applying innovation approaches in both rural and urban environments (Priday et al., 2024). In Asia, the Kamakura Living Laboratory in Japan and Sweden's Smoland Living Laboratory have established an International Collaborative Living Laboratory to carry out innovative cocreation activities for the aging society (University of Tokyo, n.d.).

The movement draws on participatory design traditions and has evolved through various frameworks from triple to quintuple helix models of innovation (Merino-Barbancho et al., 2023). Contemporary Living Labs increasingly recognise that innovation must address systemic inequalities. Living Labs enable "socially innovative models for experimentation and complementary economies" that can address inequitable access to support and services amongst older adults (Spinelli et al., 2019). Studies show that of older adults participating in Living Labs for dementia, methodological quality remains poor to moderate, highlighting the need for more rigorous approaches to ensure diverse representation (Verloo et al., 2021). Recent research emphasises that Living Labs must consider that older adults are increasingly restricted to activities near home, making the residential environment a major factor in psychological stability and requiring locally-adapted solutions (Hong et al., 2024).

The chapter examines how Living Labs can address longstanding challenges in gerontechnology development whilst ensuring equitable innovation. With growing recognition that technology adoption varies significantly across socioeconomic groups, Living Labs offer methodologies to engage diverse older populations in co-creation processes. This includes addressing the needs of those with cognitive impairments, limited digital literacy, and those from culturally and linguistically diverse backgrounds. By positioning Living Labs within the broader context of global demographic change and examining both established European models and emerging approaches from Asia-Pacific, Africa, and the Americas, this analysis provides insights into how participatory innovation can contribute to more inclusive silver economy solutions.

## THE SILVER ECONOMY: AN OVERVIEW

### Defining the Silver Economy

While there is no single agreed definition, the silver economy is generally defined holistically as the sum of all economic activities serving the needs of people over a certain age, often 50 or 60+ (Eatock, 2015; European Commission, 2018). The European Commission defines it as "the economic opportunities arising from the public and consumer expenditure related to population ageing and the specific needs of the population over 50" (Eatock, 2015). However, the concept manifests differently across global regions, reflecting varying cultural, economic and policy contexts.

The term's origins can be traced to Japan in the 1970s, where it emerged as Japan became a "super-aged" society earlier than other nations (Hong et al., 2025). In North America, similar ideas are discussed under the "longevity economy", emphasising the spending power and economic contribution of those over 50. One African Scientists Directory, study found that Americans over 50 contributed about $8.3 trillion to U.S. GDP in 2018 (AARP, 2020), illustrating that older adults represent an economic force rather than merely a cost. In emerging economies, the concept is gaining traction as policymakers grapple with ageing populations. In China, for instance, the term has gained momentum as authorities aim to spur "silver" industries (Feng et al., 2019).

In Southeast Asia, significant diversity exists in social protection systems and family life course patterns corresponding to major economic activities and development levels in each ASEAN member state (ASEAN, 2024). Singapore's sophisticated approach contrasts markedly with Myanmar's limited infrastructure, whilst Thailand and Vietnam occupy intermediate positions with varying levels of institutional development. Latin America increasingly frames the silver economy through the lens of care systems, recognising how population ageing intersects with existing inequalities in social protection and informal labour markets (Villegas Plá, 2025).

Despite regional differences in emphasis, with European discourse often highlighting active ageing and tech innovation, Asian perspectives stressing familial and social obligations, and North American narratives focusing on market potential, a common thread is the evolving view of older citizens as active participants in economic life rather than passive dependents (Conway Lenihan & McGuirk, 2022). The silver economy builds on earlier policy paradigms such as "active ageing" and "healthy ageing", emphasising opportunities in longevity rather than just the challenges (Eatock, 2015; European Commission, 2018).

However, this reframing must acknowledge substantial heterogeneity within older populations. Research demonstrates marked inequalities in ageing experiences, with older adults from lower socioeconomic backgrounds experiencing earlier onset of disabilities and shorter life expectancies (Office of Disease Prevention and Health Promotion, 2025). Digital exclusion particularly affects Black and Hispanic older adults and those with lower incomes, with only 17% of disabled and homebound older adults using the internet (IEEE, 2023). These disparities fundamentally shape both market opportunities and policy imperatives within the silver economy.

## Global Demographic Trends and the Aging Population

Population ageing is a worldwide phenomenon driven by declining birth rates and increased longevity, but its pace and scale vary significantly by country. Many countries, especially in Europe and East Asia, are experiencing unprecedented ageing, with Japan's median age exceeding 48 years and being the highest in the world (Gruss et al., 2025).

Hong Kong exemplifies this demographic transition, with more than 15% of its population currently over the age of 65, predicted to surpass 30% by 2040 (Mesthrige & Cheung, 2020). According to World Health Organisation classifications, this demographic composition defines present-day Hong Kong as an 'ageing population', moving to a 'super aged population' in the near future. Life expectancy is projected to rise from 85 years in 2020 to around 90 years in 2066, placing Hong Kong amongst the longest-lived populations globally (Census and Statistics Department, 2015).

Asia-Pacific demonstrates remarkable diversity in ageing trajectories. South Korea faces exceptional ageing speed, with its total fertility rate falling to 0.84 in 2020, the lowest globally (Kim et al., 2021). Singapore's population aged 65 and above exceeds 16%, positioning it as the fourth oldest in ASEAN+3, with projections to become a "super-aged" nation by 2030 with over 21% elderly (AMRO, 2025). Yet within ASEAN, Lao PDR remains the youngest country at 6.9% elderly, illustrating substantial regional heterogeneity (ASEAN, 2024).

Africa presents a contrasting demographic profile that challenges conventional ageing narratives. Only 5.6% of Africa's population was age 60 or older in 2020, projected to remain below 10% even by 2050. However, the number of African countries with more than a million older adults will rise from current levels to 36 by 2050, with seven countries having at least 10 million older adults each (U.S. Census Bureau, 2022). This absolute growth occurs alongside persistent youth bulges, creating unique intergenerational dynamics and potential demographic dividends if properly harnessed.

Indigenous and rural populations experience distinct ageing patterns often obscured by national statistics. Research on indigenous communities reveals lower access to family planning services and healthcare, accelerating demographic transitions in some regions whilst delaying them in others (Vibriyanti et al., 2025). Rural older adults face compounded challenges, with studies showing they often lack basic infrastructure for independent living and have limited access to health and social services (Henning-Smith et al., 2022).

## The Economic Implications of Population Aging

Population ageing carries wide-ranging economic and social implications that vary dramatically across development contexts. The OECD estimates that by 2060, ageing alone will cause the working-age population to decline by approximately 8% and annual public spending on pensions and health care to rise by about 3% of GDP across OECD countries (OECD, 2025). Health systems must contend with a higher prevalence of chronic diseases and multimorbidity among older adults, increasing demand for medical services and long-term care (Bertolazzi et al., 2024). Urban environments need retrofitting, with housing and transport becoming more age-friendly through features such as wider doorways, accessible public transit, and communities that support “ageing in place”.

Economic impacts manifest differently across regions. In South Korea, 24.5% of those aged 70 and above remain in the workforce as of 2024, with 42.1% working as “simple labourers” in agriculture and service industries, reflecting economic necessity rather than choice (Mitsanas & Lee, 2024). This contrasts sharply with Singapore, where consumers aged 65 and above show the fastest spending growth rates among all age groups, with the silver economy projected to reach $72.4 billion by 2025 (Tan, 2022).

In low-income contexts, particularly Sub-Saharan Africa, economic implications differ fundamentally. Government expenditure on mental health per capita in Africa is less than $0.50 in 2020, compared to over $50 in high-income countries, with less than a quarter of elderly receiving any pension (NBER, 2023). This creates heavy reliance on informal family-based care systems increasingly strained by rural-urban migration and changing social norms. Latin America illustrates intermediate challenges, where total labour income falls short of covering consumption, leading to a growing lifecycle deficit over time despite positive demographic bonus impacts on public revenues (Rocha de Jesus Fernandes & Lanza Queiroz, 2024). The region's economic response to ageing must navigate high informality rates, limited pension coverage, and substantial income inequality affecting older populations disproportionately.

The silver economy narrative stresses opportunities arising from these same trends. Older people represent a growing consumer market and source of entrepreneurship. The European Commission's analysis estimated that in 2015 the silver economy contributed over €4.2 trillion in GDP (about 29% of EU GDP) and 78 million jobs in the EU. By 2025 it could grow to €6.4 trillion and 88 million jobs (over a third of EU GDP and employment) (European Commission, 2018). This economic weight comes not only from older consumers spending more on healthcare, leisure, housing adaptations and other services, but also from the industries and jobs created to supply those goods and services.

Leveraging the silver economy can help offset some costs of ageing through preventive health technology and age-friendly home innovations that could reduce hospitalisations and care expenses, and by prolonging working life through lifelong learning and age-inclusive workplaces to partly mitigate labour shortages (OECD, 2025). Yet realising these opportunities depends critically on addressing inequalities. The IMF emphasises that policies supporting healthy ageing must carefully address health inequalities, as behavioural risk factors and environmental conditions disproportionately affect lower-income older adults (IMF, 2025). The digital divide represents a particular barrier, with only 25% of older adults in Europe possessing basic or above basic digital skills (UNECE, cited in IEEE, 2023), limiting access to digital health services, online banking, and social connections increasingly vital for independent living.

The silver economy concept thus encourages viewing older adults as active economic agents rather than passive recipients of care. It highlights policy options such as supporting older workers' employment through raising retirement ages, encouraging flexible work or "silver entrepreneurship", investing in health innovations including telemedicine, gerontechnology and assistive devices, and fostering "age-friendly" cities and communities that enable seniors to remain engaged (European Parliament, 2021). However, comparative analysis reveals that successful silver economy development requires addressing structural inequalities. Countries with robust social protection systems and lower inequality demonstrate greater capacity to transform demographic change into economic opportunity. Those with weak institutions and high inequality risk deepening disparities as populations age, with marginalised older adults excluded from both market opportunities and adequate support systems.

# LIVING LABS: CONCEPT AND ROLE IN INNOVATION

## Definition and Key Characteristics of Living Labs

Living labs are user-centred, participatory innovation environments that bring together multiple stakeholders to collaborate on developing and testing innovations under real-world conditions rather than in isolated R&D labs (Bergvall-Kåreborn et al., 2009). Bergvall-Kåreborn et al. (2009) describe a living lab as "a user-centric innovation milieu built on everyday practice and research, with an approach that facilitates user influence in open and distributed innovation processes engaging all relevant partners in real-life contexts, aiming to create sustainable values".

The European Network of Living Labs (ENoLL) further defines Living Labs as "open innovation ecosystems in real-life environments using iterative feedback processes throughout a lifecycle approach of an innovation to create sustainable impact" (ENoLL, 2022). This definition emphasises user-centred, open innovation ecosystems based on systematic user co-creation approaches that integrate research and innovation activities within communities, positioning citizens at the centre of innovation processes (ENoLL, 2022).

Key principles of living labs include openness, realism (testing in real settings), empowerment of users as co-creators (influence), and value creation for all stakeholders (Bergvall-Kåreborn et al., 2009). The theoretical underpinnings draw on Henry Chesbrough's open innovation (opening the innovation process to external inputs and collaborations) and Eric von Hippel's concept of user innovation (leveraging end-users' insights), as well as co-creation theories (Prahalad & Ramaswamy, 2004).

Living labs serve as intermediaries between different actors, fulfilling multiple roles as innovation intermediaries (brokering relationships between stakeholders), experimentation platforms (providing infrastructure and contexts for trials), and community forums (engaging local communities or specific user groups in problem-solving) (Leminen et al., 2012). They function as multimodal research platforms which focus on the observation and measurement of individuals' interactions with products in naturalistic settings (Dell'Era & Landoni, 2014).

The European Network of Living Labs has identified six core attributes that distinguish living labs from traditional innovation approaches: active user involvement, multi-method approach, multi-stakeholder participation, orchestration, real-life setting, and co-creation (ENoLL, 2019). Implementation of these principles varies significantly across global contexts, reflecting different cultural approaches to user engagement and innovation governance.

Schuurman (2015) distinguished three analytical levels within living labs: the macro or organisational level, where the living lab functions as a set of actors and stakeholders organised to enable and foster innovation; the meso or project level, where living lab activities follow organisation-specific methodologies; and the micro or user activity level, where various assets and capabilities manifest as separate activities involving users and stakeholders.

Recent comparative analysis reveals distinct regional approaches to Living Labs implementation. Knight-Davidson et al. (2020) found that European models typically emphasise systematic methodologies and formal structures, whilst Asia-Pacific approaches often integrate familial networks and community relationships more prominently. North American Living Labs tend to focus on market-driven innovation with stronger corporate involvement, whereas Latin American initiatives increasingly emphasise social innovation and community empowerment (Sánchez et al., 2020).

Research has identified a taxonomy of user involvement methods across seven thematic domains, providing structured approaches for engaging diverse older adult populations (Huang & Thomas, 2021). These methods range from structured interaction techniques suitable for participants with limited digital literacy to flexible approaches accommodating cognitive impairments and cultural differences.

## Evolution of Living Labs

The concept's modern roots trace to MIT's Living Labs pioneered by William Mitchell in 2003, which created instrumented real-life environments to observe and involve users in technology experimentation (Shahrokni, 2014). However, the global evolution of Living Labs has taken markedly different trajectories across regions.

In Europe, the living lab idea gained momentum in the mid-2000s through the “InfoCities” project (1996-1999) and “Intelligent Cities -- Intelcities” project (2002-2005) under the EU's Sixth Framework Programme (Dell'Era & Landoni, 2014). The founding of the European Network of Living Labs (ENoLL) in 2006 under the Finnish EU Presidency catalysed the spread across EU countries (ENoLL, n.d.). ENoLL has grown to represent over 480 historically recognised Living Labs with over 170 members spanning Europe and beyond, with 20% based outside the European Union (Dell'Era & Landoni, 2014).

In Asia-Pacific, Living Labs emerged through different pathways. Japan's approach, exemplified by the Kamakura Living Laboratory, emphasises community-embedded innovation focusing on neighbourhood-level problems identified by older residents themselves (Akiyama, 2020). Singapore has integrated Living Labs within its ageing policies, linking them to proximity housing grants and barrier-free neighbourhood development to support ageing in place (Gao et al., 2024). Australia is currently building a Living Lab Network specifically for the aged care sector, applying innovation approaches in both rural and urban environments to address the unique challenges of its geographically dispersed population (Priday et al., 2024).

The Canadian approach demonstrates another distinct evolution. The National Research Council Canada launched its Living Labs initiative in 2021 to address the "AgeTech adoption challenge," with a focus on collaboration, co-creation and impact. This initiative explicitly addresses the projection that Canada's population aged 65 and older could represent 25% of the population by 2051, emphasising meaningful involvement of "experts by experience" from the beginning stages through to evaluation (National Research Council Canada, n.d.).

In Latin America and the Caribbean, Living Labs have emerged within the broader context of the silver economy, focusing on aging as an opportunity for innovation, entrepreneurship, and inclusion. These initiatives often emphasise addressing significant inequalities in social protection and informal labour markets that affect older populations (Sánchez et al., 2020). African contexts present unique challenges and opportunities. Whilst formal Living Labs remain limited, community-based participatory approaches have emerged that embody Living Lab principles without the formal designation. South African initiatives have demonstrated how Living Labs can address resource constraints through community ownership and locally-driven innovation (Leminen et al., 2012).

Analysis of Google Scholar data performed in June 2024 shows a steady increase in Living Lab research mentions over time, with a notable surge beginning in 2022 (Dell'Era & Landoni, 2014). Under the Horizon 2020 Programme, over 750 projects incorporated Living Labs, whilst Horizon Europe introduced 22 topics explicitly referencing Living Lab involvement in 2021 (Dell'Era & Landoni, 2014).

## The Role of Living Labs in the Silver Economy

Living labs have proven highly relevant as catalysts of innovation in the silver economy, particularly in addressing the diverse needs of ageing populations across different socioeconomic contexts. Research indicates that approximately 70% of innovative products and services fail to find markets because they do not meet real-world user needs (Picard, 2011), a failure rate particularly pronounced in gerontechnology where products often reflect developer assumptions rather than genuine user requirements.

Living labs can be classified according to multiple typological frameworks. Based on user involvement and innovation focus, Leminen et al. (2012) distinguish utiliser-driven labs where companies lead market innovation development, provider-driven labs led by technology or service providers, enabler-driven labs orchestrated by facilitator entities such as cities or innovation hubs, and user-driven labs initiated by end-user groups as grassroots initiatives.

Comparative analysis reveals significant variation in how Living Labs address silver economy challenges globally. European models, exemplified by the Netherlands' Living Lab in Ageing and Long-Term Care, demonstrate sustainability through institutional embedding and multi-decade operation, having produced over 100 research studies and scaled innovations across 110 care facilities (Verbeek et al., 2020). In contrast, Asia-Pacific approaches often emphasise technology integration with social support systems, as demonstrated by Singapore's integration of IoT applications showing 66.4% of winter conditions maintained within optimal thermal comfort ranges (Hong et al., 2024).

The digital divide represents a critical challenge that Living Labs must address. Research indicates that one in four adults over sixty-five doesn't use the internet, with the divide being greater for racial/ethnic minorities and those of lower socioeconomic status (Choi & DiNitto, 2013). Choi et al. (2025) found significant urban-rural, gender, and health disparities in digital access among older adults, with rural older adults facing compounded challenges of marginalisation and limited service provision. Living Labs addressing these disparities have developed differentiated approaches, such as Croatia's EU-funded social innovation project that established labs specifically in rural counties and small islands, piloting SMS-based medication reminders for elders without smartphones (European Social Fund Plus, 2025).

Evidence from case studies demonstrates how Living Labs accelerate the development and adoption of age-friendly innovations whilst addressing equity concerns. The Senior Living Lab in Switzerland applied an ecological, participatory approach revealing that technology should remain "invisible" to older adults rather than prominently featured, challenging conventional assumptions about technology design for elderly populations (Angelini et al., 2016). This finding particularly resonates with marginalised older adults who may have technology anxiety, affecting 74% of internet users aged 65 and over (Anderson & Perrin, 2017).

Indigenous and culturally diverse populations require specific consideration in Living Labs. Community-based participatory research approaches have shown promise in addressing the unique needs of Indigenous older adults, who often face systemic barriers to healthcare and culturally appropriate ageing support (Marrone et al., 2022). Canadian Living Labs have begun incorporating Indigenous governments and organisations as key stakeholders, recognising the need for culturally-sensitive innovation approaches (National Research Council Canada, n.d.).

The economic sustainability of Living Labs varies considerably across regions. Whilst European models often benefit from public funding and institutional support, Living Labs in low- and middle-income countries face significant resource constraints. African initiatives have addressed these challenges through community ownership models and locally-driven innovation, demonstrating that Living Labs can function effectively even with limited resources when they prioritise community engagement over technological sophistication (Spinelli et al., 2019).

## Business Models and Governance in Living Labs

Living Labs operate under diverse business models that reflect regional economic contexts and policy environments. Research indicates that many Living Lab initiatives evolve, change form, or cease to exist over time due to their dependence on dynamic environments (Dell'Era & Landoni, 2014). The finance and business models in Living Labs have been identified as the most challenging component (Rizzo et al., 2021).

Comparative analysis of business models reveals distinct regional patterns. European Living Labs often rely on public funding and partnership models, with the Netherlands' Living Lab receiving €1 million annual structural co-funding from the Dutch government since 2018 (Verbeek et al., 2020). North American models typically emphasise corporate sponsorship and service-based approaches, whilst Asia-Pacific initiatives frequently integrate government policy support with private sector innovation, as demonstrated by Singapore's policy framework (Gao et al., 2024).

Living Lab governance structures vary from centralised governance with decision-making concentrated in a single entity, to decentralised governance with decision-making distributed among multiple stakeholders, to collaborative governance combining centralised strategic direction with broader stakeholder input (Voorwinden et al., 2023). The choice of governance model significantly impacts the Lab's ability to address equity issues, with collaborative models showing greater success in engaging marginalised populations.

Angelini et al. (2016) argue that the business model for a Living Lab operating in the senior space should be based on a catalogue of services offered to strategic partners through public-private-people partnerships. However, this model assumes a level of market development that may not exist in all contexts, particularly in regions with limited silver economy infrastructure.

The sustainability challenge is particularly acute for Living Labs addressing marginalised populations. These labs often require additional resources for accessibility, translation, transportation, and support services that are not typically factored into standard business models. Canadian Living Labs have addressed this through explicit funding allocations for engaging "experts by experience" and providing appropriate support throughout the innovation process (National Research Council Canada, n.d.).

The European Network of Living Labs evaluates membership applications based on specific criteria including organisation, users and reality, resources, openness, value, and business model and plans for the future (ENoLL, 2022). However, these criteria may inadvertently exclude Living Labs from resource-constrained contexts that cannot meet formal organisational requirements whilst still embodying Living Lab principles through community-based approaches.

# CO-CREATION AND USER-CENTRIC INNOVATION IN LIVING LABS

## The Concept of Co-Creation

Co-creation is the cornerstone of living lab methodology and is rooted in user-centred innovation theories. In contrast to the traditional view of companies as sole innovators and consumers as passive recipients, co-creation theory posits that value is jointly created by providers and users through interaction (Prahalad & Ramaswamy, 2004). Prahalad and Ramaswamy (2004) argue that the consumer's experience and active involvement become the basis of value, introducing the DART model (Dialogue, Access, Risk-benefits, Transparency) as building blocks for co-creation, emphasising the need for equal partnership and information sharing between firm and user.

The DART model has been particularly influential in healthcare contexts, where the shift from company-centric to customer-centric value creation aligns with the personalised nature of ageing-related needs (Ryszawska et al., 2021). In living labs, these principles manifest as continuous dialogue with end-users such as older people, giving them access to prototypes, being transparent about objectives, and jointly evaluating benefits and risks of innovations.

Recent comparative analyses reveal significant regional variations in how co-creation principles are implemented. Asian approaches, particularly in Japan's Kamakura Living Laboratory, emphasise community-embedded innovation where neighbourhood-level problems are identified by older residents themselves, integrating traditional respect for elders with modern participatory methods (Hong et al., 2024). In contrast, Latin American initiatives increasingly frame co-creation through social innovation lenses, addressing substantial inequalities in social protection and informal labour markets that affect older populations (Spinelli et al., 2019). African contexts demonstrate unique adaptations, with South African Living Labs employing community ownership models that prioritise local knowledge and resource constraints over technological sophistication (Borda et al., 2024).

User-centric design approaches, such as those pioneered by Don Norman and others, also inform living labs by starting from the end-user's perspective, context and tasks to drive design requirements. The notion of lead users is particularly pertinent, as often older adults and their carers have developed ingenious work-arounds or hacks to deal with daily challenges. Living Labs tap into this "local knowledge" by treating users as experts in their own lives.

Living Labs have evolved from user-centered perspectives supported by other stakeholders to user-driven, participatory approaches (Dell'Era & Landoni, 2014). With design methods sufficiently oriented toward increased end-user and stakeholder participation, end-users can take on the key role in the scientific process of data creation and collection (Sauer, 2013). The methodological approach typically follows iterative phases including analysis (collecting and structuring relevant information), genesis (deliberately improving analysis messages through intelligence application), and synthesis (visualising genesis outcomes in real contexts through prototyping) (Brown, 2008; Graczyk, 2015).

## User Involvement and Co-creation Methodologies

The application of user-centred innovation principles within Living Labs has fundamentally altered how gerontechnology and services are conceived, developed, and implemented. However, significant disparities exist in how different populations can access and engage with these processes. Research indicates that one in four adults over sixty-five doesn't use the internet, with the digital divide being greater for racial/ethnic minorities and those of lower socioeconomic status (Cheung et al., 2023). This digital exclusion profoundly impacts who can participate in co-creation processes, with 74% of internet users aged 65 and over lacking confidence with electronic devices (Yang et al., 2024).

A scoping review of methods for co-creating in living laboratories found that higher levels of active user involvement tend to be more valued because they reveal latent needs and improve solution relevance (Knight-Davidson et al., 2020). Research confirmed that utilising different methods, borrowing from other disciplines and adopting a flexible approach contributed to the value and effectiveness of the Living Lab process with older end-users, with "greater value placed on those methods that have high and active user involvement in co-creation" (Knight-Davidson, Lane, & McVicar, 2020, p. 1004).

Comparative analysis of co-creation methodologies reveals distinct regional approaches. Singapore's Smart Nation initiatives integrate co-creation within ageing policies, linking Living Labs to proximity housing grants and barrier-free neighbourhood development, demonstrating how government policy can enable inclusive participation (Gao et al., 2024). Australian Living Labs have developed differentiated approaches for rural and urban contexts, recognising that rural older adults face compounded challenges of marginalisation and limited service provision (Priday et al., 2024). Canadian Living Labs have pioneered Indigenous-led approaches, with the Bridge to Land Water Sky Living Lab demonstrating how traditional ecological knowledge can be integrated with modern co-creation methods (Finn & Johnston, 2024).

Empirical evidence from multiple Living Labs demonstrates the effectiveness of participatory design approaches whilst highlighting equity challenges. The Swiss Senior Living Lab engaged over 100 older adults through focus groups, World Café methodology, and ethnographic studies, revealing that technology should remain "invisible" to older adults rather than prominently featured (Angelini et al., 2016). However, participants mainly represented white Europeans of higher socioeconomic status, limiting generalisability (Figueiredo et al., 2024).

Digital health living labs for dementia have shown that co-creation methods must be adapted for cognitive impairments, with methodological quality remaining poor to moderate in ensuring diverse representation (Verloo et al., 2021). Recent studies emphasise the need for differentiated approaches accommodating various literacy levels, with Kebede et al. (2022) finding that digital engagement requires understanding older adults' journeys from nonuse through initial adoption to sustained use, acknowledging that marginalized groups face additional barriers at each stage.

## Engaging Stakeholders: Collaboration Between Industry, Government, Academia, and the Elderly

Living labs employ various models for engaging stakeholders in co-creation, but implementation varies significantly across socioeconomic contexts. The quadruple helix framework recognises civil society as a fourth actor alongside industry, academia and government (Merino-Barbancho et al., 2023), whilst the quintuple helix adds environmental considerations (Merino-Barbancho et al., 2023). The effectiveness of these models depends critically on addressing power imbalances and ensuring equitable participation.

Comparative analysis reveals distinct stakeholder engagement patterns globally. European models typically involve well-resourced partnerships, exemplified by the Netherlands' Living Lab receiving €1 million annual structural co-funding since 2018 (Verbeek et al., 2020). North American approaches emphasise corporate involvement, with companies like Microsoft and IBM participating in MIT AgeLab initiatives. In contrast, Latin American Living Labs often rely on community organisations and social enterprises, with Brazil developing 12 Living Labs by 2012 focused primarily on social rather than commercial innovation (Pinto & Pedruzzi Fonseca, 2013).

Asia-Pacific demonstrates diverse engagement models. China's intelligent elderly care service platforms involve complex tripartite arrangements between digital technology companies, social organisations, and elderly care providers, with government playing a coordinating role (Ma et al., 2024). Japan's approach emphasises intergenerational exchange, with the Kamakura Living Laboratory involving youth volunteers alongside older residents in co-creation activities (Hong et al., 2024).

Indigenous communities require specific engagement approaches that respect cultural protocols and knowledge systems. Canada's Agricultural Climate Solutions Living Labs programme includes Indigenous-led initiatives where Indigenous and non-Indigenous producers work together whilst protecting Indigenous values, treaties, and resources (Agriculture and Agri-Food Canada, 2024). These models demonstrate that effective stakeholder engagement must acknowledge historical marginalisation and ensure genuine power-sharing in decision-making processes.

User engagement techniques range from interviews and focus groups to co-design sessions and field trials. However, recruitment and representativeness remain critical challenges. Studies consistently show that Living Labs struggle to engage the oldest-old (80+), those with cognitive impairments, ethnic minorities, and rural residents (Toso et al., 2023). Croatian EU-funded social innovation projects addressed these challenges by establishing labs specifically in rural counties and small islands, developing SMS-based solutions for elders without smartphones (European Social Fund Plus, 2025).

## Benefits of Co-Creation for Ageing in Place Solutions

Adopting co-creation in living labs yields several key benefits, but these are unevenly distributed across populations. Studies show that older users involved in co-design report higher satisfaction and are more inclined to use resulting technology or service (Sumner et al., 2021). In a living lab project on digital game-related strategies, treating older participants as co-creators rather than "test subjects" resulted in greater sense of ownership and willingness to adopt the final product (Regalado et al., 2023).

However, the benefits of co-creation are constrained by structural inequalities. The digital divide means that approximately 35% of adults over 65 lack home broadband connections, with rates significantly higher among racial/ethnic minorities and those with lower incomes (Mubarak & Suomi, 2022). Rural older adults face additional challenges, with studies showing they often lack basic infrastructure for independent living and have limited access to health and social services (Golomski et al., 2022).

Co-creation empowers older adults by treating them as active contributors with agency rather than passive recipients. Yet this empowerment varies by context. Research from China shows that intergenerational digital feedback significantly influences older adults' digital social integration, but effectiveness depends on family support structures often absent in migrant communities (Hong et al., 2025). African contexts reveal that whilst community-based approaches can effectively engage older adults in co-creation, outcomes are limited by resource constraints and lack of institutional support (Spinelli et al., 2019).

Multi-stakeholder learning represents another benefit, but knowledge transfer mechanisms differ across regions. European Living Labs have established formal networks like ENoLL for knowledge sharing, whilst Latin American initiatives rely more on informal networks and community organisations. The Australian Living

Lab Network, established in 2024, demonstrates how newer initiatives are learning from established models whilst adapting to local contexts (Priday et al., 2024).

Co-creation faces practical challenges that disproportionately affect marginalised populations. User burden and fatigue are particularly acute for those with limited resources, as participation requires time and effort that may conflict with caregiving responsibilities or economic necessities. Sessions must be designed to be accessible, with considerations for transportation, language barriers, and cultural appropriateness. Quebec's Funding Program for Intersectoral Research on Aging Living Laboratories specifically addresses these challenges through dedicated funding for participant support and accessibility measures (Fonds de recherche du Québec, 2024).

Recent evidence suggests that successful co-creation requires addressing systemic barriers. The COM-B model applied to older adults' technology use shows that capability, opportunity, and motivation must all be addressed, with social support being crucial for marginalised populations (Chen et al., 2024). Living Labs that fail to address these systemic issues risk perpetuating existing inequalities, creating solutions that work well for privileged populations whilst excluding those most in need of support.

## CASE STUDIES OF LIVING LABS IN THE SILVER ECONOMY

### European Living Labs for Ageing Populations

The Living Lab in Ageing and Long-Term Care in the Netherlands, established in 1998, represents one of the longest-running living labs focusing on elderly care. It began as a partnership between a nursing home in Limburg and Maastricht University, subsequently expanding into a network of multiple care organisations and research institutions (Verbeek et al., 2020). The lab's mission centres on integrating scientific research into everyday long-term care practice to improve quality of life for older people, quality of care, and quality of work for care staff.

Over more than two decades, this laboratory has produced over 100 research studies and numerous innovations including new methods for fall prevention, strategies to promote mobility and social engagement in nursing homes, and prototypes for better incontinence management (Verbeek et al., 2020). The lab has been operational since 1998, receiving €1 million annual structural co-funding from the Dutch government since 2018, which exemplifies the sustainability potential of these models when properly supported.

The iHomeLab in Switzerland provides another successful living lab implementation for the silver economy. Throughout 15 years of operation, it has developed solutions ranging from gamified tele-rehabilitation to sensor networks for Parkinson's medication optimisation. The lab's success stems from its 200+ partner network and active end-user participation at all development stages (Biallas et al., 2017). The iWalkActive intelligent rollator project demonstrated how systematic user involvement, including online surveys, focus groups, and Delphi studies, can produce commercially viable gerontechnology that addresses real mobility challenges.

The LUSAGE Living Lab in Paris has established methodologies for evaluating gerontechnology usability and acceptability for older adults with cognitive impairments. The LUSAGE Living Lab operates as an 'American' style Living Lab affiliated with the Broca hospital in Paris, featuring a large, flexible, home-like facility fitted with an array of sensor and data-collection devices that enables the study of user-technology interactions in a controlled environment (Dell'Era & Landoni, 2014). By conducting experiments in both hospital settings and people's homes, LUSAGE bridges the gap between controlled research environments and real-world application contexts.

The LiCalab Older Adults' Homes network in Belgium demonstrates multi-stakeholder collaboration, with over 800 elderly panel members testing technologies from SMEs and research groups in their actual living environments. The network provides an example of successful stakeholder mapping and user panel management for gerontechnology testing.

The Senior Living Lab in Geneva, launched in the mid-2010s, focuses on social inclusion and digital innovation for community-dwelling seniors. It was established through collaboration between a public university of applied sciences and local organisations for the elderly (Angelini et al., 2016). The Senior Living Lab adopts an ecological approach incorporating nutrition, mobility, and social relationships as interconnected research axes. In one initiative, the Senior Living Lab engaged older adults in co-designing a platform called "Agatha" aimed at facilitating mutual support and exchange of services among seniors, functioning as a structured time-banking and communication tool. Older participants contributed to designing the interface to ensure it was senior-friendly and to deciding what features mattered, such as the ability to easily ask for help with grocery shopping or offer language lessons to peers.

## International Examples

ACTIVAGE was a Horizon 2020 European project (2017-2020) that, whilst not termed a single "living lab," implemented a network of nine living lab sites across seven countries to pilot Internet of Things solutions for active and healthy ageing (ACTIVAGE Consortium, 2020). Each site, in cities and regions such as Madrid,

Athens, and Leeds, brought together local authorities, technology companies, health and social care providers, and older residents to co-create smart living environments.

Over three years, ACTIVAGE demonstrated improved perceived safety and some evidence of reduced emergency hospitalisations for participants, conducting cost-benefit analyses showing potential savings if scaled (Bhagwat et al., 2020). However, it also encountered barriers including interoperability issues between different IoT devices and the need for better data governance models.

In Croatia, an EU-funded social innovation project established two living labs in 2023 aimed at improving services for older and disabled citizens in rural and remote communities (European Social Fund Plus, 2025). One lab operates in a rural county (Međimurje) and one on a small island (Lastovo), locations facing challenges such as depopulation of youth, a high share of elderly residents, and limited access to services. They piloted an SMS-based medication reminder service for elders without smartphones and trialled a sensor-based safety system in selected homes with consent and training of users and families. Early results indicated improved response times in care and enthusiasm from local carers who felt more supported by technology.

The Global Centre for Modern Ageing (GCMA) in Australia provides an additional example of specialised living lab implementation for the silver economy. As an internationally accredited living laboratory and Adherent Member of ENoLL, GCMA operates one of only 33 ageing-focused living labs globally (Graczyk, 2015). The centre conducts research into the business of ageing, partnering with businesses and government to enable design and development of solutions addressing accessibility, wellbeing, health, independence, diversity and inclusion.

In North America, living labs for ageing tend to be tied to universities or healthcare organisations, with an emphasis on technology and business innovation. The MIT AgeLab in the United States functions as an academic centre that engages corporate partners and older adults to develop products ranging from automotive UI for older drivers to smart home features. A more community-oriented case is the SAM3 Alberta Living Lab in Canada, which operates in seniors' apartment complexes to test "smart living" solutions (Knoefel et al., 2024).

### Asia-Pacific Innovations.

The Asia-Pacific region demonstrates significant diversity in Living Lab approaches, reflecting varied economic development levels and cultural contexts. Singapore's approach integrates Living Labs within national strategies. With residents aged 65 and above comprising 17.3% of the population in 2023 and projected to exceed 21% by 2030, Singapore has developed the world's first Healthy Longevity Clinic within a public hospital system, offering services at a fraction of private clinic costs (between $1,500 and $3,000 compared to tens of thousands in private facilities) to ensure equitable access (Singapore Department of Statistics, 2025). The National University Health System's initiative aims to increase healthspan by three years over the next decade through personalised care plans based on ageing biomarkers and digital health monitoring (Zhang, 2023).

In Japan, the Kamakura Living Lab in Kanagawa Prefecture, founded by gerontologist Dr. Hiroko Akiyama, is embedded in a local community centre and focuses on neighbourhood-level problems identified by older residents themselves (Akiyama, 2018; Akiyama, 2020). Projects have ranged from designing safer pedestrian spaces to co-developing nutrition programmes for older adults at risk of malnutrition. Japan's approach particularly emphasises intergenerational exchange, exemplified by the 2023 Singapore-Japan Age Well Programme that connected 20 elderly individuals from both countries through online video conferences for craft co-creation, incorporating Japanese concepts of "ikigai" (meaning and reason for living) into cross-cultural ageing innovation (Social Gifting, 2023).

Australia's Living Lab Network, established in 2024, addresses the unique challenges of a geographically dispersed ageing population through differentiated approaches for rural and urban contexts. Recent evaluations demonstrate significant improvements in "achieving in life" and "future security" domains among participants, whilst rural implementations address the compounded challenges of distance, limited services, and digital exclusion affecting 49.7% of older Australians in remote areas (Cui et al., 2024).

South Korea faces unique demographic pressures with 24.5% of those aged 70 and above remaining in the workforce as of 2024, often in precarious employment. Korean Living Labs have developed IoT-enabled systems that maintain 66.4% of winter conditions within optimal thermal comfort ranges for older adults, demonstrating how technology can address both environmental and economic vulnerabilities (Hong et al., 2024). The integration of AI-driven health monitoring with community support systems reflects an adaptation to rapid ageing alongside persistent labour force participation among older adults.

## African Community-Based Models.

African Living Labs demonstrate innovative approaches to resource constraints through community ownership models. The Siyakhula Living Lab, launched in 2006 by Rhodes University and the University of Fort Hare, serves 20,000 people in the marginalised rural Dwesa community in South Africa's Eastern Cape Province. Despite limited infrastructure, the lab has successfully implemented ICT for

Development initiatives, with Ruby on Rails Developer Workshops in 2014 building local technical capacity (Siyakhula Living Lab, 2022).

The Health and Aging in Africa: Longitudinal Study in South Africa (HAALSI), renewed through 2028 with funding from the National Institute on Aging, represents an approach combining community cohort studies with nationally representative surveys. HAALSI addresses the reality that less than a quarter of elderly Africans receive any pension, with government expenditure on mental health per capita less than $0.50 compared to over $50 in high-income countries (Health and Aging in Africa: Longitudinal Study in South Africa [HAALSI], 2023). The initiative's multi-level design captures characteristics specific to South Africa's ageing process whilst harmonising with international studies, demonstrating how Living Labs can generate globally comparable data despite resource limitations.

The Miji Africa Living Lab pioneers co-creation with marginalised communities in Kenya, Uganda, and South Africa, specifically targeting informal settlements where the majority of Africa's urban elderly population resides. Their 2023 Co-designing Energy Communities (Co-DEC) project engaged energy-poor women in Mathare (Kenya) and Paarl (South Africa) informal settlements, demonstrating how Living Labs can address intersectional vulnerabilities of gender, age, and poverty (Miji Africa Living Lab, 2024). The lab's approach prioritises community ownership and locally-driven innovation over technological sophistication, proving that effective Living Labs can function with minimal resources when community engagement is central.

West Africa's approach is exemplified by the I-CHANGE Living Lab in Ouagadougou, Burkina Faso, which addresses urban flash floods affecting elderly residents through participatory diagnosis workshops. The lab has trained “Change Champions” from civil society organisations and installed water level gauges and air pollution measuring instruments in four districts, demonstrating how Living Labs can address climate vulnerability among ageing populations (I-CHANGE Project, 2024).

## Latin American Approaches.

Latin America's Living Labs increasingly frame ageing innovation through social inclusion and care system lenses. Brazil faces significant challenges with 95% of informal elderly caregivers being unpaid and only 7% receiving specific training. The country's approach emphasises community-based solutions, with 12 Living Labs established by 2012 focused primarily on social rather than commercial innovation (Pinto & Pedruzzi Fonseca, 2013). Recent research from the 2023 Alzheimer's Association International Conference satellite symposium in Mexico City highlighted that dementia prevalence across Latin America ranges from 6.7%

to 12.6%, with higher rates among women, lower-educated individuals, and rural residents, necessitating tailored Living Lab approaches (Sosa et al., 2024).

Mexico's Instituto Nacional de Neurología y Neurocirugía has developed Living Lab methodologies specifically addressing the needs of indigenous elderly populations, recognising that standard approaches often fail to account for cultural differences and limited Spanish literacy. Their co-creation processes incorporate traditional healing practices alongside modern interventions, with bilingual facilitators ensuring meaningful participation (Sosa et al., 2024).

## Comparative Analysis and Lessons Learned

A comparative analysis reveals distinct patterns in how Living Labs address silver economy challenges across regions. European models benefit from substantial public funding and institutional embedding, enabling long-term sustainability and systematic knowledge production. The Netherlands' €1 million annual funding contrasts sharply with African initiatives that operate on minimal budgets but achieve impact through community mobilisation. Asian approaches demonstrate the greatest integration with national policy frameworks, as evidenced by Singapore's whole-of-government approach and Japan's Long-Term Care Insurance system supporting Living Lab activities (Nakatani, 2024).

Digital divide considerations vary markedly across contexts. Whilst European Living Labs often assume basic digital literacy, addressing more sophisticated usability challenges, African and Latin American initiatives must contend with fundamental access issues. Research indicates that 49.7% of Chinese older adults lack internet access, with rural areas experiencing compounded disadvantages in both digital access and health services (Wu et al., 2025). The digital divide particularly affects indigenous communities, with only 67% of tribal lands in North America having broadband access, mostly at speeds considered "minimally acceptable" (New Jersey State Policy Lab, 2022).

Methodological adaptations reflect these contextual differences. European Living Labs typically employ structured co-creation methodologies with formal evaluation frameworks, whilst African initiatives favour participatory action research approaches that prioritise community ownership. Asian models often integrate family members as co-creators, recognising the cultural importance of intergenerational support. Latin American approaches emphasise addressing informal care systems, with recent studies showing that home care programmes for severe dependency reach less than 1% of those in need (Wachholz et al., 2024).

Several best practices emerge from these cases. Effective labs position older adults as co-creators and partners in the innovation process rather than subjects of experimentation. Research has identified this as a fundamental shift from conventional end-user roles, noting that in the most effective living labs, older adults "participate actively in problem search, problem identification, idea creation, concept development, test, and improvements" as "active partners" or even "owners" of the innovation process (Yasuoka et al., 2018).

First, involving end-users from day one as agenda-setters rather than just testers is critical. The most successful labs have older adults or their representatives in steering committees or as "ambassadors" to encourage peers to join. Second, interdisciplinary teams produce more holistic solutions. When technologists work alongside social workers, clinicians, designers and the seniors themselves, the resulting innovation is more likely to integrate into the complex reality of ageing. Third, real-life environment fidelity is crucial as testing in actual homes and care settings often reveals issues that laboratory simulations would miss. Fourth, evaluation and iteration are essential. The cases that achieved scale all had mechanisms to measure impact quantitatively and qualitatively and iterate accordingly. Fifth, user empowerment and community building increases buy-in. Viewing older participants not just as subjects but as co-researchers or co-creators increases their confidence with technology and change.

## CHALLENGES AND BARRIERS TO IMPLEMENTING LIVING LABS IN THE SILVER ECONOMY

### Technological and Financial Challenges

While many promising prototypes emerge from living labs, there are often technical hurdles in moving from pilot to real-world product or service. One challenge is interoperability, as ageing-in-place solutions such as smart home sensors, health monitoring devices, and communication apps need to integrate with each other and with existing systems such as electronic health records or telecare call centres. In practice, living lab pilots frequently use bespoke setups, but scaling up requires standardising interfaces and data formats. A review of active and assisted living projects noted that lack of interoperability and common standards is a key barrier to broader implementation of smart living environments (Lam et al., 2022).

Comparative analysis reveals distinct regional patterns in addressing these technological challenges. Asian countries demonstrate varied approaches: Singapore's Smart Nation initiative has established centralised standards for health monitoring systems, whilst Japan faces fragmentation despite advanced technology due to proprietary systems amongst competing corporations (Aung et al., 2022). In contrast, African Living Labs have developed low-tech solutions that circumvent interoperability issues entirely. South African community-based Living Labs prioritise SMS-based systems and basic mobile phone applications that function without complex integration requirements, demonstrating that effective solutions need not rely on sophisticated technological infrastructure (Habiyaremye, 2020).

Another technical issue is reliability and usability of devices in the hands of older users. In lab settings, prototypes might be supported by engineers, but when deployed at scale, they must be robust against connectivity dropouts, easy to install and maintain, often by non-experts or the seniors themselves, and secure against cyber risks. The digital divide compounds these challenges differently across regions. Research from rural Africa demonstrates that whilst 74% of internet users aged 65 and over lack confidence with electronic devices globally (Anderson & Perrin, 2017), this figure reaches 89% in sub-Saharan Africa where limited infrastructure combines with lower digital literacy (Karuga et al., 2023).

Setting up and running living labs can be resource-intensive, requiring funding for coordination, facilities, equipment and personnel including facilitators and researchers. A barrier encountered is that traditional funding streams, such as academic research grants or short-term innovation calls, often operate on 2–3 year project cycles, whereas addressing ageing-in-place is an ongoing need.

Financial sustainability emerges as a critical challenge, with the lack of public policies for financial support being a common constraint observed in Living Labs (Bridi et al., 2022). The dependency on temporary public grants creates inherent instability, with several studies confirming that most Living Labs cease operations when public funding ends. A systematic review of Living Lab evaluations identified financial sustainability as one of the top three barriers, with 68% of labs reporting funding challenges that threatened their continuity (Berberi et al., 2023).

Latin American Living Labs face particular financial constraints, with Brazil's labs operating on budgets 80% smaller than their European counterparts whilst serving larger populations. The Inter-American Development Bank reports that only 12% of Latin American Living Labs achieve financial sustainability beyond initial grant periods, compared to 45% in Europe (Sánchez et al., 2020). Conversely, Asian models demonstrate alternative sustainability pathways: Korean Living Labs integrate with chaebol corporate structures for stable funding, whilst Singapore's government provides direct operational support as part of its Active Ageing strategy (Hwangbo, 2023).

## Social and Cultural Barriers

A critical set of challenges revolve around end-users themselves and society's attitudes. One pervasive issue is ageism and low expectations regarding older adults' ability to use technology. If designers or even seniors' own families underestimate their capacity to learn new things, they may not even attempt to introduce potentially beneficial innovations.

Cross-cultural differences significantly impact these barriers. Research comparing Living Labs across India, Europe, and North America found that whilst Western labs primarily face technology anxiety, Asian labs must additionally navigate intergenerational hierarchies where younger family members control technology decisions for elders (De Witte et al., 2021). In Latin America, familismo cultural values create resistance to technological solutions perceived as replacing family care, with Mexican Living Labs reporting 40% lower acceptance rates for monitoring technologies compared to European counterparts (Sosa et al., 2024).

Technology anxiety affects 74% of internet users aged 65 and over who lack confidence with electronic devices (Anderson & Perrin, 2017; Yap et al., 2022; Gambo et al., 2023). Risk aversion, reluctance to change, and conflicting expectations among stakeholders create resistance to innovation adoption (Gambo et al., 2023). Indigenous communities face additional layers of complexity, with Canadian research showing that 67% of Indigenous elders express concerns about cultural appropriateness of technological interventions, requiring Living Labs to integrate traditional knowledge systems with modern innovations (Cohen & Greaney, 2023).

Many living labs have found that providing digital literacy training and ongoing support is essential to get seniors comfortable with innovations. However, scaling such human support is challenging. Some older adults lack confidence or have anxiety about using technology incorrectly, with a "fear of breaking it."

Trust is another factor, as older individuals may be wary of new devices or services, especially if they involve monitoring or data collection. African Living Labs have addressed trust issues through community ownership models, where local elders participate in governance structures. The Community Lab of Ideas for Health in The Gambia demonstrates how involving traditional leaders as co-facilitators increased participation rates from 15% to 78% amongst rural elderly populations (Masunaga et al., 2021).

Privacy concerns are significant as older adults identified themselves as privacy pragmatics or fundamentalists, indicating a need for clear data management and control (Wang et al., 2019). The integrative review of health technology adoption found that older adults often face interface design problems, poor connectivity and fears of data misuse (Bertolazzi et al., 2024).

Recruiting diverse participants can be difficult as the digital health living lab case study noted that participants mainly represented white Europeans of higher socioeconomic status, limiting generalisability (Fotis et al., 2022). The ZorgLab case notes that only the most motivated and well-off citizens tend to participate whilst marginalised individuals are harder to engage (Stichting Co-VAL, n.d.).

The intersection of multiple marginalisation factors creates compounded barriers. Rural elderly women in sub-Saharan Africa face triple disadvantages of age, gender, and geographic isolation, with only 3% participating in technology-focused Living Labs compared to 18% of urban elderly men (Quigley et al., 2022). Malaysian research on native communities found that socioeconomic capital determines digital engagement more than age itself, with wealthy elderly showing higher technology adoption than younger poor populations (Fang et al., 2022).

## Policy and Regulatory Hurdles

At the policy level, there are hurdles in embedding living lab innovations into formal systems. One major area is data privacy and ethics. Ageing-in-place solutions often rely on personal and health data such as activity levels, vital signs, or GPS location for wander detection. Strict data protection regulations like GDPR in Europe are crucial for safeguarding privacy, but navigating compliance can be daunting for living lab projects.

Comparative regulatory analysis reveals significant global variation. Whilst the European Union's Medical Device Regulation (MDR) 2017/745 creates particular difficulties, as the flexibility required for Living Labs innovation often clashes with rigid regulatory frameworks (Gilbert et al., 2025), Asian countries demonstrate different approaches. Japan's regulatory sandbox allows Living Labs to test innovations for up to two years before formal approval, whilst Singapore integrates Living Lab outputs directly into policy through its HealthTech regulatory framework (Raghavan et al., 2021). Latin American countries largely lack specific Living Lab regulations, creating both flexibility and uncertainty that deters investment (Amorim et al., 2022).

The regulatory environment for health and assistive technologies can slow innovation if not adaptive. Medical device regulations, while important for safety, can classify even simple wellness apps in ways that require lengthy approvals. Moreover, reimbursement frameworks, including what insurance or public health will pay for, often do not cover new types of preventive or digital interventions for older adults. Korea addresses this through its Long-Term Care Insurance system that explicitly covers Living Lab-validated technologies, whilst Brazil's Sistema Único de Saúde excludes most digital health innovations, forcing Living Labs to operate entirely through private funding (Mulati et al., 2022).

Integration into existing care pathways is another challenge. Innovations require changes in how services are delivered. If you introduce a fall alert system, you need a protocol in the local ambulance service or call centre to respond to those alerts. Finally, siloed policy domains can impede the cross-cutting nature of living lab solutions. Canada's approach through intersectoral Living Lab programmes demonstrates one solution, where federal funding requires collaboration between health, technology, and social service ministries, though implementation remains challenging with only 23% of projects achieving true intersectoral integration (Archibald et al., 2021).

## Methodological and Quality Assurance Challenges

Living labs face specific methodological challenges that affect their effectiveness in silver economy applications. User panel management represents a particular challenge requiring advance planning regarding user selection, panel composition, activity definitions, and support structures. Critical considerations include balancing quantitative versus qualitative approaches, ensuring diversity across relevant demographics, establishing appropriate timeframes, and developing support systems including privacy protection, helpdesk services, and reward strategies (Graczyk, 2015).

Methodological challenges vary significantly across contexts. A systematic review of global Living Labs found that whilst European labs typically employ standardised co-creation methodologies, African and Latin American labs rely more on participatory action research approaches adapted from community development practice (Galway et al., 2021). This methodological diversity, whilst enabling contextual relevance, complicates cross-regional learning and comparison. Asian Living Labs demonstrate hybrid approaches, with Japanese labs integrating ethnographic methods from anthropology whilst Korean labs emphasise quantitative user experience metrics aligned with corporate innovation processes (Kim et al., 2020).

Most living labs operate at small scales and rely on short-term funding (Figueiredo et al., 2024). There is also a shortage of tailored guidelines as digital health living labs for dementia, for example, reported limited standardisation in co-creation methods and stakeholder engagement (Figueiredo et al., 2024).

The challenge of achieving representative participation particularly affects marginalised populations. Indigenous communities require culturally-specific methodologies that standard Living Lab frameworks fail to accommodate. Australian research shows that only 8% of Living Labs successfully engage Aboriginal elderly, with most failing to address cultural protocols, language barriers, and historical mistrust of research institutions (Knight-Davidson et al., 2020). Similarly, African American older adults' participation in US Living Labs remains below 5%, despite comprising 12% of the elderly population, due to methodological approaches that fail to address historical exploitation in medical research (Harrington, 2020).

The lack of standardised metrics for measuring innovation outcomes, user satisfaction, and societal impact complicates comparison and learning across different living lab initiatives. Most research originates from European contexts, with limited representation from Asia, Africa, and Latin America. Recent systematic reviews found that 73% of Living Lab publications come from Europe, 15% from

North America, 8% from Asia, 3% from Latin America, and only 1% from Africa, creating significant knowledge gaps about effectiveness in diverse contexts (Leal Filho et al., 2023).

Quality assurance represents an emerging priority for living lab operations, with leading examples implementing international standards such as ISO 9001:2015 Quality Management Systems (Graczyk, 2015). However, adapting traditional quality management approaches to the dynamic, co-creative nature of living lab activities requires innovative approaches that maintain flexibility whilst ensuring consistent quality and ethical standards. The tension between standardisation for quality assurance and flexibility for local adaptation remains unresolved, with only 31% of Living Labs achieving formal quality certification whilst maintaining user-centred innovation capacity (Tercanli & Jongbloed, 2022).

## THE FUTURE OF LIVING LABS IN THE SILVER ECONOMY

### The Role of Digitalisation and Emerging Technologies

The continued digital transformation of society offers powerful tools to enhance living labs for the silver economy. Artificial intelligence can greatly augment the analysis of data collected in living labs. AI algorithms applied to big data from smart home sensors or wearables can detect subtle health deterioration patterns or fall risks among older participants that humans might miss. Living labs are expected to experiment more with AI-driven personalised interventions, such as machine learning models that learn an individual senior's daily routine and can alert if something deviates, potentially pre-empting problems.

The integration of artificial intelligence, Internet of Things, and robotics within Living Labs signals a transformative shift in how ageing challenges are addressed. AI-powered health monitoring systems using Large Language Models demonstrate capability for personalised intervention recommendations, whilst predictive analytics enable proactive health management before issues become critical (Fuellen et al., 2025; Li et al., 2024). However, the implementation of these technologies varies significantly across global contexts, reflecting diverse digital infrastructure and equity considerations.

In high-income countries, IoT applications show particular promise. Korean studies report 66.4% of winter conditions maintained within optimal thermal comfort ranges using IoT-enabled systems, whilst Australian pilots show improvements in "achieving in life" and "future security" domains (Hong et al., 2024). Conversely, Living Labs in low- and middle-income countries face fundamental infrastructure challenges. African initiatives, exemplified by the Siyakhula Living Lab serving

20,000 people in South Africa's marginalised rural Dwesa community, demonstrate that effective innovation can occur with minimal technological infrastructure through community-based approaches prioritising local capacity building over sophisticated technology (Habiyaremye, 2020).

The digital divide presents a critical challenge that Living Labs must address when implementing emerging technologies. Recent research indicates that 23% of people living on Tribal lands lack access to high-speed Internet service compared to 7% of the overall U.S. population (Federal Communications Commission, 2024), whilst 49.7% of Chinese older adults aged 60 and above have not yet joined the internet (Wu et al., 2025). This divide is not merely about access but encompasses digital literacy, with 64% of adults aged 50-plus reporting that technology is not designed with their age group in mind (AARP Research, 2023). Latin American Living Labs have addressed these challenges through differentiated approaches, with Colombian initiatives developing SMS-based solutions for elders without smartphones and Brazilian labs focusing on social innovation rather than technological sophistication (Sánchez et al., 2020).

Internet of Things and ambient sensors will become more ubiquitous. Future living labs will likely integrate entire smart environments. Implementation approaches differ markedly across regions. Singapore's Smart Nation initiative demonstrates integration with national healthcare systems, whilst Croatian EU-funded Living Labs established in rural Međimurje County and the island of Lastovo address the needs of isolated elderly populations through simpler sensor-based safety systems requiring minimal digital literacy (European Social Fund Plus, 2024).

Robotics integration within Living Labs reveals nuanced patterns of acceptance and effectiveness. PARO robot therapy shows documented reductions in negative emotions and improved social engagement, whilst the Ryan robot from the University of Denver provides speech recognition and facial expression analysis for early-stage dementia support (Camp et al., 2022; Worth, 2024). Acceptance rates exceed 70% among adults aged 70+, compared to 55-69 age groups, suggesting greater openness to robotic assistance among the oldest populations (Hong et al., 2024). Cultural factors significantly influence acceptance. Japanese Living Labs report higher robotic technology acceptance due to cultural familiarity with assistive robots, whilst Latin American contexts show resistance to technologies perceived as replacing human care, with Mexican Living Labs reporting 40% lower acceptance rates for monitoring technologies compared to European counterparts (Sosa et al., 2024).

Indigenous communities require specific technological adaptations that respect cultural protocols. Canadian Living Labs have developed approaches integrating Indigenous knowledge systems with modern technology, with the Morning Star Lodge partnership demonstrating how culturally safe technology solutions can increase engagement among Indigenous older adults when family members are involved in the education process (Marrone et al., 2022). The Indigenous Digital Delegation at MIT exemplifies how traditional values can guide technological development, with Elder Duke Redbird emphasising the need to ensure algorithms don't replace Indigenous peoples' "symbolic symbiotic relationship with the Earth" (MIT News, 2020).

The emergence of large language models (LLMs) has introduced new possibilities for enhancing Living Lab methodologies. LLM-based opinion emulation refers to methodologies in which a powerful language model is used to generate responses that mimic the opinions or perspectives of individuals or groups (Argyle et al., 2023). Argyle et al. (2023) provide evidence that an LLM can "accurately emulate response distributions" for a wide range of human subgroups when properly prompted, suggesting potential for generating hypotheses and design ideas that can subsequently be validated in Living Labs.

However, opposing evidence suggests significant limitations. Bisbee et al. (2024) found that whilst LLMs could approximate broad trends, they often failed to capture important variations and sometimes produced misleading outputs. LLM training data systematically under-represents marginalised populations, particularly indigenous communities, rural elderly, and those from low- and middle-income countries. This limitation becomes particularly problematic when considering that approximately 22 million older Americans lack broadband access at home, meaning their perspectives are largely absent from the digital data that trains these models (Empowerline, 2022).

The literature suggests that LLMs are best viewed as complementary tools rather than replacements for Living Labs. A balanced analysis indicates promise for supplementing human-centric methods through hybrid approaches (Racine et al., 2024). LLMs could handle routine or large-scale opinion synthesis, whilst Living Labs focus on depth, validation, and genuine co-creation with real stakeholders. This approach acknowledges that the two methodologies embody different philosophies - one data-driven and synthetic, the other human-driven and experiential - each with methodological merits but not interchangeable in many respects.

## Sustainable Innovation Pathways

As the silver economy grows, there is increasing attention to ensuring that innovations are sustainable both in terms of long-term economic viability and environmental impact. Economic sustainability means finding models so that effective solutions can continue beyond pilot phase and be financially supported. Future living labs will likely explore innovative business models and financing for age-tech, such as partnering with investors focusing on the longevity economy sector.

Comparative analysis reveals distinct regional approaches to sustainable innovation in Living Labs. European models demonstrate systematic integration of circular economy principles. Engez et al. (2021) identify three ecosystem types including economic value flow, material flow, and knowledge flow ecosystems. The Hiedanranta District in Finland demonstrates circular economy implementation with material flow monitoring and optimisation, whilst the Flemish Living Labs Programme provides €1 million annually for circular transition breakthroughs (Ascione et al., 2021; Engez et al., 2021). In contrast, Latin American approaches focus on economic sustainability through social innovation, with the Inter-American Development Bank's Silver Economy Initiative addressing the region where 166 million people aged 50 and over represent 25% of the population, projected to reach 38% by 2050 (Ponce & Etchegoyen, 2025).

African Living Labs demonstrate unique sustainability pathways through community ownership models that require minimal external funding. The IST-Africa initiative, supported by the European Commission and African Union Commission, has established Living Labs that operate on principles of local resource mobilisation rather than dependency on external grants, with communities contributing labour, local materials, and traditional knowledge as forms of investment (IST-Africa, 2024). This approach contrasts with Asian models, where sustainability is achieved through integration with corporate structures. Korean chaebols provide stable funding for Living Labs as part of corporate social responsibility initiatives, whilst Chinese intelligent elderly care service platforms involve tripartite arrangements between digital technology companies, social organisations, and elderly care providers (Ma et al., 2024).

On the environmental sustainability side, there is recognition that supporting an ageing population should not come at the cost of harming the planet. This is particularly salient as older people increasingly express preferences for sustainable products (Pillemer, 2021; Ma & Xing, 2024, 2021; Pais-Magalhães et al., 2022). The concept of "green silver economy" is emerging, where the needs of an ageing society are met in ways consistent with climate goals (Zhang et al., 2024). Implementation varies by context. European Living Labs have resources to invest in sophisticated green technologies, whilst Living Labs in low-income countries focus on sustainability through traditional practices and local materials. The Community Lab of Ideas for Health in The Gambia demonstrates how traditional agricultural practices can be integrated with modern health interventions for older adults, creating sustainable solutions that don't rely on imported technologies or external energy sources (Masunaga et al., 2021).

Gender dimensions of sustainable innovation require particular attention. In Latin America, women comprise 55% of the older adult population and face unique financial challenges including lower lifetime earnings and disproportionate participation in informal labour markets (International Finance Corporation, 2024). The IFC's Silver Economy Program specifically targets financial products for silver women, recognising that sustainable innovation must address gendered economic inequalities. Similarly, indigenous approaches to sustainability offer alternative models. Canadian Agricultural Climate Solutions Living Labs include Indigenous-led initiatives where traditional ecological knowledge guides sustainable ageing solutions, demonstrating how indigenous values can inform environmentally sustainable approaches to supporting older adults (Agriculture and Agri-Food Canada, 2024).

## Policy Recommendations for Scaling Up Living Labs

To support the scaling and replication of the living lab model itself, frameworks at policy level are being developed. The OECD has advocated test-and-learn environments and involving end-users in public service innovation, essentially endorsing living lab approaches (Monteiro et al., 2020; OECD, 2022).

Effective policy frameworks must address the methodological diversity that characterises living lab approaches. While there is no single living lab methodology, successful labs combine and customise different user-centred, co-creation methodologies to fit their specific purposes (Evans, 2019). Policy support should therefore accommodate this methodological flexibility whilst establishing common quality criteria and evaluation frameworks.

Asian countries demonstrate diverse policy integration strategies. Singapore's whole-of-government approach integrates Living Labs within national ageing strategies, with the world's first Healthy Longevity Clinic within a public hospital system offering services at a fraction of private clinic costs to ensure equitable access (Singapore Department of Statistics, 2025). Japan's regulatory sandbox allows Living Labs to test innovations for up to two years before formal approval, enabling rapid iteration whilst maintaining safety standards (Raghavan et al., 2021). In contrast, China's approach involves state-led coordination of Living Labs within the broader framework of intelligent elderly care service platforms, demonstrating how authoritarian governance structures can rapidly scale Living Lab initiatives but with limited bottom-up innovation (Wu et al., 2025).

Latin American policy frameworks increasingly recognise the silver economy's potential whilst addressing regional challenges. The Inter-American Development Bank actively promotes Living Labs through technical assistance for policy formulation, with focus on three critical areas: pension systems, health, and care. With 8 million people over 65 needing help with basic functions but only 5% receiving adequate care, and 70% of paid caregivers earning minimum wage or less, policy frameworks must address fundamental structural inequalities before Living Labs can effectively scale (Inter-American Development Bank, 2025).

African contexts require different policy approaches reflecting limited institutional capacity and resources. The Department of Science and Innovation and

Technology Innovation Agency in South Africa calls for community-based rural Living Labs in marginalised communities of Limpopo and Mpumalanga provinces, demonstrating how policy can prioritise underserved populations (African Scientists Directory, 2023). With government expenditure on mental health per capita less than $0.50 compared to over $50 in high-income countries, policy frameworks must acknowledge resource constraints and focus on community-based models rather than technology-intensive approaches (National Bureau of Economic Research, 2023).

Indigenous communities require specific policy considerations that respect sovereignty and self-determination. Canadian policy frameworks increasingly recognise Indigenous governments as key stakeholders in Living Lab governance, with the Funding Program for Intersectoral Research on Aging Living Laboratories requiring collaboration with Indigenous organisations and providing dedicated funding for culturally appropriate engagement methods (Fonds de recherche du Québec, 2024).

Policy recommendations should include funding mechanisms such as multi-year grants that require multi-actor co-creation, ensuring continuity; toolkits and guidelines issued by international bodies to speed up approvals and build trust; and networks for knowledge sharing. At the EU level, the concept of "reference sites" in the European Innovation Partnership on Active and Healthy Ageing encouraged regions to showcase integrated innovation ecosystems for active ageing. Going forward, policy frameworks will likely provide more formal support and standards for living labs.

Another policy aspect is integration into healthcare and social care strategies. If national ageing strategies explicitly include "co-creation with older people" and living labs as methods, it legitimises and encourages health and social care providers to participate and allocate time to these activities. The WHO Decade of Healthy Ageing (2021-2030) calls for "changing how we think, feel and act towards age and ageism" and "developing communities that foster abilities of older people", principles that resonate with living labs.

As living labs multiply, another future consideration is evaluation and evidence. Policy frameworks will demand proof of efficacy and cost-effectiveness. We can anticipate more formal evaluation studies, including randomised trials and longitudinal studies, embedded in living lab projects to generate robust data for policymakers. Evaluation frameworks must consider equity dimensions. Living Labs serving marginalised populations may show different success metrics than those serving privileged groups. Policy frameworks should recognise that improved social cohesion or preserved cultural practices may be as valuable as technological innovation or economic returns, particularly for indigenous and rural communities where conventional economic metrics may not capture full value creation.

The digital divide must be central to policy considerations. With research showing significant disparities in digital access—from 23% of Tribal lands lacking high-speed internet in the US to 49.7% of Chinese older adults being offline—policies must address infrastructure gaps before Living Labs can effectively scale (Federal Communications Commission, 2024; Wu et al., 2025). This may require differentiated approaches, with high-tech solutions for connected urban populations and low-tech, community-based approaches for digitally excluded groups.

Finally, policy frameworks must address the sustainability challenge that affects Living Labs globally. With 68% of labs reporting funding challenges threatening their continuity (Berberi et al., 2023), policies should move beyond project-based funding toward institutional support. This might include embedding Living Labs within universities or healthcare systems, as demonstrated by the Netherlands' model, or creating dedicated budget lines for Living Lab operations within national ageing strategies.

## CONCLUSION

### Summary of Key Findings

This chapter has explored the role of Living Labs as catalysts for innovation in the silver economy, with particular focus on their impact on ageing in place solutions. Through analysis of theoretical foundations, empirical evidence, case studies, and future prospects, the investigation demonstrates how Living Labs provide a valuable framework for developing user-centred innovations that address the complex challenges of population ageing.

The analysis reveals that Living Labs have evolved from simple user testing environments into sophisticated innovation ecosystems that fundamentally transform how ageing-related solutions are conceived, developed, and implemented. Through their emphasis on co-creation and real-world testing, Living Labs enable the development of solutions that are better adapted to the actual needs and preferences of older adults, addressing the critical issue that approximately 70% of innovative products and services fail to find markets because they do not meet real-world user needs (Picard, 2011; Picard & Poilpot, 2011).

Evidence from multiple case studies demonstrates the tangible benefits of Living Labs in the silver economy context. The Living Lab in Ageing and Long-Term Care in the Netherlands has operated for over two decades, producing over 100 research studies and scaling innovations across 110 care facilities (Verbeek et al., 2020). Similarly, initiatives such as ACTIVAGE demonstrated improved perceived safety and evidence of reduced emergency hospitalisations for participants, with cost-benefit analyses showing potential savings if scaled (Bhagwat et al., 2020). These examples illustrate how Living Labs function as effective catalysts for innovation in the silver economy by ensuring practical relevance and user acceptance of developed solutions.

The examination of emerging technologies reveals how Living Labs are adapting to integrate artificial intelligence, Internet of Things, and robotics while maintaining their core user-centric principles. The analysis of large language models demonstrates both the potential for AI to augment Living Lab processes through synthetic opinion generation and the fundamental limitations that ensure human stakeholders remain central to authentic innovation processes (Argyle et al., 2023; Bisbee et al., 2024).

The research indicates that successful co-creation with older adults requires tailored approaches for diverse populations, including the oldest-old, people with cognitive impairments, ethnic minorities, and rural residents (Toso et al., 2023). Studies have shown that older users involved in co-design report higher satisfaction and are more inclined to use resulting technologies or services (Sumner et al., 2021), whilst treating older participants as co-creators rather than test subjects results in greater sense of ownership and willingness to adopt final products (Regalado et al., 2023).

## Achievement of Chapter Objectives

The chapter's exploration has been achieved through systematic examination across multiple dimensions. Living Labs catalyse innovation through several key mechanisms. First, they ensure user-centricity by positioning older adults as active co-creators rather than passive recipients, fundamentally altering the innovation process to prioritise authentic user needs over developer assumptions. Second, they facilitate multi-stakeholder collaboration through quadruple helix frameworks that bring together industry, academia, government, and civil society to address the complex, interconnected challenges of population ageing. Third, they provide real-world validation environments that test innovations in authentic contexts, significantly improving the likelihood of successful adoption and scaling.

The specific focus on ageing in place solutions has revealed how Living Labs address this critical aspect of the silver economy by developing technologies and services that enable older adults to remain in their homes and communities safely and independently. The evidence shows that ageing in place can be more resource-efficient than building new institutions and offers sustainability benefits by reducing transportation needs (Spinelli et al., 2019).

The examination of co-creation methodologies has shown how Living Labs transform the traditional innovation paradigm by treating older adults as experts in their own lives, capable of identifying problems, generating solutions, and validating outcomes. This approach addresses the fundamental challenge that gerontechnology often reflects developer assumptions rather than genuine user requirements, thereby improving both the relevance and adoption of silver economy innovations.

## Implications for the Future of the Silver Economy

The analysis reveals that the future of Living Labs in the silver economy will be shaped by advanced technologies, commitment to sustainable and inclusive innovation, and supportive policy and institutional frameworks that integrate co-creation into mainstream approaches to addressing population ageing. With these developments, Living Labs are expected to move from relatively novel experiments to a cornerstone of innovation policy for ageing societies.

The integration of emerging technologies presents both opportunities and challenges. AI-powered health monitoring systems demonstrate capability for personalised intervention recommendations, whilst predictive analytics enable proactive health management before issues become critical (Fuellen et al., 2025; Li et al., 2024). However, the analysis of large language models demonstrates that whilst AI can augment Living Lab processes, it cannot replace the authentic human engagement that provides the legitimacy and trust essential for successful innovation adoption (Racine et al., 2024; Pérez Jolles et al., 2022).

The concept of sustainable innovation is gaining prominence, with recognition that supporting an ageing population should align with environmental goals. The emerging "green silver economy" concept addresses how the needs of an ageing society can be met in ways consistent with climate goals (Zhang et al., 2024). Older adults increasingly express preferences for sustainable products (Pillemer, 2021; Ma & Xing, 2024; Pais-Magalhães et al., 2022), positioning Living Labs as crucial facilitators of this transition.

## Call to Action

The evidence presented demonstrates that Living Labs represent proven catalysts for innovation in the silver economy, particularly for developing effective ageing in place solutions. However, realising their full potential requires coordinated action across multiple stakeholder groups.

Policymakers should develop supportive frameworks that enable experimentation whilst ensuring ethical standards and user protection through regulatory sandboxes, multi-year funding mechanisms, and standardised ethics frameworks. Industry should engage authentically with older adults as co-creators through genuine partnership from agenda-setting through evaluation. Academic institutions should develop interdisciplinary approaches bridging technology, health, and social sciences.

Most importantly, the voices and expertise of older adults themselves must remain central to all innovation efforts, ensuring that solutions truly serve their needs and aspirations for ageing well in place. When done well, Living Labs overcome adoption hurdles by ensuring solutions are personalised, preserve dignity and independence, provide user control, and avoid social isolation (Pirzada et al., 2022).

The examination confirms that Living Labs serve as effective catalysts for innovation in the silver economy through their unique ability to combine user-centricity, multi-stakeholder collaboration, real-world validation, and authentic co-creation. As societies worldwide grapple with the challenges and opportunities of population ageing, Living Labs provide a proven methodology for developing solutions that truly enable older adults to age well in place whilst contributing to sustainable economic growth. The evidence supports continued investment in and expansion of Living Lab approaches as essential infrastructure for navigating the demographic transitions that define the 21st century.

## REFERENCES


AARP. (2020, January 30). *The Longevity Economy® Outlook*. AARP. Retrieved from https://www.aarp.org/pri/topics/work-finances-retirement/economics-aging/longevity-economy-outlook/

AARP Research. (2023, December 19). *2024 Tech Trends and Adults 50+*. AARP Research. https://doi.org/DOI: 10.26419/res.00772.001

ACTIVAGE Consortium. (2020). *White book: Evidence of the benefits of IoT-based solutions for ageing well in Europe (Deliverable D6.5)*. H2020 ACTIVAGE Project. Retrieved from https://cordis.europa.eu/project/id/732679/results

African Scientists Directory. (2023). *Call for proposals: Living Labs Pilot Programme in Limpopo and Mpumalanga*. Retrieved from https://africanscientists.africa/blog-post/call-for-proposals-living-labs-pilot-programme-in-limpopo-and-mpumalanga/

Agriculture and Agri-Food Canada. (2024). *Agricultural Climate Solutions — Living Labs*. Retrieved from https://agriculture.canada.ca/en/environment/climate-change/agricultural-climate-solutions/agricultural-climate-solutions-living-labs

Akiyama, H. (2018, December 16). *Users becoming the innovators: Kamakura Living Lab*. The University of Tokyo. Retrieved from https://www.u-tokyo.ac.jp/focus/en/features/z1304_00010.html

Akiyama, H. (2020). Aging well: An update. *Nutrition Reviews*, *78*(Suppl 3), 3–9. DOI: 10.1093/nutrit/nuaa084

Amorim, E. E. R., Menezes, M., & Fernandes, K. V. G. (2022). Urban living labs and critical infrastructure resilience: A global match? *Sustainability*, *14*(16), 9826. DOI: 10.3390/su14169826

Anderson, M., & Perrin, A. (2017, May 17). *Tech adoption climbs among older adults*. Pew Research Center. Retrieved from https://www.pewresearch.org/internet/2017/05/17/tech-adoption-climbs-among-older-adults/

Angelini, L., Carrino, S., Abou Khaled, O., Riva-Mossman, S., & Mugellini, E. (2016). Senior living lab: An ecological approach to foster social innovation in an ageing society. *Future Internet*, *8*(4), 50. DOI: 10.3390/fi8040050

Archibald, M., Wiebe, S., Rieger, K., Linton, J., & Woodgate, R. (2021). Protocol for a systematic review of living labs in healthcare. *BMJ Open*, *11*(2), e039246. DOI: 10.1136/bmjopen-2020-039246

Argyle, L. P., Busby, E. C., Fulda, N., Gubler, J. R., Rytting, C., & Wingate, D. (2023). Out of one, many: Using language models to simulate human samples. *Political Analysis*, *31*(3), 337–351. DOI: 10.1017/pan.2023.2

Ascione, G. S., Cuomo, F., Mariotti, N., & Corazza, L. (2021). Urban living labs, circular economy and nature-based solutions: Ideation and testing of a new soil in the city of Turin using a multi-stakeholder perspective. *Circular Economy and Sustainability*, *1*(2), 545–562. DOI: 10.1007/s43615-021-00011-6

ASEAN +3 Macroeconomic Research Office. (2025, March 7). *Silver linings: Unlocking the potential strengths in an aging Singapore*. Retrieved from https://amro-asia.org/silver-linings-unlocking-the-potential-strengths-in-an-aging-singapore/

Aung, M. N., Koyanagi, Y., Nagamine, Y., Nam, E. W., Mulati, N., Kyaw, M. Y., Moolphate, S., Shirayama, Y., Nonaka, K., Field, M., Cheung, P., & Yuasa, M. (2022). Digitally inclusive, healthy aging communities (DIHAC): A cross-cultural study in Japan, Republic of Korea, Singapore, and Thailand. *International Journal of Environmental Research and Public Health*, *19*(12), 6976. DOI: 10.3390/ijerph19126976

Berberi, A., Beaudoin, C., McPhee, C., Guay, J., Bronson, K., & Nguyen, V. M. (2023). Enablers, barriers, and future considerations for living lab effectiveness in environmental and agricultural sustainability transitions: A review of studies evaluating living labs. *Local Environment*, *28*(12), 1547–1568. DOI: 10.1080/13549839.2023.2238750

Bergvall-Kåreborn, B., Holst, M., & Ståhlbröst, A. (2009). Concept design with a living lab approach. In *42nd Hawaii International Conference on System Sciences (HICSS)* (pp. 1–10). IEEE. https://doi.org/DOI: 10.1109/HICSS.2009.123

Bertolazzi, A., Quaglia, V., & Bongelli, R. (2024). Barriers and facilitators to health technology adoption by older adults with chronic diseases: An integrative systematic review. *BMC Public Health*, *24*, 506. DOI: 10.1186/s12889-024-18036-5

Bhagwat, V. R., Paikrao, P. L., & Shrawankar, U. (2020). IoT wearable sensors and devices in elderly care: A literature review. *Sensors (Basel)*, *20*(10), 2826. DOI: 10.3390/s20102826

Bisbee, J., Clinton, J. D., Dorff, C., Kenkel, B., & Larson, J. M. (2024). Synthetic replacements for human survey data? The perils of large language models. *Political Analysis*, *32*(4), 401–416. DOI: 10.1017/pan.2024.5

Borda, A., Schuurman, D., Pedell, S., Spagnoli, F., & Konstantinidis, E. (2024). Editorial: Living labs and open innovation approaches to scale impact for human well-being. *Frontiers in Public Health*, *12*, 1378932. DOI: 10.3389/fpubh.2024.1378932

Bridi, M. E., Soliman-Junior, J., Granja, A. D., Tzortzopoulos, P., Gomes, V., & Kowaltowski, D. C. C. K. (2022). Living labs in social housing upgrades: Process, challenges and recommendations. *Sustainability, 14*(5), 2595. DOI: 10.3390/su14052595

Brown, T. (2008, June). Design thinking. *Harvard Business Review, 86*(6), 84–92. https://hbr.org/2008/06/design-thinking

Camp, N., Di Nuovo, A., Hunter, K., Johnston, J., Zecca, M., Lewis, M., & Magistro, D. (2022). Perceptions of socially assistive robots among community-dwelling older adults. In F. Cavallo, J.-J. Cabibihan, L. Fiorini, A. Sorrentino, H. He, X. Liu, Y. Matsumoto, & S. S. Ge (Eds.), *Social Robotics: 14th International Conference, ICSR 2022* (pp. 540–549). Springer. https://doi.org/DOI: 10.1007/978-3-031-24670-8_48

Census and Statistics Department. (2015). *Hong Kong Population Projections 2015–2064*. Government of the Hong Kong Special Administrative Region. Retrieved from https://www.statistics.gov.hk/pub/B1120015062015XXXXB0100.pdf

Chen, Y., Li, W., & Yang, H. (2024). Determinants of physical activity behavior among older adults with subjective cognitive decline based on the Capability, Opportunity, Motivation, and Behaviour (COM-B) model: Mediating and moderating effects. *Frontiers in Public Health, 11*, 1338665. DOI: 10.3389/fpubh.2023.1338665

Cheung, K., Chau, A. K. C., & Woo, J. (2023). The age-based digital divide in an increasingly digital world: A focus group investigation during the COVID-19 pandemic. *Archives of Gerontology and Geriatrics, 106*, 104920. DOI: 10.1016/j.archger.2022.104920

Choi, N. G., Choi, B. Y., & Marti, C. N. (2025). Digital divide among homebound and semi-homebound older adults. *Journal of Applied Gerontology*. Advance online publication. DOI: 10.1177/07334648241292971

Choi, N. G., & DiNitto, D. M. (2013). The digital divide among low-income homebound older adults: Internet use patterns, eHealth literacy, and attitudes toward computer/Internet use. *Journal of Medical Internet Research, 15*(5), e93. DOI: 10.2196/jmir.2645

Cohen, S. A., & Greaney, M. L. (2023). Aging in rural communities. *Current Epidemiology Reports, 10*, 1–16. DOI: 10.1007/s40471-022-00313-9

Conway Lenihan, A., & McGuirk, H. (2022). Small enterprises and the silver economy. *Small Enterprise Research, 29*(1), 1–5. DOI: 10.1080/13215906.2022.2048205

Cui, Y., He, Y., Xu, X., Zhou, L., & Nutakor, J. A. (2024). Can cultural capital, cognitive ability, and economic capacity help rural older adults bridge the digital divide? Evidence from an empirical study. *Frontiers in Public Health, 12*, 1393651. DOI: 10.3389/fpubh.2024.1393651

De Witte, N. A. J., Adriaensen, I., Broeckx, L., Van der Auwera, V., Van Daele, T., & De Marez, L. (2021). Cross-cultural differences in user-centred research: An international living lab survey. *Health Informatics Journal, 27*(1), 14604582211038268. DOI: 10.1177/14604582211038268

Dell'Era, C., & Landoni, P. (2014). Living lab: A methodology between user-centred design and participatory design. *Creativity and Innovation Management, 23*(2), 137–154. DOI: 10.1111/caim.12061

Eatock, D. (2015). *The silver economy: Opportunities from ageing* (EPRS Briefing 565.872). European Parliamentary Research Service. Retrieved from https://www.europarl.europa.eu/EPRS/EPRS-Briefing-565872-The-silver-economy-FINAL.pdf

Empowerline. (2022, January 19). Older People & the Digital Divide 101. https://empowerline.org/older-people-the-digital-divide-101/

Engez, A., Leminen, S., & Aarikka-Stenroos, L. (2021). Urban living lab as a circular economy ecosystem: Advancing environmental sustainability through economic value, material, and knowledge flows. *Sustainability, 13*(5), 2811. DOI: 10.3390/su13052811

European Commission. (2015). *The 2015 Ageing Report: Economic and budgetary projections for the 28 EU Member States (2013–2060)*. Publications Office of the European Union. Retrieved from https://ec.europa.eu/economy_finance/publications/european_economy/2015/pdf/ee3_en.pdf

European Commission. (2018). *The silver economy: How to stimulate the economy by hundreds of millions of euros per year*. Publications Office of the European Union. Retrieved from https://op.europa.eu/en/publication-detail/-/publication/2dca9276-3ec5-11e8-b5fe-01aa75ed71a1/language-en

European Network of Living Labs. (2019). *Adherent Member Application Guidelines: 13th Wave—2019*. Retrieved from https://enoll.org/wp-content/uploads/2019/01/enoll-application-guidelines-13th-wave-1-1.pdf

European Network of Living Labs. (2022). *ENoLL Membership Application Guidelines — Wave 2022 (16th): Empowering everyone to innovate*. Retrieved from https://enoll.org/wp-content/uploads/2021/12/application-guidelines-wave-2022.pdf

European Network of Living Labs. (n.d.). *About us*. Retrieved from https://enoll.org/about-us/

European Parliament. (2021, July 7). *Report on an old continent growing older – possibilities and challenges related to ageing policy post-2020* (A9-0194/2021). Retrieved from https://www.europarl.europa.eu/doceo/document/A-9-2021-0194_EN.html

European Social Fund Plus. (2025, May 28). *Living Labs for digital and innovative solutions for elderly and disabled citizens*. European Commission. Retrieved from https://european-social-fund-plus.ec.europa.eu/en/social-innovation-match/case-study/living-labs-digital-and-innovative-solutions-elderly-and-disabled-citizens

Evans, P. (2019). *Living lab methodology handbook*. North Wales Regional Partnership Board. Retrieved from https://www.northwalescollaborative.wales/wp-content/uploads/2020/10/Living-lab-methodology-handbook_r.pdf

Fang, Y. X., Gill, S. S., Kunasekaran, P., Rosnon, M. R., Talib, A. T., & Abd-Aziz, A. (2022). Digital divide: An inquiry on the native communities of Sabah. *Societies (Basel, Switzerland)*, *12*(6), 148. DOI: 10.3390/soc12060148

Federal Communications Commission. (2024, March). *Inquiry Concerning the Deployment of Advanced Telecommunications Capability to All Americans (Section 706 Report)* (FCC 24-27). Retrieved from https://docs.fcc.gov/public/attachments/FCC-24-27A1.pdf

Feng, C., Huang, J.-B., & Wang, M. (2019). The sustainability of China's metal industries: Features, challenges and future focuses. *Resources Policy*, *60*, 215–224. DOI: 10.1016/j.resourpol.2018.12.006

Figueiredo, T., Midão, L., Carrilho, J., Videira Henriques, D., Alves, S., Duarte, N., Bessa, M. J., Fidalgo, J. M., García, M., Facal, D., Felpete, A., Filgueira, I. R., Carlos Bernárdez, J., Rodríguez, M., Cerqueira, J. F., & Costa, E. (2024). A comprehensive analysis of digital health–focused living labs: Innovative approaches to dementia. *Frontiers in Medicine*, *11*, 1418612. DOI: 10.3389/fmed.2024.1418612

Finn, K., & Johnston, H. (2024). *Living Lab integrates Indigenous perspective into ag research. Canadian Cattlemen*. Retrieved from https://www.canadiancattlemen.ca/research/living-lab-integrates-indigenous-perspective-into-ag-research/

Fonds de recherche du Québec. (2024). *Funding Program for Intersectoral Research on Aging – Living Laboratories – 2025–2026*. Retrieved from https://frq.gouv.qc.ca/en/program/funding-program-for-intersectoral-research-on-aging-living-laboratories-2025-2026/

Fotis, T., Kioskli, K., Sundaralingam, A., Fasihi, A., & Mouratidis, H. (2022). Co-creation in a digital health living lab: A case study. *Frontiers in Public Health*, *10*, 892930. DOI: 10.3389/fpubh.2022.892930

Fuellen, G., Kulaga, A., Lobentanzer, S., Unfried, M., Avelar, R. A., Palmer, D., & Kennedy, B. K. (2025). Validation requirements for AI-based intervention-evaluation in aging and longevity research and practice. *Ageing Research Reviews*, *104*, 102617. DOI: 10.1016/j.arr.2024.102617

Galway, L. P., Levkoe, C. Z., Portinga, R. L. W., & Milun, K. (2021). A scoping review examining governance, co-creation, and social and ecological justice in living labs literature. *Challenges*, *13*(1), 1–16. DOI: 10.3390/challe13010001

Gambo, I., Bueno-Delgado, M. V., Mooses, K., Melero Muñoz, F. J., Zviel-Girshin, R., Andrushevich, A., & Taveter, K. (2023). Technology adoption review for ageing well: Analysis of technical solutions. *Frontiers in Public Health*, *11*, 1169192. DOI: 10.3389/fpubh.2023.1169192

Gao, S., Ho, E. L.-E., Chua, V., & Feng, C.-C. (2024). More than aging in place: "Aging in networks" in Singapore. *Annals of the Association of American Geographers*, *114*(9), 2132–2152. DOI: 10.1080/24694452.2024.2370922

Gilbert, S., Mathias, R., Schönfelder, A., Wekenborg, M., Steinigen-Fuchs, J., Dillenseger, A., & Ziemssen, T. (2025). A roadmap for safe, regulation-compliant living labs for AI and digital health development. *Science Advances*, *11*(20), eadv7719. Advance online publication. DOI: 10.1126/sciadv.adv7719

Golomski, C., Corvini, M., Kim, B. R., Wilcox, J., & Valcourt, S. (2022). Aspects of ICT connectivity among older adults living in rural subsidized housing: Reassessing the digital divide. *Journal of Enabling Technologies*, *16*(1), 17–27. DOI: 10.1108/JET-12-2020-0052

Gruss, B., & Noureldin, D. (2025, June). Sustaining growth in an aging world. *Finance & Development*, *62*(2), 48–51. https://www.imf.org/en/Publications/fandd/issues/2025/06/sustaining-growth-in-an-aging-world-bertrand-gruss

Habiyaremye, A. (2020). Knowledge exchange and innovation co-creation in living labs projects in South Africa. *Innovation and Development*, *10*(2), 207–222. DOI: 10.1080/2157930X.2019.1580940

Harrington, C. N. (2020). The forgotten margins: What is community-based participatory health design telling us? *Interaction*, *27*(3), 24–29. DOI: 10.1145/3386381

Health and Aging in Africa: Longitudinal Studies in South Africa (HAALSA). (2023). *About HAALSA*. https://haalsi.org/about/

Henning-Smith, C., Powell, M. A., & Lahr, M. (2022). Approaches to serving rural older adults in State Plans on Aging: A policy content evaluation. *Journal of Applied Gerontology*, *41*(10), 2132–2139. DOI: 10.1177/07334648221104085

Hong, S., Jang, E., Cho, J., Lee, J., Rhee, J. H., Lee, H., Lee, M., Cha, S. H., Koo, C., Baik, O. M., & Heo, Y. (2024). A living lab to develop smart home services for the residential welfare of older adults. *Technology in Society*, *77*, 102577. DOI: 10.1016/j.techsoc.2024.102577

Hong, W., Liang, C., Ma, Y., & Zhu, J. (2025). Intergenerational digital feedback and digital social integration of older adults: An empirical study from personal initiative perspective. *Humanities & Social Sciences Communications*, *12*, 5518. DOI: 10.1057/s41599-025-05518-z

Huang, J. H., & Thomas, E. (2021). A review of Living Lab research and methods for user involvement. *Technology Innovation Management Review*, *11*(9/10), 88–107. DOI: 10.22215/timreview/1467

Hwangbo, Y. (2023). Korea's citizen-centric smart city development by adopting living labs and design thinking methodologies and their implications for ASEAN countries. In *Sustainable Development and the Digital Economy* (pp. 225–242). Routledge., DOI: 10.4324/9781003388753-14

I-CHANGE Project. (n.d.). *Living Lab of West Africa*. https://ichange-project.eu/category/living-lab/living-lab-of-west-africa/

IEEE Connecting the Unconnected. (2023, February 9). *The elderly digital divide: Age is just a number, and so is your smartphone password*. https://ctu.ieee.org/blog/2023/02/09/the-elderly-digital-divide-age-is-just-a-number-and-so-is-your-smartphone-password/

Inter-American Development Bank. (2020). *The silver economy in Latin America and the Caribbean: Aging as an opportunity for innovation, entrepreneurship, and inclusion*. Inter-American Development Bank. https://publications.iadb.org/en/the-silver-economy-in-latin-america-and-the-caribbean-aging-as-an-opportunity-for-innovation-entrepreneurship-and-inclusion

Inter-American Development Bank. (2025, March 19). *The demographic wave drives the silver economy in Latin America and the Caribbean*. https://blogs.iadb.org/trabajo/en/the-demographic-wave-drives-the-silver-economy-in-latin-america-and-the-caribbean/

International Finance Corporation. (2024, August 27). *IFC launches Silver Economy Initiative to address growing underserved population in Latin America & the Caribbean.* https://www.ifc.org/en/pressroom/2024/ifc-launches-silver-economy-initiative-to-address-growing-underserved-population-in-latin-america-the-caribbean

International Monetary Fund. (2025, April). *World Economic Outlook, April 2025—Chapter 2: The rise of the silver economy.* https://www.imf.org/-/media/Files/Publications/WEO/2025/April/English/ch2.ashx

ISO/TC 176. (2015). *ISO 9001:2015—Quality management systems—Requirements.* International Organization for Standardization. https://www.iso.org/standard/62085.html

IST-Africa. (n.d.). *Supporting the evolution of sustainable Living Labs.* http://www.ist-africa.org/home/default.asp?page=livinglabs

Karuga, R., Kabaria, C., Chumo, I., Okoth, L., Njoroge, I., Otiso, L., & Mberu, B. (2023). Voices and challenges of marginalized and vulnerable groups in urban informal settlements in Nairobi, Kenya: Building on a spectrum of community-based participatory research approaches. *Frontiers in Public Health, 11*, 1175326. DOI: 10.3389/fpubh.2023.1175326

Kebede, A. S., Ozolins, L. L., Holst, H., & Galvin, K. (2022). Digital engagement of older adults: Scoping review. *Journal of Medical Internet Research, 24*(12), e40192. DOI: 10.2196/40192

Kim, H. K., & Lee, S.-H. (2021). The effects of population aging on South Korea's economy: The National Transfer Accounts approach. *The Journal of the Economics of Ageing, 20*, 100340. DOI: 10.1016/j.jeoa.2021.100340

Kim, J., Kim, Y. L., Jang, H., Cho, M., Lee, M., & Lee, S.-H. (2020). Living labs for health: An integrative literature review. *European Journal of Public Health, 30*(1), 55–63. DOI: 10.1093/eurpub/ckz105

Knight-Davidson, P., Lane, P., & McVicar, A. (2020). Methods for co-creating with older adults in living laboratories: A scoping review. *Health and Technology, 10*(5), 997–1009. DOI: 10.1007/s12553-020-00441-6

Knoefel, F., Wallace, B., Thomas, N., Sveistrup, H., Goubran, R., & Laurin, C. L. (2024). *Supportive smart homes: Their role in aging in place.* Springer., DOI: 10.1007/978-3-031-37337-4

Lam, L., Fadrique, L., Bin Noon, G., Shah, A., & Morita, P. P. (2022). Evaluating challenges and adoption factors for Active Assisted Living smart environments. *Frontiers in Digital Health, 4*, 891634. DOI: 10.3389/fdgth.2022.891634

Leal Filho, W., Ozuyar, P. G., Dinis, M. A. P., Azul, A. M., Will, M., & Frankenberger, F. (2023). Living labs in the context of the UN sustainable development goals: State of the art. *Sustainability Science, 18*, 1163–1179. DOI: 10.1007/s11625-022-01240-w

Leminen, S., Westerlund, M., & Nyström, A.-G. (2012). Living labs as open-innovation networks. *Technology Innovation Management Review, 2*(9), 6–11. https://timreview.ca/sites/default/files/article_PDF/Leminen_et_al_TIMReview_September2012.pdf

Li, Z., Li, F., Wang, X., Fu, Q., & Ren, W. (2024). Ethical considerations and fundamental principles of large language models in medical education: Viewpoint. *Journal of Medical Internet Research, 26*, e60083. DOI: 10.2196/60083

Ma, Y., Sun, Y., Guo, Q., & Li, H. (2024). Evolutionary game analysis of building a sustainable intelligent elderly care service platform. *Scientific Reports, 14*, 28653. DOI: 10.1038/s41598-024-79976-x

Ma, Y., & Xing, T. (2024). Encourage sustainable consumption among the elderly through generativity. *Journal of Retailing and Consumer Services, 81*, 104053. DOI: 10.1016/j.jretconser.2024.104053

Marrone, N. L., Nieman, C. L., & Coco, L. (2022). Community-based participatory research and human-centered design principles to advance hearing health equity. *Ear and Hearing, 43*(Suppl. 1), 33S–44S. DOI: 10.1097/AUD.0000000000001183

Masunaga, Y., Jaiteh, F., Manneh, E., Balen, J., Okebe, J., D'Alessandro, U., & Muela Ribera, J. (2021). The community lab of ideas for health: Community-based transdisciplinary solutions in a malaria elimination trial in The Gambia. *Frontiers in Public Health, 9*, 637714. DOI: 10.3389/fpubh.2021.637714

Merino-Barbancho, B., Abril Jiménez, P., Mallo, I., Lombroni, I., Cea, G., López Nebreda, C., Cabrera, M. F., Fico, G., & Arredondo, M. T. (2023). Innovation through the Quintuple Helix in living labs: Lessons learned for a transformation from lab to ecosystem. *Frontiers in Public Health, 11*, 1176598. DOI: 10.3389/fpubh.2023.1176598

Mesthrige, J. W., & Cheung, S. L. (2020). Critical evaluation of 'ageing in place' in redeveloped public rental housing estates in Hong Kong. *Ageing and Society, 40*(9), 2006–2039. DOI: 10.1017/S0144686X19000448

Miji Africa Living Lab. (n.d.). *Home*. https://mijiafrica.com/

Mitsanas, M., & Lee, C. (2024, February 19). How South Korea is tackling its demographic crisis. *TIME*. https://time.com/6696414/south-korea-elderly-workforce/

Mubarak, F., & Suomi, R. (2022). Elderly forgotten? Digital exclusion in the information age and the rising grey digital divide. *INQUIRY: The Journal of Health Care Organization, Provision, and Financing*, *59*, 00469580221096272. DOI: 10.1177/00469580221096272

Mulati, N., Aung, M. N., Field, M., Nam, E. W., Ma, C. H. K., Moolphate, S., Lee, H., Goto, Y., Kweun, N. H., Suda, T., Koyanagi, Y., Nagamine, Y., & Yuasa, M. (2022). Digital-based policy and health promotion policy in Japan, the Republic of Korea, Singapore, and Thailand: A scoping review of policy paths to healthy aging. *International Journal of Environmental Research and Public Health*, *19*(24), 16995. DOI: 10.3390/ijerph192416995

Nakatani, H. (2024). International promotion of Japanese aging-related health services and products: Perspective of an international agency. *Global Health & Medicine*, *6*(1), 49–62. DOI: 10.35772/ghm.2024.01004

National Bureau of Economic Research. (2023). Examining an aging population in Sub-Saharan Africa. *National Bureau of Economic Research*. https://www.nber.org/brd/20234/examining-aging-population-sub-saharan-africa

National Research Council Canada. (2021–2022). *Aging in Place: Technology and Innovation – Program plan. National Research Council Canada*. https://nrc.canada.ca/en/research-development/research-collaboration/programs/aging-place-technology-innovation-proposed-program-plan

National Telecommunications and Information Administration. (2024, November 20). *Celebrating Native American Heritage Month: Empowering Native Communities Through Digital Equity*. U.S. Department of Commerce. https://www.ntia.gov/blog/2024/celebrating-native-american-heritage-month-empowering-native-communities-through-digital-equity

New Jersey State Policy Lab. (2022, January 13). *Bridging the digital divide in Native American communities*. Rutgers University. https://policylab.rutgers.edu/publication/bridging-the-digital-divide-in-native-american-communities/

News, M. I. T. (2020, December 3). Indigenous knowledge and technology at MIT: "Is it wise?" *MIT News*. https://news.mit.edu/2020/indigenous-knowledge-technology-mit-is-it-wise-1203

Nyström, A.-G., Leminen, S., Westerlund, M., & Kortelainen, M. (2014). Actor roles and role patterns influencing innovation in living labs. *Industrial Marketing Management*, *43*(3), 483–495. DOI: 10.1016/j.indmarman.2013.12.016

OECD. (2022). *OECD Reviews of Innovation Policy: Germany 2022 — Building agility for successful transitions.* OECD Publishing. https://www.oecd.org/en/publications/oecd-reviews-of-innovation-policy-germany-2022_50b32331-en.html

OECD. (2025). *OECD Employment Outlook 2025.* OECD Publishing. https://www.oecd.org/en/publications/oecd-employment-outlook-2025_194a947b-en.html

Office of Disease Prevention and Health Promotion. (2025, March 17). *Social determinants of health and older adults.* https://odphp.health.gov/our-work/national-health-initiatives/healthy-aging/social-determinants-health-and-older-adults

Ollevier, A., Aguiar, G., Palomino, M., & Simpelaere, I. S. (2020). How can technology support ageing in place in healthy older adults? A systematic review. *Public Health Reviews, 41*, 26. Advance online publication. DOI: 10.1186/s40985-020-00143-4

Pais-Magalhães, V. (2022). A commentary regarding the link between two of today's biggest global challenges: A rapidly ageing population and energy consumption. *American Journal of Aging Science and Research, 3*(1), 27–32. https://www.probiologists.com/article/a-commentary-regarding-the-link-between-two-of-today-s-biggest-global-challenges-a-rapidly-ageing-population-and-energy-consumption

Pérez Jolles, M., Willging, C. E., Stadnick, N. A., Crable, E. L., Lengnick-Hall, R., Hawkins, J., & Aarons, G. A. (2022). Understanding implementation research collaborations from a co-creation lens: Recommendations for a path forward. *Frontiers in Health Services, 2*, 942658. Advance online publication. DOI: 10.3389/frhs.2022.942658

Picard, R. G. (2011). *Digitization and media business models* (Mapping Digital Media Reference Series No. 5). Open Society Foundations. https://www.opensocietyfoundations.org/uploads/d7f96f08-8c77-48a0-84ad-7ac6ebdbe2f1/mapping-digital-media-digitization-media-business-models-20110721.pdf

Pillemer, K. (2021). *Older people and action on climate change: A powerful but underutilized resource.* Cornell University & United Nations ESCAP. https://www.unescap.org/sites/default/d8files/event-documents/KPillemer_paper.pdf

Pinto, M. de M., & Pedruzzi Fonseca, L. (2013). Profundizando la comprensión de los Living Labs de Brasil. *CTS: Revista Iberoamericana de Ciencia, Tecnología y Sociedad, 8*(23), 231–247. https://ojs.revistacts.net/index.php/CTS/article/view/650

Pirzada, P., Wilde, A., Doherty, G. H., & Harris-Birtill, D. (2022). Ethics and acceptance of smart homes for older adults. *Informatics for Health & Social Care, 47*(1), 10–37. DOI: 10.1080/17538157.2021.1923500

Ponce, M., & Etchegoyen, J. F. (2025, July 30). *Silver opportunity: Financial innovation for an aging population in Latin America. World Bank Blogs.* https://blogs.worldbank.org/en/latinamerica/financial-innovation-aging-population-latin-america

Prahalad, C. K., & Ramaswamy, V. (2004). Co-creation experiences: The next practice in value creation. *Journal of Interactive Marketing, 18*(3), 5–14. DOI: 10.1002/dir.20015

Priday, G., Pedell, S., Livingstone, A., Margelis, G., & Gould, G. (2024). Building a living lab network to support technology innovation within the Australian aged care sector. In C. P. Lim, A. Vaidya, N. Jain, M. N. Favorskaya, & L. C. Jain (Eds.), *Advances in Intelligent Healthcare Delivery and Management* (Intelligent Systems Reference Library, Vol. 258, pp. 147–169). Springer. https://doi.org/DOI: 10.1007/978-3-031-65430-5_7

Quigley, R., Russell, S. G., Larkins, S., Taylor, S., Sagigi, B., Strivens, E., & Redman-MacLaren, M. (2022). Aging well for Indigenous peoples: A scoping review. *Frontiers in Public Health, 10*, 780898. Advance online publication. DOI: 10.3389/fpubh.2022.780898

Racine, E., D'Anjou, B., Dallaire, C., Dumez, V., Favron-Godbout, C., Hudon, A., Montreuil, M., Olivier, C., Quintal, A., & Chenel, V. (2024). Developing a living lab in ethics: Initial issues and observations. *Bioethics, 38*(2), 153–163. DOI: 10.1111/bioe.13246

Raghavan, A., Demircioglu, M. A., & Taeihagh, A. (2021). Public health innovation through cloud adoption: A comparative analysis of drivers and barriers in Japan, South Korea, and Singapore. *International Journal of Environmental Research and Public Health, 18*(1), 334. DOI: 10.3390/ijerph18010334

Regalado, F., Ortet, C. P., Costa, L. V., Santos, C., & Veloso, A. I. (2023). Assessing older adults' perspectives on digital game-related strategies to foster active and healthy ageing. *Media and Communication, 11*(3), 88–100. DOI: 10.17645/mac.v11i3.6796

Rizzo, A., Habibipour, A., & Ståhlbröst, A. (2021). Transformative thinking and urban living labs in planning practice: A critical review and ongoing case studies in Europe. *European Planning Studies, 29*(10), 1739–1757. DOI: 10.1080/09654313.2021.1911955

Rocha de Jesus Fernandes, A., & Lanza Queiroz, B. (2024). Aging, education and some other implications for the silver dividend in developing countries: Evidence from Brazil. *The Journal of the Economics of Ageing, 27*, 100497. DOI: 10.1016/j.jeoa.2023.100497

Ryszawska, B., Rozwadowska, M., Ulatowska, R., Pierzchała, M., & Szymański, P. (2021). The power of co-creation in the energy transition — DART model in citizen energy communities projects. *Energies*, *14*(17), 5266. DOI: 10.3390/en14175266

Sauer, S. (2013). *User innovativeness in living laboratories: Everyday user improvisations with ICTs as a source of innovation* (Doctoral dissertation, University of Twente). https://research.utwente.nl/files/6060272/thesis_S_Sauer.pdf

Schuurman, D. (2015). *Bridging the gap between open and user innovation? Exploring the value of living labs as a means to structure user contribution and manage distributed innovation* (Doctoral dissertation). Ghent University & Vrije Universiteit Brussel. https://biblio.ugent.be/publication/5931264

Secretariat, A. S. E. A. N. (2024, March 18). *Old age poverty and active ageing in ASEAN: Trends and opportunities. The ASEAN Magazine.* Retrieved from https://theaseanmagazine.asean.org/article/old-age-poverty-and-active-ageing-in-asean-trends-and-opportunities/

Singapore Department of Statistics. (2025). *Population and population structure — latest data.* https://www.singstat.gov.sg/find-data/search-by-theme/population/population-and-population-structure/latest-data

Siyakhula Living Lab. (n.d.). *About us.* https://www.siyakhulall.com/about-us

Social Gifting. (2023, March 2). *Japan X Singapore — Ageing well with innovative Japanese tech (What we can learn from Japan on ageing population).* https://www.social-gifting.com/en-gb/blogs/news/what-we-can-learn-from-japan-on-ageing-population

Sosa, A. L., Brucki, S. M. D., Crivelli, L., & Lopera, F. J.. (2024). Advancements in dementia research, diagnostics, and care in Latin America: Highlights from the 2023 Alzheimer's Association International Conference satellite symposium in Mexico City. *Alzheimer's & Dementia*, *20*(7), 5009–5026. DOI: 10.1002/alz.13850

Spinelli, G., Weaver, P., Marks, M., & Victor, C. (2019). Making a case for creating living labs for aging-in-place: Enabling socially innovative models for experimentation and complementary economies. *Frontiers in Sociology*, *4*, 19. DOI: 10.3389/fsoc.2019.00019

Stichting Co-VAL. (n.d.). *ZorgLab – Ageing in Place Aalst.* https://www.co-val.eu/case-studies/blog/project/zorglab-ageing-in-place-aalst/

Sumner, J., Chong, L. S., Bundele, A., & Lim, Y. W. (2021). Co-designing technology for aging in place: A systematic review. *The Gerontologist*, *61*(7), e395–e409. DOI: 10.1093/geront/gnaa064

Tan, K. (2022, July 6). Commentary: Singapore's ageing population does not only bring challenges. *CNA Lifestyle.* https://www.channelnewsasia.com/commentary/singapore-ageing-population-longevity-economy-opportunity-challenge-2790051

Tercanli, H., & Jongbloed, B. (2022). A systematic review of the literature on living labs in higher education institutions: Potentials and constraints. *Sustainability, 14*(19), 12234. DOI: 10.3390/su141912234

Tian, Y. J., Felber, N. A., Pageau, F., Schwab, D. R., & Wangmo, T. (2024). Benefits and barriers associated with the use of smart home health technologies in the care of older persons: A systematic review. *BMC Geriatrics, 24*, 152. DOI: 10.1186/s12877-024-04702-1

Toso, F., Brankaert, R., Hendriks, N., Lenaerts, L., & Wilkinson, A. (2023). Reflecting on Living Labs as multi-stakeholder collaborative networks to evaluate technological products for people living with dementia. *International Journal of Environmental Research and Public Health, 20*(3), 1673. DOI: 10.3390/ijerph20031673

UNFPA India & International Institute for Population Sciences. (2023, September 26). *India Ageing Report 2023: Caring for our elders — Institutional responses.* United Nations Population Fund India. https://india.unfpa.org/sites/default/files/pub-pdf/20230926_india_ageing_report_2023_web_version_.pdf

United Nations Economic Commission for Europe. (2021, July). *Ageing in the digital era: Key actions to ensure digital inclusion of older persons* (Policy Brief No. 26). https://unece.org/sites/default/files/2021-07/PB26-ECE-WG.1-38_0.pdf

University of Tokyo. (n.d.). *Creating the International Collaborative Living Laboratory: Towards an active aging society.* https://www.u-tokyo.ac.jp/adm/uci/en/projects/sdgs/projects_00112.html

U.S. Census Bureau. (2022, April 13). *Why study aging in Africa, region with world's youngest population?* https://www.census.gov/library/stories/2022/04/why-study-aging-in-africa-region-with-worlds-youngest-population.html

Verbeek, H., Zwakhalen, S. M. G., Schols, J. M. G. A., Kempen, G. I. J. M., & Hamers, J. P. H. (2020). The Living Lab in Ageing and Long-Term Care: A sustainable model for translational research improving quality of life, quality of care and quality of work. *The Journal of Nutrition, Health & Aging, 24*(1), 43–47. DOI: 10.1007/s12603-019-1288-5

Verloo, H., Lorette, A., Rosselet Amoussou, J., Gillès de Pélichy, E., Matos Queirós, A., von Gunten, A., & Perruchoud, E. (2021). Using living labs to explore needs and solutions for older adults with dementia: Scoping review. *JMIR Aging*, *4*(3), e29031. DOI: 10.2196/29031

Vibriyanti, D., Triyono, H., Hidayatina, A., Ikawati, D., Naviandi, U., Fasriani, A., & Yusuf, A. H. (2025). The COVID-19 pandemic and its impacts on changes in social and demographic conditions of Indigenous peoples. In Pamungkas, C., Surtiari, G. A. K., & Seftiani, S. (Eds.), *The impact of the pandemic on Indigenous People in Indonesia* (pp. 57–88). Springer., DOI: 10.1007/978-981-96-4222-9_4

Villegas Plá, B. (2025). The care agenda in Latin America: Towards a new understanding of well-being? *Development and Change*, *56*(3), 426–456. DOI: 10.1111/dech.70001

von Hippel, E. (1988). *The sources of innovation*. Oxford University Press., https://web.mit.edu/evhippel/www-old/books/sources/SofI.pdf

von Hippel, E. (2005). *Democratizing innovation*. MIT Press. https://web.mit.edu/evhippel/www/democ.htm

von Hippel, E. (2011, September 21). *The user innovation revolution. MIT Sloan Management Review*. https://sloanreview.mit.edu/article/the-user-innovation-revolution/

Voorwinden, A., van Bueren, E., & Verhoef, L. (2023). Experimenting with collaboration in the Smart City: Legal and governance structures of Urban Living Labs. *Government Information Quarterly*, *40*(4), 101875. DOI: 10.1016/j.giq.2023.101875

Wachholz, P. A., Morsch, P., Villalobos Dintrans, P., Barrientos-Calvo, I., Browne, J., Bello-Chavolla, O. Y., & Vega, E. (2024). Institutional care in four Latin American countries: The importance of fostering public information and evaluation strategies. *Pan American Journal of Public Health*, *48*, e14. DOI: 10.26633/RPSP.2024.14

Wang, S., Bolling, K., Mao, W., Reichstadt, J., Jeste, D., Kim, H.-C., & Nebeker, C. (2019). Technology to support aging in place: Older adults' perspectives. *Health Care*, *7*(2), 60. DOI: 10.3390/healthcare7020060

World Health Organization. (2025, October 1). *Ageing and health*. https://www.who.int/news-room/fact-sheets/detail/ageing-and-health

Worth, T. (2024, April 25). Are robots the solution to the crisis in older-person care? *Nature*. Advance online publication. DOI: 10.1038/d41586-024-01184-4

Wu, M., Xue, Y., & Ma, C. (2025). The association between the digital divide and health inequalities among older adults in China: Nationally representative cross-sectional survey. *Journal of Medical Internet Research*, *27*(1), e62645. DOI: 10.2196/62645

Yang, R., Gao, S., & Jiang, Y. (2024). Digital divide as a determinant of health in the U.S. older adults: Prevalence, trends, and risk factors. *BMC Geriatrics*, *24*, 1027. Advance online publication. DOI: 10.1186/s12877-024-05612-y

Yap, Y.-Y., Tan, S.-H., & Choon, S.-W. (2022). Elderly's intention to use technologies: A systematic literature review. *Heliyon*, *8*(1), e08765. DOI: 10.1016/j.heliyon.2022.e08765

Yasuoka, M., Akasaka, F., Kimura, A., & Ihara, M. (2018). Living labs as a methodology for service design—An analysis based on cases and discussions from a systems approach viewpoint. In D. Marjanović, M. Štorga, S. Škec, N. Bojčetić, & N. Pavković (Eds.), *DS 92: Proceedings of the DESIGN 2018 15th International Design Conference* (pp. 127–136). Design Society. https://doi.org/DOI: 10.21278/idc.2018.0350

Zhang, C., Liu, S., Chen, G., & Harper, S. (2024). Green finance and the silver economy: Catalyzing China's low-carbon development. *Frontiers in Environmental Science*, *12*, 1406812. DOI: 10.3389/fenvs.2024.1406812

Zhang, Q. (2023). An interpretable biological age. *The Lancet. Healthy Longevity*, *4*(12), e662–e663. DOI: 10.1016/S2666-7568(23)00213-3

## ADDITIONAL READINGS

Carroll, S., Kobayashi, K., Cervantes, M. N., Freeman, S., Saini, M., & Tracey, S. (2021). Supporting healthy aging through the scale-up, spread, and sustainability of assistive technology implementation: A rapid realist review of participatory co-design for assistive technology with older adults. *Gerontology & Geriatric Medicine*, *7*, 23337214211023269.

Chen, S., Tang, Y., Zhou, J., Lu, Y., Lei, L., & Yu, L. (2024). Facilitating co-design among older adults in a digital setting: Methodological challenges and opportunities. *CoDesign*, *20*(2), 118–135.

Jutai, J. W., Hatoum, F., Bhardwaj, D., & Hosseini, M. (2024). Implementation of digital health technologies for older adults: A scoping review. *Frontiers in Aging*, *5*, 1349520.

Li, X., Guo, S., Jin, Y., Higgs, P., Nazroo, J., & Marshall, A. (2023). Digital health for aging populations. *Nature Medicine*, *29*(7), 1623–1630.

Liu, L., Wang, X.-L., Cheng, N., Yu, F.-M., Li, H.-J., Mu, Y., Yuan, Y., Dong, J.-X., Wu, Y.-D., Gong, D.-X., Wang, S., & Zhang, G.-W. (2024). Development trends and prospects of technology-based solutions for health challenges in aging over the past 25 years: Bibliometric analysis. *Journal of Medical Internet Research*, *26*, e57031.

Paluch, R., Cerna, K., Kirschsieper, D., & Müller, C. (2023). Practices of care in participatory design with older adults during the COVID-19 pandemic: Digitally mediated study. *Journal of Medical Internet Research*, *25*, e45750.

Spinelli, G., Weaver, N., Marks, D., & Victor, C. (2019). Making a case for creating living labs for aging-in-place: Enabling socially innovative models for experimentation and complementary economies. *Frontiers in Sociology*, *4*, 19.

Wei, W., Sun, Y., Liu, B., Wang, H., & Geng, Y. (2024). How digital innovation ecosystems facilitate low-carbon transformation of the economy based on a dynamic qualitative comparative analysis. *Sustainability*, *16*(22), 9962.

Woolrych, R., Sixsmith, J., Mortenson, W. B., Rennick-Egglestone, S., Ronzi, S., Sixsmith, A., Dagios, P., & Fang, M. L. (2024). Exploring the role of smart cities in supporting ageing-in-place in Chongqing, China. *Australasian Journal on Ageing*, *43*(2), 186–194.

Zhao, J., Gao, S., Wang, J., Liu, X., & Haans, D. (2024). Older adults imagining future technologies in participatory design workshops: Supporting continuity in the pursuit of meaningful activities. In *Proceedings of the 2024 CHI Conference on Human Factors in Computing Systems* (Article 887). Association for Computing Machinery.

## KEY TERMS AND DEFINITIONS

**Active User Involvement:** Older adults are engaged as *active co-creators* across the lifecycle—not only at end-stage testing—consistent with ENoLL's user-centred, real-life, iterative principles and Bergvall-Kåreborn et al.'s emphasis on user *influence*.

**Ageing in Place:** Enabling people to continue living independently in the community, either in their current home or appropriate housing, through appropriate services and assistance (World Health Organization; Ollevier et al., 2020).

**Algorithmic Fidelity:** The degree to which a model's internal representations *appear* to capture interactions among age, gender, ideology, and culture—as explored in Argyle et al. (2023)—recognising this is not evidence of normative validity for decision-making.

**Behaviour Change Frameworks (COM-B / BCTs):** The COM-B model (Capability, Opportunity, Motivation → Behaviour) is a diagnostic framework used to design interventions. In Living Lab contexts, it helps identify enablers and barriers and link them to specific Behaviour Change Techniques (BCTs).

**Co-creation:** Value is jointly created by providers and users through interaction (Prahalad & Ramaswamy, 2004). The DART model highlights Dialogue, Access, Risk-benefits, and Transparency as the building blocks of co-creation. In Living Labs, co-creation often involves iterative feedback cycles from real-life field trials.

**Digital Divide:** Systematic disparities in access, skills, and effective use of digital technologies among older adults, shaped by income, education, geography, and disability.

**Enabler-driven Labs:** Living Labs orchestrated by facilitator entities such as cities or innovation hubs (Leminen et al., 2012).

**Equity-centred Innovation:** Designing and evaluating Living Lab interventions with explicit attention to reducing inequalities and ensuring inclusivity among diverse older adult populations.

**Green Silver Economy:** Meeting the needs of an ageing society through pathways consistent with climate goals—for example, green finance mechanisms supporting silver-economy services (Zhang, Liu, Chen, & Harper, 2024).

**Innovation Intermediaries:** Living Labs serving multiple roles as innovation intermediaries (brokering relationships between stakeholders), experimentation platforms (providing infrastructure and contexts for trials), and community forums (engaging local communities or specific user groups in problem-solving) (Leminen et al., 2012).

**Interoperability:** The ability of different Active and Assisted Living (AAL) systems, platforms, and services to work together seamlessly—critical for scaling Living Lab innovations (Lam et al., 2022).

**Lead Users:** Older adults and carers who develop ingenious work-arounds or hacks to meet daily challenges (e.g., medication reminders, fall-prevention tools), reflecting von Hippel's concept of "user innovation."

**Living Labs:** User-centred, participatory innovation environments that bring together multiple stakeholders to co-develop and test innovations under real-world conditions (Bergvall-Kåreborn et al., 2009).

**LLM-based Opinion Emulation:** Methodologies in which large language models are trained or prompted to generate responses that mimic the perspectives of individuals or groups. Such methods require safeguards to avoid amplifying biases or excluding digitally marginalised older adults (Argyle et al., 2023).

**Privacy-by-Design and Data Governance:** A principle ensuring that data minimisation, informed consent, and transparency are embedded into the design of Living Lab systems and AI-enabled interventions involving older adults.

**Provider-driven Labs:** Living Labs led by technology or service providers (Leminen et al., 2012).

**Public-Private-People Partnerships (PPPP):** Innovation ecosystems in which firms, public authorities, researchers, and citizen-users collaborate in domains ranging from health and smart cities to rural development.

**Quadruple Helix Model:** Adds users and civil society as a fourth "helix" alongside industry, academia, and government (Westerlund & Leminen, 2011).

**Quintuple Helix Model:** Integrates environmental considerations, promoting socio-ecological interactions and sustainable innovation by adding the environment as a fifth helix (Merino-Barbancho et al., 2023).

**Real-life Settings:** Living Lab testing contexts that capture the complexity of older adults' actual living environments, significantly influencing technology adoption and effectiveness.

**Silver Economy:** The sum of all economic activities serving the needs of people over a certain age, often 50 or 60+. Defined by the European Commission as "the economic opportunities arising from the public and consumer expenditure related to population ageing and the specific needs of the population over 50" (Eatock, 2015; European Commission, 2018).

**User-centric Design:** Design practice beginning from the end-user's perspective, context, and tasks to drive requirements (Don Norman et al.).

**User-driven Labs:** Living Labs initiated by end-user groups as grassroots initiatives (Leminen et al., 2012).

**Utilizer-driven Labs:** Living Labs where companies lead market-oriented innovation development (Leminen et al., 2012).

**Accessibility / Universal Design:** Designing technologies, services, and environments to be usable by all people, to the greatest extent possible, without adaptation or specialised design.

**Evaluation in Real-world Trials:** Frameworks such as RE-AIM and implementation science approaches are used in Living Labs to assess reach, effectiveness, adoption, implementation, and maintenance of innovations in complex, everyday environments.

# Chapter 5
# An Integrative Model of Senior Entrepreneurship in the Silver Economy

**Zyed Achour**
https://orcid.org/0000-0002-1578-9062
*National Institute of Labor and Social Studies, University of Carthage, Tunisia*

## ABSTRACT

*This integrative review examines senior entrepreneurship through a comprehensive analysis of academic and institutional literature, with a particular focus on OECD economies and the silver economy context. It highlights the profound heterogeneity of entrepreneurial trajectories at later stages of life, shaped by individual resources, motivational profiles, and institutional environments. Drawing on the Resource-Based View and lifespan-oriented approaches, the chapter introduces the concept of mature resources, emphasizing the dynamic configuration of human, social, and financial capital among older entrepreneurs. The analysis also explores systemic barriers and enabling factors, including social protection systems, age-related discrimination, and policy frameworks. Finally, the chapter discusses implications for public policy and entrepreneurial support practices, contributing to a more nuanced and integrative understanding of senior entrepreneurship.*

## INTRODUCTION

Demographic aging represents one of the major structural transformations reshaping contemporary economies. Across OECD and European Union countries, the rapid growth of the population aged 50 and over is profoundly altering labor markets, social protection systems, and growth dynamics. According to demographic

DOI: 10.4018/979-8-3373-6117-8.ch005

projections, this trend will intensify over the coming decades, placing mounting pressure on pension systems while raising fundamental questions about traditional forms of senior economic participation.

Against this backdrop, senior entrepreneurship—understood as the creation or takeover of economic activities by individuals aged 50 and over—emerges as both an economic and social response to these structural challenges. Far from being limited to workforce retention, this form of entrepreneurship unfolds through trajectories marked by the valorization of professional experience, the mobilization of established social networks, and the pursuit of autonomy or meaning in later career stages. Several studies show that age does not uniformly affect entrepreneurial intention and performance and that accumulated experience can constitute a decisive comparative advantage in certain entrepreneurial configurations (Lévesque & Minniti, 2006; Kautonen, Kibler & Minniti, 2017).

At the same time, the rise of the silver economy reinforces the economic relevance of senior entrepreneurship. Growing needs linked to population aging generate new entrepreneurial opportunities across diverse sectors such as personal services, healthcare, tourism, and adapted technologies. From this perspective, seniors are no longer viewed solely as recipients of goods and services but also as productive actors capable of identifying emerging needs and proposing innovative solutions—particularly in markets where deep understanding of user practices and expectations constitutes a strategic advantage.

Nevertheless, despite this potential, senior entrepreneurship continues to face persistent structural barriers. Access to financing, age-related stereotypes, and gaps in digital skills all represent obstacles that can limit senior entrepreneurial engagement. These constraints coexist with powerful drivers, notably accumulated experience, professional credibility, and dense relational networks, creating hybrid entrepreneurial configurations that oscillate between opportunity-driven and necessity-driven entrepreneurship (Weber & Schaper, 2004).

From a theoretical standpoint, analyzing senior entrepreneurship offers particularly fertile ground for interrogating dominant explanatory frameworks. The resource-based view captures the specificity of senior entrepreneurs' resource endowments, while human capital theory illuminates the central role of experience and skills accumulated throughout the life course. However, these frameworks benefit from enrichment to explicitly integrate the temporal and social dimensions of aging, as well as the resource compensation mechanisms that characterize late-career entrepreneurial trajectories (Lévesque & Minniti, 2006).

Despite growing interest in this topic, the literature on senior entrepreneurship remains fragmented, scattered across country-specific studies and partial sectoral analyses. Internationally comparable data remain limited and are often produced by a restricted number of institutions (Global Entrepreneurship Monitor, OECD,

European Commission), making it difficult to construct a coherent and current overview of the phenomenon. Moreover, theoretical frameworks mobilized to analyze entrepreneurship in general are not always adapted to the specificities of aging and late-career trajectories.

It is within this context that this chapter proposes an integrative and critical synthesis of international research on senior entrepreneurship in OECD and European Union countries. The objective is not to produce new primary empirical data but rather to systematically gather, organize, and analyze available knowledge to offer an updated and theoretically grounded overview of this phenomenon. More specifically, this chapter aims to:

1. Establish an integrative theoretical framework for understanding the specificities of senior entrepreneurship by mobilizing resource-based, human capital, and planned behavior theories;
2. Synthesize and organize available international data (GEM, OECD, Eurostat) to propose a comparative empirical mapping of senior entrepreneurship;
3. Identify and critically analyze the principal barriers and drivers of senior entrepreneurship based on existing academic and institutional literature;
4. Compare national and regional dynamics of senior entrepreneurship by highlighting the role of institutional, cultural, and economic contexts;
5. Formulate theoretical and practical implications for researchers, public decision-makers, and entrepreneurial support practitioners.

This chapter's contribution lies in its synthetic and integrative approach: rather than reproducing existing analyses, it brings them together within a coherent framework, revealing convergences and contradictions, and deriving theoretical and practical insights that go beyond simple juxtaposition of empirical results. In other words, this chapter aims to transform scattered literature into an organized and critical body of knowledge capable of guiding both future research and public action.

Methodologically, this work relies on a structured and reasoned narrative review of academic and institutional literature, complemented by comparative analysis of international secondary data. This approach, detailed in the methodological section, allows articulation of different levels of analysis (individual, institutional, and national context) and different knowledge sources (academic research, institutional statistics, and international organization reports) to construct a multidimensional understanding of senior entrepreneurship.

The chapter is organized as follows. Section 2 presents the mobilized theoretical framework, emphasizing resource-based theory, human capital theory, and planned behavior theory, while discussing their relevance for analyzing late-career entrepreneurship. Section 3 specifies the adopted methodological approach, explicating mobilized sources, selection criteria, and inherent limitations of a secondary data-based approach. Section 4 presents a structured synthesis of available international data, examining prevalence, demographic and sectoral characteristics, as well as senior entrepreneur motivations. Section 5 analyzes in depth the barriers and drivers of senior entrepreneurship identified in the literature, along with variations observed across national contexts as documented by existing comparative studies. Section 6 proposes international comparative analyses to highlight the role of institutional and cultural contexts. Section 7 discusses conceptual contributions and implications for public policies and entrepreneurial practices before Section 8 acknowledges the limitations of this synthesis and opens research perspectives. Finally, the conclusion recalls the main lessons of this integrative review and underscores the importance of developing inclusive approaches to entrepreneurship in a context of accelerating demographic aging.

## THEORETICAL FRAMEWORK

Analyzing senior entrepreneurship sits at the intersection of several complementary theoretical frameworks that help capture the specificity of entrepreneurial trajectories at an advanced stage of the life course. Among these frameworks, the Resource-Based View (RBV), human capital theory, the lifespan perspective, and planned behavior theory offer particularly relevant analytical lenses for understanding the determinants, constraints, and motivational dynamics specific to older entrepreneurs as documented in the international literature.

Originally developed in the field of strategy, resource-based theory posits that performance and competitive advantage rest on mobilizing resources that are simultaneously valuable, rare, difficult to imitate, and non-substitutable (Barney, 1991). Transposed to entrepreneurship, this approach emphasizes entrepreneurs' individual endowments and their capacity to identify, combine, and exploit economic opportunities (Alvarez & Busenitz, 2001). In the case of seniors, RBV thus highlights a distinctive resource profile, largely shaped by progressive accumulation of professional and social experiences throughout an extended career.

Senior entrepreneurs generally possess relatively solid tangible resources, notably accumulated financial capital, personal or real estate assets, and a self-financing capacity often superior to that of younger entrepreneurs. These resources can partially offset the difficulties in accessing external financing frequently encountered by this population. However, the specificity of senior entrepreneurship lies above all in the richness of mobilizable intangible resources. Human capital—understood as the cumulative stock of skills, knowledge, and professional experience acquired over the life course—constitutes a central strategic resource in this regard. Sectoral expertise, fine-grained market knowledge, and mastery of organizational processes developed over time represent difficult-to-imitate assets, conferring on senior entrepreneurs a comparative advantage in identifying and exploiting opportunities rooted in familiar industries and professional environments (Maâlaoui et al., 2014; Lévesque & Minniti, 2006).

This human capital is complemented by dense social capital, consisting of professional and personal networks built over the long term. These networks play a determining role in accessing information, financial resources, and institutional support, and positively influence both the decision to undertake entrepreneurship and the sustainability of senior entrepreneurial projects (Kautonen et al., 2011). Moreover, psychological capital—including self-confidence, resilience, and emotional maturity—appears as a key intangible resource, favoring more reflective decision-making and more stable uncertainty management. Nevertheless, these advantages may be partially counterbalanced by increased risk aversion or temporal constraints linked to proximity to retirement and a shorter planning horizon (Harms et al., 2014).

While RBV powerfully illuminates the distinctive strengths of senior entrepreneurship, it also highlights certain structural limitations. In an increasingly digitized economy, technological and digital skills constitute strategic resources whose mastery may be uneven among older entrepreneurs. Several studies thus underscore the underrepresentation of seniors in technology entrepreneurship and digitally intensive sectors, suggesting the existence of specific resource deficits in these domains (Fernández-López et al., 2022).

Human capital theory, developed by Becker (1975), complements this analysis by positing that education, training, and experience increase individual productivity and entrepreneurial capacity. Applied to seniors, this approach suggests that accumulation of professional experience constitutes a favorable lever for entrepreneurial engagement. It distinguishes general human capital, derived from formal education and transferable skills, from specific human capital, linked to deep sectoral expertise, and entrepreneurial human capital, based on prior experiences of business creation or management. Empirical research shows that senior entrepreneurs with prior entrepreneurial experience exhibit higher survival rates, reflecting cumulative learning favorable to entrepreneurial success (Unger et al., 2011).

However, human capital theory must be nuanced in the context of aging. Skills obsolescence, particularly in environments characterized by rapid technological change, can reduce the economic value of certain previously acquired knowledge. This tension between accumulation and obsolescence of human capital constitutes one of the central paradoxes of senior entrepreneurship.

The lifespan perspective, developed by Baltes (1987), offers a particularly relevant theoretical framework for understanding entrepreneurship at different ages. According to this perspective, human development is a continuous process involving both gains and losses throughout life, characterized by plasticity, multidirectionality, and the influence of historical and sociocultural contexts (Baltes, 1987). Applied to entrepreneurship, this approach recognizes that age influences entrepreneurial activity in complex and non-linear ways (Bohlmann, Rauch & Zacher, 2017). Research shows that seniors experience changes in their motivations, opportunity perceptions, and perceived entrepreneurial competencies, reflecting a continuous adaptation process to gains (experience, networks) and losses (physical energy, reduced time horizon) associated with aging (Lévesque et al., 2026). This perspective also underscores the importance of considering senior entrepreneurship not as an isolated phenomenon but as inscribed within life trajectories influenced by age-normative factors (retirement, health changes), historical influences (economic crises, technological evolutions), and non-normative events specific to each individual.

Finally, the theory of planned behavior (Ajzen, 1991) provides complementary insight by emphasizing entrepreneurial intention as the principal predictor of planned behavior; intention is shaped by attitudes toward entrepreneurship, subjective norms, and perceived behavioral control. Among seniors, these determinants are influenced by specific attitudes toward entrepreneurship, ambivalent social norms, and perceived behavioral control shaped by cumulative experience. Social representations of aging and retirement play a central role here, sometimes encouraging continued productive engagement and sometimes reinforcing norms of labor market withdrawal, as illustrated in analyses of European policy narratives on senior entrepreneurship (Stypińska, 2018). Paradoxically, seniors often express relatively high confidence in their entrepreneurial competencies, although such confidence can be undermined by age-related stereotypes and structural barriers to behavior enactment.

In synthesis, this chapter adopts an integrative conceptual framework considering senior entrepreneurship as the product of complex interactions between individual resources, entrepreneurial motivations, institutional and cultural context, structural barriers, and perceived opportunities—notably within the silver economy framework. This approach builds on the synthesis of existing empirical and theoretical work to move beyond a homogeneous vision of senior entrepreneurship and account for the diversity of observed trajectories according to specific configurations of resources, constraints, and motivations particular to each individual and national context as documented in the international literature.

Figure 1 illustrates the integrative conceptual model proposed in this chapter, capturing dynamic interactions between individual resources/motivations, systemic barriers, and institutional contexts that shape heterogeneous senior entrepreneurship trajectories within the silver economy

*Figure 1. Integrative Model of Senior Entrepreneurship in the Silver Economy*

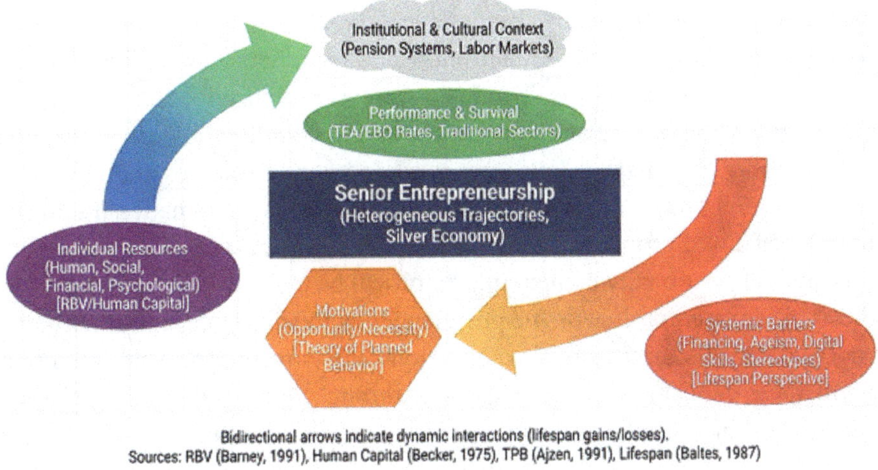


*Source: Author*

## METHODOLOGY

This integrative synthesis mobilizes a predominantly descriptive analytical methodological approach, combining critical examination of secondary quantitative data with reasoned qualitative analysis of academic and institutional literature. This choice aligns with the logic of structured narrative reviews, which allow articulation of complementary sources and levels of analysis to strengthen interpretive coherence and synthesis of results, without claiming strict causal inference (Creswell & Plano Clark, 2017).

The methodological approach rests on three main stages. First, a structured exploration of existing literature on senior entrepreneurship was conducted based on a targeted set of scientific articles and institutional reports. This is not a systematic review in the strict sense, but rather a structured and reasoned narrative review, aimed at identifying the principal theoretical frameworks, empirical results, and contemporary debates relating to late-career entrepreneurship. The Scopus, Web of Science, and EconLit databases were consulted, supplemented by publications from recognized international organizations such as the OECD, the European Commission, and the Global Entrepreneurship Monitor (GEM). The covered period extends from 2010 to 2024, with particular attention to recent work to account for transformations linked to demographic aging and the rise of the silver economy

(OECD & European Commission, 2023; GEM, 2024). Source selection criteria prioritized (a) thematic relevance to senior entrepreneurship, (b) methodological quality of studies, (c) diverse geographic coverage (OECD and EU countries), and (d) availability of internationally comparable data.

Second, secondary statistical data published by reliable institutional sources were synthesized comparatively. The main sources mobilized include Global Entrepreneurship Monitor databases for the period 2018–2024, the *Entrepreneurship at a Glance* and *The Missing Entrepreneurs* reports published by the OECD and European Commission, as well as Eurostat statistics and several national statistical institutes (OECD & European Commission, 2023; Eurostat, 2024)[1]. These data offer a robust and internationally comparable empirical base allowing identification and synthesis of senior entrepreneurship prevalence, sociodemographic profiles of concerned entrepreneurs, and their main motivations as documented by these institutions.

Third, these published data were reviewed through comparative descriptive syntheses reported in institutional analyses. These notably examine Total Early-stage Entrepreneurial Activity (TEA) rates, international comparisons, and segmentations by age, gender, sector of activity, and type of entrepreneurial motivation, distinguishing opportunity-driven from necessity-driven entrepreneurship (GEM, 2023). Where data permit, a longitudinal reading of available series is also proposed to highlight certain temporal trends and contrasting evolutions between countries as reported in consulted sources.

Conceptually, the senior entrepreneur is defined as an individual aged 50 or over engaged in creating a business or managing a business less than 42 months old, consistent with the operational definition adopted by the Global Entrepreneurship Monitor (GEM, 2024). When the literature mobilizes alternative age thresholds, notably 55 or 65 years, these variations are explicitly considered and discussed in the comparative analysis to avoid any homogenizing interpretation of late-career entrepreneurial trajectories. Total Early-stage Entrepreneurial Activity (TEA) corresponds to the percentage of the adult population involved in a nascent or recently created business, while the distinction between opportunity-driven and necessity-driven entrepreneurship illuminates the economic and institutional logics underlying senior entrepreneurial engagement (OECD & European Commission, 2023).

Finally, the analysis primarily covers OECD member countries and the European Union, while integrating specific focuses on certain key countries such as the United States, United Kingdom, Germany, France, Spain, Poland, Japan, Australia, and Chile. This geographic coverage allows comparison of contrasting institutional and socio-economic contexts while ensuring availability of reliable and methodologically comparable data (Eurostat, 2024; OECD & European Commission, 2023).

This approach involves several limitations inherent to exclusive use of secondary data. First, data comparability between countries may be affected by methodological differences in information collection and processing by different institutions (GEM, OECD, Eurostat). Second, aggregating data from slightly different periods (2014–2024) may mask certain important cyclical evolutions. Third, definitions of senior entrepreneurship vary across sources (50+, 55+, or 65+), which can introduce biases in comparisons. Fourth, self-reported survey data (notably in GEM) are susceptible to social desirability bias. Finally, this synthesis cannot capture individual longitudinal dynamics that only cohort studies would allow observing. These limitations are recognized and taken into account in the interpretation of results presented in following sections.

## RESULTS

The results presented in this section derive from analysis and synthesis of secondary data primarily from the Global Entrepreneurship Monitor (GEM) and *The Missing Entrepreneurs* reports published by the OECD and European Commission. These sources currently constitute the most reliable and comparable empirical references for identifying and comparing entrepreneurial activity according to age, motivations, and institutional contexts in developed economies (OECD & European Commission, 2023; GEM, 2024). The objective is not to produce an exhaustive causal analysis, but rather to propose a structured and critical synthesis of available empirical knowledge allowing identification of robust and comparative trends in senior entrepreneurship.

### Prevalence of Senior Entrepreneurship

Across European Union and OECD countries, seniors aged 50 to 64 exhibit lower levels of entrepreneurial participation than intermediate age cohorts. According to data compiled by the OECD in *The Missing Entrepreneurs 2023* report, approximately 4% of individuals aged 50 to 64 in Europe were engaged in Total Early-stage Entrepreneurial Activity (TEA) during the 2018–2022 period (OECD & European Commission, 2023, p. 35). This rate is lower than that of the total adult population (18–64 years), which generally stood between 6% and 8% depending on EU countries over the same period (OECD & European Commission, 2023).

Global Entrepreneurship Monitor data confirm this trend internationally. For 2024, the GEM United States report indicates that the highest TEA rates occur in the 18–24 and 25–34 age brackets (around one quarter of individuals in each group), while older age groups show significantly lower levels of entrepreneurial activity (GEM, 2024–2025 United States Report, p. 18). Although the global GEM report does not systematically provide detailed age-bracket breakdowns for all countries, available national reports convergently show that early-stage entrepreneurial activity tends to decrease with age in most developed economies (GEM, 2023–2024 Global Report).

This lower prevalence should not be interpreted as an entrepreneurial capacity deficit, but rather as reflecting late-career trajectories marked by increased risk aversion, a shorter time horizon, and specific trade-offs between economic security and entrepreneurial engagement (Lévesque & Minniti, 2006).

Moreover, seniors are proportionally more present in established entrepreneurship—that is, managing businesses existing for more than 42 months—than in recent creation phases. *The Missing Entrepreneurs 2023* report emphasizes that in the European Union, nearly one-third of senior entrepreneurs (50–64 years) are employers, a proportion slightly above the adult population average (OECD & European Commission, 2023, p. 42). In the United States, the GEM 2024–2025 report indicates that 6.6% of Americans manage established businesses (Established Business Ownership – EBO), a rate lower than the average of participating high-income economies (GEM, 2024–2025 United States Report, p. 12). These elements suggest a more pronounced orientation among seniors toward continuity, stabilization, and business sustainability rather than radical innovation or ex nihilo creation.

Table 1 synthesizes the main available indicators relating to senior entrepreneurship in the European Union and OECD, as reported in consulted institutional sources.

*Table 1. Key Indicators of Senior Entrepreneurship (50–64 years) According to Available Data*

| Indicator | European Union | OECD | Period | Source |
|---|---|---|---|---|
| TEA (Total Early-stage Entrepreneurial Activity, ages 50–64) | ~4% | Variable by country (generally <8%) | 2018–2022 | OECD & European Commission (2023) |
| Share of senior entrepreneurs who are employers (ages 50–64) | ~31% | Variable | 2018–2022 | OECD & European Commission (2023) |
| Entrepreneurial intentions (ages 50–64) | ~6% | Variable | 2018–2022 | GEM (2024); OECD & European Commission (2023) |

*Methodological note:* Data presented in this table come from aggregated institutional sources and may vary according to collection methodologies, national samples, and periods considered. International comparisons should be interpreted with caution due to these methodological differences.

## Demographic and Sectoral Characteristics

Available results reveal strong gender disparities within senior entrepreneurship. *The Missing Entrepreneurs 2023* report indicates that over the 2018–2022 period, approximately 6% of women in the EU and 9% in OECD countries were actively engaged in creating or managing recent businesses (TEA), compared to 8% and 11% respectively for men (OECD & European Commission, 2023, pp. 23–24). Although these statistics are not systematically broken down by detailed age bracket, GEM national reports and OECD analyses confirm that gender gaps persist, even widen, in age brackets above 50 years (OECD & European Commission, 2023; GEM, 2023). This persistent inequality is explained by a combination of structural factors, including more fragmented professional careers, more limited access to financial resources, and the persistence of gendered social norms that tend to strengthen with age (Kautonen et al., 2017).

Education level also appears as a central determinant. GEM data compiled by the OECD show that seniors holding higher education degrees are substantially more inclined to engage in opportunity-driven entrepreneurship, mobilizing specialized skills and high human capital. This observation aligns with GEM results showing that education increases the capacity to identify and exploit entrepreneurial opportunities, including at advanced life cycle stages (GEM, 2024).

Sectorally, available analyses from OECD and academic research suggest that senior entrepreneurs are predominantly concentrated in traditional sectors such as commerce, professional services, crafts, and certain consulting activities, while their presence remains more limited in technologically and innovation-intensive sectors. Empirical evidence indicates that being a senior entrepreneur (typically 50+ years old) is negatively associated with participation in technology-based entrepreneurial activity, highlighting an underrepresentation of older founders in tech-oriented domains (Fernández-López, Rodeiro-Pazos, Zapata-Huamaní, & Rodríguez-Gulías, 2022). This pattern has been linked in broader digital entrepreneurship studies to higher requirements in digital skills and technological adaptation capacities that may pose specific challenges for some segments of the senior population, particularly where advanced digital competences are important for opportunity recognition and exploitation.

## Entrepreneurial Motivations

Senior entrepreneurs' motivations fall along a continuum between opportunity-driven and necessity-driven entrepreneurship, strongly conditioned by institutional and macroeconomic contexts. Data compiled by the OECD in *The Missing Entrepreneurs 2023* indicate that in countries where pension systems are less generous or salaried employment opportunities limited, a significant proportion of seniors engage in entrepreneurship in response to economic constraints rather than strategic choice.

Entrepreneurial motivations present strong geographic variations. OECD reports emphasize that in certain European contexts characterized by rigid labor markets and limited social protection for older workers, necessity-driven entrepreneurship represents a substantial share of senior entrepreneurial activity (OECD & European Commission, 2023, Chapter 2). Conversely, in countries characterized by more protective pension regimes and developed entrepreneurial ecosystems, senior entrepreneurship is more associated with motivations of autonomy, personal fulfillment, and valorization of accumulated experience (Weber & Schaper, 2004).

## Performance and Survival of Senior-Led Businesses

Although seniors are less frequently engaged in creating new businesses, several empirical works cited in the literature show that businesses they lead present survival rates comparable to, even superior to, those of businesses created by younger entrepreneurs. This relative performance is explained notably by more prudent financial management, better risk anticipation, and deep managerial experience (Kautonen et al., 2017).

GEM analyses confirm that senior entrepreneurs are overrepresented among long-established business owners, particularly in the United States and certain European countries (GEM, 2023). However, their contribution to net job creation appears more moderate. OECD data on employer entrepreneurs suggest that although a significant proportion of seniors are employers, the businesses they lead tend to remain smaller in size, prioritizing stability and sustainability over rapid growth (OECD & European Commission, 2023).

## Digital and Technology Entrepreneurship Among Seniors

Seniors show strong entrepreneurial capacity in traditional sectors, yet their participation in digital and technology domains remains limited. Empirical evidence consistently documents underrepresentation in technology ventures, reflecting not just individual preferences but deeper ecosystem dynamics (Fernández-López et al., 2022). This gap stems from career trajectories less exposed to rapid digital evolution, compounded by youth-biased investment networks—despite data showing middle-aged founders achieve superior success rates. Still, seniors with strong digital skills increasingly pursue opportunity-driven tech ventures, combining technical expertise with decades of industry insight (Zhang et al., 2022).

These patterns underscore a critical insight: the challenge facing senior digital entrepreneurship lies less in age itself than in the intersection of career trajectories, ecosystem access barriers, and persistent ageist assumptions that undervalue the distinctive contributions older founders bring to innovation-intensive sectors.

# BARRIERS AND DRIVERS OF SENIOR ENTREPRENEURSHIP: LITERATURE SYNTHESIS

Analysis of academic and institutional literature reveals that senior entrepreneurship develops within an environment marked by constant tension between persistent structural obstacles and often substantial individual resources. This coexistence largely explains the heterogeneity of entrepreneurial trajectories observed among individuals aged 50 and over, both in terms of entry into entrepreneurship and project sustainability.

## Structural and Systemic Barriers

Access to financing ranks among the most frequently cited barriers in empirical studies. OECD analyses reveal that seniors face greater challenges securing external funding, particularly during startup phases, due to eligibility criteria favoring younger entrepreneurs and selection processes sometimes influenced by ageist biases (OECD & European Commission, 2023, pp. 78–82). This limits the effectiveness of public entrepreneurship support programs, which remain largely designed for early-career trajectories.

Skills gaps present a second, more nuanced constraint. While Global Entrepreneurship Monitor data show seniors reporting strong general entrepreneurial competencies—particularly in management and industry knowledge—many perceive deficits in digital and technological skills (GEM, 2024). These gaps hinder entry into technology-intensive sectors and adoption of digital business models. Academic literature emphasizes that such limitations stem less from age itself than from career paths with limited exposure to rapid digital transformations (Fernández-López et al., 2022).

Ageism operates through intertwined cognitive, affective, and behavioral channels (Posthuma & Campion, 2009). Explicit biases question seniors' adaptability; subtler ones embed in ecosystem norms favoring younger founders—despite evidence of mature entrepreneurs' superior success rates (Kautonen et al., 2011). Most damaging is "well-intentioned but inept" paternalism: condescension masked as respect that erodes credibility and fosters internalized self-doubt (Levy, 2009). Effective responses require multi-level interventions: awareness campaigns, anti-discrimination regulations, and inclusive financing/mentoring structures (OECD & European Commission, 2023).

Institutionally, public policies struggle to address senior entrepreneurship specificities. Though increasingly recognized as active aging leverage, measures remain fragmented and poorly integrated with pension systems (OECD & European Commission, 2023, Chapter 8).

## Drivers and Mobilizable Resources

Despite these constraints, several powerful drivers support senior entrepreneurial engagement as identified in the literature. The first lies in human capital accumulated over long careers. Professional experience, sectoral expertise, and managerial competencies developed over the long term constitute major assets, frequently associated with better risk management and higher survival rates for senior-led businesses (Lévesque & Minniti, 2006; Unger et al., 2011).

Social capital represents a second determining driver, widely documented. Professional and personal networks built over time facilitate access to information, partners, and informal financial resources, partially offsetting difficulties accessing institutional mechanisms. These networks also contribute to strengthening senior entrepreneurs' credibility with key stakeholders (Kautonen et al., 2011). Personal financial capital constitutes another important lever. Accumulated savings and assets allow many seniors to resort to bootstrapping strategies, reducing their dependence on external financing that is more difficult to obtain (OECD & European Commission, 2023).

Finally, intrinsic motivations play a central role in senior entrepreneurship according to motivational studies. The search for meaning, autonomy, and recognition, as well as the desire to remain socially and economically active, are frequently cited as triggering factors. These motivations are often accompanied by a desire for social or territorial contribution, bringing senior entrepreneurship closer to forms of social or impact entrepreneurship, notably in sectors linked to the silver economy (Kautonen et al., 2017; Harms et al., 2014).

While these drivers provide powerful foundations for senior entrepreneurial engagement, their mobilization and effectiveness vary substantially depending on individuals' multiple, intersecting social identities—a complexity that demands explicit analytical attention

## Intersectional Dynamics in Senior Entrepreneurship

Entrepreneurial outcomes among seniors vary significantly across intersecting social identities. Senior women, for instance, face *gendered ageism*—the combined effects of age- and gender-based discrimination that restrict access to financing, undermine credibility, and weaken network integration (Aydin et al., 2019). Socioeconomic status further shapes divergent entrepreneurial pathways: seniors with higher accumulated capital are more likely to engage in opportunity-driven ventures oriented toward self-realization, while those from lower-status backgrounds often enter entrepreneurship out of necessity under persistent resource constraints (Constantinidis et al., 2019). These inequalities are compounded for racialized and migrant seniors, who frequently encounter additional barriers related to skill recognition, market access, and participation in entrepreneurial ecosystems. Together, these dynamics challenge any notion of a uniform "senior entrepreneur" model and call for inclusive policy approaches that address multiple, overlapping disadvantages rather than age alone.

## INTERNATIONAL COMPARATIVE ANALYSES OF SENIOR ENTREPRENEURSHIP: SYNTHESIS OF EXISTING WORK

Examination of international literature and institutional reports clearly shows that senior entrepreneurship does not follow a single model but reflects great diversity in institutional, cultural, and economic configurations. Engagement rates, dominant motivations, and entrepreneurial trajectories vary strongly according to social protection regimes, labor markets, and national entrepreneurial ecosystems as documented by available comparative work.

### Anglo-Saxon Countries: Flexibility and Entrepreneurial Dynamism

In Anglo-Saxon countries, notably the United States and United Kingdom, senior entrepreneurship is relatively dynamic according to GEM and OECD analyses. GEM data indicate that seniors there display entrepreneurial intentions comparable to those of younger cohorts and engage in entrepreneurship both through opportunity and necessity (GEM, 2024). *The Missing Entrepreneurs 2023* report emphasizes that labor market flexibility, social acceptance of failure, and the density of support ecosystems—incubators, private networks, mentoring—favor these trajectories in Anglo-Saxon economies (OECD & European Commission, 2023, Chapter 4). Several studies cited in the literature emphasize that senior entrepreneurs there contribute significantly to local economic stability, particularly through managing established businesses (Lévesque & Minniti, 2006).

### Nordic Countries: Welfare State and Moderate Entrepreneurship

Nordic countries (Denmark, Finland, Norway, Sweden) present a distinct model, characterized by comprehensive policies supporting entrepreneurship within a broader welfare state context. These countries have developed extensive frameworks for entrepreneurship policy, integrating active strategies to stimulate enterprise creation and innovation in diverse population segments, including older adults

(Lundström, 2008; OECD & European Commission, 2023). The security provided by their social protection systems can reduce individual economic risk and enable seniors to consider business creation without excessive pressure (OECD & European Commission, 2023).

However, as the OECD report notes, the strong attractiveness of secure salaried employment and a culture valuing stability tend to limit the scope of senior entrepreneurship, which remains moderate compared to more liberal models. Lundström's (2008) work on Nordic entrepreneurial policies emphasizes that despite the importance of large companies (like Nokia in Finland, Ericsson and Volvo in Sweden, Maersk in Denmark), senior entrepreneurship remains relatively limited due to generous pension policies and strong job security (Lundström, 2008).

## Continental Europe: Intermediate Configurations

In continental Europe, Germany and France illustrate intermediate configurations according to OECD comparative analyses.

In Germany, *The Missing Entrepreneurs 2023* report emphasizes that the *Mittelstand* tradition (family-owned SMEs) and a robust vocational training system provide seniors with technical skills and networks favorable to entrepreneurship, particularly in industrial SMEs (OECD & European Commission, 2023, pp. 156–158). With approximately 2.6 million SMEs representing over 99% of all businesses and generating more than 55% of GDP, the German entrepreneurial fabric offers significant opportunities for experienced seniors (Statistisches Bundesamt, as cited in OECD & European Commission, 2023). Nevertheless, bureaucracy perceived as constraining and a culture of prudence sometimes limit late entry into entrepreneurship according to national studies cited by the OECD.

In France, the OECD report notes that reforms to combined work-retirement arrangements and creation of the *auto-entrepreneur* status have facilitated the rise of senior entrepreneurship, often in the form of independent activities with low capital intensity, oriented more toward income supplementation or valorization of existing skills (OECD & European Commission, 2023, pp. 162–165). These measures have enabled a significant increase in self-employment among seniors over the past decade, although these activities remain predominantly small-scale and concentrated in services.

Figure 2 reveals a clear pattern: liberal countries (USA/Chile) maximize senior entrepreneurship but driven by economic necessity, while Nordic welfare states prioritize quality (opportunity) over volume.

*Figure 2. Senior Entrepreneurship Typology by Institutional Context (GEM/OECD 2018-2024)*

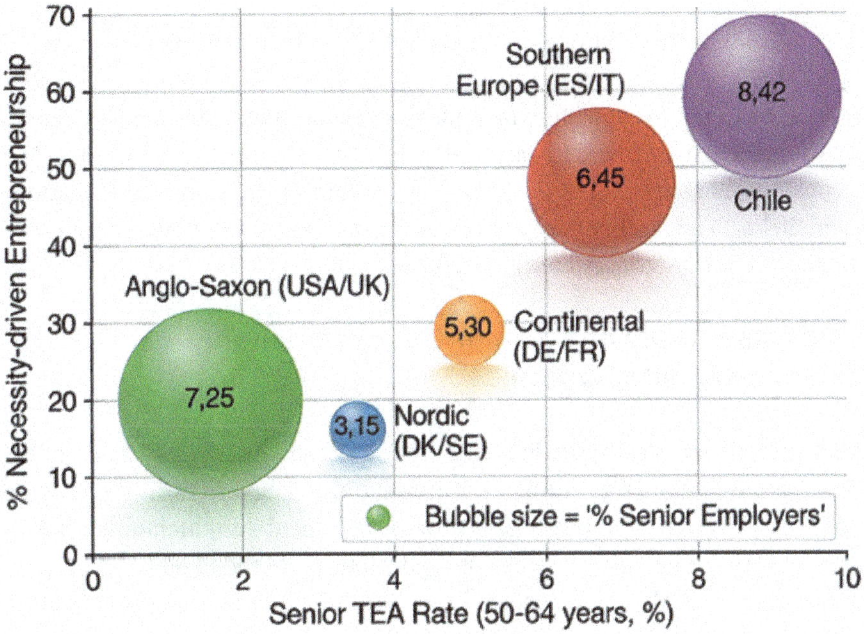


*Source: Author*

## Southern Europe: Necessity Entrepreneurship and Family Resilience

Southern European countries, such as Spain and Italy, present dynamics more marked by economic constraint according to OECD analyses.

In Spain, *The Missing Entrepreneurs 2023* report indicates that the 2008 financial crisis durably pushed many seniors toward necessity entrepreneurship, often concentrated in services, tourism, or family activities (OECD & European Commission, 2023, pp. 168–170). High unemployment rates among older workers (particularly after 2008) led to increased self-employment as an economic survival strategy rather than voluntary entrepreneurial choice.

In Italy, OECD data show that the prevalence of family-owned SMEs facilitates business takeovers by seniors, but access to credit and labor market dualism remains major barriers (OECD & European Commission, 2023). The tradition of multigenerational family businesses offers opportunities for entrepreneurial transmission and continuity, although labor market rigidities limit pure startup entrepreneurship.

## Central and Eastern Europe: Post-Socialist Transitions

In Central and Eastern European countries, such as Poland, senior entrepreneurship is inscribed in the legacy of post-socialist transitions. Smallbone and Welter's (2012) work on entrepreneurship in transition economies shows that industrial restructuring led many seniors toward self-employment, sometimes informal, with limited institutional support but a central role for family social capital (Smallbone & Welter, 2012). The duality between necessity and opportunity entrepreneurship is particularly marked there according to these analyses.

## Specific Case: Chile and Senior Entrepreneurship in OECD Emerging Economies

Chile's case illustrates a specific configuration within the OECD. Leporati, Torres Marin, and Roses' (2021) study on senior entrepreneurship in Chile, based on GEM data, reveals that high levels of senior entrepreneurship, including after age 65, are primarily explained by insufficient pensions from the capitalization-based retirement system and the importance of the informal sector (Leporati et al., 2021). The authors demonstrate that over 40% of Chilean senior entrepreneurs engage in entrepreneurship by necessity, while about a quarter do so primarily through opportunity (with the remainder reflecting mixed motivations), illustrating how social protection weaknesses can massively orient senior entrepreneurship toward economic survival logics rather than opportunity exploitation. In this context, senior entrepreneurship appears more as a subsistence strategy than as an expression of formal entrepreneurial opportunities (Leporati et al., 2021; OECD & European Commission, 2023). These results fully align with existing analyses based on GEM data and OECD comparative work, which underscore the determining role of pension systems and social protection in structuring senior entrepreneurship.

## Comparative Synthesis

Overall, these international comparisons from the literature confirm that senior entrepreneurship results from complex interactions between institutional, cultural, and individual factors. While seniors often possess the necessary human and social capital to undertake entrepreneurship, their actual engagement remains strongly conditioned by national frameworks and structural incentives. Table 2 synthesizes the main characteristics of national models identified in the literature.

*Table 2. Comparative Synthesis of National Senior Entrepreneurship Models*

| Model | Representative Countries | Main Characteristics | Primary Sources |
|---|---|---|---|
| Anglo-Saxon | USA, United Kingdom | High flexibility, failure acceptance, dense ecosystems | GEM, (2025); OECD & European Commission, (2023) |
| Nordic | Denmark, Sweden, Finland, Norway | High social protection, moderate entrepreneurship, security reduces risk | Lundström, (2008); OECD & European Commission, (2023) |
| Continental | Germany, France | Mittelstand, facilitating reforms (auto-entrepreneur), intermediate configurations | OECD & European Commission, (2023) |
| Southern European | Spain, Italy | Post-crisis necessity entrepreneurship, importance of family businesses | OECD & European Commission, (2023) |
| Post-Socialist | Poland | Family social capital, informal entrepreneurship, transition legacy | Smallbone & Welter, (2012) |
| OECD Non-European | Chile | Insufficient pensions, high necessity proportion (42.6%), informality | Leporati et al., (2021) |

Source: Author's synthesis from cited sources.

# DISCUSSION: TOWARD AN INTEGRATIVE MODEL OF SENIOR ENTREPRENEURSHIP

## Synthesis of Results from Analyzed Literature

Integrative analysis of academic and institutional literature highlights the profoundly heterogeneous character of senior entrepreneurship. Far from constituting a homogeneous group, older entrepreneurs are distinguished by strongly differentiated profiles, motivations, and trajectories, shaped both by their individual resources and by the institutional contexts in which they operate. The international comparisons presented in the previous section show marked gaps between countries, linked to social protection regimes, labor market conditions, and cultural norms associated with age (OECD & European Commission, 2023; GEM, 2023–2024).

This heterogeneity is also found at the level of entrepreneurial motivations as documented by international surveys. In certain contexts, senior entrepreneurship primarily follows an opportunity logic, associated with autonomy, personal fulfillment, or valorization of accumulated expertise. Conversely, in environments characterized by more limited social protection or exclusion of older workers from the labor market, economic necessity remains a central driver of entrepreneurial engagement (OECD & European Commission, 2023; Leporati et al., 2021). Recent crises, notably the 2008 financial crisis and the COVID-19 pandemic, have reinforced this porosity between necessity and opportunity, even in advanced economies according to OECD reports.

The results of this synthesis tend to demonstrate the relevance of a Resource-Based View reading. Human capital derived from professional experience, social capital consisting of professional and family networks, as well as personal financial capital appear as major determinants of senior entrepreneurship in the empirical studies examined (Kautonen, Down & Minniti, 2014; Lévesque & Minniti, 2006; Unger et al., 2011). Among these resources, social networks play a particularly structuring role, sometimes more decisive than formal institutional mechanisms, by facilitating access to information, financing, and market opportunities.

Despite these assets, literature analysis highlights the persistence of systemic barriers. Age-related discrimination, regulatory complexity, difficulties accessing financing, and gaps in digital skills constitute recurring obstacles to senior entrepreneurial initiative (Fernández-López et al., 2022; OECD & European Commission, 2023). By contrast, intrinsic motivations—quest for meaning, desire for autonomy, maintenance of social utility, and willingness to transmit knowledge—appear as essential levers of late-career entrepreneurial engagement identified in several works (Harms et al., 2014; Kautonen et al., 2017).

## Conceptual Contributions of This Synthesis

This integrative review contributes to existing entrepreneurship literature by enriching existing theoretical frameworks through synthesis and systematic organization of available knowledge. It first extends the Resource-Based View by identifying in the literature the notion of "mature resources," emphasizing that certain resources—such as experience, credibility, or relational capital—tend to strengthen with age, while others may transform or depreciate. The entrepreneurial potential of seniors thus rests on a dynamic resource configuration, not on a simple accumulated stock as recent work suggests (Bohlmann et al., 2017; Lévesque et al., 2026).

The analyzed work also emphasizes the central role of social capital, which often appears more determining than human or financial capital. This observation argues for more explicit integration of relational dimensions in entrepreneurial theories, particularly when dealing with aging populations. Compensation mechanisms observed in empirical studies—whereby certain resources offset deficits in other domains—provide original insight into seniors' entrepreneurial resilience.

Finally, this synthesis enriches human capital theory and planned behavior theory by highlighting from the literature a non-linear relationship between age, perceived competencies, and entrepreneurial performance, as well as age-specific subjective norms. Seniors often combine a strong sense of competence with increased risk aversion, creating a behavioral control paradox that nuances classical predictions of planned behavior theory (Ajzen, 1991; Kautonen et al., 2017).

## Implications for Public Policy

The results of this synthesis suggest the necessity of public policies specifically adapted to senior entrepreneurship, beyond generic entrepreneurial mechanisms. *The Missing Entrepreneurs 2023* report recommends targeted measures regarding continuing education, inclusive financing, and differentiated support (OECD & European Commission, 2023, Chapter 8). The articulation between pension systems and entrepreneurship constitutes a central issue: easing combined pension-income arrangements, simplifying administrative rules, and introducing adapted contribution regimes can remove major barriers to entrepreneurial initiative.

Fighting ageism also appears as a transversal priority according to OECD recommendations. It requires awareness-raising actions, effective regulation against discrimination, and better integration of seniors into entrepreneurial ecosystems. Finally, recognition of the silver economy as a strategic sector offers important opportunities for innovation, value creation, and social cohesion as several recent works emphasize (Kautonen, 2013; OECD & European Commission, 2023).

Based on comparative analysis of national models (Section 6), several action levers emerge:

1. Adapt financing mechanisms: facilitate credit access for seniors by revising discriminatory age criteria
2. Modernize pension regimes: enable flexible work-retirement combination without excessive penalties (French model)
3. Strengthen continuous digital training: target digital skills to reduce the technological divide
4. Promote intergenerational mentoring: encourage experience transmission between senior and young entrepreneurs
5. Develop inclusive ecosystems: adapt incubators and accelerators to seniors' specific needs

## Implications for Entrepreneurial Practice

For senior entrepreneurs, lessons from this review invite realistic self-assessment of available resources and personal motivations. Compensation strategies based on continuing education, intergenerational collaboration, and active network mobilization appear particularly relevant according to practical recommendations identified in the literature. Prudent risk management approaches, such as progressive startup or low-capital-intensity business models, seem well suited to late-career entrepreneurial trajectories according to analyzed case studies.

For support actors, an individualized approach is essential. It must recognize the heterogeneity of senior profiles, valorize professional experience while identifying development needs, particularly regarding digital skills. Networking and facilitating access to financial and relational resources constitute, in this regard, key levers identified in international best practices.

## LIMITATIONS AND FUTURE PERSPECTIVES

### Limitations of This Integrative Review

Our synthesis presents several limitations that should be emphasized. Methodologically, relying primarily on secondary data from institutional sources limits the scope of causal inferences. Seniors' entrepreneurial trajectories unfold across long and non-linear temporalities that only primary longitudinal studies could analyze finely.

The heterogeneity of mobilized sources—GEM, OECD, Eurostat, and national surveys—can also introduce methodological gaps and comparability problems. Moreover, analyzing existing literature is exposed to survival bias, since disappeared businesses are no longer observable, which may lead to overestimation of senior entrepreneurship performance and sustainability. Finally, certain data rely on individual declarations susceptible to social desirability bias.

The focus on developed OECD and European Union countries limits generalization of results to other institutional contexts. Additionally, the age threshold of 50 years, although widely used in the literature, remains arbitrary and masks important differences between senior sub-groups.

Our narrative review, although structured and reasoned, does not constitute a systematic review in the strict sense (PRISMA protocol). Source selection criteria, while explained in the methodological section; involve a degree of subjectivity inherent to this type of approach. A quantitative meta-analysis or systematic review with formalized protocol would allow deeper examination of certain dimensions treated here synthetically.

### Future Research Perspectives and Agendas

These limitations open rich research perspectives. Developing longitudinal studies appears essential for analyzing transitions between employment, retirement, and entrepreneurship, as well as long-term effects of entrepreneurial activity on income, well-being, and social inclusion. Qualitative comparative analyses would also allow better understanding of institutional and cultural mechanisms at work.

Digital and technological entrepreneurship among seniors constitutes a priority research axis, as does the study of intergenerational collaborations. Increased attention to gender and intersectionality dimensions would finally allow better grasping specific trajectories of senior women entrepreneurs and marginalized groups. Interdisciplinary approaches integrating psychology, behavioral economics, and cognitive sciences could enrich analysis of entrepreneurial decision-making processes at advanced ages.

Among specific future research directions identified from this synthesis:

1. Cohort longitudinal studies: follow senior entrepreneurs over 10–15 years to understand actual trajectories
2. North-South comparative analyses: extend analysis to emerging and developing countries
3. Senior digital entrepreneurship: examine technological adoption mechanisms and digital innovation
4. Intersectionality: cross age, gender, ethnic origin, and social class in entrepreneurial analysis
5. AI and automation impact: understand how emerging technologies affect senior entrepreneurship
6. Hybrid employment-entrepreneurship models: analyze intermediate forms between salaried work and pure entrepreneurship
7. Senior social entrepreneurship: explore seniors' role in the social and solidarity economy

## CONCLUSION

Senior entrepreneurship emerges as a central issue in the context of global demographic aging. This integrative synthesis of international literature highlights its profoundly heterogeneous character, shaped by institutional contexts, individual profiles, and motivations oscillating between necessity and opportunity. Analysis of existing work also shows that seniors possess distinctive resources—experience, networks, human and financial capital—capable of constituting powerful levers for economic and social value creation.

However, this potential remains partially hindered by persistent systemic barriers, such as ageism, difficulties accessing financing, inadequacy of certain public policies, and the digital divide. Senior entrepreneurship cannot therefore be envisioned solely as an individual response to aging, but as a major collective issue for growth, innovation, and social cohesion.

The international comparative analyses presented in this chapter reveal contrasting national models, ranging from entrepreneurial dynamism in Anglo-Saxon countries to necessity entrepreneurship in economies with limited social protection (such as Chile), through intermediate configurations in European countries. These variations underscore the importance of institutional and cultural factors in configuring late-career entrepreneurial trajectories.

Conceptually, this integrative review contributes to enriching existing theoretical frameworks, notably the Resource-Based View and human capital theory, by highlighting the specificities of "mature resources" and compensation mechanisms that characterize late-career entrepreneurship. Integration of the lifespan perspective offers a particularly fertile framework for understanding how gains and losses associated with aging shape entrepreneurial capacities and motivations.

By fully integrating the diversity of ages and trajectories, this work invites rethinking the dominant entrepreneurial paradigm. Developing inclusive and intergenerational models, supported by adapted policies and open ecosystems, appears as a promising path for transforming the aging challenge into a genuine societal opportunity.

Recommendations from this synthesis emphasize the necessity of coordinated actions at multiple levels: adapting financing mechanisms, modernizing pension regimes to facilitate work-retirement combination, strengthening continuous digital training, actively fighting age-related stereotypes, and developing inclusive entrepreneurial ecosystems. These measures, drawn from international best practices analyzed in this chapter, offer concrete levers for unleashing seniors' entrepreneurial potential.

Finally, this synthesis calls for renewing research agendas on entrepreneurship. Future studies should prioritize longitudinal, intersectional, and interdisciplinary approaches to grasp the complexity of entrepreneurial trajectories in the context of aging. Attention to digital dimensions, intergenerational collaborations, and hybrid forms of economic activity appears particularly promising for understanding ongoing transformations and anticipating future challenges.

In a world where the 50-and-over population will soon represent a majority share of the active population in many developed countries, senior entrepreneurship is no longer a marginal niche but an essential component of contemporary economic and social dynamics. Recognizing, supporting, and valorizing this form of entrepreneurship therefore constitutes a strategic imperative for building societies that are simultaneously innovative, inclusive, and resilient in the face of 21st-century demographic challenges.

## REFERENCES


Ajzen, I. (1991). The theory of planned behavior. *Organizational Behavior and Human Decision Processes*, *50*(2), 179–211. DOI: 10.1016/0749-5978(91)90020-T

Alvarez, S. A., & Busenitz, L. W. (2001). The entrepreneurship of resource-based theory. *Journal of Management*, *27*(6), 755–775. DOI: 10.1177/014920630102700609

Aydin, E., Cavlan, G. I., Forson, C., & Ozbilgin, M. (2019). Senior entrepreneurship, gender diversity and intersectionality. In Maâlaoui, A. (Ed.), *Handbook of research on elderly entrepreneurship* (pp. 125–138). Springer., DOI: 10.1007/978-3-030-13334-4_8

Baltes, P. B. (1987). Theoretical propositions of life-span developmental psychology: On the dynamics between growth and decline. *Developmental Psychology*, *23*(5), 611–626. DOI: 10.1037/0012-1649.23.5.611

Barney, J. (1991). Firm resources and sustained competitive advantage. *Journal of Management*, *17*(1), 99–120. DOI: 10.1177/014920639101700108

Becker, G. S. (1975). *Human capital: A theoretical and empirical analysis, with special reference to education* (2nd ed.). University of Chicago Press.

Bohlmann, C., Rauch, A., & Zacher, H. (2017). A lifespan perspective on entrepreneurship: Perceived opportunities and skills explain the negative association between age and entrepreneurial activity. *Frontiers in Psychology*, *8*, 2015. Advance online publication. DOI: 10.3389/fpsyg.2017.02015 PMID: 29250004

Constantinidis, C., Lebègue, T., El Abboubi, M., & Salman, N. (2019). How families shape women's entrepreneurial success in Morocco: An intersectional study. *International Journal of Entrepreneurial Behaviour & Research*, *25*(8), 1786–1808. DOI: 10.1108/IJEBR-12-2017-0501

Creswell, J. W., & Plano Clark, V. L. (2017). *Designing and conducting mixed methods research* (3rd ed.). SAGE Publications.

Eurostat. (2024). Business demography statistics. Statistics Explained. Retrieved from https://ec.europa.eu/eurostat/statistics-explained/index.php?title=Business_demography_statistics

Fernández-López, S., Rodeiro-Pazos, D., Zapata-Huamaní, G. A., & Rodríguez-Gulías, M. J. (2022). Senior and technology entrepreneurship: An analysis for OECD countries. *Strategic Change*, *31*(4), 447–460. DOI: 10.1002/jsc.2514

Global Entrepreneurship Monitor. (2023). *Global entrepreneurship monitor 2023/2024 global report*. GEM Consortium. https://gemconsortium.org/report

Global Entrepreneurship Monitor. (2024). *Global Entrepreneurship Monitor 2023/2024 global report: 25 years and growing*. Global Entrepreneurship Research Association. https://gemconsortium.org/report/51377

Global Entrepreneurship Monitor. (2025). *Global Entrepreneurship Monitor 2024/2025 United States report: National entrepreneurship assessment for the United States*. Global Entrepreneurship Research Association. https://gemconsortium.org/report/51640

Harms, R., Luck, F., Kraus, S., & Walsh, S. (2014). On the motivational drivers of gray entrepreneurship: An exploratory study. *Technological Forecasting and Social Change*, *89*, 358–365. DOI: 10.1016/j.techfore.2014.08.001

Kautonen, T. (2013). *Senior entrepreneurship* (OECD Local Economic and Employment Development [LEED] Papers No. 2013/19). OECD Publishing. https://doi.org/DOI: 10.1787/39915b50-en

Kautonen, T., Down, S., & Minniti, M. (2014). Ageing and entrepreneurial preferences. *Small Business Economics*, *42*(3), 579–594. DOI: 10.1007/s11187-013-9489-5

Kautonen, T., Kibler, E., & Minniti, M. (2017). Late-career entrepreneurship and retirement. *Journal of Business Venturing*, *32*(3), 432–448. DOI: 10.1016/j.jbusvent.2017.02.005

Kautonen, T., Tornikoski, E. T., & Kibler, E. (2011). Entrepreneurial intentions in the third age: The impact of perceived age norms. *Small Business Economics*, *37*(2), 219–234. DOI: 10.1007/s11187-009-9238-y

Leporati, M., Torres Marin, A. J., & Roses, S. (2021). Senior entrepreneurship in Chile: Necessity or opportunity? A GEM perspective. *European Business Review*, *33*(6), 892–917. DOI: 10.1108/EBR-11-2020-0277

Lévesque, M., & Minniti, M. (2006). The effect of aging on entrepreneurial behavior. *Journal of Business Venturing*, *21*(2), 177–194. DOI: 10.1016/j.jbusvent.2005.04.003

Lévesque, M., Stephan, U., Kautonen, T., & Bakker, R. (2026). Entrepreneurship, age, and the lifespan: Taking stock and avenues for future research. *Journal of Business Venturing*, *41*(1), 106548. Advance online publication. DOI: 10.1016/j.jbusvent.2025.106548

Levy, B. R. (2009). Stereotype embodiment: A psychosocial approach to aging. *Current Directions in Psychological Science, 18*(6), 332–336. DOI: 10.1111/j.1467-8721.2009.01662.x PMID: 20802838

Lundström, A. (Ed.). (2008). *Entrepreneurship policy in the Nordic countries: Perspectives of the development since 2003*. Nordic Council of Ministers / Swedish Foundation for Small Business Research. https://norden.diva-portal.org/smash/record.jsf?pid=diva2%3A707143&utm_source=chatgpt.com&dswid=-9615

Maâlaoui, A., Bouchard, G., & Safraou, I. (2014). Les seniorpreneurs: Motivations, profils, accompagnement. *Entreprendre & Innover, 20*(1), 50–61. DOI: 10.3917/entin.020.0050

OECD & European Commission. (2023). *The Missing Entrepreneurs 2023: Policies for inclusive entrepreneurship and self-employment*. OECD Publishing., DOI: 10.1787/230efc78-

Posthuma, R. A., & Campion, M. A. (2009). Age stereotypes in the workplace: Common stereotypes, moderators, and future research directions. *Journal of Management, 35*(1), 158–188. DOI: 10.1177/0149206308318617

Smallbone, D., & Welter, F. (2012). Entrepreneurship and institutional change in transition economies: The Commonwealth of Independent States, Central and Eastern Europe and China compared. *Entrepreneurship and Regional Development, 24*(3-4), 215–233. DOI: 10.1080/08985626.2012.670914

Stypińska, J. (2018). The enterprising self: A panacea for all or a new fictitious social role for older adults? The analysis of European policies for senior entrepreneurship. *Journal of Population Ageing, 11*(1), 43–65. DOI: 10.1007/s12062-017-9214-2

Unger, J. M., Rauch, A., Frese, M., & Rosenbusch, N. (2011). Human capital and entrepreneurial success: A meta-analytical review. *Journal of Business Venturing, 26*(3), 341–358. DOI: 10.1016/j.jbusvent.2009.09.008

Weber, P., & Schaper, M. (2004). Understanding the grey entrepreneur. *Journal of Enterprising Culture, 12*(2), 147–164. DOI: 10.1142/S0218495804000121

Zhang, T., Stough, R., & Gerlowski, D. (2022). Digital exposure, age, and entrepreneurship. *The Annals of Regional Science, 69*(3), 633–681. PMID: 35466286

## ENDNOTE

1 The empirical analysis covers data collected through 2024. Institutional reports published in early 2025 analyzing 2024 data (e.g., GEM 2024-2025 United States Report, Lévesque et al. 2026) are included as secondary sources to ensure the most current available evidence is synthesized.

# Chapter 6
# Employee Ownership and Governance as a Strategy for the Silver Economy:
## The Carris Reels Case (1995-2025)

**Cecile G. Betit**
https://orcid.org/0009-0006-4192-6362
*Independent Researcher, USA*

## ABSTRACT

*This conceptually based chapter draws from the thirty year action research case study, exploring how Carris Reels continuing efforts in 100% employee ownership and employee governance move forward concomitantly in support of its business success goals as a reel manufacturer and how these experiences might be applied to improve the quality of life in the upcoming silvering economy. Addressed in this chapter, is how the Carris Reels' experience provides and incentivizes developmental opportunities within its culture of belonging for its work-life processes at Carris to mature and increase personal capacities. Its employee ownership and governance are aimed toward improvement in quality of life, operations and production planning with safety and outputs as priorities through retirement benefits with the ESOP repurchase of company stock. As employee owners retire, their stock is repurchased by the company and then redistributed to the working employee owners.*

DOI: 10.4018/979-8-3373-6117-8.ch006

## INTRODUCTION

From the perspective that employee ownership and governance open economic, developmental and cultural pathways with expanded possibilities for improving quality of life for workers, their companies and their communities (Achour, 2024), this conceptual chapter draws from the author's longitudinal (1995-2025) Carris Reels[1] case study to illustrate the opportunities and challenges of employee ownership and employee governance as strategy to adapt to demographic ageing within the Silver Economy[2] in the manufacturing sector (Achour, Kaswan, & Rejeb, 2025; Bryson, & Freeman, 2010, 2018; Buchko, 1992). Within this context, the literature review and constructs—distributed throughout the chapter—bring together thinking from the fields of employee ownership[3], corporate governance, demographic ageing and the Silver Economy. Carris Reels' success as employee owned through its Employee Stock Ownership Plan[4] (ESOP—a trust with funds for retirement) and governed with two employee owner workers on its Board of Directors with employee owner voice distributed throughout the company, points toward possibilities to consider in facilitating well-being throughout work life in wages[5] for ageing and for retirement through the company's repurchase of stock.

The Carris experience and other efforts in building a culture of shared employee ownership and governance may serve as micro and prototype examples in discussions "to improve quality of life" in developing strategies and directions for business and policy[6] (Caryl, 2025) directed toward meaningful work with good wages and retirement funds as well as to plan for macro impacts for demographic ageing, reducing economic inequality (Chetty et al., 2024), succession planning, employee personal development, wealth distribution, organizational resilience and capacity development (Blasi, Freeman, & Kruse, 2016; Bratanova, Summers, Liu, & Vauclair, 2019; Keller & Singer, 2025). Such emphases within this chapter, are in keeping with the focus of the book, *Economic Transformations in Population Ageing: Unlocking the Silver Economy.*

## AGE DEMOGRAPHICS

The ageing trend has become clear—reflecting a new demographic phenomenon in human history caused by "people living longer than before...and a decline in the birth rate."[7] Companies are beginning to recognize the significance of the World Health Organization reports on ageing populations worldwide: "Every country in the world is experiencing growth in both the number and proportion of older persons in the population."[8]

The World Health Organization (WHO) reported that in 2023, there were approximately 1.1 billion people aged 60 or over currently alive in the world; it projects this group will reach 2.1 billion by 2050 with two thirds living in low- or middle-income countries.[9]

The workers, who will be sixty in 2050 are of working age now. Their current wages and benefits directly impact the quality of their lives and that of the communities they live in, while seeding their retirements as well as the 2050 scenarios. Later in the chapter, conversations with two Carris retirees reflect the importance of wages and retirement funding to quality of life in work life and retirement.

While the world knows a great deal about needs and interests of individuals over 60, there is limited knowledge of the health and community structures and infrastructure for quality of life required for thriving ageing populations (Ehrlich, 1968). How much can current resources, knowledge and experiential bases for caretaking and socializing the young, be applied throughout the life span is an inquiry, in process. Another involves, the current birth rates pointing to fewer adults to enter the workplace[10], while the Silver Economy is unfolding at a time in human history when digitization and robots are in full play and Artificial Intelligence's exponential growth is heartening and frightening (International Monetary Fund, 2025).

In the US, the population's median age is 38.5[11]; that of Canada is 40.6[12]; and that of Mexico is 29.6.[13] The mean (or average) age in the US was 39.60 in 2024.[14] Carris Reels posts its mean/average age as 43 (it does not post a median age). Table 1 shows the average age of Carris employees within each of its divisions for 2023 and 2024.

*Table 1. Carris Reels Average Age by Division*

| | 12/31/2023 | 12/31/2024 |
|---|---|---|
| Vermont | 44 | 44 |
| Connecticut | 45 | 44 |
| Indiana | 42 | 43 |
| Virginia | 47 | 47 |
| North Carolina | 45 | 44 |
| Texas | 42 | 41 |
| California | 41 | 40 |
| Management | 61 | 55 |
| **Company Wide** | 44 | 43 |

Workers' ages are not the only consideration in making a transition to employee ownership. The seller's age, retirement interest and company succession plan can prompt interest to sell to employees. While beyond the scope of this chapter to develop thoroughly for implications, an important aspect potentially affecting the future of US employee ownership was described in an essay by Joseph Blasi and Douglas Kruse on August 15, 2018 in *The Conversation.*[15]

The number of Baby Boomers retiring, holding US corporate ownership has been called the "Silver Tsunami."[16] Boomers at the time (2018) the article was written, owned 2.3 million—or more than half of the privately held businesses in the United States. These businesses employed one in six workers—nearly 25 million people with a payroll of $1 trillion USD a year. Their sales were about $5 trillion USD. The article's authors note, "We believe this will represent one of the largest transfers of wealth in American history."

The authors' expectation that these senior retirements would increase the number of employee owned firms is proving accurate (Oritsemolebi, Mayowa, & Munashe, 2025).[17] The National Center for Employee Ownership (NCEO) reports 1,317 new ESOPs from 2018 to 2022.[18]

Reading of the shift in age of workers, a focus in this chapter is how important conscious efforts are in strengthening shared employee ownership and governance such as that at Carris Reels (Project Equity, n.d.). Bringing all facets of a company together, reinforces shared goals, relationships and service to the common good of prospering together, through higher wages, job security and good benefits including health care and retirement (Blasi, Freeman, Mackin, & Kruse, 2010). A foundation tenet to Carris employee ownership and governance is the importance of working together for the success of the company.

From its founding and of specific focus since its corporate expansions in the 1980s, Carris Reels' experience with its work population has reflected aspects of the wide demographic diversity in the US and its regions: disability, race, language, age and ethnicities. With locations now in Canada and Mexico, the company has international reach within increasing diversity. An overview of Carris Reels is presented in the next section.

## Carris Reels Overview

Headquartered in Proctor, Vermont (Rutland County) US, the company has US locations in Arkansas, California, Connecticut, Indiana, North Carolina, Vermont, Virginia, and Texas, as well as locations in Canada, and Mexico. Carris Reels is a mid-size employee owned and governed manufacturer with $155 million in sales. There are 750 employees: 580 in the US and 170 in Canada and Mexico.

For the wire and cable industry and other applications, Carris Reels manufactures hardwood, plywood, plastic, metal, and hybrid plastic and metal reels (also known as spools and bobbins), shown in Figure 1 and wire ties, bolts, and barrels. Reel recycling is growing in importance.

*Figure 1. Sampling of Carris Reels from Carris Website*

Carris Reels was founded by Henry Carris in 1951 and purchased thirty years later by his son, William H. (Bill) Carris.[19] He said his priorities for the purchase were to move the family owned company to employee ownership with increasing employee participation. As a preparatory effort for the transition, Bill Carris participated in Harvard Business School's Executive Program, where he learned in discussions with Professor George C. Lodge of ways for employees to have significant governance voice in ongoing ways within their employee owned company.[20]

The official opening toward employee ownership began with the signing of the ESOP Trust documents on December 12, 1995; the first stock statements were issued in March, 1996 based on the outside company valuation effective December 31, 1995. The company became 100% employee owned on December 12, 2008. Employee owners are regularly informed about stock values and statements.[21]

Carris employees became participants in employee governance early in the planning for the ESOP—as employee representatives on the Long Term Plan Steering Committee with three as ESOP Trustees. Two employee-owners were elected to the Carris Board of Directors in 2014. Voice is distributed throughout the company through its Corporate Steering Committee and One Carris.

Since becoming employee owned (2008) and governed (2014) Carris Reels has seen its most profitable years. It purchased two well-established reel companies: J. Hamelin in Canada and Lone Star Reel in Texas; moved its headquarters; formed its own real estate company for its properties; and expanded its capacity to self-insure through forming and funding its own captive insurance. Carris' success seems also aligned with that of other employee-owned workplaces that aspire to be more than a place to simply work and earn a living (Blasi, Freeman, & Kruse, 2010; Kurtulus & Kruse, 2017; Scheese, 2021; Oritsemolebi, Mayowa, & Munashe, 2025).[22]

Within the ESOP legal guidelines, voting is required for significant decisions involving assets such as mergers, acquisitions, dissolutions, etc. Having an ESOP does not require employee participation in corporate governance. Research links participation positively with corporate performance (Doucouliagos, 1995; Kaswan, 2022; Del Sordo & Zattoni, 2025). The weave of Carris' governance structure, ownership and commitment in the daily life of the company, are unusually inclusive and innovative (Ellerman, 2021).

Carris Reels' ongoing efforts through its operations and culture to expand conscious awareness of its shared employee ownership and governance through One Carris are developing mutuality and belonging seeded through relationships, information and communication (Bowen & Ostroff, 2004; Boxall, 2012; Boxall & Mack, 2009). These enhance the importance of increasing internal capacities, skill-building, collaborating, cooperating in voice and work in the full context of the pieces and parts of shared ownership and governance within its larger communities (Carberry, Kim, Han, Weltmann, Blasi, & Kruse, 2024; Carey, 2004).

With ownership structured within an ESOP, Carris stock values are very important to the employee owners—they contribute to corporate health, encourage good wages and provide the determining factor for a retiree's payout for retirement. The company's repurchase obligations for retiring employee owners and the stock's redistribution to current employees will be discussed later in the chapter.

## ESOP Findings

ESOPs have a strong research base within the US. As a trust, an ESOP[23] provides a succession plan for a business from a founder/family (with good tax advantages) combined with a plan which distributes wealth and profits among employees as they retire or leave the company (after the vesting period). Research shows employee owners have between 1.4% and 7.4% higher pay throughout their employment (Kurtulus & Kruse, 2017).

The National Center for Employee Ownership has continued the Kellogg 2013 study of 28 to 34 year olds. In comparison to other retirement plans—of importance to a silvering economy, those studied "enjoyed 92 percent higher median household wealth, 33 percent higher income from wages, and 53 percent longer median job tenure" (Rosen & Case, 2022).[24] In 2021, those continuing in the 2013 study were 36 to 42 when interviewed. In comparing those who had an ESOP with those who did not:

- Their median job tenure is three years longer than those without (8.5 vs. 5.5 years).
- Their median income from wages is 23% higher ($65,000 vs. $53,000).
- Their median net household wealth is 45% higher ($66,800 vs. $46,000).[25]

In addition, with its local roots, shared employee ownership throughout working life: facilitates local economic security through jobs, philanthropy and community involvement and sustains physical and social environments.[26] Research into employee ownership points to its being good for business,[27] with companies finding their profits and productivity improving (Rosen, Case, & Staubus, 2005; Blasi, Freeman, & Kruse, 2016; O'Boyle, Patel, & Gonzales-Mulé, 2016; Blasi, Freeman, & Kruse, 2018; Paterson, & Welbourne, 2019),

From the above, the value of employee ownership throughout work life into retirement can be seen. Within the ageing demographic of the silvering economy, applying Drucker's observation to the role of innovation may be apt and will be explored in the following section.

## Peter Drucker and Innovation Strategies

Demographic shifts highlight the need to rethink innovation strategies for the ageing population. Peter Drucker's observations of the close relationship between risk and opportunity have relevance. He saw the key to success was not to avoid risk, but to manage it by focusing on opportunities rather than problems. Crises present opportunities, with innovation as a systematic process, driven by opportunities, not by solely trying to solve problems. Innovation, based on a process need, starts out with the job to be done. According to Drucker, the need "perfects a process that already exists, replaces a link that is weak, (or) redesigns an existing old process by supplying the 'missing link' (Goldstein, 2006).

These thoughts, open a line of thought to be pursued in this chapter. Using Drucker's idea for innovation above for the changing age demographic: the job to be done is to establish systems and processes to support quality of life throughout the life span. As an innovative economic strategy for well-being, in light of demographic ageing and the Silver Economy, this could involve widespread application of employee ownership with wages and capital and employee governance with voice.

Louis O. Kelso's insights as contributions to employee ownership and quality of life are explored in the next section.

## Louis O. Kelso's Insights

Suggested here, as base, is the need to clearly understand the intent of Louis O. Kelso's thoughts in the design of the Employee Stock Ownership Plan (ESOP) and to perfect the process of employee ownership that already exists in multiple forms by redesigning aspects that need changing, facilitating employee governance with voice distributed throughout the group environment. These are applied throughout the chapter.

When Louis Kelso designed the first ESOP in 1956, he "had long believed that the company's own employees should be the logical buyers and the ultimate owners; they were the ones who made the business successful in the first place, and the ones who knew the ins and outs of the business better than anyone else in the industry" (Menke, 2011).[28] Louis Kelso's brilliant innovation was seeing how applying the 1950s US tax laws could be used to finance the changing ownership to benefit both the seller and employees. "The financing transaction involves leveraging debt from third-party lenders, sellers, or a combination of both to finance the purchase of company stock. The company makes tax-deductible contributions to repay the loan, and as it's repaid, shares are released and allocated to individual employee accounts" (Employee Ownership Foundation, n.d.). It is the company repurchase of stocks from the individual employee accounts that provide individuals' retirement income. The repurchased stock is then redistributed to the other employee owners. This will be discussed later in the chapter.

An important foundation to US employee ownership, presented within binary economics, is Louis Kelso's insight that for those in modern economies, wages provide subsistence, capital provides affluence. "To enjoy affluence, all households must engage to an increasing extent in capital work, capital is more productive than wages" (Kelso & Hetter Kelso, 1986). As shown in the discussion in this chapter—through the Kelso insights and later design, ESOPs encourage good wages during work life, with capital building in shares as retirement funding.

This line of thought serves those who have ESOPs and offers potential for also improving the quality of life for ageing employees through establishing ownership provisions within the Silver Economy.

## Property Rights

It deserves to be mentioned that where capital is productive across socio-economic groups such as in the US, it has strong legal foundations in a base of property rights. Such rights allow owners to use what is owned as collateral and/or leverage for loans and investments (DeSoto, 2000). From the US founding, capital ownership through government encouragement has been used to incentivize improved outcomes: in the

1700s shares were given in the cod fisheries to encourage production; later, land grants were capital incentives, for families to settle areas in the US; today, there are tax incentives for using alternative energy as well as for owners selling to ESOPs. In the US, employee ownership has encouraged building wealth, and opened pathways to voice and power (Blasi, Freeman, & Kruse, 2013; Kaswan, 2022).

## Wages and Capital

The need for workers to have both wages and capital is seen in research that continues to suggest that wherever birth rates are rising in the world, they are not conveying economic prosperity (Simon, 2025). The Carris case and employee ownership research present options within the discussions on the global demographic shifts caused by lower birth rates and longer living elders (Adrianto et al, 2024; John T. Gorman Foundation & Federal Reserve Bank of Boston, 2023; Weissbourd, Conway & Klein, 2021). In the next section, the Carris foundations for its employee ownership and governance are discussed.

## Carris Foundations for Employee Ownership and Governance

Over a ten year period, Bill Carris wrote the *Long Term Plan* (Carris, 1994) for employees as a transition guide to transferring ownership and governance responsibility to them. He saw learning the business through participative involvement (group learning by doing and reflecting together) as a way of expanding employee owners inclusive, shared experiential base (Kolb, 1984; Mesirow, 2000) promoting success of their company and their personal wealth.[29] Their coming and learning together, sharing goals in the daily work, decision-making would enhance the well-being of their future owned company and its movement toward shared ownership and governance (Carris, 1994; Knowles & Knowles, 1955, 1959; Gibbs, 1988).

To increase shared employee ownership impact and voice in a way that would facilitate their changing relationship with their company, build confidence, employee ownership identity and experience with the process toward personal and organizational awareness and change, Bill Carris sought ways to inform and involve employees step by step in the process of change (Cady and Dannemiller, 2016; Gibbs, 1988; Kolb, 1984; Scharmer & Kaufer, 2025). As he was finishing the *LTP*, to move the process along, he reduced the sale price to 50% of fair market value, giving the employees the first 50% of ownership over the first ten years. (United States federal tax regulations, precluded giving the free portion too quickly).

## The Long Term Plan Steering Committee

As a way of providing that experience and learning from the onset, the Carris ESOP design involved nineteen employee owners, corporate managers and site managers as *the Long Term Plan* Steering Committee (LTPSC). They were charged to work with the ESOP attorney and others, to enhance participation and understanding, to establish criteria for selecting ESOP Trustees, to advise Bill Carris as seller and the Trustees regarding key legal decisions. In its first meeting, Bill Carris asked the LTPSC to consider itself and to act as if it were the corporate board of directors. Bill Carris made two decisions: the one person/one vote provision (in contrast to voting percent of stock owned) and continuing the corporate tithe to the Carris Foundation.

The LTPSC made the remaining sixteen decisions and developed the allocation formulas for employee vote. The chosen ESOP allocation formula was designed to be non-hierarchical (rather than favoring management) and reward those who had built the value of the company. The chosen formula, with ten years of service (which were later eliminated) used $30,000 as its base for compensation, with provisions in the future for increases with the US Cost of Living Adjustments (COLA). Figure 2 shows how the cost of living was added to the original $30,000 provision.

*Figure 2. Carris Salary Cap in Allocation Formula with Cost of Living Increases 1995-2023*

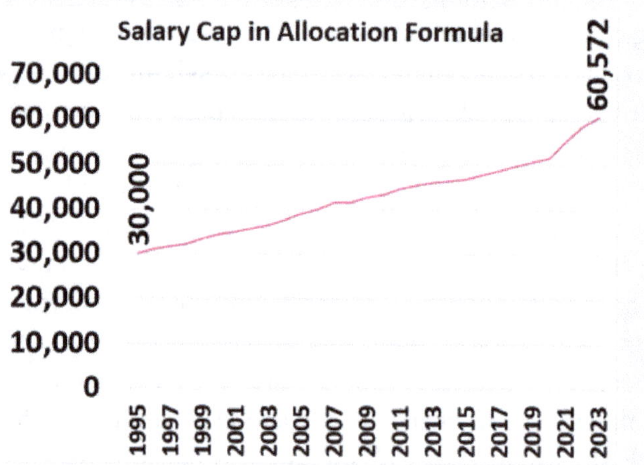


The LTPSC agreed to having consensus decision-making put in place from the beginning—an action with continuing influence.

## The Corporate Steering Committee

The Corporate Steering Committee (CSC), instituted September, 1996 is comprised of a representative from the Board of Directors, corporate managers, site managers, and elected employee representatives (one for each site and where applicable, one for every fifty employees). The CSC has been the most unusual facet of Carris employee governance. It has contributed a great deal to knowledge management and group learning and dynamics. Having everyone in the room or represented with the same freedom to speak and question, yields different levels of systemic impact over time than typical bureaucratic, hierarchical interactions (Stavros, Godwin and Cooperrider, 2016). The CSC began its work early in the transition—in September. 1996, the year following the beginning of the ESOP and its work continues.

## The ESOP Trustees

The ESOP Trustees[30] were part of the formation of the ESOP Trust Documents and continue their work with hiring the valuator and accepting the valuation report on which stock values are based (Adrianto et al, 2024; Kaswan, 2022). The ESOP Trustees are employee owners; three are elected employee owner hourly workers; two are *ex officio*: the Chief Financial Officer and the Human Resources Director.

The precedence of representation and seeking consensus have continued within many areas of the company's corporate governance and decision-making and provided precedent for One Carris described more fully below and throughout the chapter.

## Alberto Aguilar, CEO Carris Reels—Conversations August 29 and November 21, 2025

During recent conversations, Alberto Aguilar[31], Carris Reels CEO described the company's major in-house developmental investments to increase its internal capacities to achieve its goals: company employee-owner education; skill development, leadership development throughout the company, customized new equipment, robotics, automation; and site projects in Indiana, California, and Houston. While maintaining optimism in the face of uncertainty and current changes in the US marketplace, the company is cautious.

With the tariffs and supply uncertainty, pricing is a concern across companies. Carris sales are not that of our best year, but they are those of a good year. Company efforts are focused on servicing customers, increasing vertical product integration, and monitoring prices for purchases and sales to maintain company success and relationships in the marketplace. The planned major Connecticut site renovation and buildout is temporarily paused. While we can't do the major renovation, we can do smaller pieces with some automation.

In the age breakdown, we have a cross section of people in their twenties and fifties up, we have few people in their thirties and forties. It is good at this point to have some very talented and ambitious young employees coming in who want to advance as others are getting ready to retire.

We will continue the leadership training and efforts toward succession; our people are the most important. We are having community meetings to keep everyone on the same page. The same messages are going to the site managers and the community. Our ongoing continuous improvement efforts involve safety, customer service, increasing developmental capacities, and major upkeep—these are all seen as part of One Carris.

## RESEARCH DESIGN AND METHODOLOGY

The mixed methods longitudinal research of the Carris transition to 100% employee ownership and 100% employee governance began in February 1996 and concluded formally in May 2014, when the company achieved its goal of 100% employee governance (operationally defined from the beginning of the transition as having employees on the Board of Directors). Informal conversations have continued as needed as the work of the research is completed and archived. Confidentiality, proprietary information, and open access have been followed throughout.

The Carris research was designed to study the organization's change (Stouten, Rousseau, and De Cremer 2018) in transitioning from family to employee ownership and governance. There are few instances of longitudinal mixed methods research available in a whole system/large group transition and few contemporary links and bridges between actual "change" work in the field and the academy (Mohrman & Lawler, 2011).

### Qualitative

The Carris qualitative research methods included field study, participant observation and simple observation, notetaking at meetings (among others, those involving the Corporate Steering Committee, ownership, decision-making, governance, training in functional skills for ownership), interviews and ethno-methodology. Regularly scheduled conversations (at least monthly) took place with Bill Carris about his goals and plans for employee ownership and governance; less often with Mike Curran in his role as Vice President and later CEO; David Ferraro when he became

CEO; conversations occur regularly with Alberto Aguilar current CEO. Series of interviews have taken place with shared owners in a variety of roles.

During the first eighteen years of the study—there was regular attendance at a variety of meetings and activities: employee-owners training activities; corporate governance meetings; selected ESOP Trustees and Board of Directors meetings; state-of-the-company meetings (Vermont and Connecticut); strategic planning meetings (first cycles); task force meetings (health insurance); human resources (summit, presentations, and information sessions) and others that provided a direct means of working with elements within the transition. No restrictions were placed on access to information or personnel or to materials published. All sites were visited in the course of the study with interviews, meetings, and (often) photos.

## Quantitative

The quantitative study elements included: Four surveys—all US Carris Reels employees—response rate approached 70% for studies (1996), 3 (1998) and 4 (2007). Study 2 (1996) had a response rate of 41.5%. Two Corporate Steering surveys—the first had a 100% response rate and the second, 50%.

## Continuing:

Conversations with the primary foci involving archiving and reports.

## ONE CARRIS

In 2021, when Alberto Aguilar was chosen as Carris CEO, he formalized the Carris Vision process and developed ways for Carris Stakeholder Groups (the Board of Directors, Owners, Employees, Customers) to build the component plans, entitled Charters, leading to the comprehensive Vision 2025, now much expanded through company stakeholder inputs to Vision 2028—and One Carris. As a systems focus, One Carris encourages awareness and consciousness on the part of the Shareholder/Stakeholder Groups of Carris Reels' many pieces and parts within the whole—to experience its efforts and decisions in context "to improve the quality of life for our growing corporate community."

The ideas from the Long Term Plan as indicated earlier are seeded within One Carris and deepened through the life experience shared by Carris employee owners. In developing the conceptual base for One Carris, Alberto Aguilar applied Bill Carris' ideas, added his own thinking to lead the important effort to conceptualize corporate history and current Carris practice including for its future the conscious integration of culture and operations.

In Alberto Aguilar's video for Vision 2025, and plans for the future, employees were encouraged to see themselves as owners with voice: important members of the Carris community who, together, bring valuable contributions to customers that are significant to Carris' success and their benefit (Hill, Mellon, & Goddard, 2018). This continues the trend from the beginning of the transition to employee ownership and governance from the *Long Term Plan.* Bill Carris spoke of working together cooperatively for the common good. He said, that the company exists "to benefit those who work there from a financial, skill development and emotional standpoint;" that when all employees have a voice in the organization pulling in the same direction toward common goals and direction, "they should be very interested in keeping the organization healthy" (Carris 1994, p. 3). These thoughts offered strong precedence for One Carris and the basis for how Carris has approached diversity in its workplaces at it seeks to meet its purpose, "to improve the quality of life for our growing corporate community" (Carris, 1994, p. 1). Among the keys to addressing diversity in the Carris workplace, including the trend toward its ageing population can be seen in efforts, from its founding to its present that involve consciously building a sense of belonging and inclusion[32] throughout the company. Company employee owners are encouraged in their shared experience to view themselves as a consciously cohesive community—One Carris—in service with operational excellence to customers, to each other, and to their larger communities. The Carris logo, in Figure 3, shows a reel with the words *employee owned* and *customer driven.*

*Figure 3. Carris Reels Logo*

**CARRIS**REELS
employee-owned • customer-driven

The late management giant, Peter Drucker (1954), who had influence on Carris' early leadership, consistently advocated customer focus and service, as "a primary way to be as profitable as the company can be."[33]

The next section presents summaries of two conversations with Kathy Brytowski, Carris' Human Resources Director.

## Kathy Brytowski, Human Resources Director
## Conversations: September 18 and October 29, 2025 [34]

The conversations covered a variety of topics and are presented here in summary.:

**On Hiring**: The department has begun to participate in high school job fairs. We are marketing for new hires and can partner with the high schools. They are looking for employment for their students. As part of the process, we give a tour of the plants.

We have also recently hired people in their sixties, even though it is a physical job.

### On Retirement:

Because of the Carris benefit[35], employees can continue with their health insurance, and retire at 62 rather than wait to become 65. If people have a health problem, this is helpful.

Blue Ridge does our repurchase scenarios. There is no set time for people to tell us they are retiring. With the new policy, there won't be a one time payment. Payments will be over five years.

### On Retention:

Primary factors are the sense of belonging, relationships; a connection really helps as does feeling a good fit. Also, once you're at a certain point, you don't want to start over. We have an employee who is 56 and who has been here 30 years.

Seeing their stock balance can make difference. It does grow interest.

Becoming first line supervisors with training.

Pay doesn't keep people.

### Certified Employee Ownership Program:

New people are going through the program. Even at the CSC meeting, someone spoke about the program—how to be an engaged employee and reinforce something. People weave it into the discussion in the divisions.

## On the Corporate Steering Committee:

Now meets once year for two days. Representatives are expected to share with their peers. There is now a tour. The meetings are less formal than they were.

The next section introduces the Carris Vision and its implementation.

## CARRIS VISION

In Bill Carris' *Long Term Plan* for Carris employees, he wrote of taping a handwritten statement to his bookcase, "To improve the quality of life for our growing corporate community" (Carris, 1994). Community refers to the internal company, its customers, its vendors, and its locales—all for the common good. That statement became the mission for the transition, later that of the company, and is now within its corporate purpose. Figure 4 is a statement of Carris' Core Purpose.

*Figure 4. Core Purpose from the Carris Reels Annual Reports 2023 and 2024*

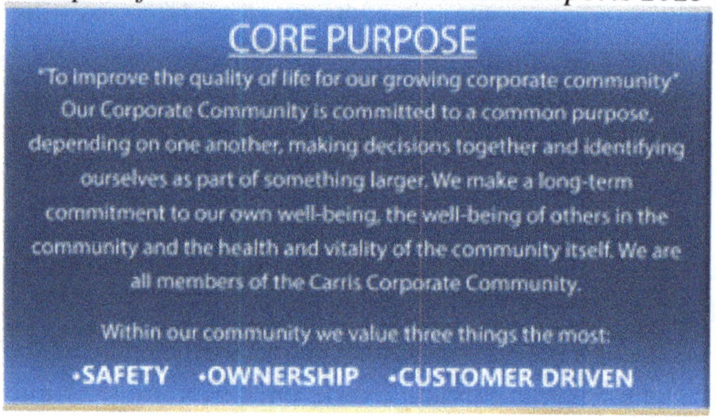


Emphasized within the corporate common purpose are relationship and commitment to the whole community. Safety, ownership and customers are the valued priorities.

In making the conscious deliberate choice to deepen its shared ownership and governance culture through its operations, the company is raising awareness of the relationship between what the company does, who is doing it, and its overall culture. Putting culture into the view of those creating it in corporate operations moves the concept into awareness and strengthens its base in succession. It deserves to be mentioned that while a great deal of its goal setting involves outcomes, Carris Reels builds awareness of how good, consistent process facilitates outcomes (Cloutier, & Langley, 2020).

Figure 5 presents the definition of Culture guiding Carris in its development.

*Figure 5. The Carris Definition of Culture in the Carris Reels Annual 2024 Report*

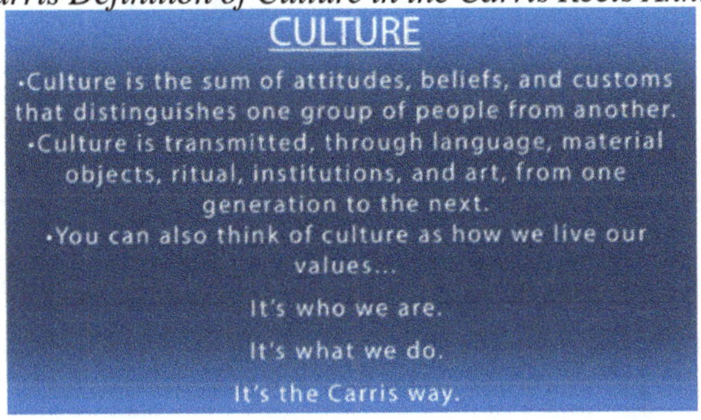


Further consideration notes the important developmental role of the shift in Carris consciousness and its culture of care in maintaining, adapting, and integrating latent patterns within its life as an organization and its succession planning. As its cultural patterns hold and transmit shared values and norms, a sense of identity ((Ravasi, Rindova, & Stiglianithe, 2019) and purpose arises among the Carris employee-owners, integrating individuals into the social system (Parsons, 1951, 1967). This is one of the benefits that older workers provide—transmission of the Carris culture and its stories.

## Ideas in Motion

Everyone at Carris is involved in Ideas in Motion. They are asked for input so that everyone can contribute to and benefit from the company's efforts and the directions being taken. The program is, in a sense, both container and dynamic for more worker input and involvement in decision-making throughout the company. It provides a way for individual employee owner's ideas to go forward for consideration and testing. There are many group efforts: structures in place for participation ranging from gap and root-cause analysis, problem solving, planning, checking, adjustments as needed, gift giving, strategic planning, etc. It deserves to be mentioned that it is quite rare in everyday work life that such participation is encouraged. Jason McKeighan, Carris Director of Manufacturing, who leads the effort, also speaks to Ideas in Motion in the segment below.

## Jason McKeighan, Carris Director of Manufacturing[36]
## Conversations April 9, and August 29. 2025,

### Ideas in Motion:

We see Ideas in Motion as the primary way of moving operations into the culture. We want to know what our people are thinking and how they think we can improve. They are the experts at what they do. We are looking at the program to increase our participation to still another level about work, about our culture. We don't want ideas to be stifled. We've used most of the ideas presented so far. A few were too expensive at the time or too time consuming. They may come up again. Some have seemed very simple and made a big difference. Sometimes we ask, "What frustrates you in a day? What tools do you need at your station so you don't need to borrow?"

At one time, Carris, R&D[37] was able to adapt equipment and refine its use. That no longer occurs. There have been code changes and new equipment is very different and more complex. Maintenance is different.

We have a mix of ages and we want to work with strengths. Older employee owners understand and have a sense about the machines. They know tools. The skill set has changed. The younger employee owners know their computerized programs. They like automation and gravitate to it. Vermont Plastics has automation. At Saint Jerome in Canada, its GENEK requires one person. There is increasing automation throughout the company plants—currently, in Indiana, North Carolina, Vermont and Texas.

Our work, making reels, is no longer as physical as it once was. Our culture is changing through operations. The new Maestro standardization program is making changes. Skills in reading are more important. We've needed more training. We now have two trainers.

Using technology, safety can be built in more easily to the equipment. We've moved to electric forklifts for materials handling. We are able to adjust speeds more carefully and have the forklifts stop as objects are sensed.

We are living the past and the future right now with our equipment and how we are set up. We have complex new machines on order.

In the following section, a conversation with Mark Chapin, Carris Retiree is presented.

## Mark Chapin, Carris Reels Retiree—
## Conversation: November 21, 2025

### How long did you work at Carris Reels?

I started January 12, 1979 and worked 42 years. I retired at 61 and I'm 66 now.

### What did you do at Carris Reels?

Everything. I started with making reels. After 3 years, I became lead person in assembly at the Mill. I also did some metal bound reels at R&D. In 1986, I became supervisor of Masonite for about 16 years. Then I became supervisor of milling (the process is that you bore the heads, saw, rout and sand) the flanges and the print shop (you the put the logos on the reels); I helped as needed to load truck at the docks. One of the machines I worked on, was moved to Masonite. Later, I moved to Tin and Bolts for the last 21 years—made barrels, ran machines that made heads for the reels. I also assembled some of the reels; put the dyes together to punch the heads out. When we were slow, I helped out in bolts. And then I went to West Rutland. I worked second shift for the first 21 years; then first shift for the second 21 years.

### What was your work experience like at Carris Reels?

I enjoyed my work there. I only had one bad experience with a supervisor who took me out of supervisory position. In the end, it worked out fine for me. In the beginning, work wasn't as high paying as GE. I think I was more comfortable than I would have been at GE. I did well enough that in 1996, I built a new house and when I retired, I had the ESOP.

### When did you retire?

I retired at 61—five years ago. The company paid for health insurance and the stocks were really good. It made it worthwhile to retire.

### Do you have a memory you can share?

All the good people that I worked with, so many came through the door that were good to work with.

### What is your retirement like?

I keep busy. I do maple sugaring in the Spring. My son and I have cows, so we hay in the summer. In spring and fall, I cut wood for heating. In the winter I relax a little and plow snow. A few days a week, I watch my three grand kids. They are six, two and a half and one. We are doing well in retirement. I retired well. My wife is still working. We are fine. With what I put in, what Carris put in and the ESOP, I feel secure. I remodeled my kitchen. My son and I are building a maple sugar house.

## DELIBERATELY DEVELOPMENTAL

The dynamism for speaking of culture at Carris is deliberately developmental (Kegan & Lahey 2016a), moving toward, emphasizing, and reflecting what workers do—in the behavioral sense (Festinger, 1954)—as basic and foundational to the idea of One Carris' shared employee ownership and governance. This emphasis consciously brings together individual intention, shared intention and action within an expanded level of awareness of shared ownership and voice in the enterprise—from shared inputs through shared processes in action to shared outcomes (Hasenkamp, 2025).

An *Everyone Culture* notes the importance of deliberately linking individual development and culture, "Imagine so valuing the importance of developing people's capabilities that you design a culture that itself immersively sweeps every member of the organization into an ongoing developmental journey in the course of working every day." (Kegan, & Lahey, 2016b, p. 5). This is happening at Carris. Through their work and a variety of practices and processes, Carris Reels share owners are encouraged to participate in the whole of company life: improvement in profitability, wages, productivity, expansion, corporate involvement (including $6.8 million in donations used locally and for broader disasters), green initiatives, energy efficiency, industry and policy influence, etc.

The trajectory of developmental change at Carris, in a sense, follows well-known observations in the fields of social psychology, organization studies, culture change, consciousness, and adult, character, and evolutionary development. Development for awareness and consciousness in such a shared enterprise requires both soft and competence skills, shared experience and an understanding of elements in the common good. Perhaps one of the unique aspects at Carris is the extent to which the company, in its shared ownership and governance, continues to refine its processes and developmental efforts from onboarding instructions through continuous improvement reflections.

In the Onboarding Phase of One Carris for new employees as potential employee owners, the company has put together a series of videos lasting from three to five minutes, ending with a short quiz. Those completing the program become "Certified Employee-Owners" for short "CEOs." The CEO program continues the efforts Carris has put together in a variety of programs, experiences and opportunities for everyone within the company—as employee owners—trademarking their watchwords: "There is Ownership in everything we do." Separation by age seems less important than the bringing together through experience—on the job and throughout Carris—in the freshness of new employee owners of younger generations who bring with them the comfort with technology that derives from being "digital natives."

Figure 6 presents a description of the Certified Employee Owner CEO Program.

*Figure 6. Certified Employee Owner CEO Program*

The topics presented in the CEO Course provide an overview of Carris as a whole:

- Introduction
- Safety
- Ownership
- One Carris
- Trust
- Engaged Owner
- Culture
- Governance
- Steps to ESOP Rewards Part 1, Valuation
- Steps to ESOP Rewards Part 2, Communication
- How to Read Your Statement
- Continuous Improvement
- Distributions
- Diversification

- Carris Cares
- ESOPs for Loved Ones

At Carris, technology is serving the company's development goals in very practical and personal ways. Everyone is learning about the new Maestro system that is standardizing some of the common work of the company. Everyone was encouraged to give input into the design. After training and working with the system, everyone is asked "what is working, what is not working and what should be changed." Maestro, invented at Carris, is being implemented in phases throughout the company. Carris wants specific areas of its work standardized across its sites as connected best practices. A company goal is also a good end-user experience.

Recently, the company reported that Maestro is clear, fast, and user-friendly. It is assuming its place as a comprehensive, integrated business solution that streamlines and automates core business processes across various departments, including finance, supply chain management, manufacturing, sales, and customer service. It offers real-time visibility into operations, facilitates data-driven decision-making, and improves efficiency and productivity by eliminating redundancies and ensuring consistency in data across the entire organization. It is a scalable, customizable, capable system that can adapt to the evolving needs of the business while ensuring compliance with industry standards and regulations.[38]

## Relationship and Participation

The relational quality of shared ownership takes on more importance as employees recognize the power of collaboration and the impacts of success. The Leadership Program currently is cohort-based by level of responsibilities within the company. The intent is to have everyone see themselves as a Carris leader (Torbert, 2004).

Participating together within the company's daily operations in the everyday work life provides rich social soil for developing shared meaning and expanding experiences promoting growth and learning. Foundational are shared perceptions and assumptions (Schein, 2004) within individual and group attention, intention, awareness, and action (Scharmer, 2025, Scharmer & Kaufer, 2025). Longevity and maturation contribute, as do new outlooks.

One Carris—bringing cultural consciousness into operations—provides the opportunity for inclusion and experiencing each other within the whole (Scharmer, 2018). This developmental focus grounded in operational excellence, opens a new direction, another level of participation for workers as employee owners sharing learning, reflecting together, refreshing ideas and foci. In a flat organization with few opportunities for role advancement, such shared effort opens inner growth and relationship opportunities. Throughout the company's history and from the very beginning of the *LTP* and the Carris Case Study, work relationships have been seen as valued and important. That they continue to be important was reaffirmed by Kathleen Byrtowski, Director of Human Resources in the recent conversations reported above.[39]

In the US, researchers not only note the ageing population but also fewer traditional kinds of mobility, in the sense of opportunities for advancement in the workplace and in social economic status. Encouraging the personal growth of Carris Reels' employee owners is seen as essential in maintaining levels of satisfaction. Similarly, for example, at the end of the two years of the Ice Bug commitment to working with the Inner Development Goals,[40] a frequent comment was, similar to the Carris experience just mentioned: how meaningful it was to have the opportunity for discussion and sharing with other employees (Wiklander, 2025).

Presented in the following section is a recent conversation with Donald Curtis, Carris retiree.

## Donald (Don) Curtis, Carris Retiree—Conversation: November 21, 2025

### How long did you work at Carris Reels?

33.5 years

### What did you do at Carris Reels?

I was a machine operator. For 33 years, I ran the drill press, put the holes in the plywood flanges. At the beginning, I worked really long hours.

### What was your work experience like at Carris Reels?

I had fun working at Carris Reels. I started September 6, the Tuesday after Labor Day.

For the first days, I thought I'll never make it. The work seemed so hard. Then I got used to it and was there for over 33 years. Carris Reels was really good to me. I learned a lot from Ted, my first supervisor. Sometimes when I'd ask him a question, he'd say, can you figure that out for yourself?

## When did you retire?

I retired 7 years ago next month after the Corporate Steering Committee said that the company would pay health insurance for workers retiring at 62 until they qualified for Medicare at 65. I still miss the people.

## What is your retirement like?

I left Carris Reels with company stock, a 401K plan and a retirement plan. I'll never spend it all. I retired debt free. We have the money invested; it is growing by leaps and bounds. We have Medicare, the Supplement and the prescription plans. We're comfortable. The main difference in my life now, is that I don't go to work. My wife and I just pick up and go as we'd like. We've been to Bar Harbor recently. We visit my wife's aunt and uncle in New Hampshire. We have new cars. We've added a deck to our home. I've been living in the same house since I was a baby.

## Do you have a memory you can share?

The first Christmas after I retired, I went to the Carris luncheon at the Mill. When I went through the door, I saw Bill Carris speaking with Dave Ferraro and Dave Fitz-Gerald. When he saw me, he stopped the conversation and came right over. He gave a big welcome, shook my hand and gave me a hug. I thanked him for the company stock and everything. He stopped me and said, if it wasn't for people like me, the company wouldn't be what it was today.

As I think about it, over the years, I did everything and anything. Because I can back up a tractor trailer, when a delivery driver would have a hard time backing to the dock, my supervisor would come to ask me to give the driver a hand.

I had a good time at Carris. I have no worries at all. We have all that we need.

In reading conversations from the Carris retirees, the idea of the corporation valuation becomes more immediate. It is presented in the following section.

# CORPORATE VALUATION

Employee owners see the results of the annual corporate valuation in their personal stock statements and the *Carris Annual Report.* Shared employee-owner stock values and profit shares have, in the majority of years, risen well ahead of projections. From 1997 to 2024, stock values more than tripled. In 2023 and 2024, Carris sales went down as the wire and cable industry experienced a bit downturn; yet—2024 employee-owner stock values increased to $75.01 through the value of company-owned real estate (operations and headquarters), reduced debt, and its new ownership of captive insurance.

Corporate valuations usually give a Fair Market Value of the Firm for the value of corporate stock. Figure 7 shows the graph of values from 1995 through 2024.

*Figure 7. Graph of Carris Reels Stock Values 1995 through 2024*

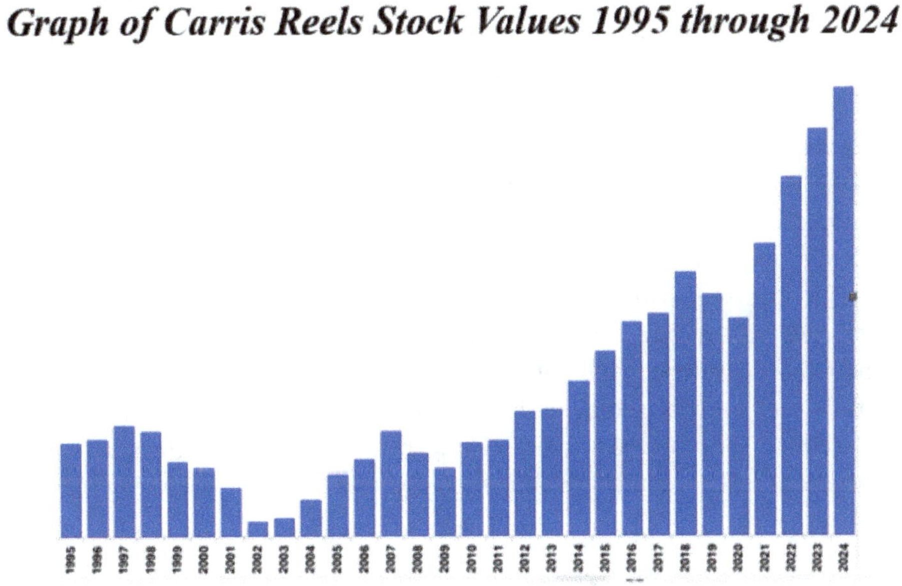


The Carris ESOP report show the number of Carris employee ownership at levels above $100,000. It also reflects that after age 55, [41] those in the ESOP can diversify their stock options. Such diversifications do not show up in the reports of Carris stock. Table 2 shows High End Carris ESOP Stock holdings for Carris employees.

*Table 2. High End Carris ESOP Stocks*

| High End ESOPS (1000 USD) | | |
|---|---|---|
| | 2022 | 2024 |
| Over 100 | 144 | 252 |
| Over 200 | 76 | 127 |
| Over 300 | 67 | 84 |
| Over 500 | 33 | 60 |

continued on following page

*Table 2. Continued*

| High End ESOPS (1000 USD) | | |
|---|---|---|
| | 2022 | 2024 |
| Over 600 | 15 | 39 |
| Over 700 | 5 | 31 |
| Over 800 | 1 | 20 |
| Over 900 | 4 | 10 |
| Over 1,000 | 1 | 7 |

To read the table, note that 252 Carris employees had 2024 stocks valued above $100,000; this is the total number of employees reported in the column; 84 had values over $300,000; 7 had values over $1,000.000.

In a very recent article Ellerman suggested that for very successful firms there were risks involved in the repurchase as currently constructed for ESOPs. He recommended alternative valuation models (2025) such as the net asset model.[42] He and Gonza developed an employee ownership model for Slovenia using other valuations seen to reduce some of the risks and cumbersome features found in US ESOPs (2024). The proposal was recently accepted by the Slovenian legislative body.

The Carris ESOP repurchase obligation is presented in the following section,

## REPURCHASE OBLIGATION

From the early years of the ESOP, the Corporate Steering Committee discussed the repurchase obligation. It became part of the Carris Strategic Planning Process in 1999. In response to questions and concerns, Bill Carris explained to employee owners that a company being purchased from its earnings was often the rule of thumb in business. On average, businesses were sold and bought using corporate profits for purchases about once a generation—about every fifteen to twenty years. The employee owners at Carris could consider their repurchase[43] obligations similarly. The company profits would go into the funds to repurchase the stock from those leaving the company based on the annual valuation. The purchased stock would go back to the ESOP for redistribution to employee owners (increasing their holdings).

Carris has a plan in place for the repurchase obligation. In a recent email from David Fitz-Gerald, Carris CFO, he said that,

Every couple of years we have a new repurchase obligation study, which helps us with planning. We have a rainy day investment fund that helps us smooth out spike years. And we changed our distribution policy, so retirees are paid in installments not lump sums. Part of why 2023 and 2024 were so large was because people were leaving in advance of the changes. We don't use Telescope/ESOP Economics anymore (was acquired by another firm) but we have repurchase obligation studies done by our recordkeeping firm, Blue Ridge Associates. (October 30, 2025)

Carris as seen in the paragraph above has a plan in place for the repurchase obligation. In 2022 the repurchase obligation was $6,962,824 (with 19 employees retired: one with over forty years of service; five with over thirty; four with over twenty; six over ten; three over one); in 2023 the repurchase was $12,680,757 (with 13 employee-owners retired four with over forty years of service; three with over thirty; three with over ten; three with six to ten years of service); in 2024 the repurchase obligation was $14,478,902 with 9 employees-owners retiring (two with over forty years; two with over thirty years; one with over twenty years; one with seventeen years; two with ten and one, nine years).

As can be read in the above paragraph, the amounts for the repurchase can be significant. What is rarely mentioned is that in the US, repurchase obligations for 100% ESOP S Corporations are offset to some extent by the fact, that the S Corporations are free of federal tax obligations and in many states are also free of state tax obligations.[44] This means that those retiring can look forward to more retirement income from their stock distribution. Those retiring, pay taxes on the distributions as they are received.

As seen above, Carris effort for employee owners throughout work life, benefits their company and their retirement.

## CONCLUDING THOUGHTS

Offered as a micro system or prototype for consideration, Carris' employee ownership and governance offer encouragement for policy makers and business practitioners to discuss how employee ownership and governance might provide a strategy to change some of the worrisome projected scenarios in areas within their purview.

The large picture in this chapter, is the difference in well-being in people's lives, a living wage and a secure retirement plan can make. This chapter's research case study provides a word picture of Carris, a successful company coming together as employee owned and governed—a scenario also experienced within other employee owned companies. Employee ownership and governance need a mix of good policy, sound business acumen and human resources to begin the process. As it is underway, developmental investments in employees, expertise and good will come to the fore to provide for the company's profitability with a good quality of life for those involved as employee owners of all ages and to provide for their quality of life retirement. The repurchase obligation is always part of ESOP planning.

Since the company became 100% employee owned in 2008, Carris has done well to plan for that responsibility. The company has now paid its retirees five times the value of their original purchase from Bill Carris. Given that Bill Carris sold the company at 50% of market value, giving them the 50% share, the company has now paid 2.5 time the market value of the company at the time of purchase. Quite amazingly that fits into Bill Carris' scenario of a company changing hands every ten to fifteen years.

As an employee owned and governed company, Carris has a kind of relational quality that meets employees where they are. There is strong effort to meet the company's purpose: "to improve the quality of life for our growing corporate community." The organization continues, as a body, to seriously apply in One Carris the ethical principle in the *Long Term Plan* "to do unto others as you would have them do unto you." As problems arise there are efforts made to resolve them quickly.

Ageing at Carris is viewed as an ongoing fact of life, a human reality to be respected, managed, and planned for within the context of the company's processes for the whole—the common good. Experience is seen as a good thing—values and stories are passed on. Those younger are teaching their elders about the computers that are being used in manufacturing. A consistent focus toward ageing may be seen in the Carris responsibility and annual budgeting requirements for the repurchase obligation. There are provisions for earlier retirement for those employee owners who find the work too demanding; the company continues to provide its portion for insured health care. Carris has moved more into automation as a way of promoting safety and well-being for employee owners, to increase production and to facilitate succession.

The responsibility for profitability in an employee owned and governed company is one shared by everyone to benefit everyone throughout work life and at retirement.

## REFERENCES

Achour, Z. (2024). Impact of employee stock ownership on firm financial performance: Does corporate social responsibility matter? *International Journal of Management and Enterprise Development, 23*(20), 155–170. https://doi.org/10.1504/IJMED.2024.139275

Achour, Z., Kaswan, M. J., & Rejeb, W. B. (2025). Towards a new paradigm of ownership: Employee share ownership as a tool for governance and CSR. In Achour, Z. (Ed.), *Integrating governance and corporate social responsibility in employee share ownership* (pp. 1–26). IGI Global., DOI: 10.4018/979-8-3693-7031-5.ch001

Adrianto, A., Ben-Ner, A., Sockin, J., & Urtasun, A. (2024). *Sharing is caring: Employee stock ownership plans and employee well-being in U.S. manufacturing* (IZA Discussion Paper No. 17233). Institute of Labor Economics. https://papers.ssrn.com/sol3/papers.cfm?abstract_id=4931402

Blasi, J., Freeman, R., & Kruse, D. (2016). Do broad-based employee ownership, profit sharing and stock options help the best firms do even better? *British Journal of Industrial Relations, 54*, 55–82. DOI: 10.1111/bjir.12135

Blasi, J., Freeman, R. B., & Kruse, D. L. (2013). *The citizen's share: Putting ownership back into democracy*. Yale University Press.

Blasi, J., Kruse, D., & Freeman, R. B. (2018). Broad-based employee stock ownership and profit sharing: History, evidence, and policy implications. *Journal of Participation and Employee Ownership, 1*(1), 38–60. DOI: 10.1108/JPEO-02-2018-0001

Blasi, J. R., Freeman, R. B., & Kruse, D. L. (2010). Do workers gain by sharing? Employee outcomes under employee ownership, profit sharing, and broad-based stock options. In Kruse, D. L., Freeman, R. B., & Blasi, J. R. (Eds.), *Shared capitalism at work* (pp. 257–290). University of Chicago Press.

Blasi, J. R., Freeman, R. B., Mackin, C., & Kruse, D. L. (2010). Creating a bigger pie? The effects of employee ownership, profit sharing, and stock options on workplace performance. In Kruse, D. L., Freeman, R. B., & Blasi, J. R. (Eds.), *Shared capitalism at work* (pp. 139–165). University of Chicago Press.

Bowen, D. E., & Ostroff, C. (2004). Understanding HRM–firm performance linkages: The role of the 'strength' of the HRM system. *Academy of Management Review, 29*(2), 203–221. DOI: 10.5465/amr.2004.12736076

Boxall, P. (2012). High-performance work systems: What, why, how and for whom? *Asia Pacific Journal of Human Resources, 50*(2), 169–186. DOI: 10.1111/j.1744-7941.2011.00012.x

Boxall, P., & Mack, K. (2009). Research and theory on high-performance work systems: Progressing the high-involvement stream. *Human Resource Management Journal, 19*(1), 3–23. DOI: 10.1111/j.1748-8583.2008.00082.x

Bratanova, B., Summers, J., Liu, S., & Vauclair, C. M. (2019). A rising tide lifts some boats, but leaves many others behind: The harms of inequality-induced status seeking and the remedial effects of employee ownership. In Jetten, J., & Peters, K. (Eds.), *The Social Psychology of Inequality*. Springer., DOI: 10.1007/978-3-030-28856-3_5

Bryson, A., & Freeman, R. B. (2010). To join or not to join? Factors influencing employee share plan membership in a multinational corporation. In Eriksson, T., Bryson, A., & Kato, T. (Eds.), *Advances in the economic analysis of participatory and labor-managed firms* (Vol. 11, pp. 1–22). Emerald Group Publishing Limited.

Bryson, A., & Freeman, R. B. (2018). The role of employee stock purchase plans—Gift and incentive? Evidence from a multinational corporation. *British Journal of Industrial Relations, 57*(1), 86–106. DOI: 10.1111/bjir.12420

Buchko, A. A. (1992). Effects of employee ownership on employee attitudes: A test of three theoretical perspectives. *Work and Occupations, 19*(1), 59–78. DOI: 10.1177/0730888492019001004

Cady, S. H., & Dannemiller, K. D. (2016). Whole system transformation: The five truths of change. In Rothwell, W., Stavros, J. M., & Sullivan, R. (Eds.), *Practicing organization development: leading transformation and change* (4th ed., pp. 440–455). John Wiley & Sons, Inc.

Carberry, E. J., Kim, J. O., Han, J. H., Weltmann, D., Blasi, J., & Kruse, D. (2025). Feeling like owners: The impact of high-performance work practices and psychological ownership on employee outcomes in employee-owned companies. *International Review of Applied Economics, 39(5), 595-616.* DOI: 10.1080/02692171.2024.240488

Carey, R. (2004). *Democratic capitalism: The way to a world of peace and plenty*. Authorhouse.

Carris, W. (1994). *The long term plan for Carris community of companies.*

Carris Reels, (2023). *Annual Report (*distributed to Employee-Owners).

Carris Reels. (2024). *Annual Report (*distributed to Employee-Owners).

Caryl, C. (2025, August 29). *Why employee ownership is a bipartisan issue*. Harvard Business School Institute for Business in Global Society. https://www.hbs.edu/bigs/corey-rosen-employee-ownership

Chetty, R., Dobbie, W. S., Goldman, B., Porter, S., & Yang, C. (2024). Changing opportunity: Sociological mechanisms underlying growing class gaps and shrinking race gaps in economic mobility. *NBER Working Paper* 32697 https://www.nber.org/papers/w32697

Cloutier, C., & Langley, A. (2020). What makes a process theoretical contribution? *Organization Theory, 1*(1). Advance online publication. DOI: 10.1177/2631787720902473

Del Sordo, E., & Zattoni, A. (2025). The role of employee ownership, financial participation, and decision-making in corporate governance: A multilevel review and research agenda. *Corporate Governance, 33*, 529–549. DOI: 10.1111/corg.12614

DeSoto, H. (2000). *The mystery of capital: Why capitalism triumphs in the West and fails everywhere else*. Basic Books.

Doucouliagos, C. (1995). Worker participation and productivity in labor-managed and participatory capitalist firms: A meta-analysis. *Industrial & Labor Relations Review, 49*(1), 58–77. DOI: 10.1177/001979399504900104

Drucker, P. (1954). The practice of management, Harper, New York, 1954; Heinemann, London, 1955; revised edn, Butterworth-Heinemann, 2007.

Ehrlich, P. R. (1968). *The population bomb*. Ballantine Books.

Ellerman, D. (2021). *The democratic worker-owned firm (Routledge Revivals): A new model for the East and West*. Routledge.

Ellerman, D. (2025, October 11). Why fair market valuations' are inappropriate for employee-owned firms and partnerships. https://ellerman.org/wp-content/uploads/2025/10/MarketValuations.pdf

Ellerman, D., & Gonza, T. (2024). A critical analysis of different forms of employee ownership. *International Review of Applied Economics, 39*(2–3), 261–276. DOI: 10.1080/02692171.2024.2435408

Employee Ownership Foundation. (n.d.). *ESOP financing*. Employee Ownership Foundation.

Festinger, L. (1954). A theory of social comparison processes. *Human Relations, 7*, 117–140.

Gibbs, G. (1988). *Learning by Doing, A guide to Teaching and Learning Methods.* Oxford Polytechnic.

Goldstein, B. B. (2006). *A guide to Drucker's systematic innovation.* Kauffman Foundation. https://www.entrepreneurship.org/articles/2006/05/a-guide-to-druckers-systematic-innovation

Hasenkamp, W. (Host). (2025, March 13). Otto Scharmer—Changing Systems [Audio Podcast Transcript]. https://podcast.mindandlife.org/otto-scharmer/

Hill, A., Mellon, L., & Goddard, J. (2018). How winning organizations last 100 years. *Harvard Business Review*. https://hbr.org/2018/09/how-winning-organizations-last-100-years

International Monetary Fund. (2025). *The rise of the silver economy: Global implications of population aging.* (World Economic Outlook, April 2025, Chapter 2). IMF. https://www.imf.org/en/Publications/WEO/Issues/2025/04/10/world-economic-outlook-April-2025

John T. Gorman Foundation & Federal Reserve Bank of Boston. (2023). *The importance of wealth to family well-being: Seeding innovation to address the structural roots of inequality.* https://www.jtgfoundation.org/wp-content/uploads/2023/05/Importance-of-wealth-to-family-well-being-full-report3.pdf accessed November 27, 2025

Kaswan, M. J. (2022). Property, ownership and employee ownership: Employee control in ESOPs. *Journal of Participation and Employee Ownership*, *5*(1), 14–31. DOI: 10.1108/JPEO-11-2020-0028

Kegan, R., & Lahey, L. (2016a). *An everyone culture: Becoming a deliberately developmental organization.* Harvard Business Review Press.

Kegan, R., & Lahey, L. (2016b). An everyone culture: Becoming a deliberately developmental organization. *Stanford Social Innovation Review.* https://ssir.org/books/excerpts/entry/becoming_a_deliberately_developmental_organization#

Keller, D., & Singer, R. (2025). *The state of play for employee share ownership.* Harvard Business School Institute for Business in Global Society. https://www.hbs.edu/bigs/joseph-blasi-employee-ownership

Kelly, M. (2012). *Owning our future: The emerging ownership revolution.* Berrett Koehler.

Kelso, L., & Hetter Kelso, P. (1986). *Democracy and economic power: Extending the ESOP revolution through binary economics.* University Press of America.

Knowles, M. S., & Knowles, H. F. (1955). *How to develop better leaders.* Association Press.

Knowles, M. S., & Knowles, H. F. (1959) *Introduction to group dynamics.* Chicago: Association Press. Revised edition 1972 published by New York: Cambridge Books.

Kolb, D. A. (1984). *Experiential learning: Experience as the source of learning and development* (Vol. 1). Prentice-Hall.

Kurtulus, F. A., & Kruse, D. L. (2017). *How did employee ownership firms weather the last two recessions?: Employee ownership, employment stability, and firm survival in the United States: 1999-2011.* W.E. Upjohn Institute for Employment Research.

Menke., & Associates. (2011). *The origin and history of the ESOP and its future role as a business succession tool.* Menke. Retrieved December 3, 2025, from https://www.menke.com/esop-archives/the-origin-and-history-of-the-esop-and-its-future-role-as-a-business-succession-tool/

Mesirow, J. (2000). Learning to think like an adult: Core concepts of transformation theory. In Mezirow, J. (Eds.), *Learning as transformation: Critical perspectives on a theory in progress* (pp. 3–33). Jossey-Bass.

Mohrman, S. A., & Lawler, E. E.III. (2011). *Useful research: Advancing theory and practice.* Berrett-Koehler Publishers.

National Center for Employee Ownership. (2018), "Employee ownership and economic well- being," accessed November 11, 2025, https://www.ownershipeconomy.org

O'Boyle, E. H., Patel, P. C., & Gonzalez-Mulé, E. (2016). Employee ownership and firm performance: A meta-analysis. *Human Resource Management Journal, 26*(4), 425–448. DOI: 10.1111/1748-8583.12115

Oritsemolebi, A., Mayowa, A., & Munashe, N. M. (2025). The use of employee ownership structures as strategies for the resilience of smaller entities in the US. *International Journal of Science and Research Archive, 14*(01), 1002–1018. DOI: 10.30574/ijsra.2025.14.1.0039

Parsons, T. (1951). *The social system.* Free Press.

Parsons, T. (1967). *Sociological theory and modern society.* Free Press.

Paterson, T. A., & Welbourne, T. M. (2019). I am therefore I own: Implications of organization-based identity for employee stock ownership. *Human Resource Management, 59*(2), 1–9. DOI: 10.1002/hrm.21985

Project Equity. (n.d.). *Build a loyal and motivated workforce with employee ownership.* https://project-equity.org/building-loyal-motivated-workforce-guide/

Ravasi, D., Rindova, V., & Stiglianithe, I. (2019). Stuff of legend: History, memory, and the temporality of organizational identity construction. *Academy of Management Journal, 62*(5), 1523–1555. DOI: 10.5465/amj.2016.0505

Rosen, C., & Case, J. (2022). *Ownership: Reinventing companies, capitalism, and who owns what.* Berrett Koehler.

Rosen, C., Case, J., & Staubus, M. (2005). Every employee an owner. Really. *Harvard Business Review, 83*(6), 122–130. PMID: 15938443

Scharmer, C. O. (2018). *The essentials of theory U: Core Principles and Applications.* Berrett-Koehler Publishers.

Scharmer, C. O., & Kaufer, K. (2025). *Presencing: 7 practices for transforming self, society, and business.* Berrett-Koehler Publishers.

Scharmer, O. (2025) The Art of Social Innovation. https://aositoronto.weebly.com/theory-u.html accessed 03/24/25/

Scheese, R. (2021). *More than a company: Leading a values-based ecosystem.* Advantage.

Schein, E. H. (2004). *Organizational culture and leadership* (3rd ed.). Jossey-Bass.

Simon, C. (2025). *Rising birth rates no longer tied to economic prosperity.* Harvard Gazette. https://news.harvard.edu/gazette/story/2025/10/rising-birth-rates-no-longer-tied-to-economic-prosperity/

Stavros, J. M., Godwin, L. N., & Cooperrider, D. L. (2016). Appreciative inquiry: Organization development and the strengths revolution. In Rothwell, W. J., Stavros, J. M., & Sullivan, R. L. (Eds.), *Practicing organization development: Leading transformation and change* (4th ed., pp. 96–116). John Wiley and Sons., DOI: 10.1002/9781119176626.ch6

Storz, C., & Pascha, W. (2011). Japan's silver market: Creating a new industry under uncertainty. In C. Storz, M. Taube, & W. Pascha (Eds.), *Institutional Variety in East Asia* (pp. 222–267). Edward Elgar Publishing.

Stouten, J., Rousseau, D. M., & De Cremer, D. (2018). Successful organizational change: Integrating the management practice and scholarly literatures. *The Academy of Management Annals, 12*(2), 752–788. DOI: 10.5465/annals.2016.0095

Torbert, B. (2004). *Action inquiry: The secret of timely and transforming leadership.* Berrett-Koehler.

Weissbourd, J., Conway, M., & Klein, J. (2021). *Race and gender wealth equity and the role of employee share ownership.* https://www.aspeninstitute.org/wp-content/uploads/2023/05/Race-and-Gender-Wealth-Equity-and-the-Role-of-Employee-Share-Ownership.pdf accessed November 27, 2025

Wiklander, M. S. (2025). *Inner growth as a team sport: Unlocking capability to create impact and smarter organizations.* Icebug AB.

## ENDNOTES

1 To see information on Carris Reels: https://carris.com/

2 Japan is cited as the first major economy to face the challenge of an ageing population. The idea of an economy, being "silver," is said to have originated with Japan's successful market efforts addressing its ageing population, beginning in the 1960's when its birthrate dropped below replacement level as life expectancy increased. (Storz and Pascha, 2011)

3 An informative resource on Employee Ownership is The Employee Ownership Project: https://www.hbs.edu/bigs/about/research/the-ownership-project

4 For additional information on ESOPs, see the National Center for Employee Ownership https://www.nceo.org/what-isemployeex-ownership/esop-employee-stock-ownership-plan and The ESOP Association https://www.esopassociation.org.

5 In speaking about employee ownership and wages, William H. (Bill) Carris, owner at the time of the sale of Carris Reels would say, "There is no logical reason why an employee owned company would not pay what it can to its employees as it meets it responsibilities and obligations."

6 In the US, employee ownership is a bipartisan issue. See C, Caryl's recent article at https://www.hbs.edu/bigs/corey-rosen-employee-ownership.

7 See https://www.ncbi.nlm.nih.gov/books/NBK148831/

8 See https://www.who.int/news-room/fact-sheets/detail/ageing-and-health

9 See https://www.who.int/news-room/fact-sheets/detail/ageing-and-health

10 See more at: https://econofact.org/immigration-and-waning-us-labor-force-growth

11 See https://www.worldometers.info/demographics/us-demographics/#median-age

12 See more information at https://www.worldometers.info/demographics/canada-demographics/

13 For more information see: https://www.worldometers.info/demographics/mexico-demographics/

14 See more at https://www.globaldata.com/data-insights/macroeconomic/the-mean-age-in-united-states-of-america-138963/

15 For the full article, see https://theconversation.com/small-business-owners-are-getting-a-new-incentive-to-sell-to-their-employees-101515

16 For the Silver Economy, the potential for a change from these facts may not be fully understood. Russe Heimlich reported for Pew Research that as of January 1, 2011 and "every day for the next 19 years, 10,000 baby boomers will reach age 65." For the full report, see https://www.pewresearch.org/fact-tank/2010/12/29/baby-boomers-retire/ See also Jena McGregor's article on the silver tsunami at https://www.washingtonpost.com/business/2018/08/30/what-silver-tsunami-retiring-baby-boomer-business-owners-could-mean-their-workers/?utm_term=.a97fbc067e50

17 With an ageing US population, employee ownership has increasing interest as a succession plan for continuing a business and its legacy. See Oritsemolebi, Mayowa, & Munashe, 2025.

18 See more at NCEO: https://www.nceo.org/research/employee-ownership-by-the-numbers

19 William H. (Bill) Carris died on October 22, 2025 as this chapter was being written. See this article from the local newspaper https://www.rutlandherald.com/news/local/rutland-remembers-bill-carris/article_b0479c43-0f41-4875-9439-31bddaae0909.html

20 In the ten years prior to the transition to employee ownership and governance, in addition to the Harvard Executive Program, Bill Carris prepared for his leadership through participation in many educational activities with broad range learning implications. As he learned of elements that would be in play for the transition, he looked for ways to learn more. He read, He attended workshops,

He studied manufacturing, management, decision making, group dynamics, adult learning, social psychology, etc.

21 Email from Kathy Brythowski, October 29, 2025.

22 Flourishing workplaces where employee owners thrive can be viewed on the video "We the Owners." See the 2025 edition at https://smlr.rutgers.edu/we-the-owners. See CLEO https://cleo.rutgers.edu/ the Curriculum Library for Employee Ownership and for additional cases on employee owned workplaces.

22 ESOP is an IRC section 401(a) qualified defined contribution plan that is a stock bonus plan or a stock bonus/money purchase plan. An ESOP must be designed to invest primarily in qualifying employer securities as defined by IRC section 4975(e)(8) and must meet certain requirements of the code and regulations. The IRS and Department of Labor share jurisdiction over some ESOP features.

24 For additional information see Employee Ownership and Economic Well-Being: A Research Project of the National Center for Employee Ownership

25 August 28, 2025 https://www.nceo.org/employee-ownership-blog/new-data-on-employee-ownership-and-economic-well-being "The content of the survey covers nearly every aspect of the labor market experience of workers, including wages, income, wealth, and benefits. The panel nature of the surveys allows for following respondents over time; e.g., their wages, wealth, and jobs are followed as each respondent moves toward retirement age.".

26 When employees become the owners/shareholders, they change the dynamic and provide a form of democratic capitalism (Kelly, 2012; Ellerman, 1992) as well as increasing the size of the capital ownership pie, reducing income inequality, thus increasing financial stability in the middle class (Blasi, Freeman, Mackin & Kruse, 2010).

27 For a listing of key studies on employee ownership and performance see https://www.nceo.org/articles/studies-employee-ownership-corporate-performance.

28 William H. (Bill) Carris wrote similar thoughts in *The Long Term Plan,* he wrote for employees. He made a similar statement shared later in this chapter in the conversation with Don Curtis.

29 Employee wealth is mentioned eleven times in the *LTP.*

30 The Carris preference is that the elected ESOP Trustees be chosen among those paid at an hourly rate. Following examination of the US Department of Labor's fiduciary accountability requirement, Carris instituted a strong pro-

gram to educate internal ESOP Trustees and to involve the employee-owners on the CSC in the Trustee selection process. It did not want to hire external ESOP Trustees as many employee-owned companies do. As fiduciaries, ESOP Trustees are responsible for meeting the standards of the Employee Retirement Income Security Act (ERISA); to act in the interests of the plan participants; to oversee the annual company (stock) valuations and processing distributions.

31 August 29 and November 21, 2025 conversations with Alberto Aguilar, CEO Carris Reels. He was first hired to put in place a new division: Carris Plastics in Mexico for sales there. He was later promoted to Vice President and, in 2021, named CEO. He has been at Carris Reels over 25 years.

32 Carris' first sawyer `in 1951, was blind. His work area was designed for his safety. For its US Hispanic population, all materials are translated into Spanish as a matter of course.

33 See listing of Peter Drucker principles on a variety of topics at https://drucker.institute/principles/

34 Kathy Brytowski shared the information sheets on stock information, benefits, ages prior to conversations.

35 When employees take early retirement between 62 and 65, the company continues to pay its portion of health insurance.

36 Jason McKeighan has had a long relationship with Carris with varied work experience. April 9 and August 29 2025 conversations.

37 R&D is the abbreviation for Research and Development.

38 From a conversation with James Brooks, IT Director: April 3, 2025.

39 September 18, 2025—shared earlier in the chapter.

40 See https://innerdevelopmentgoals.org/

41 See https://www.nceo.org/articles/how-esop-distributions-work-for-esop-participants-rules-and-guidance. As an ESOP participant, you have the right to diversify part of your ESOP account balance once you have 10 years or more of participation in the plan (defined as the ESOP or a predecessor plan whose assets were transferred to the ESOP) and are 55 years or older. You can diversify up to 25% of the shares in your ESOP account at age 55 and each year thereafter and 50% at age 60. This is cumulative;

42 For a US firm, see Chroma Tech. It uses an alternative valuation model. It is not an ESOP. Founded in 1991, by a talented group of six people committed

to scientific innovation and community, it is now a global firm with ties to Germany, Japan and China. The company is a B-Corp, employee owned and governed. It uses a custom equity-sharing plan and the book valuation model. Chroma provides a unique and prominent example for employee ownership and governance in the U.S. See https://www.chroma.com/company and https://www.electrooptics.com/article/building-better-business-together-exploring-chroma-technologys-employee-owned-culture?utm_source=webpage&utm_medium=digital&utm_content=about-us

43 In the *Long Term Plan*, Bill Carris explained the ESOP Trust's "Repurchase Liability: The requirement to purchase employees' stock when they leave the company creates what is called a repurchase liability for Carris. "The size of our repurchase liability will be determined by a number of factors, including: our annual contribution to paying off the ESOP loan, the change in value of a share of stock, the vesting schedule of the stock, the age of the employees, the turnover rate of employees, the diversification option of employees, and method of benefit distribution" (1994, p.28).

44 A primary difference between an S and C corporation is that the S corporation is a tax designation that a corporation or LLC can elect by filing Form 553: Election by a Small Business Corporation with the IRS. It's a popular tax election because it has tax-saving potential for both corporations and LLCs. See more information at https://tax.thomsonreuters.com/blog/s-corp-vs-c-corp-vs-llc-whats-the-difference-and-which-one-is-better-for-your-business/

# Chapter 7
# Digital Adoption and E-Commerce in the Silver Economy:
## A Strategic Framework for Market Entry and Growth

**Suvidhi Jain**
https://orcid.org/0009-0003-1614-5239
*Symbiosis International University, India*

**Vikas Garg**
https://orcid.org/0000-0002-1421-5980
*Symbiosis Institute of Business Management, Symbiosis International University, Pune, India*

## ABSTRACT

*The chapter explores the growing significance of the silver economy, the economic ecosystem surrounding aging populations, and its intersection with digital adoption and e-commerce. As global demographics shift toward older age groups, this segment represents an untapped market with increasing purchasing power. It proposes a multidisciplinary strategic framework integrating management, economics, and behavioural science to help businesses and policymakers engage older adults effectively. It identifies key drivers and barriers of digital adoption among seniors, emphasizing that adoption is shaped less by technology itself and more by behavioural, psychological, and social factors. Issues like age-based stereotypes, discriminatory marketing, and a lack of digital literacy hinder engagement. Conversely, social support networks and trust-building through user-friendly interfaces can foster inclusion.*

DOI: 10.4018/979-8-3373-6117-8.ch007

## INTRODUCTION

The global demographic shift to an aging population is a significant, though often unrecognized, economic change. In the past, the world's aging demographic was a perceived threat, especially a fiscal and social burden. We believe it is now a better understood as the future stimulus for a new economic sector, the digital silver economy. The digital silver economy leverages the digital economy, particularly e-commerce, to reach an emerging consumer segment of older adults, which is robust and growing. This paper presents an integrated, multidisciplinary framework utilizing management theory, behavioural economics, and public policy to propose a pathway for firms to recognize, enter, and successfully grow their businesses in the aging segment of the digital silver economy.

### The Global Demographic Shift and Its Economic Ramifications

For the first time in human history, the world is observing a rapid aging of its population; this is especially pronounced in advanced economies in North America, Western Europe, and Japan. The demographic transition, characterized by a long-term transition from high levels of fertility and mortality to low levels of both, is an essential driver of change across modern economies. The conversations surrounding this shift have been focused on the risks of economic instability for many years. Policymakers are now faced with a compounding set of complex challenges: a declining working-age population, an increase in healthcare costs, and pension plans that are, to be honest, underfunded. In economically advanced countries, where the aging population continues to grow, there is increasing dependence on a smaller group of working-age people to support the social safety net. This pattern is most evident in societies where older adults rely on fixed retirement income streams and contribute less to public tax revenue generating "concern" about the sustainability of socio-economic systems over the longer term.

This model misses a vast economic opportunity of that population. The supply side of the economy may have fewer workers, but the demand side is changing, in part, because of a new and economically strong consumer base. Older adults tend to have an extraordinary amount of a nation's wealth and often purchase goods and services based on different demand drivers, such as healthcare and home services. For example, in the United States, consumers born between 1946 and 1964 (a.k.a., the Baby Boomers) represent more than half of the total wealth in the United States, which is estimated at $83.3 trillion, representing only one-fifth of the total population. Estimates suggest that just the Baby Boomer generation represents approximately $1 million in average wealth per person. Moreover, the purchasing power of this group is emphasized as the fastest growing group (65+) of online buyers and the group with half of the disposable income (70% total) in the U.S. The goal of this approach should not be about working to relieve the weight of the aging population, but rather to understand how to actively engage the economic expense of a successful aging process, fitting into the continued booming economy.

The principal argument presented here is that businesses and governments should reconsider their perspective on labour supply. Rather than viewing it as a challenge, they ought to recognize it as an opportunity to stimulate consumer demand, thereby enhancing economic value and growth potential.

## A Strategic Imperative: Beyond Market Opportunity to Social Inclusion

The significance of the silver economy extends far beyond simple financial gain; it has become a crucial macroeconomic and social imperative. Empirical research demonstrates a clear correlation between an aging labour force and national economic health. For instance, based on figures from the International Monetary Fund (IMF), further growth in human capital for seniors, particularly through healthy aging, will sustain around 0.4 percentage points contribution to global GDP growth between 2025 and 2050. Conversely, not extending the utilization of the potential of an aging workforce may risk higher inflation.

For example, studies from a U.S. city found that each percentage point increase in the share of retirees raised the local inflation rate by an average of approximately 0.2 percentage points due to fewer workers producing the goods and services the total population demanded.

This emphasizes that engaging older adults in the digital ecosystem is about creating a market segment and a national macroeconomic and policy solution to the underlying systemic challenging economic issues of thoughtful, systemic heterodox economics and demographics.

A digital silver economy can drive consumption, innovation, and stabilize the economy by mitigating a shrinking workforce's drag. This reframes digital inclusion as a critical macroeconomic aspect, essential for economic stability and social equity. (Abubakar et al., 2023)

*Table 1. The Global Silver Economy: Market Size and Macroeconomic Impact*

| Metric | Details and Forecasts | Strategic Relevance | |
|---|---|---|---|
| Market Size & Growth | - Valued at USD 1.6 Trillion in 2023 | - Projected to reach USD 2.9 Trillion by 2031<br>- Compound Annual Growth Rate (CAGR) of 8.10% | Confirms the immense scale and rapid expansion of the market, necessitating a dedicated business strategy. |
| Purchasing Power | - Global spending power was forecast to reach $12 trillion in 2020 | - People over 50 in France hold almost half of the country's purchasing power | Highlights the financial capacity of this demographic, making them a high-value consumer segment. |
| Macroeconomic Correlation | - An aging workforce and a decline in productive capacity contribute to higher inflation | - Each percentage point increase in the share of retirees adds 0.2 percentage points to local inflation | Demonstrates that engaging this market is a critical lever for economic stability and a strategic move to address systemic headwinds. |

Source: Raksha Sharma (2025)

## The Scope of the Digital Silver Economy: Untapped Opportunities

The “silver economy” includes all economic activities catering to older adults' needs and desires. The digital silver economy is more narrowly focused on the overlap between older adults, digital technology, and e-commerce. There is a large and mostly untapped market in digital spaces, as many older adults remain either not engaged or under-engaged in a digital capacity. In some advanced economies, this presents a significant, relatively untapped market. For example, 93% of adults aged 30-49 years in the US used the internet, while only 73% of older adults aged over 65 years reported the same. Indicators show many older adults have yet to engage in the digital ecosystem, thus providing the opportunity for market engagement in a vast market. In 2024, the global silver economy market was estimated at approximately $2.75 trillion and is expected to grow to over $5.45 trillion by 2033, with a compound annual growth rate (CAGR) of 7.89%, between 2025 and 2033.

## A Multidisciplinary Approach: Merging Management, Economics, and Behavioural Science

To provide an overall framework, the report takes an interdisciplinary analytical approach. The report draws on three critical perspectives. From a management perspective, the report reviews models for strategic business models, the value creation process, and how firms create a sustainable competitive advantage.

From an economic perspective, it reviews market opportunities, the purchasing power of older adults, and the crucial importance of public policy as a lever for market development.

It looks at the psychological and social factors that may drive, inhibit, or interfere with technology adoption from the perspective of behavioural science. It involves consumer behaviour, cognitive bias, and social stereotypes. These perspectives are critical for understanding the complexities of this market and developing a holistic approach.

## THE AGE-BASED DIGITAL DIVIDE: A DETAILED ANALYSIS

### Digital Adoption Rates: A Comparative Study of Advanced and Emerging Economies

The digital divide is not a single, uniform challenge; the fundamental nature and severity of the challenges vary greatly between advanced and emerging economies. In advanced economies, there is data to suggest that the digital divide is a persistent, decreasing challenge. A recent 2024 survey by the Pew Research Center identified that approximately 90% of adults aged 65 years and older are online, versus 98% for the 50-64 age group. This would suggest that a considerable percentage of older adults remain, while that gap is decreasing, but still on the other side of the gap. In these economies, the challenge is not often the basic technology infrastructure, but is one of digital literacy, confidence, and increasing access to technology that meets older adults' needs. The pandemic for COVID-19, in particular, accelerated this transition as older adults became more comfortable using technology in the use of services (beyond extreme measures, but still substantial) and connecting with others socially. A 2020, 2024 poll of older adults reported that 36% of older adults aged 65 said COVID-19 changed their technology usage significantly. (Yuan et al., 2025)

Emerging economies experience a much more acute digital divide than exists in the context of base challenges related to access, affordability, and the technology infrastructure. For example, according to a 2023 Statista study, only 36% of adults aged 40 and older in India reported internet usage, compared to 73% of younger adults under 40.

While the number of internet users in India is growing, with a forecast to exceed 900 million by 2025, the digital divide persists, especially regarding gender and geography. A HelpAge India report 2024 revealed that 59% of participants surveyed had no access to a digital device, and only one in five felt comfortable using a digital device, which was also more common among white-collar work participants. A significant gender gap was identified, as 48% of older men who were interviewed utilized the internet somehow, compared to 33% of older women. Additionally, there were urban and rural divides. While India's overall increase in internet penetration is higher in rural settings than in urban settings, as rural populations use 488 million internet users compared to 397 million in urban settings, nearly 60% of the rural population has not used the internet and has therefore not benefited from this digital access. A 2023 ASER report on the gender and literacy gap in rural India also found this: 14-18-year-old males were twice as likely to own a smartphone (43.7%) as similarly aged females (19.8%). Thus, when considering a business model that has adapted to work in a historically digital setting, this business model would not function in a complicated market that is still navigating systemic challenges.

A corporation operating within a developed economy can consider providing solutions for design barriers and psychological barriers. In contrast, a firm in an emergent economy would first solve issues relating to access and affordability before engaging in higher-level engagement. The following chart illustrates the difference in digital engagement across these divergent environments (Sharma & Sheth, 2023).

*Table 2. Digital Engagement and E-commerce Participation by Age and Region*

| Metric | Advanced Economies (e.g., U.S. / EU) | Emerging Economies (e.g., India) | Source |
|---|---|---|---|
| Internet Usage | U.S. (65+): 90% online<br>EU-27 (65-74): 77% of internet users buy online | India (40+): 36% of adults use the internet | Pew Research Center |
| Smartphone Ownership | U.S. (65+): 91% own a smartphone | Rural India (14-18): Males are twice as likely to own a smartphone as females | AARP, ASER |
| E-commerce Participation | EU-27 (65-74): 53% of internet users purchase online | India: 312.5 million e-commerce consumers in 2022, expected to grow to 400 million by 2027 | Statista |
| Primary Challenge | Psychological, behavioural, and design-related barriers | Foundational access, infrastructure, and affordability | Research Material |

Source: Digital 2024: India — DataReportal

## The Behavioural and Psychological Dimensions of Technology Adoption

Success in digital adoption in older adults relies on a deep understanding of human behaviour and psychology. Some may mistakenly think the lack of engagement emerges from a fixed cognitive or sensory deficit; however, Behavioural Design Theory offers a more nuanced perspective, suggesting engagement with smart devices comes from an interactive relationship between motivational, ability-based, and environmental factors.

Central to the digital divide of seniors is a significant psychological barrier, namely, technology anxiety or technophobia. A state of technology anxiety is not a fixed personality trait, and thus can be manipulated by corrective intervention and the support of others. Evidence reveals that older adults who lack self-efficacy in technology engagement and/or view aging as a time of loss or feel social pressure to engage with technology are more likely to experience technology anxiety.

Negative and age-bias marketing and design exposures have potentially compounded the issue, reinforcing negative stereotypes and creating significant marketing obstacles. This historical context of negativity has contributed to a profound distrust among older consumers. Concerns over data privacy, personal data misuse, and online fraud are substantial constraints to adoption. A meta-analysis of 11 studies on technology anxiety in older adults, for example, highlights technology anxiety as a multidimensional negative influence that increases cognitive load and decreases use of digital health technologies. Socioeconomic factors such as low income, low digital literacy, and lack of family support increased technology anxiety; this suggests that hesitancy towards technology by older adults might best be understood as a rational reaction to perceived risk in the technology rather than simply 'Luddism'. (Dwivedi et al., 2022)

The effective participation of older adults in the broader digital world is fundamentally a social process. Social support networks, especially family members, friends, or groups in communities, are integral to supporting older adults to develop the competence to learn the skills to use digital products and, as a consequence, facilitate another level of experience and confidence to engage in the digital aspect of e-commerce successfully (Alam et al., 2022).

Research indicates that digital engagement is highly context contingent; social influence contributes to the older adult's technology use. For example, "intergenerational digital support" from younger family members is a salient factor in educating older adults about and furthering their use of technology and devices. When individuals receive support in navigating digital devices, technical challenges are mitigated, and a noticeable alleviation of anxiety associated with learning unfamiliar technologies. This sense of reassurance is significant in adoption. Additionally, research reveals that participation and engagement with social media platforms generate feelings of social connection, reduce perceived isolation, and encourage increased community participation among older adults. The result of these social connections appears to create a reinforcing cycle in which positive experiences with the technology encourage its continued and expanded use.

Motivation is a primary issue for older adults who are adopting technology. Although older adults can use technology, most will adopt it based on a certain goal-based motive, such as maintaining their health and social connectedness. For example, a study conducted in China observed that older adults with diminished health status were more likely to adopt smart device applications in light of specific health-related activities to organize and facilitate their health-related activities. When technology provides identifiable support for monitoring one's health or staying connected, the technology is more likely to be adopted. In this way, the use of technology should be understood in response to a real need, rather than as a generic or habitual form of behaviour (Li et al., 2023).

Usability refers to the physical usability and cognitive usability of the digital device. The design of technologies to be used must meet the physiological changes of aging, including reductions in motor skills and vision. This means the interface should be simplified, the font size should be greater, and features to allow for voice control should be included. The Technology Acceptance Model (TAM) argues that perceived ease of use and usefulness are essential in initiating adoption compared to non-adoption, especially considering cognitive and physical challenges may lower perceived ease of use and usefulness for older adults. Additionally, supporting the decision to adopt and the decision not to adopt is a Senior Technology Acceptance Model (STAM), which adds three stages to the process: objectifying(intent to use), incorporating (explore), and accepting (assimilate or reject).

To gain a better understanding of and to predict the adoption of technologies by older adults, researchers and practitioners routinely use models of behavioural economics. The Technology Acceptance Model (TAM), which is the foundational model, discusses how an individual's intention to adopt a new technology is determined by perceived usefulness (PU) and perceived ease of use (PEOU).

A meta-analysis of both TAM (Technology Acceptance Model) and the subsequent Unified Technology Acceptance and Use Theory (UTAUT) demonstrated that perceived usefulness (PU), perceived ease of use (PEOU), and social influence are all associated with older adults' intention to use new technology.

The key aspect of these models is that PU is consistently the most potent predictor of technology adoption (mainly if it addresses a critical need, such as health management and social connection). Studies found that the relationship between PU, PEOU, and social influence is moderated by geographical region and technology type. The notion that a “one-size-fits-all” approach is sufficient is fundamentally flawed. Human contexts and individual circumstances are inherently diverse, which necessitates solutions tailored to specific use cases. Rather than viewing this as a static, age-old problem, reframing it as an issue of human-centered design is more productive. Even so, the organizations that will be most successful in meeting this important market need will be those that can effectively manage the psychological complexities of trust, while still keeping their solutions simple.

Interestingly, evidence suggests that the number of children in the household reduces device engagement among younger adults living at home with their older relatives. This may indicate that the presence of family members to help with digital tasks generates lower stimulus to adopt technologies independently.

These observations illustrate the critical role of supporting social networks and interactions when adopting technology. A supportive network (family, friends, peers, etc.) can significantly impact someone's willingness or ability to act on new technologies digitally.

*Table 3. Behavioural and Psychological Factors Influencing Digital Adoption Among Older Adults*

| Barrier or Factor | Root Causes | Mitigation Strategies |
|---|---|---|
| **Technology Anxiety** | - Perceived lack of technical and cognitive resources<br>- Fear of making mistakes or damaging devices | - Pressure from social norms to engage with ICT<br>- Design for cognitive ease and simplicity<br>- Offer personalized training programs and mentorship<br>- Provide immediate, reassuring feedback in the UI |
| **Social and Age-Based Bias** | - Exposure to negative, age-biased marketing and design | - Negative self-stereotypes of aging-related loss<br>- Involve older users in participatory design and co-creation<br>- Challenge stereotypes by portraying older adults as active and capable consumers |
| **Trust Deficit** | - Concerns over data privacy and security vulnerabilities | - Lack of confidence in digital transactions<br>- Display prominent security badges and clear privacy policies<br>- Leverage social influence and endorsements from trusted networks<br>- Offer clear, multiple payment options with straightforward instructions |
| **Lack of Social Support** | - Isolation and limited access to family, friends, and community groups for help | - Design platforms with built-in social features to encourage connection<br>- Partner with community groups and non-profits for hands-on support |

## The Pervasiveness of Digital Ageism and Social Stereotypes

One crucial but often overlooked barrier to leapfrogging to digital is systemic ageism. Digital ageism constitutes making judgments about someone based on the belief that they cannot use digital technology. Digital ageism stems from the stereotype that younger people are "digital natives" and older people are incapable of being competent technology users. This goes beyond a simple observation on society's attitudes. The bias has been automated and reinforced through already biased datasets, deliberately flawed ontology designs for usability, and an a priori standard not modified for age in the technology itself. Another phenomenon of ageism that is not referenced here but speaks further to the extent to which Artificial Intelligence, designed by and for the designers of the algorithms, directly ignores older adults' interests and needs, even when older adults are the participants of the discussions about Artificial Intelligence.

The repercussions of this bias are multiplex. For example, older employees or even people suitably qualified may experience bias against them, with denials for promotions or training based on the bias that older adults do not do well in a technology-based workplace.

More alarmingly, it led to older adults becoming disenfranchised and excluded from services still considered critical and available only online, such as banking, ticketing, and government services. This lack of access further reinforces the stereotype of ageism that older adults are "frail, helpless". Consequently, self-ageism emerges, leading to a sense of being isolated, disempowered, or intimidated, further withdrawing or avoiding technology, thus withdrawing from the online world (Toni et al., 2025).

A strategic change is needed to respond to this issue. The priority should shift away from responsive strategies, such as digital literacy training, to thinking ahead about technology design and the processes involved in designing it. Participatory design is an essential response to this consideration, which recommends that older adults be involved in all decision-making about technology from the start. This changes the approach from designing for older adults to designing with older adults, putting older adults' needs and experiences at the centre of the design.

## E-COMMERCE INNOVATION AND VALUE CREATION FOR OLDER ADULTS

### Differentiating Value Proposition: Trust and Simplicity as Bedrock Of Value Proposition

In the digital silver economy sector, a value proposition which succeeds will come from much more than pricing. A winning value proposition is an intentional combination of trust, safety, and simplicity that tries to circumvent the mental roadblocks to adoption and usage. Older adults are prudent consumers who want options that allow them to do things better while minimizing risk and complexity. Ultimately, the winning value propositions provide a good customer journey that is effortless and embraces cognitive ease–meaning the mental effort of the customer has been minimized versus an experience where they have endured unnecessary obstacles leading to frustration.

This entails communicating simply, directly, and transparently the benefits of products and services while avoiding technical jargon or unclear communication (Damiyana et al., 2024).

## The Consumer Profile of the Silver Shopper: Habits and Motivations

Older adults constitute an essential and increasingly technology-friendly consumer segment that e-commerce companies cannot disregard. A recent study conducted by Google illustrated that roughly 86% of older adults who engage online will spend at least six hours online each day and own an average of five electronic devices. This data demonstrates that older adults continue to be unfairly stereotyped as being tech-phobic.The studies showed that older adults who are users of online platforms typically participate in the same activities as other generations. As a reminder, the order of their frequency of usage was; communication (91%), finance (87%), and health and wellness (73%).

The online shopping behaviour is one of caution and deliberate thought. Older adults are likely to research and price-check items before purchasing. Older adults are influenced by their social circles and reading items about items they wish to purchase. While older adults may prefer to shop in-store for non-essential items, they are open to purchasing other items online for convenience. They buy items for convenience based on need, wants based on functionality (usefulness), and value assessment for that product or service. Unlike younger generations, who communicate to share their identity through their purchase activity, older adults seem content with who they are. In contrast, older adults may have disparate levels of comfort compared to others in their own category.

This shows that the task is not a matter of convincing them to transact on the web, but developing a value proposition distinct to their needs for security, convenience, and trust.

## Designing for Inclusion: The Imperative of Usability, Accessibility, and Security

A central principle in a successful digital strategy for older consumers is a "sovereign interface." A sovereign interface is one that is intuitive and operationally simple enough to induce a sense of satisfaction and independence in the user. With older adults, sovereign interface involves designing a platform that eliminates cognitive load, or mental effort needed to sort information or complete tasks, as a critical threshold. Older adults, in general, probably incur additional cognitive load or manage cognitive load differently than younger cohorts, and finding ways to lessen cognitive load is paramount. For instance, previous studies shows older adults, on average, perform 40% slower for web tasks, and abandon more difficult tasks during work, highlighting the need for simple design.

A successful e-commerce platform for older adults is also grounded in usability, accessibility, and security. Usability is an especially critical component, which requires a platform due to its characteristics of cleanliness without clutter and simplicity in navigation (Kovalchuk et al., 2024).

Certain features should always be included to minimize cognitive load and prevent user frustration, including breadcrumb navigation, large buttons to click, and a simple checkout process with clear indicators of progress through the checkout. A simple checkout process with minimal form fields, as well as guest checkout, is critical.

Accessibility is equally essential. In particular, attention to age-related vision impairment should be addressed through larger font sizes, high contrast color schemes, and text-to-speech options. Design for motor challenges should not be overlooked either, which means avoiding rollover items and buttons that are large and touchable on mobile and tablet devices. While many of these features are considered basic best practices for web design, the significance is greater for the older population. One of the grocery delivery services, Instacart, is often cited as a solid example of accessible design because it uses pictures of products to make the virtual shopping experience intuitive by replicating the horizontal shelf structure of a grocery store.

Seniors are more concerned about online security issues than Millennials, even as online engagement increases. Online services should do what they can to foster trust, which may be accomplished through simply making security badges easily visible, having SSL certification, and, where possible, having complete transparency around privacy policies. Social proof and/or trust seals, including highlighted customer reviews and testimonials, can be powerful ways of projecting confidence if companies offer several payment options, which should aid in convenience and flexibility, mainly when they include the option of a traditional cash-on-delivery payment method. By utilizing these design principles, a company can change a user's emotional relationship with technology from that of anxiety to empowerment; this can occur when an online service is presented with an interface that not only relates function but is also empathetic and reassuring—trying to actively combat the negative stigma and frustrations that many older adults have experienced with technology (Sharma & Sheth, 2023).

*Table 4. E-commerce UX and Value Creation Principles for the Digital Silver Economy*

| Design Principle | Psychological Effect on Older Adults | Old Approach (to be avoided) | New Approach (to be adopted) |
|---|---|---|---|
| Cognitive Load Reduction | Reduces mental effort, increases confidence, and minimizes frustration. | Cluttered screens with too much information; complex user flows with unnecessary steps | Clean layouts, linear information flow; clear and simple language; use of default settings and auto-fill |
| Enhanced Readability | Accommodates age-related vision decline; reduces physical and mental strain; improves comprehension. | Small, low-contrast text; over-reliance on icons without labels | Larger fonts (min. 16pt); high-contrast color schemes (min. 7:1); labeled icons; text-to-speech functionality |
| Emotional Reassurance | Reduces anxiety; builds trust; encourages exploration; prevents abandonment. | Lack of feedback for actions; no confirmation messages for critical steps; fast-paced animations | Immediate visual and auditory feedback; clear confirmation messages and "undo" options; slow, deliberate animations |
| Simplified Navigation | It prevents feeling lost or overwhelmed and makes the user's journey logical and predictable. | Hidden or "hamburger" menus; nested sub-menus | Prominent drop-down menus with clear categories; visible navigational breadcrumbs; obvious "back" and "home" buttons |

Source: Dyachenko Anastasia (2025)

## Strategic Market Segmentation: Moving Beyond "One-Size-Fits-All"

Practical strategies for engaging the silver economy will require moving from basic age-based marketing to a more comprehensive approach. By characterizing older adults as merely an age-based market, we risk imposing a homogenized version of these consumers. Businesses should consider a behavioural segmentation approach to older adults, including how they define their own age and identity in lifestyle and behaviour.

For example, while studying Baby Boomers, we discovered that they are a consumer segment that, on average, prioritizes health and wellbeing, and they place value on experiences, especially travel experiences. Baby Boomers also seem to be phygital consumers, meaning that they look up products and services online, but would prefer to make their final purchase decision in a physical location. Therefore, the need for applied approaches that blend online and offline touch points is clear to develop an all-encompassing experience that respects consumer choice (Chauhan & Jaiswal, 2022).

## The Power of Social Support Networks in Digital Integration

Furthermore, it is essential to understand that individuals will become digitally literate and aware of technology's use, uptake, and significance, not in a vacuum. Technology uptake occurs in the context of an individual's social support environment. One social support category that consumer researchers and service designers may want to consider is generational support from family members. Family support, particularly from younger family members, tends to support older adults to learn and using new home technology. This has implications for product design, especially in creating a product that may engage caregivers or family members.

In addition, peer learning and being part of online communities offer an individual a sense of belonging and purpose, directly enhancing learning in a social context. For example, to be part of a program where older adults are brought together in a safe and supportive environment to learn digital skills has turned out to be very successful.

More specifically, the Internet-based activity (IBAs) study showed that older adults' social well-being stemmed from the idea that they would have support from others, and are happier to engage in a technology when another person is with them doing social things.

This is an opportunity for businesses to develop or collaborate with communities for peer-to-peer support. The data shows that older adults who are more socially engaged are also more stimulated to engage with digital instruments. There is evidence to suggest ways to work with these individuals to embrace another layer of adoption when concerned with digital inclusion initiatives, that being connected was an essential factor not only related to individual capacity but also engaged social networks to encourage support for adoption. (Ahmed & Garg, 2021).

# MARKETABLE STRATEGIES AND CASE STUDIES

## The Business of Well-being: Innovations in Healthcare and Wellness

The most prominent digital silver economy market entries have targeted high-value sectors aligning with older adults' essential health and wellness needs. This is because older adults are concerned about their mental and physical health and are most likely to pay for products that improve health and/or well-being, including health insurance, medications prescribed by their doctor, the category of nutrition and health, and beauty products.

## Case Study: Prescription Delivery Apps

Prescription delivery apps are increasing in popularity with a strong value proposition based on ease and safety for the user. PillPack, an Amazon company, and Alto Pharmacy are examples of how prescription delivery apps ease the burden of mobility and help manage multiple prescriptions, which can be burdensome for many older adults. For instance, PillPack dispenses various medications based on time and dose, relieving confusing and complex medication management, providing user safety, and the caregiver's peace of mind. Elements of service that foster trust and loyalty include automatic refills, same-day delivery, and communication with a pharmacist.

Evaluating consumer response to the leading prescription home delivery service providers, while PillPack was determined to be the overall best experience, CVS Simple Dose was identified as best for ease of access, presumably because of the availability of in-person support, a type of service not currently offered by other online pharmacies, and something older adults seeking support would find meaningful (Tarver; 2020). These services remove the physical and emotional labour for consumers to manage their health, a form of value-generating innovation.

Of the advantages offered by both PillPack and CVS SimpleDose, it is Alto Pharmacy that brings even more conveniences to the table, including order tracking, delivery when consumers want it, and most importantly, access to expert support any time of the day or night for any questions they may have when it's convenient for them. CVS SimpleDose is unique in that it provides an added lateral value proposition of relying on its stature as a pharmacy; allowing it to provide an opportunity for consumers to go to a pharmacy and receive in person customer care (versus pill pack's exclusive digital services), which itself may be an essential component of facilitating more older adult trust in services, especially older adults who may value human interaction as part of the medication process. It is an example of how e-commerce will provide critical services to older adults and recreational forms of social interaction, to assist with and even improve their lives.

## At Home Physical Activity Platforms Case Study

Home physical activity platforms have gained momentum and popularity, particularly with the effects of the COVID pandemic, increased interest, and opportunities for physical activity in the home environment. The global home fitness equipment market was valued at about $8.87 billion with an estimated compound annual growth rate (CAGR) of about 8.2% to reach $18.03 billion by 2033. North

America represents the largest home fitness equipment market share at 37.19% in 2024 (Lashitew, 2023).

Within this market, we can observe an interesting business model that works well for SilverSneakers. They does not use a direct to consumer (DTC) consumer subscription model, instead it uses a B2B2C (business to business to consumer) model. SilverSneakers is a fitness program offered to some of the largest Medicare insurance members in the US, free or at reduced cost to the member.

This is an exemplary case of a market entry strategy. By collaborating with Medicare providers, it is leveraging an existing trusted relationship and the inherent uncertainty of an institution. The application establishes trust among older adults and their Medicare health insurance plan, as they move from the Medicare program to the "gym."

The application is very cognizant of the user experience with dropdown low-impact classes such as Chair Yoga and Walk Strong, which inherently work for very diverse online and in-person abilities. SilverSneakers thinks about older adults' needs and wants for safely exercising with people and classes that focus on engagement in physical health, but also provide a community and connection to address social isolation.

Other applications like FitOn may have a similarly diverse workouts (vs classes). Still, those aren't necessarily engaging the audience regarding wanting them, and instead explicitly target their physical health needs, which speaks to the demand in the market for this population when it comes to engaging content.

These platforms work well because they align with an essential value of older adults: staying healthy and vibrant.

*Table 5: Key Value Propositions of Leading Silver Economy Platforms*

| Platform | Business Model | Key Value Proposition | Features |
|---|---|---|---|
| **PillPack** | DTC (Direct-to-Consumer) | Convenience, Simplicity, Medication Adherence | Free delivery, automatic refills, medications sorted by dosage and time |
| **Alto Pharmacy** | DTC (Direct-to-Consumer) | Convenience, Expert Support | Scheduled delivery, 24/7 support, expert pharmacist chat |
| **SilverSneakers** | B2B2C (Business-to-Business-to-Consumer) | Health, Trust, Community, Affordability | Free for eligible Medicare plan members, large network of gyms, online classes, community events |
| **FitOn** | Freemium (DTC) | Variety, Accessibility, Community | Unlimited free workouts, guided courses for chronic conditions, social features |

## Financial Technology (FinTech) Innovations for Seniors

Traditionally, the FinTech sector has been focused on younger, technology-native consumers, but that is rapidly shifting as companies recognize the significant financial power of the older generation. Baby Boomers hold an estimated $80 trillion in wealth, and the market for products and services designed specifically for older adults is enormous. Despite that wealth, this generation remains underrepresented in FinTech - only 24% of older adults actively use mobile banking apps, while 61% own a smartphone. (Gao et al., 2023).

Financial technology (FinTech) companies are increasingly creating products to meet older adults' needs and concerns regarding financial security and fraud prevention. Many older adults are unwilling to engage with digital banking and investment platforms primarily because of concerns about security and trust in the economic relationship, as face-to-face interactions have traditionally been done. So, effective FinTech solutions for older adults tend to focus on building trust, transparency, and ease of use. (Narayan & Narayan, 2022).

- Estate Planning and Wealth Management: The estate planning and organizing essential documents (wills, power of attorney, etc.) has become easier, cheaper, and less painful. Utilize services like Cake, which offers an easy-to-use online estate planning and document organizing platform.
- Fraud Protection and Bill Payment: True Link provides a prepaid debit card, as well as an online service which features real-time transaction alerts, fraud protection (Scamwatch), and the ability to add family member(s) to receive alerts. These services can assist users with sustaining independent living and offer peace of mind. SilverBills has a concierge bill-management service where an account manager tracks finances and pays bills for the user. Transferring responsibility to an account manager relieves the user of late fees and confusion with different payment portals and methods. These services benefit older adults with physical and/or cognitive difficulties in managing their finances.
- Simplified Financial Management: Other apps like PocketGuard link users' financial information and clearly summarize their spending. The app also helps identify opportunities to reduce monthly bills. Addressing the thrifty mindset of many Baby Boomers, the app allows users to assess whether they are getting the "right deal" on products and services, an essential element of decision-making for many individuals.

Success in this industry is predicated on providing multi-channel support, such as telephone, email, and face-to-face options, to accommodate older adults' desire for human interaction and help develop the trust necessary for negotiating the digital gap (George & Thomas, 2021).

## Technology and Travel: Enabling a New Era of Exploration

Older adults, especially retirees, typically have more discretionary time and the ability to pursue new hobbies and travel. As such, technology has become an increasingly valuable and essential resource that enables older adults to prepare, book, and travel much more easily and confidently.

The travel experiences of older adults are often not dissimilar to those of younger generations. 87% use hotel websites, 75% use an airline site, and 73% use mega-site booking when accessing travel information during planning. Travel technology is responding to their specific concerns regarding planning and mobility:

- AI-Driven Planning Tools: Artificial Intelligence is emerging as a powerful planning tool that can recommend destinations, create personalized trip itineraries, and compare costs or find deals. Research revealed that although 8 in 10 seniors were at least aware that AI was being used in travel, only one-third of respondents said they had used and wanted AI to personalize their trips. Trust is a significant barrier to use, with only 36% of older adults trusting AI to give them the most current, accurate information. However, many older adults have been using AI without knowing it in built-in services. For example, technology like Google's Gemini and Microsoft's Copilot.
- Navigation and Health Tech: Navigation apps, such as Google Maps, will continue to be an indispensable tool while planning travel and providing navigation while away from home. Health tech is also playing a massive role in making travel more accessible. Devices like the Apple Watch Series 9 and Samsung Galaxy Watch 6 have health technology that can monitor heart rhythms and detect falls, providing travel security for travelers and family. New technologies like PulseRide, a robotic wheelchair system, can streamline mobility even more.
- Community Development Platforms: The European Commission has recently supported and funded projects like ESCAPE that have tried to develop and market travel exchanges for elderly seniors in European countries. These projects aim to build upon existing tourism infrastructure to support older travelers better so they can appreciate the social aspects of travel, visiting cultural heritage sites.

Travel and technology intersecting in the silver economy offer a strong business opportunity to provide services that consider elders' unique health and mobility needs and allow seniors to strategize leisure experiences and seek convenience and new experiences.

## A COMPARATIVE POLICY AND BUSINESS ANALYSIS: THE EU AND INDIA

An effective business strategy requires continuous adaptation to local market conditions and policy environments. A comparison of EU and Indian approaches exemplifies this idea.

### The European Approach: Rights, Principles, and Digital Literacy

EU policy is based on the first principles of human rights and inclusion.

The European Declaration on Digital Rights and Principles, adopted in December 2022, is meant to guide policymakers, businesses, and other stakeholders in developing and deploying new technologies. The three main aims of the declaration are to put people at the heart of the digital transformation agenda and show how technology can help and benefit all EU citizens. Although the declaration is not legally binding, it informs EU digital law and policy and directs member states to respond to digital challenges. An OECD report published in 2024 projected that, due to inaction, only 60% of the adult population in the EU will even have at least basic digital skills by 2030, dramatically under the target of 80% (Rahayu et al., 2023).

A rights-based approach creates a regulatory atmosphere that would encourage companies to implement age-friendly design principles and ethical practices. One example is the European Accessibility Act (EAA) adopted in 2019, shaping common accessibility standards within the EU and the German Accessibility Strengthening Act (BFSG) to enact its provisions on 28 June 2025, mandating businesses to ensure that their digital presence—websites, apps, e-commerce, etc.—is accessible for all people, regardless of physical, sensory or cognitive ability. Companies face being sued and damaging their reputations for failing to ensure digital accessibility. This legislation will resonate with older adults, requiring such characteristics as font size and contrast adjustments, as well as alternative audio to visual content (Thangavel & Chandra, 2024).

Policy can also support direct intervention to remedy the digital divide through initiatives that provide digital vouchers to those unable to afford a device and in programs promoted by the Council of Europe to enhance digital literacy among seniors. Initiatives such as Mobile Money and MILEAGE (Media and Information Literacy and Digital Competences Enhancement for Active Aging) are two of several

European Union-based programs designed to increase digital skills and lessen fear of new technologies among older adults in ways that are fun and promote "learning by doing".

A community-based initiative in Latin America, AMID (Adultos Mayores a la Inclusión Digital), effectively provides technology training through its own methodology, and makes available various socialization and recreational opportunities for older adults in Peru, allowing them to gain confidence in their digital self-sufficiency and counter the high-risk factor of isolation. In Singapore, the government's community-based program, Seniors Go Digital, provides subsidized smartphones and mobile data plans for seniors and free, in-person training in digital skills at hundreds of community centers and roving counters island-wide (Badran et al., 2025).

## The Indian Model: Foundational Infrastructure and Affordability

### The Role of Public-Private Partnerships in Scaling Digital Inclusion

In emerging economy settings worldwide, the government's role is not to regulate but to be the key market enabler and investor in infrastructure. The private sector is rarely motivated to create costly networks in rural or remote areas with sparse population densities and low short-term profit potential.

Government investment mitigates the risk of private investors by investing in and building foundational Digital Public Infrastructure (DPI) such as BharatNet. After substantial coverage has been established in remote areas, the private sector can start to innovate, thinking of inclusive, profitable service delivery. It transforms market failure in rural infrastructure development into a market opportunity. In this ecosystem of government and private-sector innovative ways to solve problems, non-governmental organizations (NGOs) are also critical participants (Goyal & Arora, 2021).

Organizations such as HelpAge India have started and are working on delivering on-site workshops and digital literacy sessions to the community. Staff and youth volunteers work directly with older adults to move through practical how-to training on mobile phones, for convenience with everyday tasks such as utility bill payment and cab ordering. These capacity-building ventures promote the importance of digital technology for everyday functioning while providing competence and confidence in support of older adults staying autonomous and independent (Singh, A; 2025).

The situation in emerging markets, such as India, involves an essential challenge, more than a rights-based issue. The Digital India project is the flagship program of the Indian government, designed to launch the nation into a digitally empowered society through access to high-speed broadband utility and digital literacy for all citizens. Among the initiatives for the Digital India program are broadband highways, expanding mobile connectivity, a digital identity, and public access to the internet. These initiatives show how a strategy focusing on infrastructure will be key to accelerating the digital divide, especially in rural areas (Jain & Kumar, 2020).

The business model of Jio provides a textbook example of how a corporation can function as both a business partner and supporter of this national ambition. Rather than merely competing with existing telecom providers, Jio created a new market by commencing its growth trajectory with a freemium model that allowed for massive onboarding of early-stage data and calls, while accumulating millions of users and changing consumption behaviour dramatically. After Jio was launched, its business model was based on investment and infrastructure, including the most up-to-date available product, 4 G technology, for reliable and affordable internet access at the national level.

By being offered under refundable deposit contracts, the JioPhone put mobile internet in reach of the very bottom of the socio-economic ladder, including even the lowest income earners, such as daily wage workers, who could not afford the entry-level price that would allow them to use a smartphone.

## Case Study on JioMart Ecosystem as a Low-Literacy Market Model

JioMart in India serves an excellent case study of a scalable business model to remove the digital barrier for customers with low insight and digital literacy. At the centre of the JioMart e-commerce case in India is the "phygital" (physical + digital) model, which does not eliminate the importance of the brick-and-mortar, but embraces and integrates with brick-and-mortar stores. JioMart plugged into the already existing network of retail that exists in India and is worth over a trillion dollars in retail; created over many decades, established as part of the Indian culture and community, with existing personal relationships and trust with the retailers, which included the traditional kirana (small local store) shops (Jha & Agarwal, 2023).

JioMart has identified three strategic levers for low-literacy adoption:

- **WhatsApp Commerce**: JioMart's most significant development in its push to low-literacy shoppers is end-to-end shopping within WhatsApp, a place that shoppers in India are already comfortable with. This removes the giant hurdle of needing to learn a new mobile application or navigate a complicated website, because the consumer is already in the point of sale application.
- **Ecosystem Integration**: The Jio business model provides a data-rich example of bundling different services to drive increased consumption of services. The MyJio app is a single platform to access services like JioPay, JioMart, and JioCinema, even when they require transactions to navigate through separate apps. Such characteristics help bond consumers to the services and de-

velop a single digital identity that allows for hyper-personalization, lowering customer acquisition costs for new customers and existing services.

- **Building on Local Relational Trust:** JioMart leveraged local kirana (grocery) stores to build on the background and relationship that consumers had with their local shopkeeper – a trusted relationship. This model again enables a more rapid hyperlocal delivery experience from a trusted source, while simultaneously modernizing local retail ecosystems with the power and sophistication of digital tools and inventory management systems.

This strategic approach addresses the digital literacy gap through assisted selling in a more than 100,000 retail partner stores network. This model combines the confidence of a trusted local retailer with the online ease of product discovery, presenting the lowest entry barriers to consumers with limited digital skills. This illustrates how a private sector-led business can produce profit and support a government's nation-building agenda by tackling those initial gaps in access and infrastructure. (Kapuria, 2021)

Public-private partnerships (PPPs) will be fundamental in bridging digital exclusion, as they require the public sector to provide universal connectivity, which it does not have the resources to address. In contrast, the private sector lacks the incentive to invest in areas with financial sustainability concerns. As policymakers consider these issues, they must a) promote transparency; b) encourage engagement with local communities; and c) provide 'positive discrimination' to demand-side beneficiaries.

## THE STRATEGIC FRAMEWORK FOR MARKET ENTRY AND SUSTAINABLE GROWTH

### A Holistic Model: Reconciling Management, Behaviour, and Public Policy

The examination outlined in this report leads to an inclusive framework for digitally engaging with the silver economy. This framework comprises three interconnected components, which involve, beyond a technological aspect, a human dimension, a social dimension, and an economic dimension, all having critical relationships. (Rana, N. P; 2020)

#### Behavioural and Human-Centered Design

This pillar acknowledges that the challenge of adopting the digital is, in essence, a human issue and therefore can't be resolved with technological solutions. The bedrock of participatory design, namely, including older adults in designing technologies meaningful and understood by the older adult community, such that trust is established and maintained, might require an alternate salutogenic approach to how technology is designed and developed. This means, among other things, that trust-creating and effective security mechanisms that lessen cognitive load would be the starting point.

### Strategic Business Models

This pillar promotes an innovative business model not confined to the traditional direct-to-consumer (DTC) strategy. In practice, to attract older adults, the company may devote its product offering to health, home, and groceries, as these are the three areas they are most attached to, and will explore other measures to leverage trust and reach. As a member of B2B2C, for example, SilverSneakers is entering this space with existing institutional trust and partnerships, resulting in a negligible cost for building the brand and time to market it relative to its entirely new premise. This is essentially a competitive advantage to seize on while in this situation.

### Specific Policy Engagement

This pillar explains policy as another key factor driving market opportunity, especially in emerging economies. Enterprises wishing to succeed must be compatible with national frameworks emphasizing infrastructure and affordability. In contrast, enterprises in developed markets can thrive in a more restrictive policy environment that encourages inclusive design and consumer protections and rights, such as the EU Declaration on Digital Rights. As a result, sound business strategies, in this instance, require a solid understanding of the local policy environment and the willingness to go the extra mile to partner with public sector objectives. (Singh & Hess, 2022).

## Recommendations for Businesses: Building a Competitive Advantage

With these principles in mind, we propose the following actions for companies that are interested in strengthening their presence in the digital silver economy while enhancing their competitive advantage:

## Make Trust and Security a Priority:

Be sure that each step you take is to ease the fears of older adults, such as ensuring safe payments, badges of trust, and simple privacy policies. Visibility of social proof, like customer reviews and testimonials, is critical to longevity.

## Make the User Journey Simple:

Design user-friendly interfaces that reduce the cognitive load and make checkout of the shopping experience as short as possible. Use large font/high contrast colors and progress indicators to instill users' trust in the transaction. It's important to note that older adults tend to be slow computer users and do not want their interaction to feel like a burden.

## Establish A Value-Focused Targeted Marketing Strategy:

Directly create and market products for the spaces where older adults are most willing to purchase online, namely health, home, and food. In particular, think through digital service ideas for older adult consumers that promote health, while making their lives easier, such as home-delivered medications or fitness programs delivered in their home. (Udayana et al., 2024).

## Engage With Social and Community-Based Models:

Build in features that make it easy for family or caregiver support, as intergenerational support was identified as a reason for adoption. Leverage business-to-business-to-consumer (B2B2C) opportunities to leverage the supportive institutions of your partners and community members. Utilize peer-learning techniques to promote the development of a trusting community of users.

## Be Active Against Digital Ageism:

Building product and marketing strategies, taking an active stance against ageist stereotypes, and using the most appropriate, truthful imagery depicting older adults in their lives. Also, remember to facilitate the engagement of older adults in the development process, as this will support the claim that the products are genuinely inclusive (Dwivedi et al., 2023).

## Recommendations for Governments: Fostering an Inclusive Digital Future

Governments play an essential role in creating a more market-friendly landscape that will be good for the economy in a broader sense, and for developing greater social inclusion:

### Investment in foundational infrastructure:

In an emerging economy, high-speed internet must be considered one of the most essential foundational utilities that will also aid in closing the foundational digital divide by providing universal digital literacy. This will help provide the basis for new business models and the facilitation of growth.

### Create a rights-based framework:

In developed economies, follow the EU's approach of a human-centered digital transformation that protects citizens¡ rights, clarifying expectations for business with regards to inclusive design, and data privacy, with laws such as the BFSG, which was passed in Germany, and makes accessibility mandatory, and gives everyone a voice, offering them an option, in a digital environment wherein exclusion is never an option.

### Encourage Digital Literacy Initiatives:

Offer support and partnership possibilities to non-tech-related organizations that support peer-learning and inter-generational training, focusing on behavioural barriers to accessing technology, such as technophobia or low confidence. For example, in India, this would involve funding projects focused on digital literacy and safety with rural and elderly women to bridge the ongoing issue of the gender gap. (Venkatesh et al., 2023).

### Encourage Public-Private Partnerships:

Pursue and foster partnerships with private sector companies that have a mission aligned with national digital inclusion goals. By combining the public sector's convening power and the private sector's entrepreneurship, governments can enable a pace of digital transformation while ensuring that those who are not financially viable, whether people or places, are not left behind. (Kapoor et al., 2021).

## CONCLUSION

The Digital Silver Economy represents a new, groundbreaking paradigm for an ageing world. The global shift in demographics should not be viewed as a burden to be carried, but instead as an opportunity to be seized for economic and social benefit. The report makes it clear that winning in this market won't come from hoping to fight against the so-called weaknesses of the elder generation but rather from discovering their tremendous value and building a system that will support the unique needs of the elder generation, as well as their activities and social systems. Overall, this has a value and a role that is not only an organisational success but also delivers considerable social good by optimising a kinder, more inclusive, and ultimately prosperous and dignified digital future for all in an ageing society.

A primary need academically is a transition from qualitative analysis to quantitative measure. Furthermore studies should identify and use neuroeconomic methods such as eye-tracking or cognitive load measurement to rigorously quantify sovereign frameworks performance in comparison to standard e-commerce designs. The empirical testing would provide objective physiological evidence that core design principles of simplified navigation, high contrast layouts and other recommendations significantly reduce cognitive friction, directly supporting the recommendation that technology designs will improved task completion rates and generally decrease technology anxiety for older users. In addition, as human technology interaction changes, studies should also consider how new ubiquitous interface paradigms, such as voice activated commerce and AI driven conversational platforms, impact senior adoption. Importantly, specifically test the hypothesis that voice activated commerce will effectively bypass traditional literacy and manual dexterity barriers to use for the senior user diminishing technology anxiety as a universal access point for the silver economy.

In the case of policymakers, future studies should explore comparative effectiveness trials using intervention models that may differ by studying a region receiving digital vouchers versus a region receiving the equivalent funding earmarked entirely for community-based, peer-to-peer training. The essential unit of analysis must be actual participation in e-commerce and related economic impacts, rather than simply measuring basic internet use. Likewise, firms can operationalize the framework immediately by running A/B tests to compare a control group (a standard interface) against an experimental group using principles of the sovereign interface (larger font size, fewer steps, redo/undo prominently offered). In deciding which metrics to compare, key indicators will include conversion, time to purchase (total time spent completing a transaction), and call center volume related to technical problems (easy, medium, and hard), and you will be able to straightforwardly calculate the ROI of design elegance and/or simplicity.

Ultimately, companies need to assess the financial impact of their high-trust acquisition strategies. This will require tracking the customer acquisition cost (CAC) and customer lifetime value (CLV) for both types of segments recruited by human-centered high trust channels (local partners, 24/7 personalized support, etc.) versus coded purely digital channels. Assuming CLV and associated high loyalty is produced and driven by high-trust human engagement, the CLV built over time will exceed the cost of initial acquisition. For emerging markets, companies should also view that access gap as a strategic investment by partnering with local providers to track the adoption curve within rural/senior segments. The goal should be an increase in regional internet usage by way of making educational and other forms of access adopt, closing the gap and before launching high engagement digital services. This all requires a combination with specific types of customer segmentation and rigor of behavioural drivers such as Perceived Usefulness or Social Influence to candidly and effectively develop, deploy and measure the efficacy of marketing campaigns in reality and to dynamically optimize -both demographic and behavioural segments while matching resources to realistic psychological and infrastructural realities.

## CONFLICT OF INTEREST STATEMENT

The authors declare that they have no conflicts of interest regarding the publication of this chapter.

## REFERENCES


Abubakar, A. M., Bala, K., & Shneikat, B. H. T. (2023). Impact of social commerce adoption on SME performance: Evidence from emerging markets. *Journal of Retailing and Consumer Services*, *70*, 103107. DOI: 10.1016/j.jretconser.2022.103107

Agarwal, S., & Narain, R. (2020). Digital payment adoption in India: The role of trust and technology readiness. *International Journal of Bank Marketing*, *38*(7), 1585–1607. DOI: 10.1108/IJBM-12-2019-0498

Ahmed, A., & Garg, V. (2021). E-commerce logistics and digital transformation: Challenges for Indian SMEs. *International Journal of Physical Distribution & Logistics Management*, *51*(7), 655–673. DOI: 10.1108/IJPDLM-08-2020-0294

Alam, S. S., Ali, M. Y., & Jani, M. F. M. (2022). An empirical study of factors affecting electronic commerce adoption among SMEs in Malaysia. *Journal of Business Economics and Management*, *23*(2), 240–258. DOI: 10.3846/jbem.2022.16010

Badran, M., López, R., Valarezo, A., & Pérez-Amaral, T. (2025). E-commerce in Spain: Trends, growth, and market dynamics (2018–2021). *Telecommunications Policy*, *49*(7). Advance online publication. DOI: 10.1016/j.telpol.2025.103003

Chauhan, S., & Jaiswal, M. P. (2022). Determinants of small business adoption of digital payment services in India: A SEM–ANN approach. *Journal of Enterprise Information Management*, *35*(6), 1660–1680. DOI: 10.1108/JEIM-08-2021-0338

Damiyana, D., Maulina, E., Muftiadi, A., Auliana, L., & Kurniadi, K. (2024). The influence of innovation, knowledge management, and e-commerce adoption on MSME performance, and its impact on MSMEs' sustainability. Journal of Infrastructure. *Policy and Development*, *8*(11). Advance online publication. DOI: 10.24294/jipd.v8i11.7994

Dwivedi, Y. K., Hughes, L., Coombs, C., Constantiou, I., Duan, Y., Edwards, J. S., Gupta, B., Lal, B., Misra, S., Prashant, P., Raman, R., Rana, N. P., Sharma, S. K., & Upadhyay, N. (2023). Digital and social media marketing: Implications for marketing strategies. *International Journal of Information Management*, *68*, 102518. DOI: 10.1016/j.ijinfomgt.2022.102518

Dwivedi, Y. K., Ismagilova, E., Hughes, L., Carlson, J., Filieri, R., Jacobson, J., Jain, V., Karjaluoto, H., Kefi, H., Krishen, A. S., Kumar, V., Rahman, M. M., Raman, R., Rauschnabel, P. A., Rowley, J., Salo, J., Tran, G. A., & Wang, Y. (2022). Setting the future of digital and social media marketing research: Perspectives and research propositions. *International Journal of Information Management*, *59*, 102168. DOI: 10.1016/j.ijinfomgt.2020.102168

Gao, J., Siddik, A., Abbas, S., Hamayun, M., Masukujjaman, M., & Alam, S. (2023). Impact of E-Commerce and Digital Marketing Adoption on MSMEs' Financial and Sustainability Performance during the COVID-19 Pandemic: An Empirical Study. *Sustainability (Switzerland)*, *15*(2). Advance online publication. DOI: 10.3390/su15021594

George, G., & Thomas, S. (2021). Sustainable business models for digital platforms: Lessons from India. *Strategic Entrepreneurship Journal*, *15*(4), 561–580. DOI: 10.1002/sej.1407

Goyal, N., & Arora, S. (2021). Impact of government policies on SME e-commerce adoption: A longitudinal analysis. *Government Information Quarterly*, *38*(3), 101594. DOI: 10.1016/j.giq.2021.101594

Jain, P., & Kumar, R. (2020). Digital ecosystems and SME performance in India: The moderating role of government support. *Journal of Small Business Management*, *58*(5), 923–945. DOI: 10.1080/00472778.2019.1709382

Jha, A. K., & Agarwal, S. (2023). E-commerce adoption among Indian SMEs: An innovation diffusion perspective. *Journal of Business Research*, *157*, 113484. DOI: 10.1016/j.jbusres.2022.113484

Kapoor, K., Dwivedi, Y. K., Piercy, N. F., & Lal, B. (2021). Digital transformation in emerging markets: Enablers and challenges for SMEs. *Business Horizons*, *64*(5), 599–611. DOI: 10.1016/j.bushor.2021.04.002

Kapuria, P. (2021). Digitising Indian Retail: Analysing Challenges and Exploring Growth Models. Observer Research Foundation. Retrieved from https://www.orfonline.org/research/digitising-indian-retail-analysing-challenges-and-exploring-growth-models

Kovalchuk, O., Ruslan, S., & Banakh, S. (2024). Cryptocurrency Crime Risks Modeling: Environment, E-Commerce, and Cybersecurity Issues. *IEEE Access : Practical Innovations, Open Solutions*, *12*, 50673–50688. DOI: 10.1109/ACCESS.2024.3386428

Lashitew, A. (2023). When businesses go digital: The role of CEO attributes in technology adoption and utilization during the COVID-19 pandemic. *Technological Forecasting and Social Change*, *189*. Advance online publication. DOI: 10.1016/j.techfore.2023.122324 PMID: 36718420

Li, F., Su, X., & Hu, Y. (2023). Digital transformation and organizational resilience: Evidence from Chinese manufacturing firms. *Technovation*, *124*, 102711. DOI: 10.1016/j.technovation.2023.102711

Narayan, B., & Narayan, P. (2022). FinTech adoption by Indian MSMEs: Drivers and barriers. *International Journal of Bank Marketing*, *40*(4), 783–802. DOI: 10.1108/IJBM-07-2021-0301

Rahayu, R., Dayani, F., & Wibowo, A. (2023). Determinants of digital payment adoption in MSMEs in Indonesia: The role of financial literacy and technology acceptance. *Journal of Entrepreneurship in Emerging Economies*, *15*(4), 1230–1250. DOI: 10.1108/JEEE-02-2022-0090

Rana, N. P., Luthra, S., Mangla, S. K., Islam, R., Roderick, S., & Dwivedi, Y. K. (2020). Barriers to adopting e-commerce in Indian SMEs: A combined DEMATEL and AHP approach. *Technological Forecasting and Social Change*, *152*, 119908. DOI: 10.1016/j.techfore.2019.119908

Sharma, R., & Sheth, J. (2023). Resurgence of e-commerce in post-pandemic India: A consumer behavior perspective. *Journal of Retailing and Consumer Services*, *70*, 103113. DOI: 10.1016/j.jretconser.2022.103113

Singh, A., Bothra, V., Sen, A., & Chakraborty, D. (2025). Navigating the Digital Marketplace: Understanding the E-Commerce Adoption Journey of Emergent Users in India. *Proceedings of the ACM on Human-Computer Interaction*, *9*(5). Advance online publication. DOI: 10.1145/3743728

Singh, S., & Hess, T. (2022). Digital transformation strategies of Indian SMEs: A resource-based view. *Information & Management*, *59*(8), 103675. DOI: 10.1016/j.im.2022.103675

Thangavel, P., & Chandra, B. (2024). Digital Immigrants Versus Digital Natives: Decoding Their E-commerce Adoption Behavior. *SAGE Open*, *14*(4). Advance online publication. DOI: 10.1177/21582440241282437

Toni, N., Goh, T., Edward, Y., & Calen. (2025). Supply Chain Sustainability And Financial Performance: The Role Of E-Commerce, Digital Banking, And Digital Marketing Of Smes. Economics - Innovative and Economics Research Journal, 13(1), 487–507. https://doi.org/DOI: 10.2478/eoik-2025-0027

Udayana, A., Fatmawaty, A., Makbul, Y., Priowirjanto, E., Ani, N., Siswanto, E., Susanti, W., & Andriani, S. (2024). Investigating the role of e-commerce application and digital marketing implementation on the financial and sustainability performance: An empirical study on Indonesian SMEs. *International Journal of Data and Network Science*, *8*(1), 167–178. DOI: 10.5267/j.ijdns.2023.10.007

Venkatesh, V., Thong, J. Y. L., & Xu, X. (2023). Unified Theory of Acceptance and Use of Technology: A decade of research. *Management Information Systems Quarterly*, *47*(2), 425–478. DOI: 10.25300/MISQ/2023/15210

Yuan, Z., Wang, Y., Sun, T., & Xu, H. (2025). Democratizing Data Analytics Products to Drive SME Growth: A Natural Experiment. *Manufacturing & Service Operations Management*, *27*(4), 1053–1067. DOI: 10.1287/msom.2024.1138

# Chapter 8
# Retail Grocery and the Silver Economy:
## Rethinking Strategies and the Retailing Mix for an Inclusive Shopping Experience

**Francesca Negri**
https://orcid.org/0000-0001-9929-2848
*Catholic University of the Sacred Hearth, Italy*

## ABSTRACT

*Italy, one of the world's oldest countries, offers a preview of how population ageing will reshape Grocery Retail. For over-65s, grocery shopping is both a functional activity and a social ritual that supports autonomy and well-being. Yet retailers still overlook this segment or rely on outdated stereotypes, despite its size and growth. Grocery stores must serve multiple generations simultaneously, making inclusion a strategic priority. Drawing on 1,005 survey responses collected in 2025 by REM Lab, this chapter analyses how older shoppers behave, what they value, and where gaps emerge across pricing, assortment, services, private labels and communication. The goal is to highlight opportunities for more inclusive, evidence-based strategies that enhance the shopping experience for all ages.*

## INTRODUCTION

Italy stands at the forefront of the demographic transition that is reshaping consumer markets worldwide (EU, 2025). With one of the highest proportions of people aged 65 and over in the world, the Country offers both a compelling case study and

DOI: 10.4018/979-8-3373-6117-8.ch008

a predictive lens for understanding the future of Retail Grocery in ageing societies. For this segment, grocery shopping holds a dual significance. Functionally, it is an essential, recurrent activity that ensures access to food, household essentials, and health-related products. From a values-based perspective, it is also a meaningful social and personal ritual - one that helps older consumers remain active, engaged, and connected to their communities. The act of grocery shopping can serve as a routine anchor, reinforcing independence and social interaction, and thus contributing to overall well-being.

For retailers, the over-65 segment represents a substantial and growing market opportunity, amplified by the demographic curve's trajectory: the Italian demographic structure is characterised by an inverted population pyramid, reflecting one of the highest proportions of older adults in the world (Istat, 2025). Yet, preliminary data suggest that this potential is far from fully realised. Too often, older consumers are either overlooked or addressed through outdated stereotypes - remnants of past segmentation practices that fail to capture the diversity, agency, and evolving lifestyles of today's older shoppers. In the Grocery sector, this oversight is particularly striking because stores frequently host multiple generations at the same time, creating a uniquely complex environment. Unlike service contexts such as cafés or hotels, where generational overlap is often more limited, Grocery Retail must simultaneously satisfy the needs, preferences, and expectations of diverse age cohorts sharing the same physical and digital spaces.

This reality poses a strategic and operational challenge: to design and implement solutions that can deliver a pleasant, safe, and satisfying shopping experience for every generation. Addressing this challenge requires rethinking segmentation and targeting approaches, as well as innovating across the retailing mix - assortment, pricing, store formats, services, and communication - both online and offline. It also calls for an evolution in the representation of older adults in marketing communications, moving beyond tokenistic imagery towards authentic and inclusive narratives.

The Chapter will examine both the strategic and operational dimensions of inclusion within the grocery sector, framing the discussion within broader Diversity, Equity, and Inclusion (DEI) agendas. Strategically, the analysis will draw on available corporate reporting to assess how inclusivity is embedded in organisational priorities, both in terms of the shopper experience and workforce composition. Operationally, the study will evaluate retailing mix variables and communication practices, informed by panel data collected through 1,005 surveys conducted in early 2025 by REM Lab, our research Centre. These data will shed light on the sentiment of over-65 consumers and their concerns for the future; the strategies they adopt to mitigate reduced purchasing power caused by inflation; their loyalty levels and assessments of reward programme effectiveness; preferred store formats; the role of online channels and information sources; assortment preferences; price and promotion sensitivity; perceptions of store staff; and the relevance of private label (MDD) products. For each of these variables, the Chapter will compare the responses of over-65 shoppers with those of other generational cohorts, allowing for a nuanced intergenerational analysis.

By examining the interplay between demand and supply, the study will identify both critical gaps and promising practices in terms of effectiveness and inclusivity. In the domain of private label development, for instance, findings reveal a market opportunity for protein-enriched product lines targeted at older consumers. While the food industry currently tends to position protein and high-protein products towards younger demographics, the prevalence of age-related issues such as sarcopenia and the market size of the over-65 segment would fully justify a strategic repositioning of these products as part of an inclusive offering.

The overarching aim is to gain a deep understanding of both the functional and values-based aspects of the over-65 grocery shopper, moving beyond stereotypes and discriminatory mechanisms to foster genuinely age-inclusive organisational strategies.

By aligning strategic priorities with operational execution, retailers can capture the economic potential of this segment while contributing to a more equitable and inclusive shopping environment for all generations.

## Literature Review and Conceptual Framework

Academic scholarship on retail marketing, consumer behaviour, and ageing provides a robust foundation for analysing the inclusion of older consumers and workers within contemporary retail systems. Classic retail marketing literature conceptualises retailing as the coordinated management of the marketing mix, store environment, and service encounter to create value for heterogeneous consumer segments (Berman et al., 2021; Levy et al., 2022). Within this tradition, the shopping experience is co-created through both physical and social dimensions of the store, including layout, signage, service design, and frontline employees, making workforce composition and competencies a central lever of retail strategy. As demographic ageing reshapes both labour markets and consumption patterns, the integration of elderly people into retail workforces and shopping environments becomes not merely a social concern but a strategic imperative. Consumer gerontology has extensively documented how ageing affects cognitive, emotional, and motivational processes relevant to consumption. Moschis (1994; 2012; 2007; 2012; 2019) frames ageing as a multidimensional life-course process influencing needs, preferences, and marketplace behaviours, challenging simplistic chronological age classifications. Empirical research on cognitive ageing demonstrates that changes in information processing speed, memory, and decision strategies affect how older consumers evaluate assortments, promotions, and service interactions (Yoon et al., 2009; Cole et al., 2008). These insights are particularly relevant for retail contexts, where decision-making often occurs under time pressure and sensory overload. Consequently, retail environments that rely heavily on complexity, rapid choice, or technology-mediated interactions risk systematically disadvantaging older consumers if age-inclusive principles are not embedded in design and service delivery.

*Drivers of main grocery store choice.* Literature has observed that ageing involves social, biological and psychological changes with the elderly people cohort, having different necessities and wants when shopping compared to younger cohorts (Park and Farr 2007; Wilson et al., 2004). For example, elderly people experience a decline in appetite, food consumption and dietary tolerability (Hughes et al 2004). Moreover, their ability to see, hear, move, learn, remember, taste, smell, chew and handle products decreases (Popper and Kroll, 2003). With reference to the overall shopping experience, Meneely *et al.* (2009) focus their research on product access, price and customer service as crucial areas among Senior shoppers. Yin et al. (2013) pointed out that layout, lighting, product information, shopping facilities, accessibility, location, temperature, service, smell and atmosphere (Hare et al. 1999; Leighton and Seaman 1997) directly impact the shopping experience for older consumers. The "age-related supermarket design" could reflect six different categories: trolleys and baskets, store layout and aisles, shelves and freezers, product-related issues, customer service and checkout (Yin et al. 2013). In addition to these physical design elements, older consumers traditionally rely on small local retail stores for their grocery needs and as a means of socialising (Yin et al 2013).

*Generational Cohort Theory (GCT).* While the increased average age of shoppers and consumers seems widely recognized, scholars largely ignore the societal change, and also that service provision, customer experience and research need to address this structural change. Marketing research explores the behavioral differences between "old" and "young" consumers. Conventionally, this branch of research posits a normative, chronological age-related decline in extrinsic and intrinsic motivation and individuals' behavior (Homburg and Giering 2001; Kohijoki 2011; Kohijoki and Marjanen 2013; Lambert-Pandraud et al 2005). Chronological age has been found to explain several possible changes that occur in people's psychological, social, and societal functioning during their life cycle. Indeed, the general process of ageing consists of many dimensions of which chronological ageing is only one (Cleveland and Shore, 1992).

Literature has pointed out (Parment 2013) that generational cohorts are characterized by different needs, perceptions, expectations, and shopping/ consumption behaviors. In the words of Parment (2013) "While birth age has been a useful way to create groups, it describes segments but does not help to understand segment motivations". This could be marketing myopia in the light of ageing society. At this point, marketing scholars use the Generational Cohort Theory (GCT) to investigate the descriptive surface in order to understand behaviors and motivations associated with age in more depth (Lancaster and Stillman 2002; Parment 2013). The idea that people differ in the amount and type of effort they put into shopping experience is not new in the field of marketing (Katona 1958; Slama and Tashcian, 1985): moreover, many studies indicate that customers' spending patterns differ over the course of their life cycle (Bleichrodt and Quiggin, 2000).

*Retail and DEI policies.* At the macro level, the silver economy literature - particularly within European policy discourse - positions population ageing as a driver of economic innovation rather than a constraint. European Commission reports emphasise the growing purchasing power of consumers aged 65 and over and the need for age-friendly retail spaces, services, and employment practices that support active ageing (European Commission, 2018, 2020). Complementing this perspective, management scholarship on the silver market highlights the strategic potential of products, services, and retail formats tailored to later life stages, while warning against deficit-based representations of ageing (Kohlbacher & Herstatt, 2008). However, critical contributions argue that traditional age-based segmentation risks reinforcing stereotypes and obscuring intra-cohort diversity, calling for more nuanced, needs-based and context-sensitive approaches (Sudbury-Riley, 2009). This critique aligns with emerging work at the intersection of DEI and marketing, which frames inclusion as both an ethical obligation and a source of competitive advantage. DEI scholarship in service and retail contexts underscores how inclusive practices influence employee wellbeing, service quality, and customer trust. From this perspective, age inclusion extends beyond communication or product adaptation to encompass workforce policies, training, and intergenerational service encounters. Age-inclusive design research further reinforces this view, demonstrating how universal and inclusive design principles can enhance usability and dignity for older consumers while improving experiences for all shoppers (Coughlin, 2017; Coleman et al., 2008).

The present Chapter applies Generational Cohort Theory (GCT) as a framework to examine the over-65 in-store shopping experience. The idea of "cohort" assumes that people are influenced by events occurring during their coming-of-age years; many previous studies have proven this phenomenon (Parment 2013; Lemon and Verhoef 2016). Taken together, these streams suggest a conceptual framework in which DEI functions as an enabling governance lens that aligns retail marketing mix decisions, workforce strategies, and consumer behaviour insights. By integrating consumer gerontology with retail strategy and DEI, this Chapter positions age inclusion not as a niche response to demographic change but as a structural component of contemporary retail value creation.

To the best of our knowledge, the retail literature still lacks a contribution that systematically integrates a cohort-based perspective on ageing with a comprehensive analysis of inclusivity in retail, encompassing both internal dimensions (i.e., older employees and age-diverse workforces) and external dimensions (i.e., older shoppers and the shopping experience). Existing studies are xisting contributions are scarce and insufficiently recent, and tend to address these themes in isolation: research on ageing consumers predominantly focuses on behavioural, cognitive, or experiential aspects of later-life consumption, while contributions on diversity, equity, and inclusion in retail largely concentrate on gender, ethnicity, or disability, with age remaining a comparatively underexplored dimension. Similarly, workforce-related studies often examine ageing employees from a human resources or labour economics perspective, without explicitly linking internal age inclusion to customer-facing outcomes and retail marketing strategy. This fragmentation results in a significant theoretical gap, as retail is inherently a socio-technical system in which employees, shoppers, and organisational practices interact in the co-creation of value. Addressing this gap is particularly relevant for the research agenda, as it opens the possibility of moving beyond traditional cohort-based segmentation, which has been widely criticised for its rigidity and risk of stereotyping, toward more distinctive, needs-based, and context-sensitive approaches to understanding ageing in retail environments. At the same time, the absence of an integrated framework has important managerial implications. Retail managers are increasingly confronted with ageing workforces and ageing customer bases simultaneously, yet they lack conceptual tools to align DEI policies, retail marketing mix decisions, and service design choices in a coherent way. A more holistic perspective on age inclusivity could therefore support managers in designing retail environments, service encounters, and organisational practices that are not only more equitable, but also more resilient and competitive in ageing societies.

## Objective and Contribution

The main objective of this chapter is to analyse the evolving role of over-65 consumers in the Italian grocery retail sector, identifying both the functional and symbolic value that grocery shopping holds for this segment and exploring how retailers are (not) adapting their strategies to meet these needs inclusively. The research aims to:

1. Evaluate the extent to which DEI principles are embedded in grocery retail strategies and operations, with a focus on age inclusivity.
2. Suggest innovative segmentation and targeting approaches that avoid stereotyping and address the heterogeneity of older shoppers, allowing for a deeper under-

standing of key life events, which are far more relevant than chronological age in defining an individual. These milestones form the basis for subsequent operational decisions, starting with the development of communication campaigns.

3. Map the behavioural patterns, preferences, and expectations of over-65 grocery shoppers, comparing them with those of younger cohorts.
4. Identify gaps between the supply-side offer and the demand-side expectations of older consumers.

The Chapter contributes to four main streams of literature and discussions:

- **Retail Marketing**: by providing granular, age-segmented insights into grocery shopping habits, preferences, and expectations.
- **Age-Inclusive Marketing and DEI**: by integrating the concept of age diversity into both strategic and operational retail planning, addressing a gap in current DEI discourse that often overlooks age as a key dimension.
- **Research Agenda**: drawing on the analysis of existing literature alongside primary and secondary data discussion, the Chapter concludes by outlining a Research Agenda intended to foster an increasingly nuanced and realistic understanding of this target group.
- **Managerial Implications**: the Chapter offers an evidence-based framework for designing retail strategies that can simultaneously serve multiple generations in shared spaces, increasing both customer satisfaction and store performance.

Findings from this study have direct implications for grocery retailers seeking to future-proof their strategies in ageing markets:

- **Leverage DEI as a Strategic Asset:** embed age inclusivity into DEI programmes for both customers and staff, ensuring that older employees are seen as valuable contributors to the shopping experience.
- **Rethink Segmentation:** move beyond chronological age to include variables such as health status, lifestyle, and digital literacy. Such rethinking also provides the foundation for renewing loyalty programmes, by developing more effective targeting mechanisms and designing rewards and incentives that hold genuine relevance and appeal for the over-65 segment.
- **Optimise Store Design:** ensure physical accessibility, intuitive navigation, and adequate seating areas without creating an "age-segregated" feel. Offline, bust also online, in the light of an omnichannel shopping experience.
- **Revise Communication Strategies:** replace outdated portrayals of ageing with realistic, aspirational, and diverse representations.

- **Enhance Digital Onboarding:** provide simple tutorials, in-store digital assistance, and hybrid shopping options that bridge online and offline experiences.
- **Innovate in Private Label:** develop product lines tailored to age-related nutritional needs (e.g., high-protein ranges for older adults), positioned as inclusive rather than niche.

## Methodology

The study adopts a mixed-method approach, combining:

1. **Secondary Data Analysis:** Review of corporate DEI and CSR reports from major Italian grocery retailers to assess strategic inclusion efforts.
2. **Quantitative Analysis:** Primary survey data from 1,005 respondents collected in early 2025, representing multiple generations of grocery shoppers, with oversampling of the over-65 segment for robust comparisons. Variables analysed include shopping frequency, preferred store formats, online/offline channel usage, information sources, price and promotion sensitivity, loyalty programme participation, staff interaction, and private label perceptions.
3. **Comparative Generational Analysis:** Statistical comparisons between over-65 shoppers and younger cohorts to identify convergences, divergences, and potential areas for operational adaptation.
4. **Case-Based Insights:** Selected examples of successful and unsuccessful age-inclusive strategies in the grocery sector, drawn from both the Italian context

## NEEDS AND CHARACTERISTICS OF AGING

This section will discuss some of the aspects that require a rethinking of purchasing and consumption behaviours for people over 65.

The impact of population aging on food consumption is shaped by a complex interplay of individual, sensorial, situational, social, and psychological barriers. A comprehensive understanding of these dimensions is essential to redesign purchasing and consumption behaviours among older adults, particularly in light of their evolving nutritional needs.

At the *individual level*, aging is associated with physiological changes that directly affect food intake. Reduced oral health - including lower salivation, impaired mastication, and difficulties in swallowing - coupled with a decline in sensory functioning and a general loss of appetite, significantly decreases eating pleasure and dietary variety. Moreover, diminished motor abilities limit independence in purchasing and preparing food (Geny et al., 2025; Norton et al., 2020).

The latest Italian demographic data indicate that 2024 marked the end of the excess mortality associated with the pandemic. Italy reaffirms its position among the world's longest-living countries, and its age structure continues to reflect the progressive ageing of the population.

In Italy, the economic significance of the population aged 65 and over is substantial and multifaceted, extending across consumption, wealth, and contributions to national economic activity. Individuals in this age group have become a pivotal economic force. Estimates of the economic impact attributable directly to goods and services consumed by the over-65 cohort range between approximately €297 billion and €350 billion annually, representing around 16.6 to 19.7 percent of Italy's GDP in recent years, highlighting their role as a core driver of domestic demand (Itinerari Previdenziali analysis). Additional assessments indicate that the broader Silver Economy, which encompasses the array of products and services oriented to older adults, contributes between €323.5 billion and €500 billion, equivalent to roughly 20-30 percent of Italian GDP, reflecting both direct spending and the longer value chain linked to housing, food, transportation, health services, and leisure sectors. Beyond consumption, the over-65 population also holds a disproportionate share of wealth: older Italians are major holders of both financial and real estate assets, contributing to overall economic stability and intergenerational transfers of income and resources. These figures underscore the economic weight of the elderly segment not only as consumers but also as holders of wealth and contributors to labour and employment patterns, rendering the over-65 demographic a strategic market and policy priority for both researchers and managers seeking to engage with ageing societies.

Life expectancy at birth reached 83.4 years in 2024, confirming a long-term trend of population longevity. The number of individuals aged 80 and above now stands at 4.6 million, while the country counts approximately 23,500 centenarians. These figures illustrate not only the extension of life expectancy, but also the growing weight of very old age groups within the national demographic profile.

The combined effect of declining mortality and sustained longevity poses significant implications for welfare systems, consumption patterns, and service provision. As the population structure shifts upward, understanding the needs, preferences, and behavioural dynamics of older adults becomes increasingly central for both policymakers and market actors.

Recent demographic data reveal a new historic low in fertility and an increasing imbalance in the population's age structure. Italy continues to rank among the world's oldest countries: one quarter of its population is now aged 65 or older, and more than 4.5 million individuals are aged 80 and above. Meanwhile, births continue to decline, with only 370,000 newborns recorded in 2024 and a fertility rate that has fallen to 1.18 children per woman.

Italy holds the highest share of older adults globally, with older individuals representing 24.3% of the population at the start of 2024 and 24.7% at the beginning of 2025. Within the over-65 segment (14.57 million people), the most notable increase concerns the "oldest-old": those aged 80 and above now number 4.59 million, nearly 50,000 more than in 2024. Remarkably, this group exceeds the population of children under age 10 (4.33 million), marking a profound shift in generational balance.

*Figure 1. An aging world*

**The share of seniors within a population varies greatly among countries, as does total population size.**

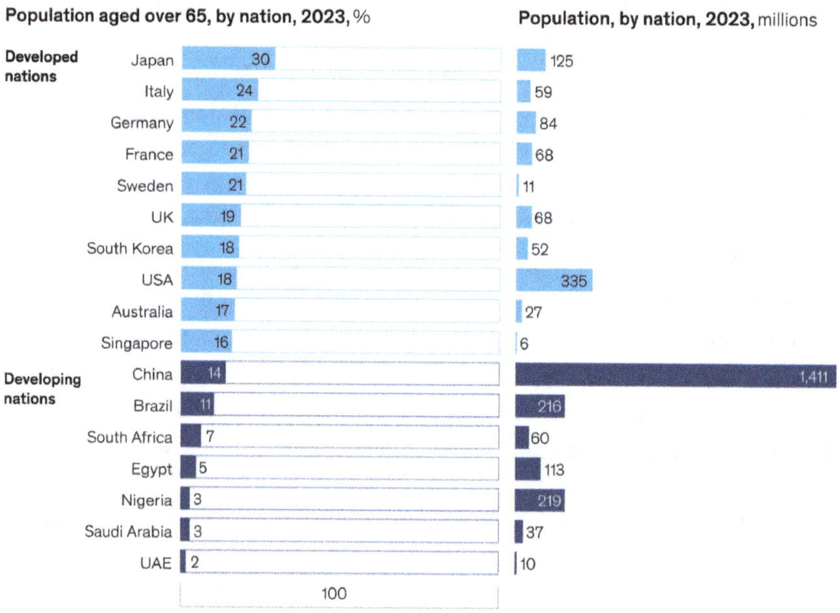


Source: World Bank

McKinsey & Company

This expansion in the proportion of older adults is commonly described as "top-heavy ageing" of the population pyramid, highlighting the structural transformation of Italian demography and its far-reaching implications for social policy, healthcare, welfare systems, and market dynamics.

Improvements in longevity and living conditions have significantly transformed what it means to be 65 years old today. Many individuals at this age enjoy good health and remain active participants in social, economic, and community life. This shift reflects not only longer lifespans but also a redefinition of ageing itself.

Adopting a dynamic approach to ageing, the threshold traditionally used to mark the onset of old age would move considerably forward - to 74 years for men and 75 for women. This suggests that chronological age alone is no longer an adequate indicator of functional capacity or social participation.

However, the increase in overall life expectancy does not always correspond to an equivalent extension of healthy life years. While many older adults experience prolonged vitality, others face health limitations that emerge earlier, highlighting persistent inequalities in ageing trajectories.

Overall, the concept of the "new elderly" points to a more heterogeneous, active, and dynamic older population - one that challenges outdated stereotypes and calls for a reconsideration of how ageing is defined, measured, and addressed in policy and societal discourse.

The generations born after the Second World War experienced significantly improved living conditions, the expansion of universal healthcare in the 1970s, and higher levels of educational attainment. These combined factors supported healthier lifestyles and produced long-term positive effects on health in later life, delaying the onset of frailty and functional limitations. Adopting balanced diets, engaging in regular physical activity, refraining from smoking, and limiting alcohol consumption contribute to preventing - or at least postponing - the emergence of conditions such as overweight and chronic degenerative diseases.

A crucial characteristic of today's older cohorts is the marked increase in human capital. Compared to previous generations, contemporary older adults are better educated, generally enjoy higher levels of well-being, remain active for longer, and possess broader cultural resources. Nevertheless, inequalities persist. Internal and rural areas show substantially lower proportions of residents with medium-to-high educational attainment compared to urban centres, and this educational disadvantage is reflected in wider disparities in individual well-being.

Digital adoption patterns further differentiate older generations. For individuals born in the 1940s and 1950s, the uptake of digital technologies has been slow, increasing by less than two percentage points per year between 2003 and 2024 - a considerably modest pace even when compared to other non-digital natives (those born before 1980). More positive results emerge for the 1960s cohorts, who experienced a stronger acceleration in regular Internet use (an average of 2.6 percentage points per year), partly because they encountered digitalisation during their prime working years. Within this group, women - benefiting from higher education levels and greater participation in the labour market relative to earlier generations - have closed the digital gap with men, even surpassing them among women born between 1965 and 1969.

Digital skills play a decisive role in supporting the digital transition while mitigating inequalities that may undermine social inclusion and equity. The EU's

*Digital Decade* strategic programme explicitly aims to ensure that, by 2030, 80% of the population aged 16–74 possesses at least basic digital skills.

However, digital competencies remain strongly associated with both age and educational level. In Italy in 2023, the gap in basic digital proficiency between individuals aged 16–24 (59.1%) and those aged 45–54 (48.7%) reached ten percentage points, widening further among older age groups. Notably, educational attainment acts as an equaliser: age-based gaps disappear entirely among individuals with higher levels of education. Overall, digital skills tend to be more widespread among men (+3.1 percentage points compared with women), although this female disadvantage is observed exclusively among women aged 45 and above.

As individuals age, their social networks tend to shrink. Retirement, the loss of loved ones, and deteriorating health or economic conditions can all reduce opportunities for social interaction. Yet, precisely in this stage of life, having access to supportive relationships becomes a crucial resource for overall well-being. In Italy, data from 2023 show that 94.2% of older adults report having at least one person - whether a family member, friend, or neighbour - whom they can rely on, a proportion comparable to that of younger individuals. This indicates a notable resilience of social ties even in advanced age.

Alongside these relational dynamics, important signs of transformation are emerging. New generations of older adults exhibit significantly higher levels of education compared to their predecessors. This improvement in human capital has tangible positive effects on health, autonomy, and social participation. However, the distribution of these benefits remains uneven across the country, with territorial disparities continuing to shape differences in well-being and opportunities.

These developments unfold against the backdrop of broader demographic change. In the EU27, individuals of working age (15-64 years) currently represent 63.8% of the population, while those aged 65 and over account for 21.6%, an increase of 2.9 percentage points over the past decade. This upward trend is observed across all EU member states, highlighting a continental shift toward older population structures and underscoring the growing relevance of ageing-related policies and interventions.

Approximately 30% of Italian firms are particularly exposed to the ageing of their workforce. These are predominantly small economic units, often characterised by self-employment and limited organisational capacity, making them especially vulnerable to demographic shifts. The gradual exit of older workers - combined with the insufficient inflow of younger cohorts - raises concerns about business continuity, knowledge transfer, and long-term sustainability.

A critical dimension highlighted in the slide concerns the role of younger workers, especially those with higher qualifications, in sustaining the innovative and competitive capacity of firms. Regardless of the specific economic sector, the presence of skilled young people is strongly associated with greater adoption of new technologies, enhanced productivity, and improved adaptability to market transformations.

The concept of "successful ageing" is becoming increasingly widespread: as the years pass, it is possible to maintain autonomy and good physical and mental health, provided that the appropriate environmental and genetic conditions are present. The **"fourth age** is distincted from the third age more on health status and level of autonomy than on chronological age.

## Managing Multiple Generations in the Workplace: Opportunities, Threats, and Strategic Approaches

In this context, demographic ageing is not only a social issue but also an economic challenge, shaping the vitality, resilience, and strategic potential of the productive system. Policies that support youth employment, intergenerational collaboration, and the upgrading of workforce skills emerge as essential levers for ensuring that firms can continue to innovate and compete in an increasingly complex environment.

The presence of multiple generations within today's organisations - ranging from Baby Boomers to Generation X, Millennials, and increasingly Generation Z - constitutes one of the most significant demographic transformations affecting the contemporary workforce. This shift introduces a complex mix of opportunities and challenges, requiring companies to adopt structured and inclusive management strategies. Understanding the dynamics of generational diversity is therefore essential for sustaining organisational performance, fostering innovation, and ensuring long-term competitiveness.

A multigenerational workforce offers a unique reservoir of complementary skills, experiences, and perspectives. Older employees often bring decades of tacit knowledge, organisational memory, and industry-specific expertise. Such knowledge is especially valuable for decision-making, problem-solving, mentoring, and ensuring continuity in processes and client relationships. Senior workers frequently exhibit strong work ethic, reliability, and a deep understanding of the company's culture and history.

Younger generations, by contrast, typically contribute enhanced digital literacy, openness to innovation, and a natural familiarity with emerging tools and technologies. Millennials and Generation Z tend to adopt agile working styles, promote experimentation, and encourage the use of new methodologies, such as data-driven decision-making or collaborative platforms. These capabilities are essential in environments shaped by rapid technological change, digital transformation, and evolving consumer expectations.

When effectively integrated, these generational strengths produce intergenerational complementarities: younger employees benefit from mentorship and guidance, while older workers gain support in adapting to technological advancements. Multigenerational teams often show increased creativity, broader cognitive diversity, and improved capacity for innovation. Furthermore, companies that embrace generational inclusion can strengthen their employer brand, attract a wider talent pool, and better reflect the demographic diversity of their customer base.

Despite these opportunities, generational diversity also introduces potential risks that may undermine organisational cohesion and performance. A key challenge concerns divergent work values, shaped by different socio-economic contexts. Older workers may prioritise stability, hierarchy, and structured routines, whereas younger employees often seek flexibility, meaningful work, continuous learning, and rapid advancement. These contrasting expectations can generate misunderstandings, perceived inequities, or tension across teams.

Communication styles represent another source of conflict: younger generations may prefer immediate, digital communication channels, while older colleagues often rely on more traditional, face-to-face interactions. These differences may lead to inefficiencies or reduced collaboration if not mediated effectively.

A further threat involves resistance to change. Senior workers may feel threatened by fast-paced technological evolution or fear that their skills are becoming obsolete. Conversely, younger employees may question existing organisational practices, potentially destabilising established routines or hierarchies.

Generational stereotypes - such as portraying Baby Boomers as technophobic or Millennials as entitled - can reinforce biased attitudes and obstruct trust-building. These stereotypes may lead to discrimination, reduced morale, and disengagement. If unmanaged, such tensions undermine knowledge transfer, slow down innovation, and reduce organisational resilience.

Finally, demographic ageing creates structural challenges: firms may face higher retirement turnover, difficulty in replacing specialised roles, and increased risks related to the loss of critical expertise. At the same time, younger generations may experience limited upward mobility if older workers remain in key positions for longer.

To leverage the benefits of a multigenerational workforce while mitigating its risks, organisations must adopt deliberate and evidence-based management strategies. Several models and organisational practices have emerged as particularly effective.

1. **Intergenerational mentoring and reverse mentoring.** Traditional mentoring allows older workers to transfer tacit knowledge to younger colleagues, supporting career development and organisational continuity. Reverse mentoring, by contrast, enables younger employees to share digital skills and innovative mindsets with senior staff. Together, these practices foster mutual respect, bridge skill gaps, and promote collaborative learning.

2. **Lifelong learning and upskilling.** Providing continuous training opportunities - especially in digital competencies - helps reduce the fear of obsolescence among older workers and supports adaptability. At the same time, offering leadership training and skills-development programmes to younger employees enhances organisational readiness for future challenges.
3. **Flexible work arrangements.** Workplace flexibility, including hybrid work, adjustable hours, and personalised job design, addresses diverse generational needs. Older workers may value reduced workloads or phased retirement, while younger employees often seek autonomy and a better work-life balance. Flexibility contributes to higher engagement and retention across age groups.
4. **Inclusive leadership and communication.** Managers play a critical role in mediating generational differences. Inclusive leadership that values diversity, encourages open dialogue, and avoids stereotypes is essential. Adapting communication practices - combining digital and traditional formats - ensures that all employees can participate effectively.
5. **Job redesign and crgonomic adaptation.** For ageing workers, ergonomic adjustments and task redesign can extend work ability and improve safety. Simultaneously, involving younger employees in cross-functional teams increases engagement and promotes knowledge exchange.
6. **Organisational culture that values diversity.** A culture of respect, collaboration, and shared purpose is crucial. Companies benefit from articulating clear values on age inclusion, addressing implicit biases, and promoting intergenerational teamwork.

Generational diversity represents both a strategic resource and a managerial challenge. When inclusive practices are adopted, firms can harness the unique strengths of each generation, enabling innovation, adaptability, and long-term sustainability. Conversely, failing to manage generational differences risks undermining cohesion, knowledge continuity, and competitive capacity.

In an era marked by demographic change, workforce ageing, and rapid technological evolution, organisations must view generational management not as a peripheral HR initiative but as a central component of organisational strategy and competitive advantage.

The retail sector is uniquely exposed to the opportunities and challenges generated by an ageing workforce and the coexistence of multiple generations within the same organisation. Unlike other industries, retail operations depend heavily on frontline, customer-facing roles, continuous physical activity, and rapid adaptation to evolving consumer expectations. These features amplify both the value and the complexity of managing generational diversity.

On the opportunity side, older employees represent a strategic asset for retailers. Their long-standing experience, deep product knowledge, and well-developed interpersonal skills often translate into higher-quality customer service and stronger customer loyalty-elements that are critical in sectors such as grocery, fashion, and specialty retail. Senior workers also embody institutional memory and operational stability, supporting the continuity of store routines, mentoring younger colleagues, and reducing short-term turnover. Younger employees, by contrast, bring agility, digital fluency, and a natural orientation toward omnichannel practices, online–offline integration, social media communication, and retail technologies such as self-checkout, CRM tools, and clienteling systems. When effectively combined, these generational contributions can enhance service innovation, accelerate the adoption of new formats, and strengthen the retailer's competitive positioning.

However, the retail sector also faces disproportionate risks linked to ageing employees. Retail jobs often involve physically demanding tasks-prolonged standing, lifting, stocking shelves, working irregular hours-that may become increasingly challenging with age. As the average age of employees rises, companies may face higher rates of work-related fatigue, ergonomic injuries, and reduced physical capacity, potentially affecting productivity and increasing absenteeism. At the same time, generational tensions may emerge around customer service expectations, pace of technological change, or willingness to adopt digital tools, particularly in areas such as e-commerce fulfilment, mobile POS systems, or AI-driven inventory management. If unmanaged, these tensions can weaken operational efficiency and slow down innovation.

Moreover, retail is experiencing rapid digital transformation, and companies that cannot leverage younger generations' digital competences while maintaining the experiential strength of senior staff risk losing competitiveness. The sector's traditionally high turnover rates also complicate knowledge transfer, making intergenerational mentoring both more necessary and more challenging. Finally, demographic ageing among consumers mirrors that of the workforce: understanding the needs of older shoppers becomes an internal and external imperative, requiring retailers to rely on multigenerational teams that can effectively interpret diverse customer expectations.

In this context, retailers must adopt targeted strategies-such as ergonomic redesign of tasks, flexible scheduling, digital upskilling, and structured intergenerational collaboration-to fully exploit generational complementarities while mitigating the sector-specific vulnerabilities amplified by workforce ageing.

## LEVERAGE DEI AS A STRATEGIC ASSET: THE ITALIAN CASE

In recent years, retailers worldwide-particularly those operating in the grocery sector - have increasingly embedded Diversity, Equity and Inclusion (DEI) principles into their corporate strategies. What began as a compliance-oriented response to regulatory and social pressures has progressively evolved into a strategic lever that shapes organisational culture, customer experience, talent management, and long-term competitiveness. International grocery leaders such as Walmart, Tesco, Carrefour, Kroger, Ahold Delhaize and Woolworths have formalised DEI frameworks, set measurable targets, and implemented board-level governance structures to ensure accountability. Their strategies typically span multiple dimensions of inclusion-gender, ethnicity, disability, socio-economic background-but the age dimension has become increasingly salient as demographic shifts reshape consumer markets and workforce composition.

The ageing of the population, especially evident in Europe, North America and parts of Asia, is transforming both labour pools and consumer bases. As a result, DEI strategies in retail are now explicitly addressing age inclusivity, recognising that older employees and older consumers represent not only a challenge but a significant source of value. From a workforce perspective, leading retailers are adopting initiatives such as age-diverse recruitment, programmes for mid- and late-career development, flexible scheduling for senior employees, ergonomic adaptations to reduce physical strain, and intergenerational training models where younger and older staff exchange digital and operational competencies. These policies aim to retain experienced workers, leverage their tacit knowledge, and mitigate labour shortages-especially relevant in grocery, where physical presence and service interactions remain critical.

On the customer side, DEI in grocery retail increasingly includes a dedicated focus on the accessibility, usability and inclusiveness of stores for older shoppers, who constitute a growing share of total grocery spending. International retailers have introduced solutions such as:

- **Age-friendly store layouts**, wider aisles and clearer signage to improve navigation.
- **Enhanced lighting and shelf-labelling systems** to support visual accessibility.
- **Longer or flexible checkout times**, assisted checkouts, and “slow lanes” for customers who prefer a less hurried environment.
- **Customer service training** focused on empathy, patience and communication with older adults.

- **Transportation partnerships** or shuttle services to improve store access for customers with mobility limitations.
- **Online shopping support**, including simplified digital interfaces, telephone ordering assistance, and hybrid delivery–pickup solutions tailored to older consumers who may experience digital barriers.
- **Healthy-ageing product ranges**, such as easy-to-open packaging, fortified foods, and meal solutions that meet the nutritional needs of over-65 consumers.

In parallel, several retailers have piloted "quiet hours", intergenerational community initiatives, and in-store health services to strengthen social inclusion and support older adults' wellbeing. These interventions reflect a broader strategic recognition: age-inclusive practices generate commercial value, foster customer loyalty, improve brand reputation, and position retailers as community anchors in ageing societies.

Taken together, the evolution of DEI practices in grocery retail demonstrates a shift from symbolic commitments to operational, measurable, and customer-centric interventions. Age inclusion is no longer peripheral-it is emerging as a core dimension of responsible and future-oriented retail strategy.

The Italian grocery retail landscape is highly fragmented and characterised by low levels of internationalisation, especially when compared with other European markets. Unlike countries where a small number of large multinational chains dominate the sector, Italy presents a complex mosaic of regional and national players, each with distinct strategic positioning, store formats, and customer bases. This structural fragmentation has historically limited consolidation and has contributed to a competitive environment in which price dynamics, promotional pressure, and localised differentiation play a central role.

The following section reports the 2025 market shares of the main grocery retail groups operating in Italy, expressed as a percentage of total FMCG sales (LCC – Largo Consumo Confezionato) at value as of 30 June 2025. These figures (Fig. 2 and Table 1) provide an updated snapshot of the competitive balance within the sector and highlight the relative weight of the principal banners active across the country.

*Figure 2. Main retail Banners in Italy (2025)*

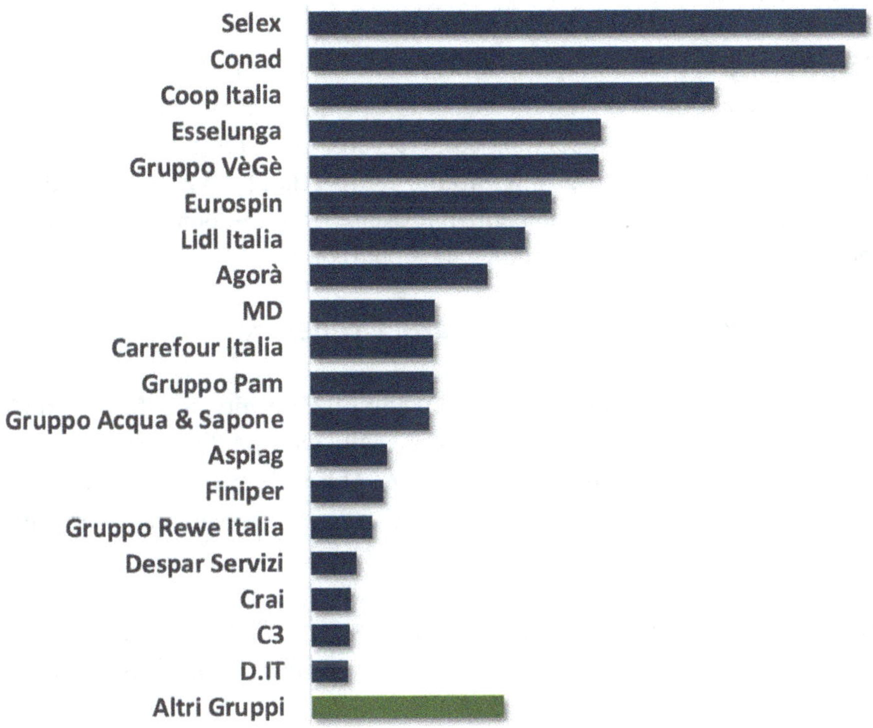


*Source: REM Lab/Circana, UCSC, 2025*

*Table 1. Number of Grocery Retail Outlets by Channel (2022–2025)*

| Grocery Retail Channels (GDO) | 2022 | 2023 | 2024 | 2025 | Change 2025 vs. 2022 |
|---|---|---|---|---|---|
| Hypermarkets | 405 | 393 | 387 | 385 | –20 |
| Superstores | 555 | 563 | 556 | 546 | -9 |
| Supermarkets | 8,630 | 8,683 | 8,766 | 8,779 | +149 |
| Proximity stores/LSP | 6,260 | 6,202 | 6,217 | 6,216 | –44 |
| Discount stores | 5,413 | 5,522 | 5,623 | 5,672 | +259 |
| Drugstores | 3,348 | 3,492 | 3,575 | 3,659 | +311 |
| Total GDO channels | 24,611 | 24,855 | 25,124 | 25,257 | +646 |

Source: REM Lab/Circana, UCSC, 2025

The evolution of store formats between 2022 and 2025 highlights a structural transformation in the Italian grocery retail ecosystem.

## Formats in Decline: Hypermarkets and Traditionl Proximity Stores

- **Hypermarkets (–20 units)** and **superstores (–9 units)** continue their long-term decline, a trend driven by changing consumer habits, the shift toward convenience, and rising operating costs for large-scale formats.
- **Proximity stores (LSP) show a notable contraction (–44 units)**, signalling consolidation, increasing competitive pressure from discounters, and possibly the closure of underperforming neighbourhood outlets.

## Formats in Expansion: Discount and Drugstore

- **Discount stores register strong expansion (+259 units)**, confirming their relevance in a price-sensitive market, especially during inflationary periods.
- **Drugstores show the highest growth (+311 units)**, driven by demand for personal care, household goods, and convenience-oriented shopping missions.

**Supermarkets remain the backbone of the system.** With +149 units, supermarkets continue to represent the most stable and resilient channel, maintaining their central role in everyday grocery shopping.

**Overall system growth.** The total number of GDO outlets increases by +646 units over the period, reflecting both sector dynamism and ongoing reconfiguration of the competitive landscape.

In the following pages there is a synthetic table of what is visible from public sources for the main Italian retail banners. It focuses on:

1. support for senior employees,
2. policies for a multi-generational workforce,
3. offers/solutions for senior customers (mostly 60/65+).

*Table 2. Strategic and Operational solutions for aging society: a focus on Italian retail banners*

| Retail Banner | 1) Senior employees/age support | 2) Co-existence of generations | 3) Senior customers (65+ etc.) |
|---|---|---|---|
| Coop | Coop Alleanza 3.0[1] explicitly mentions *"age management e ricambio generazionale"* in its Diversity & Inclusion section, with actions on training, internal mobility and work–life balance that take age into account. There is also a connection with ONU DSG: 5, 8, 10 | Same page stresses a heterogeneous workforce and programs that value different life stages and experience levels (inter-generational knowledge transfer, mentoring). | Many Coop stores offer a 10% discount day for over-60/65, often combined with home-delivery and click-and-collect; over-65 discount is cited in trade press[2] and store descriptions. |
| Conad | Social-responsibility reports (2022[3]) emphasise employee welfare, training and work–life balance but do not single out formal "age management" tools; support for workers with care duties indirectly benefits older workers and caregiver. | No explicit Italian "multi-generation" program found; coexistence of generations is treated within broader HR and welfare initiatives. | Articles on supermarket age benefits indicate free or discounted home delivery for over-70 and for people with disabilities, in some cooperatives, and occasional pensioners' promotions. |
| Coop (other cooperatives) | Several local Coop systems are reported[4] to ppparticipate in projects on *age management* in the cooperative world (training for older workers, gradual retirement, flexible roles), usually framed within territorial welfare projects. | Coops are often cited as case studies in Italian research on age-diverse organisations, but policies are fragmented by cooperative and territory. | Besides discounts, some stores highlight age-friendly services: home delivery, assisted check-out, clear signage and smaller formats with "over 65 discount" as a communication hook. |
| Esselunga | 2024 sustainability reports[5] include a Diversity & Inclusion section that commits to equal opportunities and monitoring of workforce composition by age, seniority and contract type; age is treated as one of the protected dimensions, with training and welfare open across age groups. | Corporate material stresses collaboration and inclusion but does not describe specific inter generational programs; knowledge transfer and internal training are the main levers. | For seniors and people with disabilities Esselunga provides reduced home-delivery fees for 70+ customers and periodically runs price initiatives aimed at protecting their purchasing power, as reported by consumer guides and press[6]. |
| Selex group (Selex, Dimar, Alì, Mercatò, etc.) | 2022 Selex's sustainability reports[7] monitor workforce by age bracket and explicitly commit to avoiding discrimination based on age, but do not detail specific senior-only programs. | Some member companies[8] run training and digital-upskilling initiatives that implicitly support older staff, yet they are framed as general HR development rather than age-programs. | At customer level, several Selex banners position themselves on proximity and service; senior-specific benefits appear more at local banner level (e.g. home delivery, "pensioners' day") than in national communication, and are not systematically reported online. |

continued on following page

*Table 2. Continued*

| Retail Banner | 1) Senior employees/age support | 2) Co-existence of generations | 3) Senior customers (65+ etc.) |
|---|---|---|---|
| Aldi Italia | Aldi states that "diversity is a strength" and has signed the Italian "Carta per le Pari Opportunità"; HR policies[9] commit to inclusive, non-discriminatory practices but there is no visible age-specific program. | Internal communication highlights equal opportunities and gender empowerment; nothing explicit on structured inter-generational management in Italy was found. | No national-level over-65 promotion surfaced; the banner competes mainly through everyday low prices and broad affordability rather than age-targeted deals. |
| Lidl Italia | "Insieme in Lidl" is a corporate statement[10] on Diversity & Inclusion that commits to equal treatment and a workplace "free from barriers", explicitly prohibiting discrimination (including by age) and offering neutral support contacts for employees. | Career pages[11] highlight a "diverse team by age, gender and background"; inter-generational mix is described as a value, but without concrete Italian age-management tools publicly detailed. | There's no systematic senior-only promotions; Lidl's promise is more about uniform low prices and simplified shopping rather than specific "over-65" schemes. |
| Eurospin | Public sources[12] show Eurospin participating in general DEI and people-analytics discussions, but without clear age-specific HR policies published. | Multi-generation aspects are mostly implicit (mass hiring across ages); no structured Italian program surfaced. | No stable national over-65 initiative was found; the focus is on discount positioning for all. |
| Carrefour Italia | At group[13] level, Carrefour frames inclusion and diversity as core to its CSR and talent strategy; in Italy this includes labour-inclusion projects (e.g. for refugees and disabled people) and training on inclusion. | Diversity programs explicitly mention age as one of the dimensions and promote inclusive teams, though specific tools for seniors vs. juniors are not very detailed in public docs. | Carrefour offers percentage discounts to over-60s on specific days, and in the past launched a *"Senior Card"* that effectively cut VAT on fresh groceries for over-65s; current media also underline regular senior-day initiatives. |
| Pam/Pam Panorama | CSR communication highlights inclusion and work–life balance, but not senior-targeted HR measures. | No explicit age-management scheme found; inclusion is mostly framed around gender and disability. | Multiple sources[14] point to over-65 discounts and free delivery (e.g. 10% on Sundays for 65+ and a dedicated free-delivery weekday for seniors). |
| Despar/Aspiag | Sustainability reports emphasise proximity, local employment and general diversity principles; nothing strongly age-specific is visible. | No detailed public program on inter-generational management found. | Despar Nordovest and other banners communicate over-65 discounts on specific days (e.g. 10% Monday–Thursday beyond a minimum spend). |

continued on following page

*Table 2. Continued*

| Retail Banner | 1) Senior employees/age support | 2) Co-existence of generations | 3) Senior customers (65+ etc.) |
|---|---|---|---|
| Crai | Crai appears in events[15] on empowerment and inclusion in retail, indicating an interest in DEI, but age-targeted HR measures are not clearly documented online. | Inter-generational aspects are mentioned only generically (family-owned, local retailers working with "people of all ages"). | There's no stable national over-65 schemes; some local affiliates may run pensioners' promotions, but they are not consistently reported on the corporate site. |
| Vegè, Agorà, C3, Finiper/ Iper, Rewe (Italian operations) | For these groups, public sustainability material focuses on community support, local employment and in some cases gender equality; no explicit, branded age-management programs for senior staff emerged. | Multi-generation topics are largely implicit (family business narrative, "people at the centre") rather than structured policies. | Press and consumer guides mention senior discounts mainly for Iper/Unes (linked to Finiper) and local banners (e.g. some over-65 discounts and home-delivery advantages), but information[16] is fragmented and often store-specific rather than group-wide. |

## RETAIL STORES PUT TO THE TEST BY THE OVER-65S

The following data were collected by REM Lab – Research Centre on Retail & Consumer Experience at Università Cattolica del Sacro Cuore in early 2025 as part of a broader investigation into grocery shopping behaviours and generational differences in consumption. The survey was administered using the Qualtrics platform, which enabled the distribution of the questionnaire, the management of responses, and the secure processing of the dataset. The insights presented below therefore reflect a robust and systematically collected empirical base, grounded in a methodologically rigorous data-collection process. The filter question for this set is: 'do you personally take care of grocery shopping for yourself and/or your family?

*Table 3. Age of Respondents*

| Age Range | Percentage | Count |
|---|---|---|
| 18 to 30 years | 21% | 207 |
| 31 to 60 years | 51% | 515 |
| Over 60 years | 28% | 283 |

Source: REM Lab, UCSC, 2025

The sample presents a balanced distribution across age groups, with a slight predominance of respondents aged 31 to 60, who represent just over half of the total.

Notably, individuals over 60 account for 28% of the sample-an unusually high share compared to many consumer surveys and particularly relevant for studies on ageing, consumption patterns, or intergenerational dynamics. This strong representation of older adults enhances the robustness of insights related to senior behaviours, needs, and attitudes, making the dataset especially valuable for research on ageing and market segmentation.

*Table 4. In the last few months, has concern about the near future increased in your family? (Single response)*

| Response | Total | 18–30 years | 31–60 years | Over 60 years |
|---|---|---|---|---|
| Yes, it has increased | 76.9% | 76.3% | 78.6% | 74.2% |
| No, it has decreased | 10.9% | 11.6% | 11.5% | 9.5% |
| I don't know | 12.1% | 12.1% | 9.9% | 16.3% |

Source: REM Lab, UCSC, 2025

The data reveal a strong and widespread sense of growing concern about the near future across all age groups. Approximately three out of four respondents report an increase in family-level worry, with relatively small differences between age segments. Adults aged 31–60 show the highest levels of rising concern (78.6%), likely reflecting their exposure to both economic pressures and family responsibilities. Respondents over 60 also show high concern (74.2%), but they have the largest share of uncertainty ("I don't know"), suggesting more variable perceptions or possibly lower exposure to day-to-day economic decision-making. Overall, the results indicate a generalised climate of anxiety, with implications for consumer confidence and purchasing behaviour across generations.

*Table 5. Price sensitivity. Level of Attention to Product and Brand Prices When Grocery Shopping (0–10 scale) (0 = minimum attention, 10 = maximum attention)*

| Score Group | Total | 18–30 years | 31–60 years | Over 60 years |
|---|---|---|---|---|
| 1 to 6 | 18.4% | 26.7% | 19.6% | 10.2% |
| 7 to 8 | 39.6% | 43.2% | 41.7% | 33.2% |
| 9 to 10 | 41.9% | 30.1% | 38.6% | 56.5% |

Source: REM Lab, UCSC, 2025

The data show that price sensitivity in grocery shopping is very high overall, with more than four in ten respondents scoring their attention to prices at the maximum level (9–10). Age differences are significant. Consumers over 60 display the highest price vigilance: 56.5% report maximum attention, reflecting fixed incomes, inflation pressure, and habit-forming frugality. In contrast, respondents aged 18–30 are less price-focused, with a larger share in the low–medium attention category (scores 1–6). The 31–60 age group sits in between but leans strongly toward medium–high attention (scores 7–10). Overall, the results reinforce the idea that older consumers are the most attentive and price-conscious segment, a factor with direct implications for promotions, retailer loyalty strategies, and assortment decisions.

*Table 6. Adopted behaviours, compared to the past, with reference to grocery shopping*

| Behaviour | Response | Total | 18–30 years | 31–60 years | Over 60 years |
|---|---|---|---|---|---|
| We shop more often at discount supermarkets (Lidl, Eurospin, ALDI, MD, etc.) | Yes | 70.8% | 70.4% | 72.0% | 68.9% |
| | No | 29.2% | 29.6% | 28.0% | 31.1% |
| We buy more discounted products/brands | Yes | 86.0% | 78.6% | 87.2% | 89.0% |
| | No | 14.0% | 21.4% | 12.8% | 11.0% |
| We buy more supermarket private labels (Coop, Conad, Esselunga, etc.) | Yes | 76.0% | 68.9% | 78.3% | 77.0% |
| | No | 24.0% | 31.1% | 21.7% | 23.0% |
| We buy more "no-brand"/first-price products | Yes | 70.8% | 74.8% | 71.1% | 67.5% |
| | No | 29.2% | 25.2% | 28.9% | 32.5% |
| We buy fewer non-essential products (sweets, snacks, crisps, etc.) | Yes | 82.1% | 77.2% | 82.1% | 85.5% |
| | No | 17.9% | 22.8% | 17.9% | 14.5% |
| We buy fewer "expensive" products (e.g., meat, oil, etc.) | Yes | 67.9% | 62.6% | 70.7% | 66.8% |
| | No | 32.1% | 37.4% | 29.3% | 33.2% |
| We try to minimise waste, buying only what we really need | Yes | 85.4% | 79.6% | 85.0% | 90.1% |
| | No | 14.6% | 20.4% | 15.0% | 9.9% |
| We visit multiple supermarkets to look for the best prices/discounts | Yes | 73.6% | 70.4% | 74.4% | 74.6% |
| | No | 26.4% | 29.6% | 25.6% | 25.4% |
| We buy fewer premium/well-known brands | Yes | 73.6% | 72.8% | 74.4% | 72.8% |
| | No | 26.4% | 27.2% | 25.6% | 27.2% |
| We shop more frequently, buying fewer items each time | Yes | 46.9% | 53.4% | 46.4% | 43.1% |
| | No | 53.1% | 46.6% | 53.6% | 56.9% |

Source: REM Lab, UCSC, 2025

Across all age groups, the data highlight a strong shift toward value-driven grocery behaviour, reflecting economic uncertainty and heightened price sensitivity. Three trends stand out:

1. **Discount and promotion-driven purchasing is widespread.** More than 70% of respondents across every age group report shopping at discount chains, and

86% buy more discounted products. Older adults (89%) are the most responsive to promotions.

2. **Strong movement toward private labels and low-cost alternatives.** Private labels and first-price products are increasingly preferred, especially among those aged 31-60. This suggests a structural reorientation toward affordability rather than temporary behaviour.
3. **Waste reduction and essentialism are becoming universal norms.** A remarkable 85% of respondents try to minimise waste, with the share rising to 90% among those over 60-indicating deeply internalised frugality in older consumers.

Younger consumers (18–30) stand out for:

- higher frequency of small-basket shopping (53%),
- slightly greater willingness to buy no-brand products,
- lower discipline around waste reduction compared to seniors.

Overall, the table paints a clear picture: across generations, Italian consumers are recalibrating their grocery habits toward savings, necessity, and efficiency, with older adults showing the most consistent and structured cost-management behaviours.

*Table 7. Factors Considered Important When Choosing a Supermarket, by Age Group*

| Factor | Total | 18–30 years | 31–60 years | Over 60 years | Mean Delta (60+ vs. others) |
|---|---|---|---|---|---|
| Convenience/reachability (distance, parking, etc.) | 35.0% | 32.0% | 30.9% | 44.5% | 9.6% |
| Cleanliness, hygiene, sanitisation of spaces and staff | 39.8% | 34.0% | 36.3% | 50.5% | 10.7% |
| Professionalism/kindness of staff | 26.7% | 21.8% | 23.7% | 35.7% | 9.0% |
| Variety/completeness of assortment | 33.5% | 27.2% | 30.5% | 43.5% | 10.0% |
| Speed at checkout | 22.7% | 19.4% | 22.5% | 25.4% | 2.7% |
| Clarity of product display and ease of product search | 28.5% | 23.3% | 25.8% | 37.1% | 8.6% |
| Quality of fresh and ultra-fresh products (cold cuts, meat, etc.) | 40.7% | 32.5% | 35.5% | 56.2% | 15.4% |
| Overall price convenience | 49.0% | 37.4% | 47.4% | 60.4% | 11.4% |
| Average price increase since the beginning of the year | 29.8% | 24.3% | 28.0% | 37.1% | 7.3% |
| Promotions, discounts, offers | 50.0% | 48.5% | 45.6% | 59.0% | 9.0% |
| Quality and convenience of supermarket private labels | 38.1% | 30.1% | 35.7% | 48.4% | 10.3% |
| Presence of self-checkout/automatic tills | 19.4% | 21.4% | 19.0% | 18.7% | –0.7% |
| Convenient/extended opening hours | 28.2% | 25.2% | 26.0% | 34.3% | 6.1% |
| Constant availability of the products I look for | 34.0% | 28.2% | 31.8% | 42.0% | 8.1% |
| Visibility of food preparation in fresh departments | 23.8% | 20.9% | 21.7% | 29.7% | 5.9% |

Source: REM Lab, UCSC, 2025

The table reveals a pronounced generational gradient in supermarket choice criteria. Older consumers (60+) consistently attribute higher importance to nearly all store attributes, especially those linked to freshness (56.2%), cleanliness (50.5%), assortment quality (43.5%), and convenience of prices (60.4%). These priorities reflect their stronger orientation toward product quality, safety, and economic value-all amplified by fixed incomes and higher sensitivity to inflation.

Younger respondents (18–30) show lower sensitivity across most dimensions, but slightly higher interest in self-checkout (21.4%), signaling greater digital familiarity. The 31–60 group generally sits between the two extremes.

The largest "mean deltas" (differences between 60+ and all others) occur for:

- quality of fresh products (+15.4%)
- overall price convenience (+11.4%)
- cleanliness (+10.7%)
- assortment completeness (+10%)

This confirms that older adults behave as hyper-selective, quality-driven, and value-conscious shoppers, placing them at the centre of competitive strategies in grocery retail-especially for fresh departments, store standards, and pricing policies.

*Table 8. Average Time Spent in the Supermarket (in minutes)*

| Age Group | Average Time (minutes) |
|---|---|
| Total | 32.6 |
| 18–30 years | 32.4 |
| 31–60 years | 30.7 |
| Over 60 years | 36.1 |

Source: REM Lab, UCSC, 2025

The data indicate that older shoppers (60+) spend significantly more time in the supermarket, with an average of 36.1 minutes, compared to 30.7 minutes for those aged 31–60 and 32.4 minutes for young adults. This suggests that seniors approach grocery shopping as a more deliberate and slower-paced activity, possibly due to a combination of factors such as greater attention to price and quality, lower time pressure, or mobility differences. For retailers, this longer dwell time represents both an opportunity-to engage older consumers through services, clear layout, and assistance-and a responsibility, requiring store environments that are more accessible, comfortable, and easy to navigate.

*Table 9. Number of Different Stores Visited for Grocery Shopping in the Last Month*

| Age Group | Average Number of Stores Visited |
|---|---|
| Total | 5.5 |
| 18–30 years | 7.6 |
| 31–60 years | 5.4 |
| Over 60 years | 4.3 |

Source: REM Lab, UCSC, 2025

The data show a clear generational divide in store-hopping behaviour. Younger consumers (18–30) visit by far the most supermarkets, with an average of 7.6 different stores per month. This suggests higher mobility, more experimentation, and possibly greater price sensitivity combined with digital search/price-comparison habits.

In contrast, older consumers (60+) visit the fewest stores, averaging 4.3 locations per month. This reflects a more stable shopping routine, greater preference for familiar environments, and potentially mobility or convenience constraints. Shoppers aged 31–60 fall close to the total average, indicating balanced but still selective behaviour.

For retailers, these findings highlight two strategic imperatives:

- Younger shoppers demand variety and competitive pricing, pushing retailers to strengthen multichannel visibility and promotions.
- Older shoppers reward consistency, accessibility, and trust, making store experience, clarity, and service quality key retention levers.

*Table 10. Perceptions of Supermarket Private Labels, by Age Group*

| Statement | Total | 18–30 years | 31–60 years | Over 60 years |
|---|---|---|---|---|
| They are good quality at a convenient price | 24.7% | 20.4% | 23.7% | 29.7% |
| In some cases, they are my first choice | 25.7% | 19.9% | 25.8% | 29.7% |
| They reflect the supermarket's values | 22.6% | 18.9% | 20.2% | 29.7% |
| They are riskier to buy than well-known brands | 11.3% | 13.6% | 11.7% | 8.8% |

Source: REM Lab, UCSC, 2025

The data show that older consumers (60+) consistently express the strongest trust and preference for supermarket private labels. For every positive statement-quality at a good price, first-choice usage, and alignment with supermarket values-the 60+ group scores around 30%, well above younger respondents. They are also the least likely to perceive private labels as "risky", with only 8.8% expressing concerns.

Younger shoppers (18–30) show more hesitation:

- they rate private-label quality and value lower,
- and show the *highest* perceived risk (13.6%).

Consumers aged **31–60** sit close to the total average, indicating moderate but growing confidence.

Overall, the findings highlight that private labels are particularly appealing to older customers, both economically and symbolically. This segment sees private labels as reliable, aligned with the store's identity, and offering strong value-making them a strategic lever for retailers aiming to retain and grow loyalty among senior shoppers.

*Table 11. Importance Assigned to Different Information Sources When Deciding Which Food Products to Buy (Scale: 1 = minimum importance, 10 = maximum importance)*

| Information Source (Average Score) | Total | 18–30 years | 31–60 years | Over 60 years |
|---|---|---|---|---|
| TV | 5.4 | 6.0 | 5.4 | 5.0 |
| Radio | 4.8 | 5.4 | 4.9 | 4.1 |
| Daily newspapers | 4.7 | 5.5 | 4.7 | 4.1 |
| Magazines | 4.8 | 5.7 | 4.9 | 4.0 |
| Supermarket flyers/leaflets | 6.7 | 6.5 | 6.8 | 6.7 |
| Brand websites | 5.0 | 5.7 | 5.2 | 4.1 |
| Supermarket websites | 5.6 | 6.1 | 5.7 | 4.9 |
| Supermarket apps | 5.7 | 6.1 | 5.8 | 5.3 |
| Social networks | 4.8 | 5.8 | 4.9 | 3.8 |
| Supermarket shelves (in-store observation) | 6.8 | 6.9 | 6.8 | 6.8 |
| Product packaging | 6.3 | 6.5 | 6.3 | 6.0 |
| Supermarket staff | 5.8 | 6.1 | 5.7 | 5.7 |
| Word of mouth (friends/relatives) | 6.2 | 6.5 | 6.2 | 6.0 |
| Blogs/forums on the Internet | 4.6 | 5.5 | 4.8 | 3.5 |

Source: REM Lab, UCSC, 2025

This table highlights clear generational differences in the information sources consumers rely on when choosing food products.

1. **Younger shoppers (18–30) are the most omnichannel.** They consistently score higher across nearly all digital and media-driven sources:
   - social networks (5.8)
   - brand websites (5.7)
   - supermarket websites and apps (6.1)
   - online blogs/forums (5.5)

They also attribute greater importance to traditional media than older groups (TV, newspapers, magazines), suggesting broader media exposure and a more exploratory approach to information.

2. **Middle-aged consumers (31–60) show stable, moderate reliance on all sources.** Scores hover around the total average, indicating a balanced use of digital, in-store, and interpersonal cues. This group mirrors mainstream shopping behaviour.
3. **Older adults (60+) favour in-store and interpersonal information.** Their highest scores cluster around:
    - supermarket shelves (6.8)
    - supermarket flyers (6.7)
    - word of mouth (6.0)
    - product packaging (6.0)
    - staff advice (5.7)

They show significantly lower reliance on:

- social media (3.8)
- brand websites (4.1)
- newspapers/magazines (4.0–4.1)

This indicates that older shoppers prefer tangible, direct, and trusted sources, and remain less influenced by digital channels.

4. **Universal touchpoints.** Across all ages, the most influential information sources are:
    - supermarket shelves (6.8)
    - supermarket flyers (6.7)
    - product packaging (6.3)
    - word of mouth (6.2)

These represent the core high-impact levers for retailers and brands.

## MAIN RESULTS DISCUSSION: CRITICAL GAPS AND PROMISING PRACTICES IN TERMS OF EFFECTIVENESS AND INCLUSIVITY

Examined initiatives *(paragraph 3)* show that Italian grocery retailers are already reading population ageing mainly through the customer lens; the HR/age-management side is less codified and often embedded in generic D&I language. Almost all the large groups (Coop, Conad, Esselunga, Carrefour, Lidl, Aldi, Selex) now position Diversity & Inclusion as a strategic pillar in sustainability reports and HR branding. However, only a minority make age and "senior workers" a visible, dedicated chapter - Coop is the clearest example with explicit "age management & generational turnover". Inter-generational co-existence is usually framed in broad terms - "team diversity", "different backgrounds and ages" - rather than through formal tools (e.g. phased retirement, reverse mentoring). Evidence of structured age-management projects is sporadic and often appears in external case-study reports, not in mainstrcam corporate communication. By contrast, promotions and services for older customers are widespread and very visible in Italian grocery retail. Many chains offer: dedicated "over-60/65 days" with 5-10% off the bill, reduced or free home-delivery for over-70 and/or disabled customers, senior-friendly services (assisted checkout, smaller formats, click-and-collect). In a certyain way, most of the solutions offered today are customer-oriented but essentially tactical rather than strategic - primarily focused on discounts and price reductions. These measures are likely insufficient to grasp the magnitude of the demographic shift in the years ahead, and even less adequate to address the multifaceted needs of this target group today.

On the other side, shopper analysis *(paragraph 4)* suggests that over-65 shoppers demonstrate:

- High loyalty to familiar store formats but growing interest in convenient, smaller-format stores located in neighbourhood settings.
- A cautious but increasing adoption of online grocery shopping, particularly for heavy or bulky items.
- Strong sensitivity to price and promotions, with inflation significantly influencing purchasing patterns.
- An appreciation for clear in-store signage, accessible layouts, and knowledgeable staff interaction.
- A preference for Private Label products when they deliver quality comparable to branded alternatives - especially in categories linked to health and nutrition.

The data also highlight gaps in communication, with many older shoppers perceiving advertising as either irrelevant to their needs or based on outdated stereotypes. At the same time, there are signs of potential cross-generational alignment in certain categories, such as sustainable packaging and local product sourcing, which could serve as unifying themes in intergenerational retail strategies. In the case of loyalty programmes, an excessive focus on reward catalogue items designed for young families renders these collections largely irrelevant to the over-65 segment, who have little interest in products such as bed linen or cookware.

By focusing on Italy, this Chapter provides insights with predictive value for other markets on similar ageing trajectories. The integration of consumer insight, operational adaptation, and inclusive strategy development offers a roadmap for grocery retailers to serve the over-65 market effectively. In doing so, retailers can transform a demographic challenge into a strategic advantage, ensuring that grocery shopping remains a functional necessity, a social connector, and a pleasurable experience for all generations.

## A Research Agenda

To catch this demographic challenge, a new segmentation logic is urgently needed: adults aged 65 and over cannot be treated as a homogeneous block, since their behaviours are profoundly shaped by life events that may or may not occur in the ageing process. Experiences such as widowhood, menopause, the birth of grandchildren, changes in health status, retirement transitions, or shifts in caregiving responsibilities generate distinct emotional, social, and practical needs that directly influence purchasing and consumption patterns. Rather than relying on chronological age alone, companies should adopt a more dynamic, event-based segmentation approach that recognises the heterogeneity of later life. Each of these life-course moments should be assessed-ideally through a positioning map-to evaluate both their relevance in terms of inclusion and their commercial implications. This perspective enables firms to identify high-potential touchpoints (see Table 12), tailor offerings and communication strategies, and design solutions that respond meaningfully to the diverse experiences of older consumers, rather than assuming a monolithic "senior" market.

*Table 12. Life-Event–Based Segmentation of Older Consumers: Impacts on Consumption Behaviour and Retail Responses*

| Key Life Event/ Disruptive Moment | Impact on Purchasing and Consumption Behaviour | Examples of Retail Solutions/Services/Products |
|---|---|---|
| Retirement | More time to evaluate quality/ price ratios; more time to compare offers, including online; increased spending on travel, hobbies, and health. | Loyalty programmes for active seniors; travel and experience packages; hobby and craft product lines; in-store health corners; extended-time services (e.g., early-morning shopping). |
| Children leaving home (empty nest) | Personal care and wellbeing; home renovation or redecoration; reduction in household consumption; more individual desires; interest in pets. | Home makeover services; modular furniture; wellness products; personalised beauty routines; pet-care sections; classes/workshops (cooking, decor, personal development). |
| Own illness or illness of partner | Higher spending on medicines and care; modified diets; interest in accessible housing solutions; telehealth services. | Retail pharmacy integrations; health-food aisles (low-sugar, high-protein, allergen-free); home-care equipment; partnerships with telehealth providers; ergonomic home products. |
| Bereavement (spouse or peers) | Increased sociality/spirituality; new habits; higher use of social media. | Community in-store events; book clubs; gentle fitness classes; guided digital-literacy sessions; products for mindfulness and spiritual wellbeing. |
| Birth of a grandchild | Spending for grandchildren; intergenerational activities; savings and wealth transfer. | Expanded baby/kids sections; grandparent–grandchild experience kits; gift registries; educational toys; financial services or saving plans offered via retail partners. |
| Forced digitalisation | Increase in online shopping; need for simplicity and human support; attention to digital safety. | Senior-friendly e-commerce interfaces; "human helpline" or live chat; step-by-step app tutorials; secure payment options; in-store digital coaching desks. |
| Economic crisis or inflation | Reduction of discretionary spending; search for deals; attention to economic sustainability. | Clear discount architecture; private-label value lines; dynamic promotions; bulk-buy options; sustainability + savings bundles; price-comparison tools. |
| Menopause (and post-menopause) | Purchases for women's health; comfortable clothing; psychological/physical wellbeing. | Menopause-specific product ranges (supplements, skincare); breathable and adaptive clothing; wellbeing and relaxation products; targeted communication avoiding stigma; in-store female-health advisors. |

While segmentation grounded in Customer Management (CM) datasets remains essential for understanding behavioural patterns at scale, companies increasingly need complementary tools to capture the subtle, qualitative nuances that define today's older consumer segments. Transactional data, loyalty programmes, and ICT-based analytics can effectively map purchasing frequency, basket composition, and customer lifetime value. However, these instruments often miss the deeper motivations, emotional drivers, life-event transitions, and identity-related dynamics that shape consumption among adults aged 65 and above. To obtain a more holistic understanding, firms can integrate these traditional data-driven approaches with the construction and discussion of buyer personas, anchored in the use of digital twins-virtual profiles that simulate real consumers' characteristics, behaviours, and decision-making pathways. This hybrid methodology enables retailers and consumer-facing firms to move beyond purely descriptive segmentation and toward a richer, experience-oriented and anticipatory understanding of their senior customer base.

Digital twins, when applied to marketing and consumer research, are virtual representations of specific customer archetypes built from real data-behavioural analytics, demographic variables, feedback loops, and qualitative insights. Unlike static personas, digital twins can be dynamically updated: as new data flows in, their preferences, constraints, and behavioural predictions evolve. This allows companies to test product concepts, store formats, communication styles, and service innovations in a simulated environment, anticipating how different senior subgroups-such as active retirees, caregivers, widowed individuals, or digitally reluctant customers-might respond. In the context of ageing consumers, digital twins are particularly valuable because they incorporate life events (e.g., retirement, illness, becoming a grandparent) that strongly influence purchasing patterns but are not always visible in standard CM data.

The integration of CM analytics and digital twins is further strengthened by generative research, a methodological approach aimed at uncovering latent needs, unarticulated motivations, and deeper cultural meanings that do not emerge through quantitative data alone. Generative research uses tools such as in-depth interviews, co-creation sessions, ethnographic observation, diary studies, and creative tasks to understand how people make sense of their experiences. For older adults, this might involve exploring emotional relationships with food, changes in identity after retirement, or perceived challenges in digital environments. The goal is not merely to validate hypotheses but to generate new insights, inform innovation pipelines, and reveal frictions or desires that traditional data may overlook.

However, this integrated approach also presents limitations. Among its advantages, digital twins offer scalability, predictive value, and the capacity to run scenario-based analyses at low cost. They enable cross-functional teams to visualise and discuss consumer behaviours more concretely, improving alignment between marketing, design, and retail operations. Generative research, meanwhile, brings depth, empathy, and cultural sensitivity, allowing companies to design solutions that resonate with the lived experiences of their senior customers. Yet both approaches require expertise, time, and careful data governance. Digital twins risk oversimplification or bias if the input data lacks diversity or if life events are modelled inaccurately. Generative research, while rich in insight, may be resource-intensive and difficult to generalise across large populations.

Ultimately, the integration of CM datasets, ICT analytics, buyer personas, digital twins, and generative research provides a multi-layered understanding of ageing consumers. It allows companies not only to track what seniors do, but also to grasp why they do it-and how their needs evolve across different phases of later life. This holistic lens is crucial for developing inclusive, responsive, and commercially relevant strategies in a market in which the over-65 population is increasingly heterogeneous and influential.

## CONCLUSION

This Chapter has examined the implications of population ageing for grocery retail, positioning the Italian market as an advanced laboratory for understanding retail dynamics in ageing societies. The findings demonstrate that consumers aged 65 and over represent not only a growing economic force, but also a segment for which grocery shopping retains strong functional, social, and symbolic value. Despite this relevance, retail responses remain largely partial and unbalanced: while customer-oriented initiatives targeting older shoppers are widespread, they are predominantly tactical and price-focused, and insufficiently integrated into broader strategic and organisational frameworks. Age inclusion on the workforce side is even less structured, often embedded in generic DEI narratives rather than articulated through dedicated age-management policies. Empirical evidence highlights that over-65 shoppers are loyal, highly price-conscious, quality-oriented, and particularly receptive to private labels, while valuing staff professionalism, clarity, and store accessibility. These behaviours challenge stereotypical representations of ageing consumers and underscore the heterogeneity of later life. Overall, the Chapter shows that traditional cohort-based segmentation is increasingly inadequate for capturing the complexity of ageing markets. Advancing both theory and practice requires a shift toward more dynamic, life-event-based and inclusion-oriented approaches that align retail marketing mix decisions, workforce strategies, and DEI principles.

By embracing age inclusivity as a strategic asset, grocery retailers can transform demographic change from a structural challenge into a source of long-term competitiveness and social value.

## CONFLICT OF INTEREST

The authors declare that they have no conflicts of interest regarding the publication of this Chapter.

## REFERENCES

Berman, B., Evans, J. R., & Chatterjee, P. M. (2021). *Retail management: A strategic approach* (13th ed.). Pearson.

Bleichrodt, H., & Quiggin, J. (2000). Life-cycle preferences over consumption and health: When is cost-effectiveness analysis equivalent to cost-benefit analysis? *Journal of Health Economics, 18*, 681–708. DOI: 10.1016/S0167-6296(99)00014-4

Cleveland, J. N., & Shore, L. McF. (1992). Self-and Supervisory Perspectives on Age and Work Attitudes and Performance. *The Journal of Applied Psychology, 77*(4), 469–484. DOI: 10.1037//0021-9010.77.4.469

Cole, C., Laurent, G., Drolet, A., Ebert, J., Gutchess, A., Lambert-Pandraud, R., Mullet, E., Norton, M. I., & Peters, E. (2008). Decision making and brand choice by older consumers. *Marketing Letters, 19*, 355–365. DOI: 10.1007/s11002-008-9058-x

Coleman, R., Clarkson, J., & Cassim, J. (2008). *Design for inclusivity: A practical guide to accessible, innovative and user-centred design*. Routledge.

Coughlin, J. F. (2017). *The longevity economy: Unlocking the world's fastest-growing, most misunderstood market*. PublicAffairs.

European Commission. Directorate-General for Communications Networks, Content and Technology, Oxford Economics & Technopolis. (2018). The silver economy: final report. Publications Office. https://data.europa.eu/doi/10.2759/685036

European Commission. (2020). Green paper on ageing: Fostering solidarity and responsibility between generations. Publications Office of the European Union. https://op.europa.eu/en/publication-detail/-/publication/d918b520-63a9-11eb-aeb5-01aa75ed71a1

Hare, C., Kirk, D., & Lang, T. (1999). Identifying the expectations of older food consumers - more than a 'shopping list' of wants. *Journal of Marketing Practice: Applied Marketing Science*, 5 (6/7/8), 213-232. https://doi.org/DOI: 10.1108/EUM0000000004575

Homburg, C., & Giering, A. (2001). Personal Characteristics as Moderators of the Relationship Between Customer Satisfaction and Loyalty – An Empirical Analysis. *Psychology and Marketing, 18*(1), 43–66. DOI: 10.1002/1520-6793(200101)18:1<43:AID-MAR3>3.0.CO;2-I

Hughes G, Bennett KM, Hetherington MM.(2004). Old and alone: barriers to healthy eating in older men living on their own. *Appetite*. Dec;43(3):269-76. doi: DOI: 10.1016/j.appet.2004.06.002

Istat (2025). Demo. https://demo.istat.it/

Katona, G. (1958). Attitude change: Instability of response and acquisition of experience. *Psychological Monographs, 72*(10), 1–38. DOI: 10.1037/h0093789

Kohijoki, A. M. (2011). The effect of aging on consumer disadvantage in grocery retail services among the Finnish elderly. *Journal of Retailing and Consumer Services, 18*(4), 370–377. DOI: 10.1016/j.jretconser.2011.04.0

Kohijoki, A. M., & Marjanen, H. (2013). The effect of age on shopping orientation—Choice orientation types of the ageing shoppers. *Journal of Retailing and Consumer Services, 20*(2), 165–172. DOI: 10.1016/j.jretconser.2012.11.004

Kohlbacher, F., & Herstatt, C. (2008). *The silver market phenomenon: Business opportunities in an era of demographic change*. Springer.

Lambert-Pandraud, R., Laurent, G., & Lapersonne, E. (2005). Repeat Purchasing of New Automobiles by older consumers: Empirical Evidence and Interpretations. *Journal of Marketing, 69*(2), 97–113. DOI: 10.1509/jmkg.69.2.97.60757

Lancaster, L., & Stillman, D. (2002). *When Generations Collide: Who They Are. Why They Clash. How to Solve the Generational Puzzle at Work*. Collins Business.

Leighton, C., & Seaman, C. E. A. (1997). The elderly food consumer: Disadvantaged? *International Journal of Consumer Studies, 21*(4), 363–370. DOI: 10.1111/j.1470-6431.1997.tb00294.x

Lemon, K. N., & Verhoef, P. C. (2016). Understanding Customer Experience Throughout the Customer Journey. *Journal of Marketing, 80*, 69–96. DOI: 10.1509/jm.15.0420

Levy, M., Weitz, B. A., & Grewal, D. (2022). *Retailing management* (11th ed.). McGraw-Hill Education.

Meneely, L., Burns, A., & Strugnell, C. (2009). Age associated changes in older consumers retail behaviour. *International Journal of Retail & Distribution Management, 37*(12), 1041–1056. DOI: 10.1108/09590550911005010

Meneely, L., Strugnell, C., & Burns, A. (2009). Elderly consumers and their food store experiences. *Journal of Retailing and Consumer Services, 16*(6), 458–465. DOI: 10.1016/j.jretconser.2009.06.006

Moschis, G. P. (1994). Consumer Behavior in Later Life: Multidisciplinary Contributions and Implications for Research. *Journal of the Academy of Marketing Science*, *22*(3), 195–204. DOI: 10.1177/0092070394223001

Moschis, G. P. (2007). Life course perspectives on consumer behavior. *Journal of the Academy of Marketing Science*, *35*, 295–307. DOI: 10.1007/s11747-007-0027-3

Moschis, G. P. (2012). Consumer Behavior in Later Life: Current Knowledge, Issues, and New Directions for Research. *Psychology and Marketing*, *39*(2), 57–75. DOI: 10.1002/mar.20504

Moschis, G. P. (2019). *Consumer Behavior over the Life Course – Research Frontiers and New Directions*. Springer Nature Switzerland., DOI: 10.1007/978-3-030-05008-5

Park, N., & Farr, C. (2007). Retail Store Lighting for Elderly Consumers: An Experimental Approach. *Family and Consumer Sciences Research Journal, 35*(4), 316–337. DOI: 10.1177/1077727X07300096

Parment, A. (2013). Generation Y vs. Baby Boomers: Shopping Behavior, Buyer Involvement and Implication for Retailing. *Journal of Retailing and Consumer Services, 20*(2), 189–199. DOI: 10.1016/j.jretconser.2012.12.00

Popper, R., & Kroll, B. (2003). Food Preference and Consumption Among the Elderly. *Food Technology*, •••, 57.

Slama, M. E., & Tashchian, A. (1985). Selected Socioeconomic and Demographic Characteristics Associated with Purchasing Involvement. *Journal of Marketing*, *49*, 72–82. DOI: 10.1177/002224298504900107

Sudbury-Riley. Lynn, A Multivariate Segmentation Model of Senior Consumers (December 3, 2009). *Journal of Consumer Marketing*, 26/4 (2009), 251–262, Available at SSRN: https://ssrn.com/abstract=2362843

Teller, C., & Gittenberger, E. (2011). Patronage behaviour of elderly supermarket shoppers–antecedents and unobserved heterogeneity. *International Review of Retail, Distribution and Consumer Research, 21*(5), 483–499. DOI: 10.1080/09593969.2011.619701

Wilson, L., Alexander, A., & Lumbers, M. (2004). Food Access and Dietary Variety Among Older People. *International Journal of Retail & Distribution Management*, *32*, 109–122. DOI: 10.1108/09590550410521789

Yin, Y., Pei, E., & Ranchhod, A. (2013). The shopping experience of older supermarket consumers. *Journal of Enterprise Information Management*, *26*(4), 444–471. DOI: 10.1108/JEIM-05-2013-0025

Yoon, C., Cole, C. A., & Lee, M. P. (2009). Consumer decision making and aging: Current knowledge and future directions. *Journal of Consumer Psychology*, *19*(1), 2–16. DOI: 10.1016/j.jcps.2008.12.002

## ENDNOTES

1 https://www.coopalleanza3-0.it/cooperativa/sostenibilita/per-persone/diversita-inclusione-pari-opportunita.html

2 https://www.corriere.it/cook/news/25_giugno_15/supermercati-le-agevolazioni-e-gli-sconti-riservati-dalle-diverse-catene-a-pensionati-disoccupati-e-disabili-b1735391-884d-4213-b0ab-5053d5a1dxlk.shtml

3 https://chisiamo.conad.it/assets/documents/Bilancio%20Sociale%20Conad%20Centro%20Nord%202022.pdf?_u=7c5b84ea7ba5e9479fa082a44774ec1ad3fcbf52&

4 https://www.rivistaimpresasociale.it/rivista/articolo/pratiche-di-age-management-nella-cooperazione-sociale

5 https://www.esselunga.it/media/investor-relations/financial-information/2025/bilancio-consolidato-31-12-2024-ita.pdf

6 https://www.pensionati.cisl.it/public/pdf/pdf_7716_Guida%20al%20risparmio.pdf

7 https://www.bilanciosostenibilitagrupposelex.it/download/Selex-BS2022.pdf

8 https://images.selex-insegne.stormreply.com/mediaObject/superemme/pan/bilanciosostenibilita24/Pan_BdS_2024_WEB/original/Pan_BdS_2024_WEB.pdf

9 https://carriera.aldi.it/informazioni/la-diversita-come-forza

10 https://lavoro.lidl.it/old_perche-lavorare-in-lidl/cosa-offriamo/diversity-inclusion/insieme-in-lidl-statement

11 https://lavoro.lidl.it/lavoro-formazione/neodiplomati/lidl-2-your-career

[12] https://www.hr-link.it/politiche-attive-e-people-analytics-imprese-e-pa-insieme-per-lemployability

[13] https://www.carrefour.com/sites/default/files/2025-04/CFR_URD_2024_EN_250328_MEL.pdf

[14] https://www.money.it/pensioni-sconti-chi-fa-spesa-questi-supermercati-quali-giorni

[15] https://www.donnedelretail.it/eventi/empowerment-femminile-conoscere-i-propri-diritti-e-guidare-il-cambiamento

[16] https://www.unes.it/it

# Chapter 9
# Exploring the Silver Economy:
## Public Finance Sustainability Using a Mathematical Model and Proof

**Öner Gümüş**
https://orcid.org/0000-0002-3231-3293
*Kutahya Dumlupinar University, Turkey*

## ABSTRACT

*This study aims to analyze the effects of the increasingly visible demographic transformation in the 21st century on Turkey's public finances in terms of the silver economy and uses deterministic dynamic modeling to analyze the dynamic relationships between public revenues, public expenditures, nominal interest rates, and public debt stock. The findings reveal that the silver economy has a double impact on public finance. On the one hand, the aging population creates budgetary pressure by increasing health care and pension expenditures. On the other hand, the elderly population's consumption potential, saving tendencies, and demand for new sectors may contribute to economic vitality. This dual effect makes the silver economy a strategic area not only for social policy but also for fiscal policy.*

## INTRODUCTION

A key demographic shift in the 21st century is the aging of people worldwide. This movement is indicated by the increase in life expectancy and decrease in fertility rates, leading to a higher number of older individuals in most countries. High-income countries are the epicenter of this trend, but it has gradually extended to low- and middle-income countries. 80% of older adults worldwide are predicted to live in

DOI: 10.4018/979-8-3373-6117-8.ch009

less affluent areas by 2050 (The Lancet Healthy Longevity, 2021, April; Hong et al., 2023; Bloom et al., 2015a; Harper, 2014; Fang et al., 2020). Economic growth, labor markets, social security, and health systems will all be significantly impacted by this shift (Bloom et al., 2015b; Harper, 2014; Bloom et al., 2010; Maestas et al., 2023). One area where these findings are evident is public finance.

One of the major changes that modern public finance must confront is an aging population. People are also living longer, and the working-age population is shrinking, as fertility rates remain low for an extended period of time. All of these have lasting consequences for the budget's bottom line. This demographic transformation, the so-called silver economy, poses new mathematical limits not only for social security systems, health expenditures, and care services, but also for budget sustainability and fiscal stability. In such an environment, determining which combinations of revenue and expenditure growth rates are necessary to maintain fiscal balance is possible not only by observing past trends but also through a formal proof framework. This study aims to develop a model that mathematically analyzes budget sustainability, which can be calibrated using hypothetical parameters when data is unavailable and with real statistics when data is available.

This study makes an original contribution to the silver economy literature by providing a closed-form mathematical proof of financial sustainability thresholds under demographic pressure, an approach that is rarely applied in existing research. While most studies on the silver economy focus on sectoral analyses, market dynamics, or qualitative policy debates, this study identifies the necessary and sufficient conditions for long-term fiscal balance through deterministic dynamic modelling. The model specifically captures how demographic aging directly affects two key parameters: the expenditure-growth ratio (g_E) and the revenue-growth ratio (g_R). On the expenditure side, an aging population increases g_E by raising mandatory expenditures such as pensions, healthcare, and long-term care services. On the revenue side, the shrinking working-age population is reducing the tax base and limiting g_R by restricting revenue tax collection. The interaction between these two dynamics, combined with the nominal interest rate (i), determines whether public debt will converge towards a stable level or grow unsustainably. By generating open thresholds (g_R ≥ g_E for sustainability; g_R > i for stability), this study provides policymakers with a quantitative framework for assessing fiscal trajectories and designing targeted interventions. This formal modelling approach distinguishes the study from descriptive and empirical studies in the literature and provides a tool that is applicable and replicable in different national contexts.

The conventional debt sustainability analyses employed by organizations like the IMF and the World Bank, which are mostly predicated on forecasts of the debt-to-GDP ratio and fiscal balance objectives, are essentially different from this modeling framework. Conventional debt sustainability analyses use scenario-based stress tests and financial rules that look backward to evaluate sustainability. However, they do not derive analytically clear growth rate thresholds that directly link demographic aging to fiscal balance conditions. Nevertheless, this study demonstrates the two demographic mechanisms of the silver economy by presenting the necessary and sufficient mathematical conditions as follows: On the expenditure side, aging directly increases the silver economy by raising compulsory expenditures; on the revenue side, the shrinking working-age population erodes the tax base, thereby constraining the silver economy. By formulating these demographic-fiscal linkages within a deterministic dynamic framework, the model provides a closed-form analytical solution that definitively identifies which combinations of income and expenditure growth rates ensure long-term fiscal balance and which inevitably lead to unsustainable debt accumulation. In the silver economy literature, where fiscal sustainability is usually discussed qualitatively rather than through formal mathematical proof, the integration of demographic economics with public finance theory through open-threshold derivation represents a conceptual advance beyond descriptive analysis and closes a significant gap.

In this model, the public budget is a system that changes over time. Three key variables are defined: public revenues R(t), public expenditures E(t), and public debt stock D(t). On the revenue side, the tax base depends heavily on the proportion of the working-age population; the lower this proportion, the lower the potential for revenue growth. On the expenditure side, the increase in the elderly population increases the growth rate of mandatory items such as health care, pension payments, and long-term care expenses. An important assumption here is that spending growth is fueled not only by price inflation but also by demographic pressures. In a simple formulation, the expenditure function is defined as $E(t)=E_0e^{gEt}$ and the revenue function as $R(t)=R_0e^{gRt}$, where gE represents the expenditure growth rate and gR represents the revenue growth rate.

A differential equation shows how the amount of debt changes over time:

$$\frac{\partial D}{\partial t} = E(t) - R(t) + iD(t) \tag{1}$$

The letter ‘i’ in this equation stands for the nominal interest rate. This equation shows that the budget deficit (E-R) is added directly to the debt stock, which shows how much interest is owed on existing debt.

The theorem’s proof also depends on the budget balance’s sign and the growth rates’ difference. One possibility is that the budget is in surplus, and debt dynamics are unit-root-like rather than explosive; if R(t)-E(t)>0, then output growth suffices to ensure that government debt grows only at the interest rate. If R(t)-E(t)<0, there is a deficit, and debt goes up because of both interest and the deficit. In the initial scenario, gR is present. This condition leads to unlimited growth in the debt stock.

In the second case, when gR=gE, revenues and expenditures grow at the same rate; in this case the debt ratio depends on the interest rate. If gR>I, the debt ratio stabilizes; otherwise, it increases. In the third case, when gR>gE, the deficit decreases over time and may even be in surplus. In this scenario, the debt stock converges to an upper bounded value. Consequently, the necessary and sufficient condition for sustainability is gR>gE, and for stability, gR>i.

This approach can be applied both when data is unavailable and when data is available. When data is unavailable, parameters are taken from the literature or policy objectives. For instance, let's assume that the contribution of the elderly population to expenditure growth is 2% and the overall growth rate of other items is 1%. In this case gE=0.03 can be taken. If the revenue growth rate targeted by reforms to broaden the tax base is 3,5%, gR=0.035. In this scenario, the condition that the revenue growth rate (gR) is greater than the economic growth rate (gE) is satisfied, and the model predicts that the debt ratio will converge to a constant value over time. Such an analysis allows for rapid policy simulation for data-poor countries.

Parameters are calculated directly when data is available. For instance, the growth rate of health and social security expenditures for the last ten years can be determined as gE from OECD or TurkStat data. The average rate of increase in tax revenues is taken as gR. Suppose gR=0.028 and gR=0.025. In this situation, because gR is less than gE, the debt ratio is expected to rise over the long term. This sends a clear policy signal to either accelerate revenue growth or restrain expenditure growth.

This model provides clear guidance for policy implementation. Gradually raising the retirement age would increase the working-age population, raising the revenue growth rate. Technological investments and digitalization that increase efficiency in health reduce treatment costs and lower gE. Expanding the tax base, reducing the size of the informal economy, or structurally adjusting consumption taxes directly affects revenue growth. The model can be used to predict the long-term effects of such policy interventions on the fiscal balance.

The mathematical framework's strength is that it presents policymakers clear rules to follow. The model shows precisely which combinations of revenue and expenditure growth rates make fiscal balance sustainable and which will inevitably increase the debt ratio. Thus, macroeconomic decisions can be handled within measurable limits, rather than randomly. In addition, the flexible nature of the model facilitates its adaptation to different countries, regions, or local governments.

As a result, the sustainability of public finance under silver economy conditions can be assured not only by extrapolating from historical data but also by establishing mathematically necessary conditions. The model presented here can be applied with or without data, can be recalibrated as parameters change, and is a reliable tool to anticipate the fiscal consequences of different policy scenarios. This approach provides a scientific, repeatable, and robust basis for maintaining fiscal stability.

The Turkish Lira (TL) was used as the currency in the study. This is because public revenues, public expenditures, debt stock, and interest rates are officially published in TL. The conversion of TL into foreign currency would have included exchange rate volatility in the analysis, overshadowing the main focus on fiscal dynamics. Moreover, since fiscal policy implementations in Turkey are made in TL, the national currency is preferred in order for the findings to be meaningful for policymakers.

There are three reasons for the selection of Turkey in the study: the first reason is the availability of long-term, reliable data; the second reason is that Turkey is undergoing a rapid aging process and feeling the effects of the silver economy intensely; and the third reason is that the main purpose of the study is to test the model. Although the choice of a single country is a methodological limitation, this study provides a strong basis for future comparative research.

Although the model used in the study works even without data, Turkey's 2006-2024 data was obtained from the official website of the Republic of Turkey's Ministry of Treasury and Finance. Since 2006, Turkey's public finance data, including revenues, expenditures, debt stock, and interest rates, has been regularly released in accordance with international standards. Furthermore, the model could be tested in a variety of scenarios because the 2006-2024 timeframe encompassed a range of economic events, including the global financial crisis of 2008, currency shocks, and pandemics. As a result, the chosen time frame offers a suitable framework for methodology, policy, and data reliability. In this context, the data are applied to the model, and the findings are interpreted in the discussion section. Afterwards, recommendations are made according to the findings, and the study is concluded by emphasizing the managerial, practical, and theoretical implications.

The data used in this study are available within the article. There is no conflict of interest between the authors of the study. This study did not receive any external funding. The study does not require ethical approval, as it does not involve any work with human or animal subjects. This article has been proofread and linguistically edited using GenAI tools to improve grammar and fluency. No part of the article, including data analysis, interpretations, or conclusions, was generated by AI tools. The author takes full responsibility for the content of this publication.

## LITERATURE REVIEW

The silver economy refers to economic activities and opportunities arising from an aging population, usually focused on people aged 50 or 55 and over. As populations worldwide age, this sector is growing rapidly and influencing markets, public policies, and technological innovation. The silver economy includes a wide range of goods and services for older people, such as healthcare, financial management, smart products, tourism, and housing. Peru, China, Japan, South Korea, and many countries in Europe are actively developing strategies to capitalize on the economic potential of their aging populations, with various levels of progress and focus areas (Ramos, 2024; Griva et al., 2024; Guo et al., 2023; Gschwendtner, 2020). Technological advances, in particular AI-enabled financial management, smart home products, telemedicine, and digital platforms, play a central role in supporting the independence, health, and economic participation of older people. In addition, the entrepreneurship of older individuals is increasingly recognized. This phenomenon includes support for older entrepreneurs and digital business models that enable older people to remain active in the labor force (Wang, 2025; Caridà et al., 2022; Kamberidou, 2020; Gschwendtner, 2020). Governments have put policies in place to encourage the silver economy, including retirement community support, tax breaks, and subsidies. There are still issues, though, like disparities between rural and urban areas, inadequate pension savings, and the possibility of social exclusion or unsustainable development particularly in rural areas (Ramos, 2024; Guo et al., 2023; Krzyminiewska, 2019; Wierzbicka & Farelnik, 2024; Gschwendtner, 2020). Additionally stressed are ethical issues like privacy and nondiscrimination (Griva et al., 2024; Caridà et al., 2022). A dynamic, multidisciplinary field, the silver economy is influenced by policies, innovation, and changing demographics. There are a lot of chances for social inclusion and economic growth as the silver economy expands. Coordinated strategies are necessary to overcome the obstacles and guarantee fair and long-lasting benefits for aging populations.

The silver economy has been the subject of numerous studies, each with its own methodology, conclusions, and outcomes. These studies are summarized in Table 1.

*Table 1. A literature review of studies that have focused on silver economy*

| References | Methods | Results | Outcomes |
|---|---|---|---|
| Klimczuk (2016) | Model development and comparative analysis | Typology of silver economy models | A new typology of silver economy models in the European Union was proposed using the active aging index |
| Álvarez-Diez et al. (2023) | Bibliometric analysis and literature mapping | Coherence between the silver economy and disruptive technologies | The Silver Economy, driven by demographic changes, is a growing field of knowledge, with key themes, agents, and countries identified using SciMAT-based tools and techniques. |
| Krzyminiewska (2020) | Comprehensive review | There isn't enough discussion of ethical issues in the silver economy, which could lead to a lower quality of life for older people. | Ethical concerns in the silver economy and the quality of life for seniors |
| Wu et al. (2025) | Study of market analysis and consumer behavior | The silver economy market is growing quickly, and older customers are becoming more loyal to brands and paying more attention to quality. | Patterns of consumption, market size and growth trends, industry diversification, brand loyalty, and preferences for quality and safety |
| Shestakova et al. (2022) | Surveying and analyzing data | There aren't many specialized products for seniors available, and people don't know about them. | Awareness of silver economy products, availability of specialized products for the elderly, localization of silver economy production |
| Wang et al. (2022) | Epidemiological examination | The aging population caused a net 7.86% change in the way people spend their money. | Improving the structure of consumption |
| An et al. (2024) | Using Structural Equation Modelling for surveys and data analysis | The most important factor in deciding to use digital public services was how useful they seemed. | Subjective well-being, anxiety about technology, self-efficacy, perceived usefulness, and the desire to use digital public services |
| Csoba & Ladancsik (2022) | Surveying and analyzing data | Only 2.7% of people over 65 work for pay, but 68.7% do unpaid work to save money. | Labor market participation, informal work activities, willingness to work, barriers to employment |
| Palomino et al. (2022 | Focus group study with machine learning data analysis | Depression, sadness, and anger were the most prominent moods identified by the classifier | Depression, sadness, anger |
| Liu et al. (2025) | Model development and evaluation using expert consensus methods | Service resources and smart technology infrastructure were identified as the most crucial quality indicators | Quality of smart elderly care services |

continued on following page

*Table 1. Continued*

| References | Methods | Results | Outcomes |
|---|---|---|---|
| Roszkowska (2020) | Data analysis and measure development study | Poland's regions show significant differences in elderly age structure | Similarity of elderly population age structures across regions |
| Smith (2021) | Qualitative study with interviews and observations | Older adults aged 75+ use technology for diverse purposes but face physical, cognitive, and conceptual barriers | Technology use patterns, needs, and challenges among older adults |
| Demirbilek & Öktem Özgür (2017) | Content analysis | Elderly poverty is increasing in developing countries / elderly unemployment rates are increasing | Providing employment opportunities for the elderly who want to work according to their qualifications and supporting the elderly to stay in working life as much as possible |

Source: (Table by author).

The existing literature mostly analyzes the silver economy at the sectoral/representative level. Most of the studies present results based on bibliometric mapping, market analysis, ethical/strategic discussions, or surveys. However, a closed-form equilibrium conditional analysis of the debt dynamics of the public budget is not available in the literature. This study closes this gap by linking the revenue-expenditure pressure created by the silver economy to budget sustainability in a dynamic modeling-based framework.

The study will demonstrate the necessary and sufficient conditions for sustainability and stability, with a focus on dynamic modelling. This provides a theoretical contribution that distinguishes this study from the descriptive/empirical works in the literature. In other words, the study answers the question of which growth combinations will make the fiscal balance sustainable for the silver economy with proven thresholds.

The model used in this study can be run with a parametric scenario if no data are available and with calibration if data are available. This flexibility provides a practical methodological advantage over the data dependency of most literature.

This study compares the closed form of the model with Turkey's real revenue-expenditure-debt-interest series, providing a macro-fiscal application that is rare in the silver economics literature.

The model quantitatively illustrates how policy actions affect $g_R$ and $g_E$ on the debt path. Therefore, the study supplements the qualitative policy recommendations in the literature with a quantitative threshold.

Underlining that revenue/expenditure is flow and debt is stock will eliminate measurement error/interpretation confusion, and unit standardization will increase the comparability of results.

In this context, the following hypotheses will be tested in this study:

**$H_1$:** Public expenditure growth will exceed public revenue growth in the long term due to demographic pressures created by the shadow economy in Turkey (gE > gR).
**$H_2$:** Public revenue growth will remain above the nominal interest rate to ensure debt stability (gR > i).
**$H_3$:** If the sustainability condition (gR ≥ gE) is not met, the debt stock will show an upward trend in the long term.
**$H_4$:** A small increase in public revenue growth (gR) or a small decrease in public expenditure growth (gE) will cause significant changes in the debt stock trajectory.
**$H_5$:** The pressure on health, pension and care expenditure created by the silver economy will systematically increase the expenditure growth rate (gE).
**$H_6$:** The deviation between model estimates calculated using fixed average parameters and the actual debt stock will not undermine the purpose of testing the model's sustainability conditions.

Within the scope of these hypotheses, the study will try to answer the following questions:

- Are public revenues sufficient to cover public expenditures in Turkey?
- Is debt dynamics a threat under interest burden in the comparison of the growth rate of public revenues and nominal interest rate in Turkey?
- How does the growth difference between public revenues and public expenditures determine the long-run trend of debt stock in Turkey?
- How would debt sustainability in Turkey be affected if public revenues were increased or public expenditures were reduced?
- What is the impact of an aging population on health, care, and pension expenditure?
- What are the reasons for the deviation of the debt stock to be estimated with fixed average parameters from the actual debt stock?

## METHODOLOGY

Deterministic dynamical modeling is a fundamental approach in systems science, engineering, and applied mathematics that focuses on systems whose future states are completely determined by current conditions and governing equations, typically differential or difference equations.

Deterministic dynamical models usually use state variables and parameters to describe system evolution over time through ordinary differential equations (ODEs) or discrete-time updates.

Deterministic dynamic modeling is a key part of both economic theory and practice. It gives us structured ways to look at and predict how economic systems will change over time. These models presume that the future states of the system are entirely dictated by present conditions and model parameters, devoid of stochastic disturbances, rendering them especially valuable for comprehending economic stability, cycles, and policy ramifications. Deterministic models are often used to study the economy as a whole, plan production, and model financial markets. They yield clear and predictable outcomes in stable conditions, rendering them advantageous for long-term planning and policy assessment. Deterministic models have been utilized in macroeconomic systems to investigate intricate phenomena such as chaos and bifurcation, demonstrating that even straightforward economic principles can yield unpredictable, non-periodic dynamics at specific parameter values (Stutzer, 1980; Sterman, 1989; Ashley & Patterson, 1989). Deterministic multi-period models assist in optimizing scheduling and costs in production and inventory management, particularly when demand and costs are predetermined (Zangwill, 1966). Deterministic dynamic modeling is employed in this study for the silver economy.

This study seeks to examine a particular phenomenon associated with public finance via mathematical proof. The method is based on a theoretical framework that uses inductive and deductive techniques together. Firstly, basic economic/fiscal indicators and related variables in the literature will be defined, and the relationships between these variables will be formulated mathematically. If the data set is available, real data will be used; in the absence of data, synthetic data will be generated to represent the characteristics of the parameters. Synthetic data will be used to test the logical and theoretical consistency of the model. The aim here is to prove the logic and mathematical validity of the model rather than the data.

The model is based on the following fundamental assumptions:

- Public revenues and public expenditures exhibit exponential growth: $R(t) = R_0 e^{g_R t}$ and $E(t) = E_0 e^{g_E t}$. This formulation assumes that revenues and expenditures increase at constant and steady growth rates.
- The nominal interest rate (i) is assumed to be fixed throughout the modelling period. This assumption allows us to focus on long-term structural relationships by excluding the short-term effects of interest rate fluctuations.
- Expenditure growth (gE) stems not only from price inflation but also from demographic pressures. In particular, the increase in the elderly population

is driving up the growth rate of mandatory expenditure items such as healthcare, pension payments and long-term care.

- Revenue growth (gR) is largely dependent on the size of the working-age population and the breadth of the tax base. The decline in the working-age population limits the growth potential of tax revenues.
- Debt dynamics are determined as the direct sum of the budget deficit (E-R) and interest payments accrued on the current debt stock (iD): $dD/dt = E(t) - R(t) + iD(t)$.

These assumptions represent the demographic and financial mechanisms necessary for the model to capture the effects of the silver economy on fiscal sustainability.

The use of fixed average parameters over an 18-year period is a purposeful methodological choice based on long-term fiscal sustainability analysis. This approach aligns with the body of research on demographic fiscal pressures and prioritizes structural trends over cyclical volatility (Bloom et al., 2015; Maestas et al., 2023). By averaging growth rates over about 20 years, the model distinguishes between temporary macroeconomic fluctuations and the long-term demographic pressures of the silver economy. Accounting for changes in annual growth rates brought on by business cycles, financial crises, or policy shocks reveals the underlying long-term trajectory of fiscal balance. Alternative approaches that employ time-varying parameters or stochastic simulations shift the analytical focus from determining mathematical sustainability thresholds to predicting specific debt levels, which is a different research objective outside the scope of this study. Both the applicability of the policy and the availability of the data affect the decision to use nominal variables. Turkish public finance statistics are officially published in nominal Turkish lira, and inflation effects are symmetrically embedded in both gR and gE. The situation in question limits the effects on the relative growth differential (gR-gE), which is a critical determinant of sustainability. Conversion to real variables introduces additional assumptions regarding deflator selection and complicates direct comparability with official fiscal reports used by policymakers.

In the process of constructing the model, firstly the dependent and independent variables and the functional relationships between them will be defined. Algebraic expressions, inequalities, and limit cases will then be used to demonstrate the interactions between variables. The aim of this process is to demonstrate, both analytically and through logical deductions, how the selected financial phenomenon behaves under certain economic assumptions. In mathematical proof, we first make the necessary definitions and assumptions, then we put forward the propositions, and finally we prove the theorem. The results will be assessed from both theoretical and practical perspectives. This method aims to establish causal relationships through the principles of formal logic and mathematical rigor, in contrast to conventional statistical correlation or regression analyses. Thus, some hypotheses, which are usually discussed in the field of public finance based on observation, will be directly tested with logical and mathematical tools.

## RESULTS

Since public revenues, public expenditures, nominal interest rates, and debt stock will be discussed in terms of the silver economy in this study, these data were obtained from the Republic of Turkey Ministry of Treasury and Finance. These data are given in Table 2.

*Table 2. Data on public revenues (in million TL), public expenditures (in million TL), nominal interest rate and debt stock in Turkey*

| | Public Revenues (million TL) | Public Expenditures (million TL) | Nominal Interest Rate | Debt Stock (million TL) |
|---|---|---|---|---|
| **2006** | 196884.045 | 178126.033 | %18,12 | 345.502 |
| **2007** | 218592.972 | 204067.683 | %18,01 | 333.862 |
| **2008** | 245448.402 | 227030.562 | %19,19 | 380.830 |
| **2009** | 260645.106 | 268219.185 | %12,81 | 442.049 |
| **2010** | 321571.293 | 294358.724 | %8,49 | 474.146 |
| **2011** | 387208.286 | 314606.792 | %8,62 | 519.070 |
| **2012** | 460968.248 | 361886.686 | %8,75 | 532.901 |
| **2013** | 535088.806 | 408224.560 | %7,88 | 586.193 |
| **2014** | 593732.671 | 448752.337 | %9,62 | 612.517 |
| **2015** | 687385.872 | 506305.093 | %9,17 | 678.246 |
| **2016** | 829919.425 | 584071.431 | %9,95 | 759.952 |
| **2017** | 933141.327 | 678269.193 | %11,03 | 876.494 |
| **2018** | 1142422.362 | 830809.401 | %16,06 | 1.067.115 |
| **2019** | 1321751.406 | 1000026.856 | %15,88 | 1.329.054 |
| **2020** | 1575451.503 | 1203737.135 | %8,82 | 1.812.849 |
| **2021** | 2128400.057 | 1603545.136 | %14,64 | 2.747.828 |
| **2022** | 3855705.088 | 2942747.715 | %16,96 | 4.035.455 |
| **2023** | 6773142.048 | 6588015.612 | %20,77 | 6.736.632 |
| **2024** | 10718615.729 | 10780614.067 | %38,61 | 9.257.422 |

Source: Turkey Republic Ministry of Treasury and Finance, 2025.

Budget equilibrium is the positive or negative difference between the revenues and expenditures of the government for a year. It is mathematically formulated as follows:

$$Equilibrium_t = R_t - E_t \quad (2)$$

If $R_t > E_t$, it means that there is a budget surplus. If $R_t < E_t$, it means that there is a budget deficit. Analysis of the state budget from 2006 to 2024 shows a tendency toward surplus. In 2009 and 2024, there is a deficit in the budget, while in other years, the budget equilibrium is positive. Considering the fact that the years with positive state budgets are long-term, it would be correct to argue that a general discipline prevails in public finance. In 2009, it is possible to argue that the deficit emerged due to the global financial crisis. In this period, the slow increase in public revenues and the high level of transfer items in expenditures had a negative impact on the budget balance. Consequently, a budget deficit of 7.6 billion TL emerged. Since 2011, a significant increase in revenues has been observed, and the budget surplus has increased steadily. Particularly noteworthy are the increases in budget surpluses of approximately 525 and 913 billion TL in 2021 and 2022, respectively. These increases in budget surpluses prove that both revenue performance and expenditures have improved and are relatively under control, and these years can be considered the strongest examples of budget discipline. The year 2024 closed with a small deficit of approximately 62 billion TL. The convergence of revenues and expenditures explains this small difference. This situation shows that there is still discipline in public finance, but the pressure on expenditures has increased.

After the budget deficits are calculated, it is necessary to calculate the annual nominal growth rates of public revenues and public expenditures. The purpose of this calculation is to measure how public revenue and public expenditure series grow from year to year. Table 3 summarizes the period, 2006-2024, in one go. In other words, instead of the individual growth rates of each year, they are averaged to determine the average logarithmic growth rate and its equivalent compound annual growth rate, which is a more understandable form. Therefore, Table 3 shows the long-run overall growth trend with a single figure. Table 6 answers the question of what the average trend is in the long run.

*Table 3. Summary (Average Log and Equivalent Compound Growth)*

| Indicator | Value | Explanation |
|---|---|---|
| **Average logarithmic growth (revenue)** | 0.22206235250820366 | g_= mean [ln(R_t/R_{t-1})] |
| **Average logarithmic growth (expenditure)** | 0.22794519200443786 | g_= mean [ln(E_t/E_{t-1})] |
| **Equivalent compound growth (revenue)** | 0.24864923184853494 | exp(g_) - 1 |
| **Equivalent compound growth (expenditure)** | 0.25601648379995545 | exp(g_) -1 |

In Table 3, two different but consistent methods are used. One of them is logarithmic growth (equation 3), and the other is arithmetic percentage growth (equation

4). The logarithmic difference is fully consistent with the exponential structure of the model and is a summable rate definition for the long run. The arithmetic percentage provides the reader with understandable language. The use of both methods preserves theoretical accuracy and readability.

$$g_R(t) = \ln\left(\frac{Rt}{Rt-1}\right), \quad g_E(t) = \ln\left(\frac{Et}{Et-1}\right) \tag{3}$$

$$\%\Delta R_t = \left(\frac{Rt}{Rt-1} - 1\right) \times 100, \quad \%\Delta E_t = \left(\frac{Et}{Et-1} - 1\right) \times 100 \tag{4}$$

Table 3 shows that the average logarithmic growth of revenues is approximately 22.2%, while the average logarithmic growth of expenditures is 22.7%. According to this value, expenditures exceed revenues to a limited extent. In the 2006-2024 period, the equivalent compound nominal growth rate of revenues is 24.8%, while expenditures have a slightly higher rate of 25.6%. Therefore, despite the closeness of the values, we observe a slight acceleration in expenditures.

Following this process, we will subject these average growth rates and nominal interest rate series to sustainability and stability tests. Additionally, we will employ the debt equation to create a straightforward projection.

Table 4 showcases the sustainability and stability tests, displaying the averages of public revenues, public expenditures, and nominal interest rates.

*Table 4. Tests of Sustainability and Stability (Summary)*

| Condition | Result | | | |
|---|---|---|---|---|
| Sustainability ($g_R \geq g_E$) | False | 0.22206235250820366 | 0.2279451920043778 | 0.14388421052631578 |
| Stability ($g_R > i$) | True | 0.22206235250820366 | 0.2279451920043778 | 0.14388421052631578 |

Table 4 shows that the average logarithmic growth of public revenues () is approximately 22.2%, the average logarithmic growth of public expenditures () is approximately 22.8%, and the average nominal interest rate () is approximately 14.4%. The sustainability condition is $g_R \geq g_E$. However, since 22.2%<22.8%, the condition of the sustainability test cannot be met. This situation indicates that in the long run, revenues may be insufficient to cover public expenditures, and debt pressure may arise.

In the stability test, the condition is $g_R > i$. Since 22.2% exceeds 14.4%, the stability test's condition is satisfied. This data proves that interest alone does not constitute a negative situation for public finance since the growth in public revenues is faster than the interest cost.

## DISCUSSION

The first finding of the study indicates that the growth rate of public revenues (22.2%) is below the growth rate of public expenditures (22.8%). This situation reveals that the sustainability condition of $g_R \geq g_E$ inequality is not satisfied. Although the difference may seem mathematically small, in the long run, it has critical importance in determining the direction of the debt stock. The main emphasis of the silver economy in the literature is that health, social security, and care expenditures will increase rapidly due to the aging population. The results of this study confirm the theoretical expectations expressed in the literature using data from Turkey. In other words, the expenditure pressure brought about by the elderly population exceeds the increase in revenue, making sustainability in public finance difficult. Therefore, the sustainability problem is not only a matter of fiscal discipline but also a natural consequence of the demographic transformation.

The second finding of the study is that the growth rate of public revenues (22.2%) is higher than the average nominal interest rate (14.4%). This indicates that the debt dynamics are stable against interest rate pressure. In other words, while interest rates accelerate the increase in debt, the faster growth of revenues compared to interest rates prevents the debt from becoming completely threatening. This result is in line with many studies in the literature, especially the findings that financial crises are usually caused by revenue-expenditure imbalances rather than interest rate pressures. In the case of Turkey, high interest rates alone do not pose a threat. The main problem is the inability of revenues to cover expenditure increases. This finding emphasizes the following point for policymakers: Interest rate control affects debt dynamics, but the main factor ensuring sustainability should be the balance between revenue and expenditure. In this case, the silver economy constitutes an obstacle to the sustainability of public finance for Turkey.

The model demonstrates that as long as expenditure growth remains higher than revenue growth, the debt stock will tend to increase in the long term. This situation is directly in line with the findings in the literature that the aging population will burden public finances. Extraordinary developments such as the currency crisis after 2018 and the 2020 pandemic caused significant fiscal pressures, confirming the model's sustainability predictions. In other words, Turkey's debt stock dynamics concretely reflect the pressure of the silver economy on public expenditures.

One of the most striking findings of the study is that a small increase in revenue growth or a small decrease in expenditure growth would be sufficient to fulfill the sustainability condition. This finding provides a critical roadmap for policymakers. Policy recommendations frequently mentioned in the literature (widening the tax base, combating informality, reforms to increase efficiency in health and care services, etc.) are verified with the threshold values of the mathematical model.

Essentially, these proposals are not just theoretical discussions but rather tangible policy instruments that can undergo testing against specific thresholds. This study's contribution is to show mathematically what size of intervention would be sufficient for the recommendations in the literature.

The aging population increases expenditure on health, care, and pensions, which are at the center of the silver economy. The findings demonstrate the presence of this pressure in Turkey. The convergence of public revenues and public expenditures in the 2023-2024 period is one of the most concrete indicators of this trend. The literature primarily discusses the silver economy in terms of new market opportunities and the consumption power of the elderly population. This study shows the burden of the silver economy on public finance from a different perspective. While the consumer potential of the elderly population has positive reflections on the economy, it makes sustainability difficult in terms of public finance, especially social security and health expenditures. This dual effect makes the silver economy a source of both opportunity and risk.

The results of this study largely confirm the general expectations in the literature on the effects of the silver economy on public finance. The growth in revenues is sufficient to cover the interest burden, but the increase in expenditures faster than revenues weakens sustainability. The long-term trend of the debt stock has a significant impact on even seemingly small differences. Even a small-scale policy implementation can have major impacts. For instance, a 2% or 3% expansion of the tax base or a similar reduction in health/care expenditure could strengthen sustainability. However, as the demographic pressure of the silver economy continues, structural reforms are inevitable in the long run.

Beyond Turkey, these findings have broader implications for aging economies worldwide. For example, countries such as South Korea, Thailand, Poland, and Chile face comparable fiscal pressures. The model's explicit thresholds ($gR \geq gE$ for sustainability; $gR > i$ for stability) provide a repeatable analytical framework that can be adapted to country-specific data or applied in contexts with weak data access using parametric scenarios. This methodological flexibility makes the framework valuable for international comparative research and policy benchmarking in the field of the silver economy.

In line with these explanations and calculations, it is possible to emphasize the following points regarding the acceptance or rejection of the hypotheses:

- Although revenues are increasing in Turkey, expenditures are growing slightly faster. This proves that the sustainability condition is not satisfied. Therefore, hypothesis $H_1$ is accepted.

- Since the growth in public revenues is higher than the growth in interest rates, the debt dynamics are stable against interest rate pressure, which means that interest rates alone cannot be a threat. Therefore, hypothesis $H_2$ is accepted.
- Since the growth in public expenditures exceeds the growth in public revenues, the upward trend of debt stock is confirmed in the model. Therefore, hypothesis $H_3$ is accepted.
- We accept hypothesis $H_4$ because we see that even small adjustments in the model ensure sustainability.
- Since the findings show that the silver economy puts pressure on health and pension expenditures in particular, hypothesis $H_5$ is also accepted.
- The 2018 currency shock, the 2020 pandemic, and the 2021-2023 fiscal expansions explain the differences in the model. Therefore, hypothesis $H_6$ is also accepted.

The acceptance of all hypotheses shows that the theoretical claims in the study are supported by the data. As a result, the study aligns with the expectations in the literature and has undergone numerical testing specifically for Turkey.

## CONCLUSION

This study analyzes the effects of the silver economy on public finance using mathematical proof methods and empirical data for the case of Turkey and examines the relationships between public revenues, public expenditures, nominal interest rates, and public debt stock by using the deterministic dynamic modeling method. The calculations based on the data for the period 2006-2024 allowed for the testing of sustainability and stability conditions and the formulation of projections for the debt stock.

The obtained results confirm many expectations expressed in the literature in the context of the silver economy. In particular, the increasing effect of the aging population on public expenditures puts pressure on public finance through health, social security, and care expenditures, which exceeds the growth rate of revenues and leads to long-term sustainability problems. In this respect, the silver economy is not only an area of social transformation but also a potential problem for fiscal discipline and budget management.

As a result, the silver economy harbors both risks and opportunities for Turkey. If the risks are managed correctly, the financial pressures created by the aging population can be reduced and new economic opportunities can be utilized, but to manage this process well, we need to make significant changes to the structure, stick to strict fiscal policies, and plan for the future.

## MANAGERIAL IMPLICATIONS

This study's findings suggest that academic, practical, and managerial levels should consider the effects of the silver economy on public finance. The analysis within the framework of a mathematical model has produced important policy signals for decision makers regarding revenue, expenditure, interest, and debt stock data for the period 2006-2024 in Turkey.

One of the most important findings of the study is that expenditures grow faster than revenues. Even this small difference causes the debt stock to follow an upward trend in the long run. For managers, this finding suggests that public revenues and public expenditures should be managed not only by their nominal size but also by the difference between their growth rates. Therefore, managers should carefully plan expenditure programs to avoid falling below the revenue growth capacity.

The model results reveal that interest rates alone are not a threatening factor for debt dynamics. The fact that public revenues have increased faster than interest costs proves that Turkey has a stable outlook in this respect. This finding suggests that managers should prioritize policy management of the revenue-expenditure balance over interest rate control. However, it is critical to minimize fluctuations in interest rates through long-term borrowing strategies.

While the aging population puts pressure on public expenditure, at the same time, consumption potential and savings tendencies offer opportunities for the development of new sectors. Managers should consider this dual effect and manage the silver economy not only from the perspective of financial burden but also from the perspective of economic opportunity. By creating new revenue-generating sectors, we can mitigate risks to fiscal sustainability.

The model indicates that either a small increase in income growth or a small decrease in expenditure growth is enough to meet the sustainability conditions. This finding is crucial for public administrators. This discovery is important because it demonstrates that targeted small and feasible steps, as well as major structural transformations, can have a significant impact on debt dynamics. For instance, a small efficiency improvement in health expenditure can significantly support fiscal sustainability.

Reforms such as gradual age adjustments in the pension system, widening the contribution base, digitalization in health and care services, and combating the informal economy are the most critical strategies to alleviate the fiscal pressures of the silver economy. Instead of being content with short-term fiscal balances, managers must build a fiscal framework that is resilient to long-term demographic pressures.

The mathematical model used in this study shows managers which revenue-expenditure combinations will ensure fiscal sustainability. Unlike traditional observational analyses, this tool guides management through measurable thresholds and conditions. Managers should therefore make more use of such model-based tools in their decision-making processes and test different scenarios through policy simulations.

Managers need to assess the silver economy not only in terms of the current budget balance but also in terms of long-term debt stock trends. This is because income-expenditure imbalances that start with small differences can rapidly increase the debt stock over time and narrow the fiscal space. Thus, doing something now can help stop a worse financial crisis from happening in the future. The silver economy is not just a problem for fiscal discipline; it is also a change that comes with both strategic chances and dangers. Public administrators can keep spending under control, bring in money by encouraging new sectors, and ensure long-term fiscal stability by taking small but focused steps.

## PRACTICAL IMPLICATIONS

The findings of this study indicate that the silver economy has concrete and practical implications for the administration of public finance. In particular, the findings on public revenues, public expenditures, interest rates, and debt stock reveal several practical lessons for decision-makers.

Because public expenditure is growing faster than public revenue, it is important to set priorities when managing the budget. Public administrators have to balance health and social security expenditures necessitated by the aging population with other expenditure items. This leads to the need to identify which areas are strategic priorities. Early and small-scale interventions can prevent major financial crises, as model results indicate that even small differences change the direction of the debt stock in the long run. In addition, since the increase in the elderly population creates a permanent pressure on public finances, it is necessary to adopt more cost-effective methods in services for the elderly population. To reduce future financial risks, public institutions must consider demographic projections.

The findings of the study show that public revenues may be insufficient to meet public expenditures. Therefore, it is imperative to adopt diversification strategies to create revenue sources.

Since nominal interest rates are below public revenues, it is possible to argue that debt dynamics are based on the revenue-expenditure gap rather than interest rates. Therefore, decision-makers in debt management should prioritize long-term planning and risk allocation. At the practical level, extending borrowing maturities and diversifying borrowing costs support fiscal sustainability.

An aging population is not only a financial burden, but it can also create new business opportunities. Public authorities can create new markets that will generate indirect income for public finance through policies that support the consumption and investment behavior of the elderly population. This approach has the potential to offset some of the spending pressure.

Thanks to the mathematical model used in the study, managers can make their decisions based on evidence-based thresholds. For instance, the model indicates the specific level of revenue growth or expenditure reduction required to meet the sustainability condition. Such an approach can make the policy design of public institutions more transparent and accountable.

## THEORETICAL IMPLICATIONS

This study makes a theoretical contribution to the literature by using a deterministic dynamic model approach to analyze the effects of the silver economy on public finance. Firstly, the relationship between public revenues, public expenditures, nominal interest rate, and debt stock is analyzed based on mathematical proofs, and the net thresholds for sustainability and stability conditions are presented. Thus, a formal modeling framework clarifies the fiscal effects of the silver economy.

Secondly, the approach developed in this study can be applied through scenario analysis when data is not available and empirical calibration when data is available. This flexibility provides a more generalizable and testable theoretical framework for silver economics studies, which are mostly limited to observational and sectoral analyses in the literature.

Finally, the findings show that even small differences are a determinant of the long-run course of the debt stock. This result emphasizes at the theoretical level that the effects of the silver economy on public finance are a non-linear and dynamic process. Therefore, the study contributes to the literature both in terms of methodology and conceptual aspects.

## RECOMMENDATIONS

The realization of certain policy implementations within the scope of the results may limit the negative effects of the silver economy on public finance and ensure sustainability.

Effectively combating the informal economy and expanding the tax base will increase the growth rate of revenues. The model indicates that even small increases in revenue growth can sufficiently meet the sustainability condition.

It is possible to control expenditure growth through digitalization in health and care services, preventive health policies, and efficient resource allocation. Even a small efficiency increase in expenditures can positively change the long-term path of the debt stock.

Gradual age adjustments in the pension system, widening of the contribution base, and transparency in fund management will reduce pressure in the long run. In the context of the silver economy, such reforms would support fiscal sustainability while protecting the social rights of the elderly population.

Although revenue growth above interest rates provides profitability in the short term, it creates a risk of volatility in interest rates. Therefore, it is critical to favor long-term and low-cost instruments in the borrowing strategy.

Channeling the consumption power of the elderly population into innovative sectors can create new economic value in areas such as health tourism, age-friendly housing projects, and technology-enabled care services. Such initiatives have the potential to generate income to compensate for spending pressure.

Regularly assessing public finance indicators in the context of the silver economy will enable the establishment of early warning mechanisms. Thus, we can control demographic pressures on the fiscal system.

## REFERENCES


Álvarez-Diez, R. C., Vega-Esperza, R. M., Bañuelos-Garcia, V. H., & López-Robles, J. (2023). The evolution research on silver economy: Current researches, trends, and implications for future directions. *Transinformação, 35*, 1–16. DOI: 10.1590/2318-0889202335e237325

An, J., Zhu, X., Wan, K., Xiang, Z., Shi, Z., An, J., & Huang, W. (2024). Older adults' self perception, technology anxiety, and intention to use digital public services. *BMC Public Health, 24*, 1–13. DOI: 10.1186/s12889-024-21088-2 PMID: 39702092

Ashley, R. A., & Patterson, D. M. (1989). Linear versus nonlinear macroeconomies: A statistical test. *International Economic Review, 30*(3), 685–704. DOI: 10.2307/2526783

Bloom, D. E., Canning, D., & Fink, G. (2010). Implications of population aging for economic growth. *Oxford Review of Economic Policy, 26*(4), 583–612. DOI: 10.1093/oxrep/grq038

Bloom, D. E., Canning, D., & Lubet, A. (2015a). Global population aging: Facts, challenges, solutions & perspectives. *Daedalus, 144*(2), 80–92. DOI: 10.1162/DAED_A_00332

Bloom, D. E., Chatterji, S., Kowal, P., Lloyd-Sherlock, P., McKee, M., Rechel, B., Rosenberg, L., & Smith, J. P. (2015b). Macroeconomic implications of population aging and selected policy responses. *Lancet, 385*(9968), 694–657. DOI: 10.1016/S0140-6736(14)61464-1 PMID: 25468167

Caridà, A., Varrone, N., Altimari, A., & Melia, M. (2022). The transformative power of technology to turn the silver economy into a gold society: A systematic literatüre review. *Sinergie Italian Journal of Management, 40*(3), 19–49. DOI: 10.7433/s119.2022.02

Csoba, J., & Ladancsik, T. (2022). The silver generation in the labor market: Work and time management of the 65+ age group in North-Eastern Hungary. *Journal of Women & Aging, 35*(4), 319–342. DOI: 10.1080/08952841.2022.2048591 PMID: 35324394

Demirbilek, T., & Öktem Özgür, A. (2017). Gümüş ekonomi ve aktif yaşlanma bağlamında yaşlı istihdamı. *Yaşlı Sorunları Araştırma Dergisi,* 10(1), 14-28. https://dergipark.org.tr/tr/pub/yasad/issue/27680/291744

Fang, E. F., Xie, C., Schenkel, J. A., Wu, C., Long, Q., Cui, H., Aman, Y., Frank, J., Liao, J., Zou, H., Wang, N. Y., Wu, J., Liu, X., Li, T., Fang, Y., Niu, Z., Yang, G., Hong, J., Wang, Q., . . . Woo, J. (2020). A research agenda for ageing in China in the 21st century (2nd edition): Focusing on basic and translational research, long term care, policy and social networks. *Aging Research Review,* 64, 1-26. https://doi.org/DOI: 10.1016/j.arr.2020.101174

Griva, A., Mitroulia, M., & Armakolas, S. (2024). Strategic management of the silver economy. *European Journal of Management and Marketing Studies, 9*(1), 1–17. DOI: 10.46827/ejmms.v9i1.1693

Gschwendtner, P. (2020). Silver economy strategies: A comparative study of Japanese and South Korean governmental measures. *Vienna Journal of East Asian Studies, 12*(1), 62–91. DOI: 10.2478/vjeas-2020-0003

Guo, Y., Liu, M., Wang, J., Xia, Y., & Zhao, D. (2023). Demographic challenge: The rise of the silver economy in China. *Advances in Economics, Management, and Political Sciences, 34*, 120–125. DOI: 10.54254/2754-1169/34/20231688

Harper, S. (2014). Economic and social implications of aging societies. *Science, 346*(6209), 587–591. DOI: 10.1126/science.1254405 PMID: 25359967

Hong, C., Sun, L., Liu, G., Guan, B., Li, C., & Luo, Y. (2023). Response of global health towards the challenges presented by population aging. *China CDC Weekly, 5*(39), 884–887. DOI: 10.46234/ccdcw2023.168 PMID: 37814614

Kamberidou, I. (2020). "Distinguished" women entrepreneurs in the digital economy and the multitasking whirlpool. *Journal of Innovation and Entrepreneurship, 9*(3), 1–26. DOI: 10.1186/s13731-020-0114-y

Klimczuk, A. (2016). Comparative analysis of national and regional models of the silver economy in the European Union. *International Journal of Ageing and Later Life, 10*(2), 31–59. DOI: 10.3384/IJAL.1652-8670.15286

Krzyminiewska, G. (2019). Silver economy in rural areas in the context of (un) sustainable development. *Annals of the Polish Association of Agricultural and Agribusiness Economists, XXI*(3), 212–219. DOI: 10.5604/01.3001.0013.2858

Krzyminiewska, G. (2020). Ethical dilemmas of the silver economy. *Ekonomia i Prawo, 19*(1), 61–71. DOI: 10.12775/EiP.2020.005

Liu, X., Chau, K.-Y., Liu, X., & Wan, Y. (2025). Synergistic evaluation system of "technology and service" in smart elderly care institutions. *Digital Health, 11*. Advance online publication. DOI: 10.1177/205520762513266 PMID: 40290271

Maestas, N., Mullen, K. J., & Powell, D. (2023). The effect of population aging on economic growth, the labor force, and productivity. *American Economic Journal. Macroeconomics, 15*(2), 306–332. DOI: 10.1257/mac.20190196

Palomino, M., Allen, R., Aider, F., Tirotto, F. A., Giorgi, I., Alexander, H., & Masala, G. (2022). The mood of the silver economy: A data science analysis of the mood states of older adults and the implications on their wellbeing. *Annals of Computer Science and Information Systems, 32*, 251–258. DOI: 10.15439/2022F50

Ramos, E. R. A. (2024). Economía plateada: Development in Peru and its growing perspectives. *Economía y Sociedad, 29*(65), 1–24. DOI: 10.15359/eys.29-65.1

Roszkowska, E. (2020). Similarity of regions in terms of the elderly population-proposition of a measure. *Optimum. Economic Studies, 2*(100), 148–162. DOI: 10.15290/oes.2020.02.100.11

Shestakova, N. N., Djanelidze, M. G., & Skvortsova, M. B. (2022). Prospects for silver economy development in the Russian megapolis. *Advances in Gerontology, 35*(6), 948–956. PMID: 36905600

Smith, A. W. (2021). *Digital age: a study of older adults' user experiences with technology* [unpublished dissertation]. Purdue University, Indiana, USA. https://doi .org/DOI: 10.25394/PGS.15044157.v1

Sterman, J. D. (1989). Deterministic chaos in an experimental economic system. *Journal of Economic Behavior & Organization, 12*(1), 1–28. DOI: 10.1016/0167-2681(89)90074-7

Stutzer, M. J. (1980). Chaotic dynamics and bifurcation in a macro model. *Journal of Economic Dynamics & Control, 2*, 353–376. DOI: 10.1016/0165-1889(80)90070-6

The Lancet Healthy Longevity. (2021, April). Care for ageing populations globally. *The Lancet,* 2(4), e180. https://doi.org/DOI: 10.1016/s2666-7568(21)00064-7

Turkey Republic Ministry of Treasury and Finance. (2025). İstatistikler. https://www.hmb.gov.tr/kamu-finansmani-istatistikleri

Wang, Y., Zhao, W. & Meng, W. (2022). Bilateral effect of aging population on consumption structure: evidence from China. *Frontiers in Public Health,* 10, 01-16. https://doi.org/DOI: 10.3389/fpubh.2022.941485

Wang, Z. (2025). Technological innovations in the silver economy: AI-driven financial management, smart products, and entrepreneurial support for aging populations. *Applied and Computational Engineering, 118*, 101–106. DOI: 10.54254/2755-2721/2025.20844

Wierzbicka, W., & Farelnik, E. (2024). Population aging and the potential for developing a silver economy in the Polish national cittaslow network. *Sustainability, 16*, 1–19. DOI: 10.3390/su16166768

Wu, W., Ying, S., & Wu, Y. (2025). Silver economy industry market consumption characteristics research. *Journal of Modern Social Sciences, 2*(1), 94–98. DOI: 10.71113/JMSS.v2i1.187

Zangwill, W. I. (1966). A deterministic multi-period production scheduling model with backlogging. *Management Science, 13*(1), 105–119. DOI: 10.1287/mnsc.13.1.105

## KEY TERMS AND DEFINITIONS

**Debt Stock:** It is the total public debt arising from the borrowings of the government from domestic and foreign markets and which has not yet been paid.

**Deterministic Dynamic Modeling:** It is a method used in economics and finance, modelling variables that change over time with predetermined mathematical rules.

**Nominal Interest Rate:** Interest rate showing the cost of borrowing.

**Public Expenditures:** All expenditures made by the state to carry out public services.

**Public Finance:** It is the branch of science that analyses the government's revenue and expenditure policies, budget balances, borrowing processes and fiscal sustainability.

**Public Revenues:** It is all kinds of revenue obtained by the state to finance public services.

**Silver Economy:** It is the whole of the economic and social dynamics that arise with the increase in the elderly population (especially over 60 years of age) in socicty.

# Chapter 10
# Healthy Aging and Resource Sustainability:
## Integrating Health Economics and Natural Resource Management in the Silver Economy

**Lawal Olamilekan Abdulwahab**
https://orcid.org/0000-0003-4955-244X
*School of Business and Economics, Universiti Brunei Darussalam, Brunei*

## ABSTRACT

*The rapid aging of populations poses significant challenges for healthcare, resource allocation, and sustainability. This chapter proposes an integrative framework linking health economics, natural capital theory, and eco-health to address these issues within the silver economy. It shows that aging is inseparable from ecological systems and that investments in green infrastructure, ecosystem services, and sustainable governance provide co-benefits for health and resilience. Global case studies highlight nature-based interventions such as therapeutic green spaces and eco-health hubs that improve elder well-being, reduce costs, and support climate adaptation. The chapter also examines ethical dilemmas in commercial wellness markets, stressing the need for safeguards, equity, and participatory governance. Advances in digital health, IoT, AI, and ecosystem valuation tools are identified as key enablers. Ultimately, it calls for a shift from fragmented, treatment-focused eldercare to holistic eco-health approaches that align healthy aging with environmental stewardship.*

DOI: 10.4018/979-8-3373-6117-8.ch010

## INTRODUCTION

The 21st century has ushered in one of the most profound demographic transformations in human history: the global aging of populations. Increasing life expectancy and declining fertility rates significantly alter the age structure in both developed and developing economies. According to the World Health Organization, by 2050, the number of people aged 60 and older is expected to double, reaching more than 2 billion globally. This silver shift has cascading effects on social systems, healthcare financing, labor markets, and economic productivity. The implications of aging populations are particularly acute in healthcare systems, where demand is rising for the management of chronic diseases, long-term care, and age-sensitive medical interventions. As the elderly population grows, healthcare costs escalate, stretching public resources and challenging fiscal sustainability. Recent studies have shown that aging leads to disproportionate use of medical services and exacerbates structural imbalances in healthcare delivery, labor supply, and economic output (Shrivastava & Ali, 2025). Moreover, in countries experiencing rapid aging without concurrent economic growth, such as China and many Eastern European nations, the sustainability of healthcare financing and pension systems is at risk (Kanev et al., 2024; Yi, 2023). At the same time, this demographic challenge also presents an untapped opportunity for innovation and reform.

The concept of the silver economy, which encompasses a set of economic activities and services catering to older adults, has gained momentum as a strategic policy frontier. This includes sectors such as healthcare, wellness tourism, age-friendly housing, digital health technologies, and preventive care markets. The silver economy has the potential to enhance well-being and serve as a catalyst for sustainable economic growth if aligned with social and environmental objectives (He, 2024; Mason & Lee, 2019). However, mainstream economic discourse often neglects a crucial dimension: the intersection between healthy aging and natural resource sustainability. Ecosystems such as forests, parks, coastal areas, and thermal springs promote physical and mental health, especially among older adults. These nature-based health interventions reduce disease burden and offer cost-effective alternatives to expensive medical treatments. Despite growing awareness of the silver economy, a gap remains in linking healthy aging to natural resource management. Existing approaches often treat health and environmental sustainability as separate policy areas. This chapter addresses this gap by proposing a unified framework that integrates health economics, natural capital, and eco-health principles.

The demographic transformation illustrated in Figure 1 underscores the magnitude of global aging, which represents one of the most consequential structural shifts in human history. The number of individuals aged 60 and above is projected to more than double between 2020 and 2050, reaching over two billion. This transformation reshapes the global economic landscape through increased healthcare spending, rising dependency ratios, and mounting fiscal pressure on pension and welfare systems. At the same time, it presents a strategic opportunity to redesign health and resource systems around sustainability and prevention rather than treatment and consumption.

By visualizing the rapid expansion of older populations, the figure reinforces the argument that demographic trends must be treated not merely as social challenges but as ecological and economic catalysts. Integrating healthy aging strategies with sustainable natural resource management thus becomes a necessity for maintaining long-term societal stability. The visual narrative bridges the abstract notion of population aging with tangible policy imperatives, including the need for investment in green infrastructure, equitable access to health resources, and the reallocation of fiscal priorities toward resilience and longevity.

*Figure 1. Global Population Aged 60+ (1950–2050): Historical and Projected Growth*

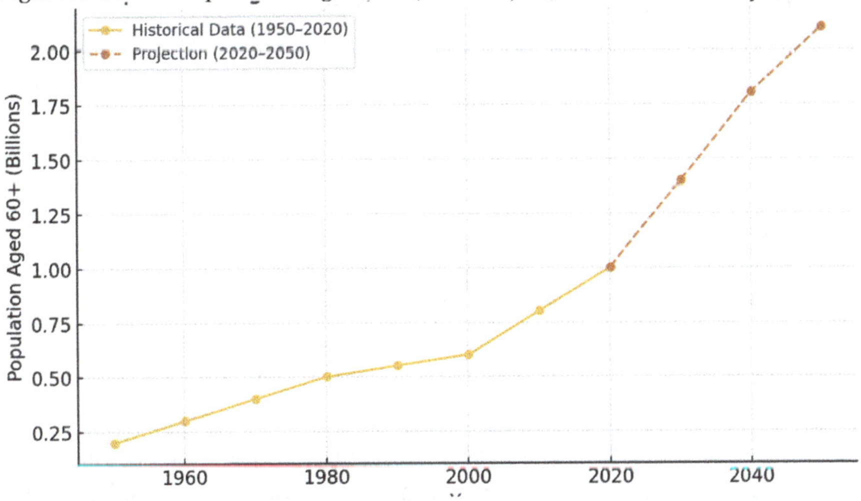


*Sources: Data from World Health Organization (WHO, 2024) & United Nations Department of Economic and Social Affairs, World Population Prospects 2024.*

## Historical Evolution of the Silver Economy and Eco-Health Concepts

The foundations of the silver economy and eco-health paradigms are rooted in earlier policy and theoretical milestones. The Brundtland Report first formalized the concept of sustainable development, linking human well-being to ecological integrity (Bermejo, 2014). In health economics, Arrow's seminal work on uncertainty and welfare economics established the analytical basis for understanding health as both a social good and an economic asset (Gutowski et al., 2009). Building on these, the Madrid International Plan of Action on Ageing positioned aging within global development goals and sustainability discourse (Choy, 2015). The study introduced the ecosystem-services framework, connecting natural capital to human welfare and the valuation of environmental goods (Duxbury & Dickinson, 2007). Collectively, these historical foundations underpin contemporary eco-health approaches, situating this chapter within a broader lineage of integrated sustainability thinking.

This chapter develops a cross-sectoral framework connecting health economics and natural resource management to promote healthy aging. It is organized into seven sections covering theory, evidence, Governance, innovation, and future research. The structure of this chapter is as follows: This chapter is divided into six sections. Section 2 reviews the literature linking health economics, ecosystem management, and aging, concluding with an integrative eco-health framework. Section 3 presents the core analysis, combining quantitative and Governance perspectives. Section 4 outlines financial and policy mechanisms for implementation, while Section 5 examines future directions in technology and research. Section 6 concludes with policy implications and recommendations for advancing healthy aging within sustainable ecosystems.

## LITERATURE REVIEW

### Health Economics and the Cost of Aging

Health economics offers a structured framework for evaluating, allocating, and optimizing healthcare resources within the constraints of an aging demographic. As global populations age, healthcare systems are increasingly pressured by the rising demand for managing chronic diseases, providing long-term care, and implementing preventive interventions. The growing imbalance between care needs and the available labor force, along with constrained fiscal environments, makes it imperative to assess the cost-effectiveness of policy responses and interventions. Recent studies confirm that aging significantly influences healthcare sustainability, with escalating costs and demand leading to fiscal imbalances unless proactive reforms are enacted. Implementing predictive health analytics, remote monitoring, and personalized care models has proven effective in controlling costs and improving patient outcomes in aging populations (Olamijuwon & Zouo, 2024).

Additionally, models integrating health service decentralization and preventive care promise to reduce system burdens (Cristea et al., 2020). Furthermore, environmental policies that incorporate cost-benefit frameworks tailored to the aging population can enhance the effectiveness of public health expenditures (Festa et al., 2022). While economic reforms shape the affordability of aging, environmental conditions determine its quality, a link examined in the next section.

Table 1 illustrates that aging populations not only increase healthcare costs but also create new economic opportunities. Nations like Japan and Germany, which adopted preventive and digital health strategies early on, achieved cost savings and an improved quality of life. In contrast, slower adopters, such as the U.S. and China, face rising expenses due to chronic diseases and inefficiencies. The evidence suggests that aging can be viewed as an investment opportunity, rather than a burden. Preventive eco-health approaches, evaluated through QALYs and ICERs, yield greater long-term returns than conventional care, emphasizing that aging economics must include ecological and preventive health factors for sustainable human and planetary well-being.

*Table 1. Comparative Healthcare Expenditure and Cost-Effectiveness Strategies in Aging Societies*

| Country/ Region | % of GDP on Healthcare (2022) | Elderly (65+) as % of Population | Primary Cost Pressure | Key Reform Strategy | Reported Cost Outcome |
|---|---|---|---|---|---|
| Japan | 11.0% | 29% | Long-term care & chronic disease | Integrated community-based care, robotics | Reduced hospital stay lengths by 20% |
| Germany | 12.8% | 22% | Long-term care financing | Preventive care networks, digital monitoring | Healthcare spending growth slowed by 1.3% annually |
| China | 7.1% | 14% | Rapid aging without income growth | Community health insurance, telemedicine | Improved access, moderate cost containment |
| U.S. | 17.3% | 17% | Chronic diseases & high medical costs | Value-based care models, AI health analytics | Projected savings of 8% in Medicare expenditure |
| Nordic Countries (avg.) | 10.5% | 21% | Aging labor & welfare pressure | Preventive & digital public health | Increased QALYs, improved cost-effectiveness ratios |

**Sources:** OECD Health Statistics (2025), WHO Global Health Expenditure Database (2025), and synthesized from Olamijuwon & Zouo (2025), Cristea et al. (2020), Festa et al. (2022).

## Ecosystems and Environmental Health

The aging process does not occur in a vacuum; environmental determinants influence it. Ecosystems, such as parks, urban green spaces, and clean air and water systems, play a direct role in the physical and mental health of older adults. However, traditional health policy and economic models often overlook these non-market contributions. The concept of ecosystem services, which refers to the benefits humans derive from nature, should be extended to include aging-related health benefits. Emerging literature emphasizes that integrating green infrastructure into urban and community planning leads to improved health outcomes among older adults, including enhanced cardiovascular health, increased mobility, and reduced loneliness (Dennis et al., 2022; Lazzarini & Lucia, 2024). These nature-based solutions enhance healthspan and alleviate the burden on conventional medical systems, making them both economically and ecologically viable. However, evidence from the Global South remains underrepresented in existing analyses. Studies on urban ecosystem services in Latin America, which highlight socioecological inequalities and regional governance challenges, as well as inequitable access to natural capital and ecosystem service benefits across Latin American communities, illustrate the importance of regional and cultural diversity in eco-health applications (Dobbs et al., 2018; Laterra et al., 2019).

## Theoretical Framework From Health Economics to Eco-Health

The theoretical foundations of this chapter draw on the convergence of health economics, natural capital theory, and eco-health models. Each framework contributes uniquely to understanding how aging, environmental systems, and health outcomes can be aligned for sustainability. Health economics has traditionally emphasized the efficient distribution of scarce medical resources, maximizing outcomes such as Quality-Adjusted Life Years (QALYs) and Incremental Cost-Effectiveness Ratios (ICERs). These tools provide critical benchmarks for evaluating the value of medical interventions, but are often limited to narrowly defined clinical outcomes (Fisher et al., 2021). However, health economists are increasingly recognizing the necessity of expanding their evaluative lens to account for non-market ecosystem services, including mental health improvements from access to green spaces, reduced healthcare demand due to cleaner air, and resilience benefits from biodiversity. Natural capital theory reframes ecosystems, biodiversity, and ecological functions as critical assets that yield long-term societal and economic returns. The concept emphasizes that human prosperity and health cannot be decoupled from the preservation and regeneration of ecological systems. Scholars emphasize that sustainable development is attainable only if natural capital stocks are maintained or enhanced, positioning ecosystems as indispensable components of human well-being.

Recent analyses suggest that failure to preserve natural capital undermines ecological stability and accelerates public health crises by exacerbating risks of climate-sensitive diseases and food insecurity (Cheng, 2020). Eco-health theory provides a critical bridge between health economics and natural capital approaches by explicitly situating health outcomes within social-ecological systems. This model argues that chronic disease patterns, mental health, and life expectancy are co-produced by both environmental quality and healthcare delivery. For example, empirical studies increasingly highlight the co-benefits of eco-health interventions, showing that investments in green infrastructure reduce environmental degradation and lower long-term health expenditures (Polasky & Daily, 2021). Bringing these strands together, emerging integrated frameworks propose that health outcomes, aging dynamics, and environmental resilience must be modeled in a coordinated manner. Such interdisciplinary approaches allow policymakers to evaluate co-benefit strategies where chronic disease prevention aligns directly with ecological restoration and climate resilience (Rambaud, 2024). The shift from traditional health economics to an eco-health paradigm reframes the determinants of healthy aging as inseparable from ecological well-being. By embedding natural capital into economic and health models, societies can better anticipate long-term costs, optimize preventive interventions, and foster sustainable longevity.

The integrative model presented in Figure 2 situates healthy aging at the intersection of three foundational theories: health economics, natural capital, and eco-health. Health economics provides the fiscal lens, emphasizing efficiency and long-term returns on preventive interventions. Natural capital theory reframes ecosystems as productive assets that sustain human health through services such as air purification, food provision, and climate regulation. The eco-health paradigm, in turn, unites these concepts within a systems-based understanding of human–environment co-dependence. The intersection that this chapter defines as eco-health economics represents a transformative policy framework in which healthcare systems internalize ecological value. Instruments such as Payments for Ecosystem Services (PES), green healthcare bonds, and sustainability-linked insurance models operationalize this integration. The outcome is a self-reinforcing cycle: ecological investment improves population health, which in turn reduces healthcare expenditure and strengthens resource regeneration. By visualizing this theoretical synthesis, Figure 2 reinforces the central argument that sustainable aging requires systemic, cross-disciplinary alignment not only between health and environment but also between fiscal planning, Governance, and ethical responsibility. Together, these frameworks provide the foundation for the eco-health economics model developed in this chapter. Building on this theoretical foundation, the following section translates these insights into economic, environmental, and Governance analyses that form the core of the chapter.

*Figure 2. Integrative Framework Linking Health Economics, Natural Capital, and Eco-Health*

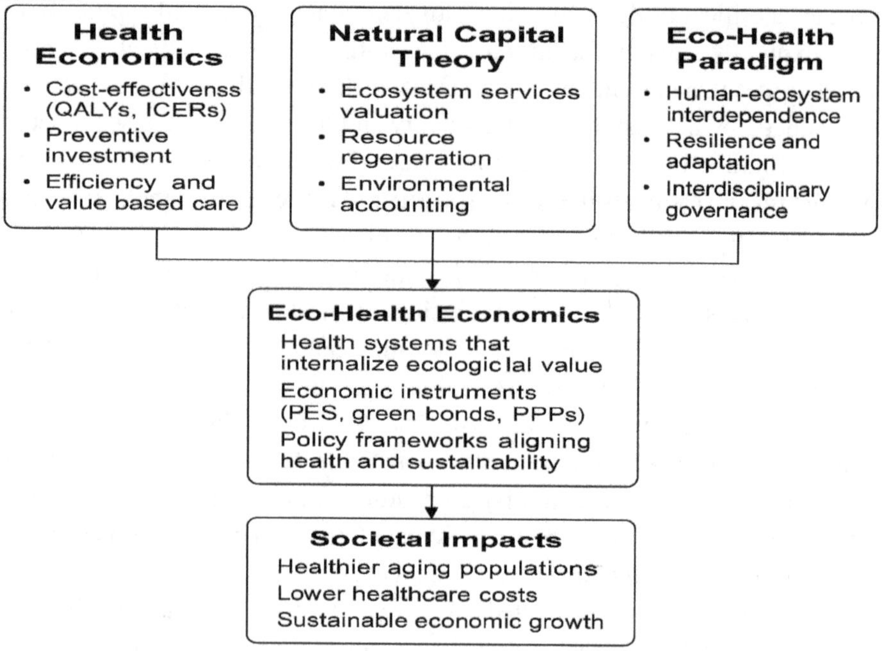


*Source: Adapted from Drummond et al. (2015), Costanza et al. (2017), Polasky & Daily (2021), Bunch (2017), and Richardson et al. (2016).*

# CORE ANALYSIS

## The Economics of Healthy Aging

The demographic shift toward an aging population presents a profound global challenge for health financing and social welfare systems. As the proportion of older adults increases, so does the demand for complex and chronic healthcare services, long-term care, and support for individuals with disabilities. Traditional models, centered on acute, treatment-focused interventions, are economically unsustainable in the face of growing healthcare utilization. Therefore, the emerging subfield of healthy aging economics emphasizes a strategic shift toward preventive, cost-effective, and person-centered models of care. Central to this approach is the investment in upstream interventions designed to delay or prevent the onset of age-related morbidity. These include mobility support programs, nutritional optimization, mental health services, and community-based social engagement platforms. Evidence suggests that such interventions enhance quality of life and yield long-term cost savings for healthcare systems. For instance, structured community participation programs for seniors have been linked to significant reductions in hospitalizations and care dependency (Bethune et al., 2024). Integrating digital health innovations, including telemedicine, wearable health trackers, AI-assisted diagnostics, and mobile health applications, revolutionizes preventive care for older populations. These tools enable remote monitoring of chronic conditions, early detection of health risks, and patient engagement in self-care. Economic modeling studies show that such technologies can reduce the cost of elderly care by lowering hospital admissions and minimizing unnecessary clinical visits (Wong et al., 2022; Zhang et al., 2022).

Table 2 demonstrates that preventive, eco-integrated health systems yield significant fiscal and health benefits compared to treatment-oriented models. Community-based physical activity, nutrition programs, and eco-therapy deliver high QALY gains at low costs, with nature-based interventions achieving cost-effectiveness under $600 per QALY. These measures lower hospitalizations, delay morbidity, and enhance independence, generating multimillion-dollar savings per 100,000 older adults. The Eco-Health Economics model (Figure 4) illustrates how aligning ecological, fiscal, and behavioral policies maximizes efficiency. Overall, early investment in preventive and eco-health strategies yields superior long-term returns, promoting sustainable and cost-effective healthy aging.

*Table 2. Economic Impact of Preventive Health Interventions in Aging Populations*

| **Intervention Type** | **Target Group** | **Cost per Capita (USD)** | **Health Impact (QALYs Gained)** | **Cost-Effectiveness (USD per QALY)** | **Estimated Public Savings (per 100,000 older adults)** |
|---|---|---|---|---|---|
| Regular Physical Activity Programs (community-based) | 60+ | $300 | +0.45 | $670 | $2.8 million |
| Nutritional Support (Mediterranean-style diet subsidy) | 65+ | $420 | +0.52 | $808 | $3.1 million |
| Green Exercise / Park Access Programs | 55+ | $150 | +0.38 | $395 | $1.9 million |

continued on following page

*Table 2. Continued*

| Intervention Type | Target Group | Cost per Capita (USD) | Health Impact (QALYs Gained) | Cost-Effectiveness (USD per QALY) | Estimated Public Savings (per 100,000 older adults) |
|---|---|---|---|---|---|
| Home-based Chronic Disease Prevention (telemonitoring, AI diagnostics) | 70+ | $750 | +0.60 | $1,250 | $4.5 million |
| Community Garden and Eco-therapy Projects | 60+ | $180 | +0.35 | $514 | $2.2 million |

Source: WHO, *Global Report on Ageing and Health, 2022, 2023, 2024, and 2025, and Empirical studies, 2025.*

Research indicates that strategic investment in aging-in-place solutions, such as smart home devices, fall prevention tools, and telehealth services, can delay institutionalization and associated expenditures (Rhodes & McNichols, 2025). The economic rationale for healthy aging is robust; investing in proactive, technology-enabled, and socially embedded care strategies reduces future public expenditure while improving life expectancy, autonomy, and well-being in older age. This shift represents not only a cost-saving strategy but also a societal imperative for sustainability in the face of accelerating demographic change.

## Natural Resources as Health Assets

As populations age globally, a holistic view of health economics must recognize the value of natural environments not merely as ecological or aesthetic amenities, but as integral, cost-effective assets for promoting public health and enhancing the quality of life among older adults. The intersection of environmental sustainability and health economics becomes especially pertinent when examining the benefits of green infrastructure, blue spaces (such as lakes and rivers), and other natural resources in facilitating physical activity, psychological well-being, and social engagement among elderly populations. Empirical evidence consistently shows that proximity to green and blue spaces is correlated with improved mental and physical health outcomes in older adults. A 2024 longitudinal study using UK Biobank data found that older adults living within 300–1000 meters of natural environments experienced a significantly lower incidence of psychiatric disorders, including dementia and depression, with hazard ratios improving by up to 30% compared to those without such access (B.-P. Liu et al., 2024). From an economic perspective, such natural resource-based interventions offer significant cost-effectiveness advantages. Rather than investing solely in reactive healthcare systems, embedding nature into urban design reduces hospital admissions, prescription use, and mental health crises in aging populations.

For example, structured exposure to green environments has been shown to lower blood pressure, improve mobility, and enhance cognitive resilience among older adults, a preventive model that reduces dependency on costly long-term care (Ribeiro et al., 2024). Climate change compounds the vulnerabilities of aging populations by intensifying heat stress, vector-borne diseases, and air pollution. Older adults are disproportionately affected by extreme weather events such as heatwaves, which exacerbate chronic conditions like cardiovascular and respiratory diseases (J. S. Kim & Kim, 2024). Evidence from population-level vulnerability mapping demonstrates that heat exposure risks are strongly correlated with urbanization levels and demographic aging, emphasizing the need for local adaptation strategies (Q. Wang et al., 2021). Integrating eco-health into climate adaptation planning through measures such as urban greening, heat-resilient housing, and vulnerability indices for the elderly can mitigate these impacts and align public health resilience with environmental sustainability (Holsman, 2023).

Beyond direct health effects, green and blue spaces serve as social infrastructure, enabling informal care networks, intergenerational engagement, and reduced loneliness, which are recognized determinants of aging well. The design of accessible, age-friendly environments becomes a public health imperative. Studies emphasize that urban green spaces tailored to the preferences of the elderly, characterized as serene, partially enclosed, and equipped with walking paths and seating, promote both physical activity and restorative experiences (Qiu et al., 2021). Environmental gerontology also provides a robust framework for evaluating the interplay between elderly behavior and outdoor environments. A 2021 review of the literature, grounded in environmental gerontology, emphasized that nature-based environments not only increase physical activity but also support cognitive engagement, social connectivity, and psychological well-being in older adults (Sánchez-González & Egea-Jiménez, 2021). Natural resources serve as dynamic, low-cost health assets that enhance public health, mitigate healthcare expenditures, and promote a resilient aging population.

Table 3 demonstrates that access to natural environments is a key social determinant of health for older adults. Studies show that even a 10% increase in green space coverage can improve physical and mental well-being, reduce morbidity, and extend life expectancy. Parks, wetlands, and coastal zones serve as health assets, providing preventive benefits comparable to medical care. Economically, this reduces hospitalizations, medication use, and healthcare costs while supporting seniors' independence. Within the eco-health framework, protecting and expanding natural spaces emerges as both an environmental and public health investment that aligns sustainability with healthy aging.

*Table 3. Association Between Access to Green and Blue Spaces and Health Outcomes in Older Adults*

| City/ Region | Green/Blue Space Coverage (%) | Mean Self-Reported Health Score (0–100) | Life Expectancy (years) |
|---|---|---|---|
| Helsinki | 38 | 82 | 84.2 |
| Copenhagen | 35 | 80 | 83.5 |
| Tokyo | 27 | 76 | 82.8 |
| Lisbon | 24 | 74 | 82.3 |
| Shanghai | 22 | 72 | 81.4 |
| São Paulo | 18 | 68 | 80.1 |
| Los Angeles | 17 | 66 | 79.9 |
| Delhi | 10 | 59 | 77.8 |

Sources: Drawn from empirical studies Ribeiro et al., 2024, Liu et al., 2024, Ribeiro et al., 2024, Liu et al., 2022

Strategic investment in green and blue infrastructure tailored to the needs of the elderly not only enhances environmental sustainability but also aligns with fiscal responsibility and ethical imperatives for equitable aging. Therefore, urban and rural planning, health policy, and environmental management must integrate these resources as foundational to healthy longevity economics. While the quantitative results demonstrate economic efficiency, effective implementation depends on governance mechanisms that can align health and environmental objectives.

## Governance Mechanisms for Sustainable Aging

The integration of environmental and health sectors demands not only innovative policy frameworks but also transformative governance structures that enable cross-sectoral coordination. With the growing body of evidence affirming the bi-directional relationship between environmental quality and aging population health outcomes, governance models must move beyond traditional silos to embrace holistic, systems-level planning. Eco-health governance models prioritize institutional collaboration across health, environment, urban planning, tourism, and aging services. This is particularly critical in aligning health impact assessments (HIA) with environmental impact frameworks to support informed decisions on infrastructure. Countries such as China have introduced fiscal mechanisms, like the Environmental Protection Tax (EPT), which not only reduce emissions but also improve the health of middle-aged and older adults by mitigating chronic diseases and enhancing psychological well-being through environmental improvements (H. Wang et al., 2024). Incorporating nature-based infrastructure into urban planning policies is a key tenet of effective eco-health Governance. For instance, empirical studies in Hong Kong have demonstrated how strategic urban design, including access to green spaces, proximity to public transportation, and mixed land use, directly enhances the functional ability of older adults and supports gender-sensitive health outcomes (Chen et al., 2022). These findings support the deployment of environment-sensitive public health programs in municipalities, aligning zoning laws and transportation policies with the principles of aging in place.

Figure 3 illustrates the institutional framework required for integrating eco-health into sustainable aging systems. Effective implementation relies on cross-sector policy alignment among environmental, financial, and Governance institutions. National governments provide enabling policies, while local authorities deliver community-based eco-health actions such as urban greening and age-friendly infrastructure. Civil society, academia, and the private sector foster innovation by linking environmental restoration with the well-being of older adults. Financial tools, such as Payments for Ecosystem Services and Green Health Bonds, connect ecological value to public finance. This multi-level governance model embeds eco-health economics into policy, ensuring measurable sustainability and resilience for both ecosystems and aging populations.

*Figure 3. Governance Framework for Eco-Health Integration*

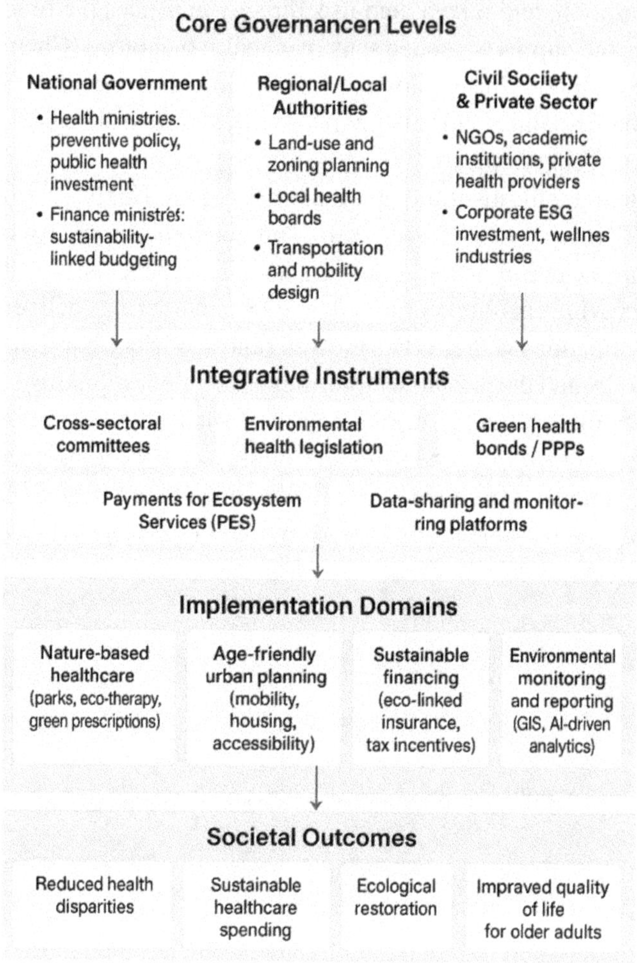


*Source: Author, 2025*

Furthermore, integrated governance strategies have been successful in Europe, where national governments have incorporated public environmental policies into their efforts to improve public health. Countries that align their environmental directives with the Sustainable Development Goals (SDGs) have achieved measurable improvements in life expectancy and reductions in disease burden, especially among older populations (Cau an, 2024). Public trust and perceptions of environmental Governance also significantly influence the success of eco-health policies. A study from Washington state found that community beliefs about environmental management correlated strongly with local health outcomes and ecological conditions. This suggests that governance structures must be participatory and transparent to mobilize public support for integrated interventions (Fleming et al., 2022). Finally, institutional frameworks that embed Health in All Policies (HiAP) approaches, especially in small- to mid-sized urban contexts, can unlock intersectoral innovation. The AFOOT Project in Germany exemplifies how transdisciplinary urban planning and public health collaboration can enhance walkability and active living among seniors, thus contributing to broader health equity and sustainability goals (Brüchert et al., 2017). The future of eco-health Governance lies in institutionalizing environmental determinants within health systems. Through shared Governance, investment in natural infrastructure, and public engagement, policy frameworks can create resilient, age-inclusive environments that mitigate health disparities and enhance environmental stewardship across generations. Governance structures alone cannot achieve integration without ethical guidance, which is examined in the following section.

## Ethical and Equity Challenges in Eco-Health Implementation

The integration of environmental and health systems introduces complex ethical questions regarding equity, access, and the commercialization of wellness. Three interrelated challenges dominate this discourse: distributive equity, ecological exploitation, and informed consent. Distributive equity concerns the uneven availability of ecosystem-based healthcare resources. Marginalized or rural communities often face limited access to green spaces, exposing them to disproportionate health risks. Equitable eco-health design, therefore, requires inclusive spatial planning and community-led management to ensure fair benefit distribution. Ecological exploitation arises when wellness industries commodify nature, such as exclusive eco-retreats, without reinvesting in conservation or respecting local resource rights. Sustainable governance frameworks must regulate these practices through transparent standards and benefit-sharing mechanisms to ensure equitable distribution of benefits. Informed consent and data ethics have emerged as additional concerns in the digital era of eco-health, where wearable sensors and environmental monitoring may collect personal data. Ensuring ethical AI use and privacy safeguards is vital to protect older adults from data misuse and surveillance. Integrating Traditional Ecological Knowledge (TEK) further strengthens ethical Governance by recognizing Indigenous perspectives on reciprocity and stewardship (Chaudhary et al., 2018). TEK offers a moral and ecological compass that balances modern technologies with cultural integrity. Collectively, these ethical considerations highlight that eco-health systems must not only be efficient and sustainable but also just and inclusive. Addressing these moral dimensions ensures long-term legitimacy and social acceptance of eco-health as a cornerstone of the silver economy. With ethical parameters established, the following section turns to concrete financial and policy strategies to operationalize eco-health in practice.

## SOLUTIONS AND RECOMMENDATIONS

### Financing Models via green bonds/blockchain

Integrating nature-based solutions into eldercare and public health systems necessitates innovative, equitable, scalable, and sustainable financing frameworks. Conventional health budgets alone cannot accommodate the emerging demand for eco-health models. Financing mechanisms, such as Payments for Ecosystem Services (PES), Public–Private Partnerships (PPPs), and climate adaptation funds, represent strategic avenues for mobilizing the capital required to embed ecosystem services into health and aging strategies. Payments for Ecosystem Services (PES) offer direct financial incentives for landowners and stakeholders to maintain and enhance ecosystem functions that deliver measurable health co-benefits. For example, PES schemes can be directed toward maintaining forested areas near aging communities to ensure air purification, temperature regulation, and mental health benefits through access to green spaces. A global review of 118 PES projects revealed that those funded through public–private partnerships adhered more closely to ecological principles and adaptive management practices, making them more viable long-term solutions for integrating ecosystem health (Prager et al., 2016). In this context, PES should be seen not merely as a conservation tool but as a health promotion and climate adaptation strategy. Another critical innovation is the application of hybrid governance models, combining PES with market-driven carbon insetting strategies and rancher-friendly policies. In California's rangelands, such models facilitated private sector financing to support soil health, enhance food security, and promote ecological integrity while offering indirect health benefits through improved environmental conditions (Biggs et al., 2021). Public–Private Partnerships (PPPs) also provide significant potential for enhancing healthcare infrastructure with nature-based solutions.

In Saudi Arabia, PPPs were shown to improve service efficiency, distribute financial risks, and promote investment in health infrastructure, which can be extended to eco-health models such as urban parks, green hospitals, and restorative health resorts (Almalki & Al-Hanawi, 2018). Recent financial innovations expand the toolkit for eco-health investment. Green bonds are increasingly used to finance health-linked environmental projects, channeling capital toward sustainable infrastructure that benefits aging communities (Malorgio et al., 2021). These instruments not only attract environmentally conscious investors but also enhance the protection of natural capital and ecosystem resilience (Tamula et al., 2024). These mechanisms demonstrate how digital finance, including blockchain verification and smart-contract automation, can bridge the gap between ecosystem restoration and health expenditure, creating innovative pathways for public–private partnerships in the evolving silver economy (Ranjan, 2024). Such financing partnerships can be particularly valuable for retrofitting existing eldercare facilities with biophilic design elements or integrating community gardens and green corridors into care homes. Adaptation financing, especially from multilateral climate funds and resilience-building programs, has proven instrumental in supporting eco-health infrastructure.

For instance, PES-funded conservation of riparian buffers in the U.S. through the Conservation Reserve Enhancement Program reduced flood impacts and insurance costs, indirectly safeguarding community health and financial systems (Y. Kim, 2024). To broaden geographic representation, eco-health innovations from the Global South offer valuable insights. For instance, Brazil's Amazon Elder Wellness Initiative integrates forest-based therapies into geriatric care, while Kenya's Urban Greening Program demonstrates how city parks reduce healthcare costs in low-income communities. In Pacific Island nations, community-based coastal restoration serves a dual purpose, promoting health while reducing malnutrition and heat stress among older adults. These cases illustrate that eco-health strategies are globally adaptable across diverse socioeconomic contexts. Policy coherence, transparency, local capacity building, and inclusive governance mechanisms are essential for maximizing the benefits of these models. Future financing frameworks should consider co-benefits in health, biodiversity, and climate mitigation to optimize returns on investment and sustainably support aging populations.

## Implementation and Participation Frameworks

The increasing interdependence between public health, aging, and environmental sustainability necessitates a paradigm shift in policy design. Traditional policy frameworks, often compartmentalized within ministries or sectors, lack the cross-sectoral agility required to integrate eco-health principles effectively. To ensure inclusive, resilient, and equitable health outcomes for aging populations, eco-health policy design must be transdisciplinary, rights-based, and rooted in evidence-based Governance. Eco-health integration begins with recognizing environmental determinants as essential components of national health strategies. Forward-looking countries are now embedding environmental indicators into health policy instruments. For instance, Taiwan's Healthy City initiative integrates green infrastructure, pollution control, and active aging interventions through city-level coordination, resulting in health gains and a reduction in chronic diseases among seniors (Jaušovec & Gabrovec, 2023; Mahani et al., 2023). A foundational principle of eco-health policy is the Health in All Policies (HiAP) approach, which requires health considerations to be integrated across multiple domains, such as urban planning, housing, and transportation. Localized examples in Denmark and the Netherlands show how HiAP frameworks have enabled municipalities to create age-friendly communities with safe mobility, social participation, and nature-based interventions, strengthening equity and elder well-being (Christensen et al., 2018; Weber, 2019). Policy coherence between national and municipal levels is critical.

To trial eco-health initiatives, national frameworks should empower local governments with resources, legal safeguards, and innovation capacity. Case studies from Nepal's Ageing and Health Agenda and integrated care strategies in East Asia illustrate how ecosystem services can be systematically aligned with elder health strategies, particularly in rural regions (Dhakal & Aryal, 2022). Adaptive Governance is equally essential. Singapore and other innovation-driven nations utilize longitudinal health and environmental data to refine eco-health programs, such as fall prevention in parks or cognitive therapies in green settings. Such feedback loops demonstrate the value of flexible, data-driven policy cycles for resilient aging populations (Rosa & Ourique, 2024). Crucially, eco-health policy must also incorporate ethical and legal protections. Safeguards are required to prevent green gentrification, inequitable access, and the commercial exploitation of older populations. Embedding elder rights, anti-discrimination measures, and ecosystem justice into eco-health frameworks ensures that health equity is upheld (Alamgir & Shan, 2023; Sadana et al., 2018). Eco-health policy design must transcend siloed health frameworks and integrate nature, justice, and systems thinking into its core. Governments can ensure eco-health systems that deliver inclusive, resilient, and dignified care for aging populations by promoting co-benefits across health and sustainability, mobilizing multi-sectoral coalitions, and embedding adaptive regulation.

## Actionable Roadmap for Health–Environment Alignment

A comprehensive roadmap for aligning health and environmental systems must be visionary yet operational, particularly in aging societies. It should translate eco-health principles into practical, measurable, and scalable actions. To achieve this, the roadmap can be structured across three domains: governance innovation, community-based implementation, and cross-sectoral monitoring and evaluation (M&E). At the national level, governments should institutionalize eco-health coordination platforms that integrate stakeholders from health, environment, urban planning, agriculture, and social welfare. These platforms must be legally mandated and adequately resourced to execute multi-sectoral programs. Evidence shows collaborative governance frameworks can strengthen elderly health resilience and promote eco-health alignment by combining digital, institutional, and environmental approaches (R. Liu & Meng, 2023). Embedding aging priorities into national development agendas and health–environment strategies is crucial.

Models like the One Health approach, which integrates ecological, social, and health governance, demonstrate the value of unified structures for long-term sustainability (Morand, 2022). To be effective, governance models must empower municipalities to innovate locally while aligning with national and global health and environmental targets (Souza & Machado, 2018). Eco-health strategies need local implementation hubs that combine access to green spaces, traditional ecological knowledge, elder-focused wellness programs, and climate-resilient infrastructure. These hubs should be embedded in rural and urban contexts, particularly where aging populations face social or health vulnerabilities. Participatory co-design is vital. For example, Ecohealth Villages have emerged as models for linking ecological stewardship with health by fostering community ownership, ecological restoration, and cultural equity (Orlando et al., 2022). Localized eco-health hubs reduce costs and improve elder well-being by promoting social inclusion, resilience, and environmentally sustainable practices (Seah et al., 2020). A robust monitoring and evaluation (M&E) framework ensures accountability and guides policy. This should include eco-health impact assessments, equity audits of green access for elderly populations, and performance indicators that link ecosystem services with health outcomes, such as air quality, mobility, and mental health.

Advances in geospatial science (GIScience) now enable precise assessments of how environmental exposures impact elderly health, providing insights into risks and opportunities (Tian et al., 2025). At the international level, knowledge-sharing networks such as Healthy Cities and eco-health research consortia facilitate the transfer of innovations, thereby reinforcing the scalability of interventions (Bunch, 2017). Aligning environmental and health systems for aging populations is no longer optional; it is imperative. A practical roadmap must be grounded in governance reform, community-driven eco-health hubs, and standardized monitoring and evaluation (M&E) systems. By embedding eco-health principles into policy, infrastructure, and data-driven accountability, societies can ensure that aging is dignified and ecologically sustainable. The emerging trends and research frontiers discussed in the next section illustrate how innovation can sustain these frameworks over time.

## FUTURE RESEARCH DIRECTIONS

### Future Research Priorities

The empirical measurement of eco-health outcomes is a crucial but still underdeveloped area within health–environment research. Although recognition of nature's role in human well-being has expanded significantly, the absence of standardized indicators, harmonized datasets, and longitudinal tracking mechanisms hinders causal inference and international comparability. To advance the field, it is essential to develop validated metrics that capture ecological integrity and population-level health impacts. One promising contribution is the Community EcoHealth Index (CEHI), developed from the EnviroAtlas ecosystem services metrics. By aggregating high-resolution spatial data such as greenspace access, air quality, and tree canopy density, the CEHI creates neighborhood-level indicators of exposure to ecosystem services. This tool enables policymakers and planners to visualize eco-health disparities, target resources, and integrate ecological equity into public health agendas (Cochran et al., 2019). Complementing such indices, multi-dimensional evaluation frameworks are emerging. For example, reservoir and aquatic ecosystem health assessments employ multimetric indices that combine biodiversity, water quality, and ecosystem resilience indicators, thereby linking ecological status with human exposure and risk (Biney et al., 2025).

Other innovative approaches integrate socioecological systems thinking into health research. The One Health ecological dimension framework emphasizes quantifying biodiversity, soil quality, and water sustainability as determinants of human health outcomes, reinforcing the systemic interdependencies between ecosystems and well-being (McIntyre et al., 2018). Moreover, ecological health indices applied in forest and urban ecotone areas have provided robust models for assessing ecosystem vigor, organization, and resilience while correlating them with community health and satisfaction indicators (Jafari et al., 2024). Recent empirical studies also underscore the causal health benefits of ecological interventions. For instance, the establishment of ecological reserves in China has been shown to significantly improve both physical and mental health among older residents, offering compelling evidence for measurable eco-health gains (M. Wang et al., 2023). The field must integrate these models into a globally standardized measurement architecture. This requires empirically validated causal pathways, stronger adjustment for socioecological confounders, and interoperability between data systems such as GIS-based environmental exposure assessments and health registries. Eco-health metrics can provide reliable, comparative evidence for policy and practice only through such integration.

## Interdisciplinary Data and Indicators

Accurately estimating the cost-effectiveness of eco-health interventions, particularly for aging societies, requires an interdisciplinary toolkit that integrates economics, public health, and ecological sciences. Traditional health economics often focuses on medical interventions and treatments. However, the broader cost-benefit landscape of nature-based solutions demands innovative models that incorporate non-market ecosystem services, long-term health impacts, and social externalities. One significant advancement is the use of ecosystem service valuation frameworks, such as integrated cost–benefit and Multicriteria Decision Analysis (MCDA) models. Recent applications demonstrate how combining environmental and social criteria can quantify cost savings from urban greening initiatives and ecological restoration by linking avoided healthcare costs with improved well-being outcomes (Oppio et al., 2024). System Dynamics Modeling (SDM) has also become a powerful tool for forecasting. It enables policymakers to simulate the long-term health and financial effects of preventive green infrastructure investments, such as walkable parks and therapeutic gardens. Studies show that these interventions reduce geriatric care costs, enhance mobility, and lower risks of chronic illness, offering substantial public savings over time (Pimpin et al., 2016).

Furthermore, Multicriteria Decision Analysis (MCDA) has proven particularly effective in supporting decision-making related to health. Unlike conventional cost-effectiveness analysis, MCDA accommodates broader indicators such as environmental quality, equity, and patient-centered well-being, enabling more nuanced evaluations of eco-health strategies. For example, in elderly care contexts, MCDA has complemented cost-effectiveness analysis by integrating stakeholder perspectives, providing richer evidence for local-level investment decisions (Hoedemakers et al., 2022). As eco-health modeling evolves, future research must prioritize scalability across diverse geographic and socioeconomic contexts, align findings with real-world financing mechanisms, and incorporate dynamic monitoring data into these interdisciplinary frameworks. By advancing these tools, policymakers can more credibly demonstrate that eco-health interventions foster sustainability and generate measurable, long-term cost savings.

## Technology's Role in Eco-Health Innovation

Emerging technologies, including the Internet of Things (IoT), Artificial Intelligence (AI), and remote sensing, are transforming the design and management of eco-health systems, particularly in aging societies. These innovations enable predictive analytics, real-time monitoring, and personalized interventions, creating scalable, precise, and adaptive health–environment integrations. For example, the FEEL framework leverages federated learning with IoT and AI to provide eco-contextual health recommendations tailored to elderly populations. By aggregating biometric and environmental data such as air quality and temperature, this system facilitates decentralized, privacy-preserving healthcare in green urban environments, achieving strong accuracy in activity and fall detection (Ghosh & Ghosh, 2023). Beyond urban Health, AI-integrated drones and satellite systems are increasingly deployed for ecological monitoring and climate adaptation planning. These approaches reduce human intrusion while enhancing resilience in ecosystem stewardship and health-related infrastructure (Cabri et al., 2023). In the context of aging populations, wearable sensors and robotic systems now integrate AI to continuously monitor vital signs, detect falls, and analyze behavior.

These tools improve clinical responsiveness and provide caregivers with actionable, real-time data (Maity et al., 2024). Reviews of recent remote monitoring technologies further emphasize their potential to reduce costs, strengthen autonomy, and improve equity in elder healthcare while stressing the need for stronger safeguards around data accuracy, privacy, and accessibility (González-Baldovinos et al., 2025). Equally, geospatial and remote sensing tools provide actionable insights for eco-health planning. By mapping urban heat islands, pollution hotspots, and access to green infrastructure, these technologies support the design of age-friendly, climate-resilient neighborhoods (Arsanjani, 2017). Looking ahead, eco-health innovation must be grounded in interdisciplinary collaboration among health scientists, technologists, and urban ecologists. While IoT, AI, and remote sensing provide powerful tools, ethical issues such as privacy, informed consent, and digital literacy, especially among older adults, must remain central to design and deployment (Shrestha & Ghosh, 2025). Emerging technologies further expand the operational capacity of eco-health systems. Blockchain platforms enhance transparency in Payments for Ecosystem Services (PES) transactions, ensuring that environmental credits are traceable and verifiable across stakeholders (Villares, 2020). Blockchain integration within digital ecosystems has been shown to improve transaction accountability, data integrity, and governance efficiency (Gurram et al., 2025).

Meanwhile, Virtual Reality (VR) and immersive technologies are emerging as promising therapeutic tools offering digital nature experiences that enhance psychological well-being and cognitive engagement among older adults, particularly those with mobility limitations (Malamas et al., 2024). However, these innovations must be implemented in conjunction with strategies to close digital divides, particularly in rural and low-income settings where access to digital infrastructure remains limited (Hussain et al., 2024). Ultimately, innovative eco-health systems powered by interoperable technologies will drive the next generation of elder-centered innovations, ensuring that healthier aging is achieved in harmony with ecological sustainability.

## CONCLUSION

Synthesizing the analyses and evidence across economic, ecological, and Governance dimensions, this final section outlines the key lessons and policy takeaways. Integrating health promotion and environmental sustainability, as captured through the dual-benefit framework, represents a transformative paradigm in Governance, planning, and aging welfare. This framework emphasizes that interventions that enhance ecosystem integrity concurrently deliver significant health benefits, particularly for older populations. It reframes natural ecosystems not merely as environmental assets but as social determinants of health, positioning ecological well-being as central to elder care strategies. In doing so, the framework highlights how policy innovation can simultaneously advance individual longevity and planetary resilience. Recent empirical findings demonstrate that access to ecosystem services, such as clean air, urban greenery, and biodiversity, measurably improves cardiovascular function, mental resilience, and social connectivity among elderly populations (Lindgren & Elmqvist, 2017). Epidemiological evidence further confirms that proximity to blue and green spaces is associated with reduced morbidity, improved mental health, and lower healthcare utilization among older adults (Hazell, 2020). These benefits extend beyond the individual level, generating macro-scale cost savings and resilience dividends for healthcare systems. In urban development, green infrastructure has emerged as a dual vehicle for adaptation and mitigation, providing climate regulation, air purification, and psychosocial enrichment. Long-term studies, such as those in Barcelona, demonstrate how integrating ecosystem services into city planning enhances sustainability outcomes and public health, particularly under demographic aging pressures (Luca et al., 2021). This positions the dual-benefit model not only as a scientific construct but also as a pragmatic governance strategy.

However, realizing its potential requires embedding social equity at the core. Research on forest-based ecosystem services in Nepal highlights how inequities, such as elite capture, can exacerbate disparities in access to ecological benefits (Chaudhary et al., 2018). Likewise, urban case studies reveal that marginalized communities often have less access to natural amenities, undermining the promise of dual-benefit systems (Geneletti et al., 2019). Integrating traditional ecological knowledge (TEK) is gaining traction as a culturally sensitive pathway for sustainability. Embedding TEK within eco-health strategies preserves biodiversity, enhances intergenerational learning, and creates elder-centered models of ecological stewardship (Shemshad et al., 2025). This highlights the flexibility of the dual-benefit framework in adapting to diverse socio-cultural contexts. Future-ready ecosystems, urban or rural, must be designed to withstand climate shocks, demographic transitions, and public health crises. The dual-benefit model provides a systems-thinking framework for structuring investments in natural capital, yielding co-benefits such as disease regulation, thermal comfort, and disaster risk reduction (DeClerck et al., 2016). The dual-benefit framework emphasizes that sustainability and health are not parallel goals, but rather deeply interconnected imperatives. A reconfiguration of policies, financing, and community planning around this nexus is not optional; fostering inclusive longevity in the Anthropocene is essential.

## Call for Holistic, Cross-Disciplinary Aging Strategies

As the global population ages rapidly, traditional sectoral approaches to eldercare, which are often siloed into healthcare, urban development, or social welfare, are increasingly inadequate for addressing the interconnected needs of older adults. A paradigm shift toward holistic, cross-disciplinary aging strategies is urgently required. Such strategies must integrate health sciences, environmental planning, gerontology, digital innovation, and social equity to ensure comprehensive well-being in the 21st century. At the core of this integrated approach is recognizing that aging occurs within broader social, spatial, ecological, and technological contexts. For instance, the built environment can significantly shape healthy aging outcomes depending on accessibility, inclusivity, and integration with natural infrastructure. Research from Europe suggests that cross-disciplinary models integrating public health and urban planning promote active mobility and social engagement among seniors, underscoring the importance of coordinated planning in both small towns and dense cities (Dorato, 2020). Equally vital are educational interventions that bridge the knowledge divide between biology, design, and gerontology. Pedagogical initiatives have demonstrated that incorporating the biology of aging into interdisciplinary curricula equips professionals with the skills necessary to support age-inclusive practices and design adaptable urban environments (Ding & Ran, 2021). Such academic innovation empowers the next generation of practitioners to address the complex challenges of aging collaboratively.

The growing field of environmental gerontology offers further insights into how spatial design affects the quality of life for older adults. Urban design approaches that incorporate biophilic principles, wayfinding systems, and adaptive technologies have enhanced the social participation, psychological well-being, and autonomy of elders (Lak et al., 2020). These findings underscore the importance of integrating environmental considerations into geriatric care and policy frameworks. Exemplary initiatives illustrate the promise of cross-disciplinary collaboration. The European Innovation Partnership on Active and Healthy Ageing (EIP-AHA) brings together regional governments, researchers, and civil society to co-design integrated solutions, emphasizing inclusive design, health equity, and technological innovation across various fields, including architecture, IT, and transportation (Chi et al., 2021). Community participation must also be prioritized. Programs that empower seniors as social entrepreneurs and co-creators of local solutions show how active aging can generate social value while reducing isolation and promoting cultural integration (Socci et al., 2020). These experiences demonstrate that older adults can play a pivotal role in shaping resilient and inclusive communities. Finally, addressing socioeconomic disparities requires coordinated policy efforts. Studies show that integrated neighborhood and campus-based models, where health systems, educational institutions, and local governments collaborate, transform environments into age-friendly ecosystems (Wood et al., 2022). By establishing shared metrics and fostering interdisciplinary collaboration, such models reduce inequities and foster collective resilience. To realize this vision, policymakers must institutionalize eco-health frameworks across sectors, invest in nature-based infrastructure, and promote cross-disciplinary collaboration. Healthy aging and environmental sustainability are not competing goals; they are mutually dependent imperatives for future resilience.

## CONFLICT OF INTEREST

The authors declare that they have no conflicts of interest regarding the publication of this chapter.

## AI USE DECLARATION

The authors acknowledge that artificial intelligence tools were used solely to improve language clarity and readability. The authors reviewed and approved all content and are fully responsible for the final version of this chapter.

## REFERENCES


Alamgir, W., & Shan, H. (2023). Clinical Leadership and Integration of Triple Bottom Line for Planetary Health. *Life Sciences*. Advance online publication. DOI: 10.37185/lns.1.1.439

Almalki, A., & Al-Hanawi, M. K. (2018). Public Private Partnerships and Collaboration in the Health Sector in the Kingdom of Saudi Arabia: A Qualitative Study. *Global Journal of Health Science*, *10*. Advance online publication. DOI: 10.5539/GJHS.V10N6P10

Arsanjani, J. J. (2017). Remote Sensing, Crowd Sensing, and Geospatial Technologies for Public Health: An Editorial. *International Journal of Environmental Research and Public Health*, *14*, 4. DOI: 10.3390/ijerph14040405 PMID: 28398268

Bermejo, R. (2014). *Sustainable Development in the Brundtland Report and Its Distortion*. 69–82. https://doi.org/DOI: 10.1007/978-94-017-8981-3_5

Bethune, T., Grant, C., Bayer, E., & Leavitt, T. S. (2024). Designing for Lifelong Health – A Commentary on Integrating Community Design and Healthy Aging Across the Life Course. *Journal of Public Health Management and Practice*, *31*, 143–144. DOI: 10.1097/phh.0000000000002081 PMID: 39808761

Biggs, N. B., Hafner, J., Mashiri, F. E., Huntsinger, L., & Lambin, E. (2021). Payments for ecosystem services within the hybrid governance model: Evaluating policy alignment and complementarity on California rangelands. *Ecology and Society*, *26*. Advance online publication. DOI: 10.5751/ES-12254-260119

Biney, E. E., Gyamfi, C., Karikari, A., & Darko, D. (2025). Reservoir ecological health assessment Methods: A systematic review. *Ecological Indicators*. Advance online publication. DOI: 10.1016/j.ecolind.2025.113130

Brüchert, T., Quentin, P., Baumgart, S., & Bolte, G. (2017). Intersectoral collaboration of public health and urban planning for promotion of mobility and healthy ageing: Protocol of the AFOOT project. *Cities & Health*, *1*, 83–88. DOI: 10.1080/23748834.2017.1312086

Bunch, M. (2017). Ecosystem Approaches: Navigating Complexity. *Promoting Health*, *1*, •••. https://consensus.app/papers/ecosystem-approaches-navigating-complexity-promoting-bunch/7c4c045cb46a5fecabddc89c0dc6e860/

Cabri, A., Rovetta, S., Masulli, F., Sharma, A., Meo, P. G., & Magliulo, M. (2023). *Remote Healthcare System Based on AIoT*. 215–221. https://doi.org/DOI: 10.1007/978-3-031-48121-5_30

Cau an, C. (2024). Implementation of European Public Environmental Policies in the Context of Improving Public Health. *2024 E-Health and Bioengineering Conference (EHB)*, 1–4. https://doi.org/DOI: 10.1109/EHB64556.2024.10805664

Chaudhary, S., McGregor, A., Houston, D., & Chettri, N. (2018). Reprint of: Environmental justice and ecosystem services: A disaggregated analysis of community access to forest benefits in Nepal. *Ecosystem Services*, *29*, 316–332. DOI: 10.1016/J.ECOSER.2018.01.009

Chen, S., Bao, Z., & Lou, V. (2022). Assessing the impact of the built environment on healthy aging: A gender-oriented Hong Kong study. *Environmental Impact Assessment Review*. Advance online publication. DOI: 10.1016/j.eiar.2022.106812

Cheng, E. (2020). *Theories and Interpretations of Environmental Policy*. https://consensus.app/papers/theories-and-interpretations-of-environmental-policy-cheng/8154bb700b3452209a955ec1c061e410/

Chi, Y.-C., Wu, C.-L., & Liu, H.-T. (2021). Effect of a multi-disciplinary active aging intervention among community elders. *Medicine*, *100*. Advance online publication. DOI: 10.1097/MD.0000000000028314 PMID: 34941126

Choy, Y. (2015). 28 Years Into Our Common Future: Sustainable Development In The Post-Brundtland World. *WIT Transactions on the Built Environment*, *168*, 1197–1211. DOI: 10.2495/sd151032

Christensen, J., Bloch, P., Møller, S. R., Søgaard, C. P., Klinker, C., Aagaard-Hansen, J., & Bentsen, P. (2018). Health in All local Policies: Lessons learned on intersectoral collaboration in a community-based health promotion network in Denmark. *The International Journal of Health Planning and Management, 34*. Advance online publication. DOI: 10.1002/hpm.2620 PMID: 30118138

Cochran, F., Jackson, L., Neale, A., Lovette, J., & Tran, L. (2019). A Community EcoHealth Index from EnviroAtlas Ecosystem Services Metrics. *International Journal of Environmental Research and Public Health, 16*. Advance online publication. DOI: 10.3390/ijerph16152760 PMID: 31382383

Cristea, M., Noja, G.,  tefea, P., & Sala, A. L. (2020). The Impact of Population Aging and Public Health Support on EU Labor Markets. *International Journal of Environmental Research and Public Health, 17*. Advance online publication. DOI: 10.3390/ijerph17041439 PMID: 32102277

de Luca, C., Langemeyer, J., Vaňo, S., Baró, F., & Andersson, E. (2021). Adaptive resilience of and through urban ecosystem services: A transdisciplinary approach to sustainability in Barcelona. *Ecology and Society*. Advance online publication. DOI: 10.5751/es-12535-260438

DeClerck, F., Jones, S., Attwood, S., Bossio, D., Girvetz, E., Chaplin-Kramer, B., Enfors, E., Fremier, A., Gordon, L., Kizito, F., Noriega, I., Matthews, N., McCartney, M., Meacham, M., Noble, A., Quintero, M., Remans, R., Soppe, R., Willemen, L., & Zhang, W. (2016). Agricultural ecosystems and their services: The vanguard of sustainability? *Current Opinion in Environmental Sustainability, 23*, 92–99. DOI: 10.1016/J.COSUST.2016.11.016

Dennis, M., Barker, A., Anderson, J., Ashton, J. C., Cavan, G., Cook, P. A., French, D., Gilchrist, A., James, P., Phillipson, C., Tzoulas, K., Wheater, C., Wossink, A., & Lindley, S. (2022). Integrating knowledge on green infrastructure, health and well-being in ageing populations: Principles for research and practice. *Ambio, 52*, 107–125. DOI: 10.1007/s13280-022-01765-5 PMID: 35932422

Dhakal, S., & Aryal, M. M. (2022). *Ageing and Health Agenda for Nepal: Challenges and Policy Responses for Sustainable Development*. Ageing Asia and the Pacific in Changing Times., DOI: 10.1007/978-981-16-6663-6_10

Ding, X., & Ran, M. (2021). *Research on the Application of Role Theory in Active Aging Education Service System Design*. 205–222. https://doi.org/DOI: 10.1007/978-3-030-90328-2_13

Dobbs, C., Escobedo, F. J., Clerici, N., de la Barrera, F., Eleutério, A., MacGregor-Fors, I., Reyes-Paecke, S., Vásquez, A., Camaño, J. D. Z., & Hernández, H. (2018). Urban ecosystem Services in Latin America: Mismatch between global concepts and regional realities? *Urban Ecosystems*, *22*, 173–187. DOI: 10.1007/s11252-018-0805-3

Dorato, E. (2020). *Participatory experiences supporting more healthy and active cities. The research-intervention Anziani&Città.* 240–244. https://doi.org/DOI: 10.1201/9781003027379-45

Duxbury, J., & Dickinson, S. (2007). Principles for sustainable Governance of the coastal zone: In the context of coastal disasters. *Ecological Economics*, *63*, 319–330. DOI: 10.1016/j.ecolecon.2007.01.016

Festa, N., Hsu, J., Hammitt, J., & Gill, T. (2022). Reappraising the public health benefits conferred by environmental policy: Considerations for an aging society. *Journal of the American Geriatrics Society*, *71*, 1291–1299. DOI: 10.1111/jgs.18219 PMID: 36585900

Fisher, B., Wit, L. A., & Ricketts, T. (2021). Integrating Economics into Research on Natural Capital and Human Health. *Review of Environmental Economics and Policy*, *15*, 95–114. DOI: 10.1086/713024

Fleming, W., Hallman, T. A., Hoek, J. V. D., Johnson, S. M., & Biedenweg, K. (2022). Measuring Spatial Associations between Environmental Health and Beliefs about Environmental Governance. *Environmental Management*, *70*, 1038–1050. DOI: 10.1007/s00267-022-01706-8 PMID: 36167922

Geneletti, D., Cortinovis, C., Zardo, L., & Esmail, B. A. (2019). *Towards Equity in the Distribution of Ecosystem Services in Cities*. SpringerBriefs in Environmental Science., DOI: 10.1007/978-3-030-20024-4_6

Ghosh, S., & Ghosh, S. (2023). FEEL: FEderated LEarning Framework for ELderly Healthcare Using Edge-IoMT. *IEEE Transactions on Computational Social Systems*, *10*, 1800–1809. DOI: 10.1109/TCSS.2022.3233300

González-Baldovinos, D. L., Sánchez-Fernández, L. P., Cano-Rosas, J. L., López-Chau, A., & Guevara-López, P. (2025). Innovations and Technological Advances in Healthcare Remote Monitoring Systems for the Elderly and Vulnerable People: A Scoping Review. *Applied Sciences (Basel, Switzerland)*. Advance online publication. DOI: 10.3390/app15063200

Gurram, H., Trehan, A., Pradhan, C., Bhadade, D. P., Mathurkar, P. K., & Rane, D. S. R. (2025). Blockchain Integration in Information Systems: Transforming Data Security and Transaction Transparency. *Journal of Information Systems Engineering & Management*. Advance online publication. DOI: 10.52783/jisem.v10i11s.1585

Gutowski, T., Sekulic, D. P., & Bakshi, B. (2009). Preliminary thoughts on the application of thermodynamics to the development of sustainability criteria. *2009 IEEE International Symposium on Sustainable Systems and Technology*, 1–6. https://doi.org/DOI: 10.1109/issst.2009.5156699

Hazell, E. (2020). Disaggregating Ecosystem Benefits: An Integrated Environmental-Deprivation Index. *Sustainability*. Advance online publication. DOI: 10.3390/su12187589

He, R. (2024). The Influence of Population Aging on China's Economy. *Advances in Economics, Management and Political Sciences*. https://doi.org/DOI: 10.54254/2754-1169/2024.ld18195

Hoedemakers, M., Tsiachristas, A., & Mölken, M. R. R. (2022). Moving Beyond Quality-Adjusted Life-Years in Elderly Care: How Can Multicriteria Decision Analysis Complement Cost-Effectiveness Analysis in Local-Level Decision Making. *Value in Health : The Journal of the International Society for Pharmacoeconomics and Outcomes Research*. https://doi.org/DOI: 10.1016/j.jval.2022.04.1728

Holsman, D. K. K. (2023). *Climate Change 2022 – Impacts, Adaptation and Vulnerability*. https://doi.org/DOI: 10.1017/9781009325844

Hussain, N. Y., Babalola, F. I., Kokogho, E., & Odio, P. E. (2024). Blockchain Technology Adoption Models for Emerging Financial Markets: Enhancing Transparency, Reducing Fraud, and Improving Efficiency. *International Journal of Multidisciplinary Research and Growth Evaluation*. https://doi.org/DOI: 10.54660/.ijmrge.2024.5.1.1281-1292

Jafari, A., Keivan-behjou, F., & Mostafazadeh, R. (2024). Ecosystem health assessment using multicriteria approach in a forested ecotone area in northwest Iran. *Journal for Nature Conservation*. Advance online publication. DOI: 10.1016/j.jnc.2024.126589

Jaušovec, M., & Gabrovec, B. (2023). Architectural Evaluation of Healthcare Facilities: A Comprehensive Review and Implications for Building Design. *Buildings (Basel, Switzerland)*. Advance online publication. DOI: 10.3390/buildings13122926

Kanev, A., Kobyakova, O., Kurakova, N., & Shibalkov, I. (2024). *Population ageing and national healthcare systems sustainability. A review of world practices*. National Health Care., DOI: 10.47093/2713-069x.2023.4.4.5-13

Kim, J. S., & Kim, S. K. (2024). Ageing population and green space dynamics for climate change adaptation in Southeast Asia. *Nature Climate Change*. Advance online publication. DOI: 10.1038/s41558-024-01980-w

Kim, Y. (2024). Payments for Ecosystem Services Programs and Climate Change Adaptation in Agriculture. SSRN *Electronic Journal*. https://doi.org/DOI: 10.2139/ssrn.4746066

Lak, A., Rashidghalam, P., Amiri, S. N., Myint, P., & Baradaran, H. (2020). An ecological approach to the development of an active aging measurement in urban areas (AAMU). *BMC Public Health, 21*. Advance online publication. DOI: 10.1186/s12889-020-10036-5 PMID: 33388040

Laterra, P., Nahuelhual, L., Vallejos, M., Berrouet, L., Pérez, E. A., Enrico, L., Jiménez-Sierra, C., Mejía, K., Meli, P., Rincón-Ruíz, A., Salas, D., Špirić, J., Villegas, J. C., & Villegas-Palacio, C. (2019). Linking inequalities and ecosystem services in Latin America. *Ecosystem Services*. Advance online publication. DOI: 10.1016/j.ecoser.2018.12.001

Lazzarini, G., & Lucia, M. G. (2024). Demographic aging: Challenges and opportunities for ecological transition. *Journal of Emerging Perspectives*. https://doi.org/DOI: 10.36253/jep-16902

Lindgren, E., & Elmqvist, T. (2017). *Ecosystem Services and Human Health*. https://doi.org/DOI: 10.1093/ACREFORE/9780199389414.013.86

Liu, B.-P., Huxley, R., Schikowski, T., Hu, K.-J., Zhao, Q., & Jia, C.-X. (2024). Exposure to residential green and blue space and the natural environment is associated with a lower incidence of psychiatric disorders in middle-aged and older adults: Findings from the UK Biobank. *BMC Medicine, 22*. Advance online publication. DOI: 10.1186/s12916-023-03239-1 PMID: 38221612

Liu, R., & Meng, X. (2023). Exploration on the Construction of a Big Data Ecosphere for the Rural Elderly Health Promotion from the Perspective of Collaborative Governance. *2023 13th International Conference on Information Technology in Medicine and Education (ITME)*, 795–799. https://doi.org/DOI: 10.1109/ITME60234.2023.00163

Mahani, A., Lyeo, J., Fung, A., Husack, K., Muhajarine, N., Diener, T., Brown, C., & Conceptualization. (2023). *At the end of the day, it is Council's decision: Integration of health and equity into urban design and urban planning decisions and policies in Regina Saskatchewan.* https://doi.org/DOI: 10.1101/2023.12.05.23299446

Maity, S., Maji, S., Sil, S., Roy, A., Sarkar, S., Dhabal, S., & Venkateswaran, P. (2024). Homecare Robotic Systems: Wearable Remote Sensing with Interactive AI Features. *2024 IEEE Applied Sensing Conference (APSCON)*, 1–4. https://doi.org/DOI: 10.1109/APSCON60364.2024.10465959

Malamas, V., Koutras, D., Dasaklis, T. K., Vassilakopouls, V., & Kotzanikolaou, P. (2024). Blockchain Revolution in the Metaverse: Challenges, Applications and Future Directions. *2024 International Conference on Artificial Intelligence, Metaverse and Cybersecurity (ICAMAC)*, 1–6. https://doi.org/DOI: 10.1109/icamac62387.2024.10829333

Malorgio, A., Teti, E., & Dallocchio, M. (2021). Green Bonds: The Evolution of a Sustainable Financial Instrument on the Cutting Edge. *International Review of Environmental and Resource Economics*. Advance online publication. DOI: 10.1561/101.00000134

Mason, A., & Lee, S.-H. (2019). *The economic impact of population aging: How should policymakers respond?* https://consensus.app/papers/the-economic-impact-of-population-aging-how-should-mason-lee/373ef245b7b75f84943ed085fea2a8f8/

McIntyre, K. M., Vogler, B., Chantziaras, I., Coelho, A., Díez, J. G., Esteves, A., Igrejas, G., Lurz, P., Martins, S. B., Mastin, A., Murray, A., Parnell, S., Poeta, P., Ramos, S., Saraiva, C., Speranza, C. I., McMahon, B. J., Rüegg, S., Häsler, B., & Zinsstag, J. (2018). *Assessing the ecological dimension of One health.* 126–169. https://doi.org/DOI: 10.3920/978-90-8686-875-9

Morand, S. (2022). *ONE HEALTH: AN ECOSYSTEM-BASED ECOLOGY OF HEALTH.* https://consensus.app/papers/one-health-an-ecosystembased-ecology-of-health-morand/5cb3ace534135d95aa9abea88ba3a026/

Olamijuwon, J., & Zouo, S. J. C. (2024). The impact of health analytics on reducing healthcare costs in aging populations: A review. *International Journal of Management & Entrepreneurship Research*. https://doi.org/DOI: 10.51594/ijmer.v6i11.1690

Oppio, A., Caprioli, C., Dell'Ovo, M., & Bottero, M. (2024). Assessing Ecosystem Services through a Multimethodological Approach Based on Multicriteria Analysis and Cost-Benefits Analysis: A case study in Turin (Italy). *Journal of Cleaner Production*. Advance online publication. DOI: 10.1016/j.jclepro.2024.143472

Orlando, L., DePinto, A. J., & Wallace, K. (2022). Ecohealth Villages: A Framework for an Ecosystem Approach to Health in Human Settlements. *Sustainability*. Advance online publication. DOI: 10.3390/su14127053

Pimpin, L., Pérez-Ferrer, C., Knuchel-Takano, A., Retat, L., Jaccard, A., Brown, M., & Webber, L. (2016). Modelling the long-term epidemiological and cost impact of a multicomponent lifestyle intervention and a sugar-sweetened beverage tax in the European Union: Results from the EConDA project. *Lancet, 388*. Advance online publication. DOI: 10.1016/S0140-6736(16)32324-8

Polasky, S., & Daily, G. (2021). An Introduction to the Economics of Natural Capital. *Review of Environmental Economics and Policy, 15*, 87–94. DOI: 10.1086/713010

Prager, C., Varga, A., Olmsted, P., Ingram, J., Cattau, M., Freund, C., Wynn-Grant, R., & Naeem, S. (2016). An assessment of adherence to basic ecological principles by payments for ecosystem service projects. *Conservation Biology, 30*. Advance online publication. DOI: 10.1111/cobi.12648 PMID: 26502915

Qiu, L., Chen, Q., & Gao, T. (2021). The Effects of Urban Natural Environments on Preference and Self-Reported Psychological Restoration of the Elderly. *International Journal of Environmental Research and Public Health, 18*. Advance online publication. DOI: 10.3390/ijerph18020509 PMID: 33435508

Rambaud, A. (2024). How Can Accounting Reformulate the Debate on Natural Capital and Help Implement Its Ecological Approach? *International Journal of Political Economy, 53*, 67–95. DOI: 10.1080/08911916.2024.2321428

Ranjan, R. (2024). Creating synergies between payments for ecosystem services, green bonds, and catastrophe insurance markets for enhanced environmental resilience. *Land Use Policy*. Advance online publication. DOI: 10.1016/j.landusepol.2023.106970

Rhodes, A., & McNichols, C. C. (2025). Aging in Place and Healthcare Equity: Using Community Partnerships to Influence Health Outcomes. *Health Care, 13*. Advance online publication. DOI: 10.3390/healthcare13101132 PMID: 40427968

Ribeiro, A., Soares, R., Barbosa, L., Silva, A., Ferreira, R., Terroso, S., Andriolli, A. C., Silva, L., & Ribeiro, C. A. (2024). Green Environments and Healthy Aging: Analyzing the Role of Green Infrastructure in the Functional Well-Being of Seniors A Pilot Study. *International Journal of Environmental Research and Public Health, 22*. Advance online publication. DOI: 10.3390/ijerph22010035 PMID: 39857487

Rosa, G. B., & Ourique, M. (2024). Clean-up actions as catalysts for sustainability and physical activity promotion. *European Journal of Public Health, 34*. Advance online publication. DOI: 10.1093/eurpub/ckae144.1369

Sadana, R., Soucat, A., & Beard, J. (2018). Universal health coverage must include older people. *Bulletin of the World Health Organization*, *96*, 2–2. DOI: 10.2471/BLT.17.204214 PMID: 29403091

Sánchez-González, D., & Egea-Jiménez, C. (2021). *Outdoor Green Spaces and Active Ageing from the Perspective of Environmental Gerontology*. 235–251. https://doi.org/DOI: 10.1007/978-3-030-58031-5_14

Seah, B., Espnes, G., Ang, E., Lim, J. Y., Kowitlawakul, Y., & Wang, W. (2020). Supporting the mobilization of health assets among older community dwellers residing in senior-only households in Singapore: A qualitative study. *BMC Geriatrics*, *20*. Advance online publication. DOI: 10.1186/s12877-020-01810-6 PMID: 33076833

Shemshad, M., Synowiec, A., Kopyra, M., & Benedek, Z. (2025). The Community-Driven Ecosystem Resilience and Equity Framework: A Novel Approach for Social Resilience in Ecosystem Services. *Sustainability*. Advance online publication. DOI: 10.3390/su17083452

Shrestha, S. T., & Ghosh, A. (2025). Enhancing Elderly Care with AI: A Review of Artificial Intelligence and Machine Learning Applications. *SoutheastCon*, *2025*, 900–905. DOI: 10.1109/SoutheastCon56624.2025.10971504

Shrivastava, P., & Ali, S. S. A. S. S. (2025). Analyzing the impact of aging populations on healthcare system sustainability. *Journal of Neonatal Surgery*. Advance online publication. DOI: 10.52783/jns.v14.1554

Socci, M., Clarke, D., & Principi, A. (2020). Active Aging: Social Entrepreneuring in Local Communities of Five European Countries. *International Journal of Environmental Research and Public Health*, *17*. Advance online publication. DOI: 10.3390/ijerph17072440 PMID: 32260209

Souza, M. S. E., & Machado, C. (2018). [Governance, intersectoriality and social participation in public policy: The National Council on the Rights of the Elderly]. *Ciencia & Saude Coletiva*, *23*(10), 3189–3200. DOI: 10.1590/1413-812320182310.14112018 PMID: 30365839

Tamula, K. E., Navidad, N. C., Peregrino, T. D., Abing, M. J. J., Teves, M. R. Y., Capulong, C. M., & Laygan, R. M. C. (2024). The Effect of Green Bonds on Natural Capital Protection: Worldwide Evidence. *Journal of Economics Research and Social Sciences*. https://doi.org/DOI: 10.18196/jerss.v8i2.21604

Tian, W., Cao, K., & Feng, Q. (2025). The Impact of Environmental Exposure on the Health of Older Adults: A Review From the GIScience Perspective. *Transactions in GIS*, *29*. Advance online publication. DOI: 10.1111/tgis.70056

Villares, L. (2020). *Blockchain and Conservation: Why Does It Matter*. 346–355. https://doi.org/DOI: 10.1007/978-3-030-55374-6_34

Wang, H., Zhou, R., Luo, H., Liang, S., & Kong, Y. (2024). The impact of environmental protection tax on the health of middle-aged and older adults: Evidence from CHARLS data in China. *Frontiers in Public Health, 12*. Advance online publication. DOI: 10.3389/fpubh.2024.1446248 PMID: 39234086

Wang, L., Liang, J., & Wang, B. (2024). Population Aging and Sustainable Economic Development: An Analysis Based on the Role of Green Finance. *Finance Research Letters*. Advance online publication. DOI: 10.1016/j.frl.2024.106239

Wang, M., Huang, H., Xiong, J., Yuan, Z., & Zeng, K. (2023). Impact of ecological reserves on the local residents' health: Evidence from a natural experiment in China. *Social Science & Medicine, 336*. Advance online publication. DOI: 10.1016/j.socscimed.2023.116186 PMID: 37778142

Wang, Q., Zhang, Y., Ban, J., Zhu, H., Xu, H., & Li, T. (2021). The relationship between population heat vulnerability and urbanization levels: A county-level modeling study across China. *Environment International, 156*. Advance online publication. DOI: 10.1016/j.envint.2021.106742 PMID: 34224997

Weber, M. (2019). How the City of Utrecht develops a Health and Equity in all Policies approach. *European Journal of Public Health*. Advance online publication. DOI: 10.1093/eurpub/ckz185.733

Wong, A., Bayuo, J., Wong, F., Yuen, W. S., Lee, A. Y. L., Chang, P. K., & Lai, J. C. (2022). Effects of a Nurse-Led Telehealth Self-care Promotion Program on the Quality of Life of Community-Dwelling Older Adults: Systematic Review and Meta-analysis. *Journal of Medical Internet Research, 24*. Advance online publication. DOI: 10.2196/31912 PMID: 35311680

Wood, G., Pykett, J., Daw, P., Agyapong-Badu, S., Banchoff, A., King, A., & Stathi, A. (2022). The Role of Urban Environments in Promoting Active and Healthy Aging: A Systematic Scoping Review of Citizen Science Approaches. *Journal of Urban Health, 99*, 427–456. DOI: 10.1007/s11524-022-00622-w PMID: 35587850

Yi, P. (2023). *Chinas Population Aging: Economic Problems, Solutions and Prospect*. Advances in Economics, Management and Political Sciences., DOI: 10.54254/2754-1169/32/20231570

Zhang, Y., Leuk, J. S. P., & Teo, W. (2022). Domains, Feasibility, Effectiveness, Cost, and Acceptability of Telehealth in Aging Care: Scoping Review of Systematic Reviews. *JMIR Aging*, *6*. Advance online publication. DOI: 10.2196/40460 PMID: 37071459

# Compilation of References


AARP Research. (2023, December 19). *2024 Tech Trends and Adults 50+*. AARP Research. https://doi.org/DOI: 10.26419/res.00772.001

AARP. (2020). *The longevity economy outlook: How people age 50 and older are fueling economic growth, stimulating jobs, and creating opportunities for all.* AARP. https://www.aarp.org/pri/topics/work-finances-retirement/economics-aging/longevity-economy-outlook/

AARP. (2020, January 30). *The Longevity Economy® Outlook.* AARP. Retrieved from https://www.aarp.org/pri/topics/work-finances-retirement/economics-aging/longevity-economy-outlook/

Abid, I. (2025a). *Drivers of Labor Force Participation and Economic Growth in Gulf Cooperation Countries Region: A Dynamic Panel Analysis.* International Journal of Sustainable Development and Planning, 20(5), 2065–2077. https://doi .org/ IIETA+1DOI: 10.18280/ijsdp.200523

Abid, I. (2025b). *Balancing Growth and Sustainability: The Role of Economic Factors in Adjusted Net Savings in South Asia.* International Journal of Sustainable Development and Planning, 20(4), 1487–1497. https://doi.org/ IIETA+1DOI: 10.18280/ijsdp.200412

Abid, I., Goaied, M., & Ben Ammar, M. (2019). *Conventional and Islamic Banks' Performance in the Gulf Cooperation Council Countries; Efficiency and Determinants.* Journal of Quantitative Economics, 17(3), 623–665. https://doi.org/ IDEAS/RePEc+1DOI: 10.1007/s40953-018-0139-2

Abramson, C. M. (2016). Unequal aging: Lessons from inequality's end game. *The Public Policy and Aging Report*, *26*(2), 68–72. DOI: 10.1093/ppar/prw006

Abubakar, A. M., Bala, K., & Shneikat, B. H. T. (2023). Impact of social commerce adoption on SME performance: Evidence from emerging markets. *Journal of Retailing and Consumer Services*, *70*, 103107. DOI: 10.1016/j.jretconser.2022.103107

Aburto, J. M., Schöley, J., Kashnitsky, I., Zhang, L., Rahal, C., Missov, T. I., & Kashyap, R. (2022). Quantifying impacts of the COVID-19 pandemic through life-expectancy losses: A population-level study of 29 countries. *International Journal of Epidemiology, 51*(1), 63–74. DOI: 10.1093/ije/dyab207 PMID: 34564730

Achour, Z. (2024). Impact of employee stock ownership on firm financial performance: Does corporate social responsibility matter? *International Journal of Management and Enterprise Development, 23*(20), 155–170. https://doi.org/10.1504/IJMED.2024.139275

Achour, Z., Kaswan, M. J., & Rejeb, W. B. (2025). Towards a new paradigm of ownership: Employee share ownership as a tool for governance and CSR. In Achour, Z. (Ed.), *Integrating governance and corporate social responsibility in employee share ownership* (pp. 1–26). IGI Global., DOI: 10.4018/979-8-3693-7031-5.ch001

ACTIVAGE Consortium. (2020). *White book: Evidence of the benefits of IoT-based solutions for ageing well in Europe (Deliverable D6.5)*. H2020 ACTIVAGE Project. Retrieved from https://cordis.europa.eu/project/id/732679/results

Adrianto, A., Ben-Ner, A., Sockin, J., & Urtasun, A. (2024). *Sharing is caring: Employee stock ownership plans and employee well-being in U.S. manufacturing* (IZA Discussion Paper No. 17233). Institute of Labor Economics. https://papers.ssrn.com/sol3/papers.cfm?abstract_id=4931402

African Scientists Directory. (2023). *Call for proposals: Living Labs Pilot Programme in Limpopo and Mpumalanga*. Retrieved from https://africanscientists.africa/blog-post/call-for-proposals-living-labs-pilot-programme-in-limpopo-and-mpumalanga/

Agarwal, S., & Narain, R. (2020). Digital payment adoption in India: The role of trust and technology readiness. *International Journal of Bank Marketing, 38*(7), 1585–1607. DOI: 10.1108/IJBM-12-2019-0498

Agriculture and Agri-Food Canada. (2024). *Agricultural Climate Solutions—Living Labs*. Retrieved from https://agriculture.canada.ca/en/environment/climate-change/agricultural-climate-solutions/agricultural-climate-solutions-living-labs

Ahmed, A., & Garg, V. (2021). E-commerce logistics and digital transformation: Challenges for Indian SMEs. *International Journal of Physical Distribution & Logistics Management, 51*(7), 655–673. DOI: 10.1108/IJPDLM-08-2020-0294

Ajzen, I. (1991). The theory of planned behavior. *Organizational Behavior and Human Decision Processes, 50*(2), 179–211. DOI: 10.1016/0749-5978(91)90020-T

Akiyama, H. (2018, December 16). *Users becoming the innovators: Kamakura Living Lab*. The University of Tokyo. Retrieved from https://www.u-tokyo.ac.jp/focus/en/features/z1304_00010.html

Akiyama, H. (2020). Aging well: An update. *Nutrition Reviews, 78*(Suppl 3), 3–9. DOI: 10.1093/nutrit/nuaa084

Alamgir, W., & Shan, H. (2023). Clinical Leadership and Integration of Triple Bottom Line for Planetary Health. *Life Sciences*. Advance online publication. DOI: 10.37185/lns.1.1.439

Alam, S. S., Ali, M. Y., & Jani, M. F. M. (2022). An empirical study of factors affecting electronic commerce adoption among SMEs in Malaysia. *Journal of Business Economics and Management, 23*(2), 240–258. DOI: 10.3846/jbem.2022.16010

Albertini, M., & Kohli, M. (2013). The generational contract in the family: An analysis of transfer regimes in Europe. *European Sociological Review, 29*(4), 828–840. DOI: 10.1093/esr/jcs061

Alhammadi, K., Santos-Roldán, L., & Cabeza-Ramírez, L. J. (2021). *A Theoretical Framework on the Determinants of Food Purchasing Behavior of the Elderly: A Bibliometric Review with Scientific Mapping in Web of Science*. Foods, 10(3), 688. https://doi.org/ MDPI+1DOI: 10.3390/foods10030688

Almalki, A., & Al-Hanawi, M. K. (2018). Public Private Partnerships and Collaboration in the Health Sector in the Kingdom of Saudi Arabia: A Qualitative Study. *Global Journal of Health Science, 10*. Advance online publication. DOI: 10.5539/GJHS.V10N6P10

Álvarez-Diez, R. C., Vega-Esperza, R. M., Bañuelos-Garcia, V. H., & López-Robles, J. (2023). The evolution research on silver economy: Current researches, trends, and implications for future directions. *Transinformação, 35*, 1–16. DOI: 10.1590/2318-0889202335e237325

Alvarez, S. A., & Busenitz, L. W. (2001). The entrepreneurship of resource-based theory. *Journal of Management, 27*(6), 755–775. DOI: 10.1177/014920630102700609

Alves Martins, T., Arriscado Nunes, J., Dias, I., & Menezes, I. (2022). Learning and the Experience of Social, Civic, and Political Participation in Old Age. *Adult Education Quarterly, 72*(4), 401–421. DOI: 10.1177/07417136221080432

Amorim, E. E. R., Menezes, M., & Fernandes, K. V. G. (2022). Urban living labs and critical infrastructure resilience: A global match? *Sustainability, 14*(16), 9826. DOI: 10.3390/su14169826

Anderson, M., & Perrin, A. (2017, May 17). *Tech adoption climbs among older adults*. Pew Research Center. Retrieved from https://www.pewresearch.org/internet/2017/05/17/tech-adoption-climbs-among-older-adults/

Angelini, L., Carrino, S., Abou Khaled, O., Riva-Mossman, S., & Mugellini, E. (2016). Senior living lab: An ecological approach to foster social innovation in an ageing society. *Future Internet*, *8*(4), 50. DOI: 10.3390/fi8040050

An, J., Zhu, X., Wan, K., Xiang, Z., Shi, Z., An, J., & Huang, W. (2024). Older adults' self perception, technology anxiety, and intention to use digital public services. *BMC Public Health*, *24*, 1–13. DOI: 10.1186/s12889-024-21088-2 PMID: 39702092

Archibald, M., Wiebe, S., Rieger, K., Linton, J., & Woodgate, R. (2021). Protocol for a systematic review of living labs in healthcare. *BMJ Open*, *11*(2), e039246. DOI: 10.1136/bmjopen-2020-039246

Argyle, L. P., Busby, E. C., Fulda, N., Gubler, J. R., Rytting, C., & Wingate, D. (2023). Out of one, many: Using language models to simulate human samples. *Political Analysis*, *31*(3), 337–351. DOI: 10.1017/pan.2023.2

Arsanjani, J. J. (2017). Remote Sensing, Crowd Sensing, and Geospatial Technologies for Public Health: An Editorial. *International Journal of Environmental Research and Public Health*, *14*, 4. DOI: 10.3390/ijerph14040405 PMID: 28398268

Ascione, G. S., Cuomo, F., Mariotti, N., & Corazza, L. (2021). Urban living labs, circular economy and nature-based solutions: Ideation and testing of a new soil in the city of Turin using a multi-stakeholder perspective. *Circular Economy and Sustainability*, *1*(2), 545–562. DOI: 10.1007/s43615-021-00011-6

ASEAN +3 Macroeconomic Research Office. (2025, March 7). *Silver linings: Unlocking the potential strengths in an aging Singapore*. Retrieved from https://amro-asia.org/silver-linings-unlocking-the-potential-strengths-in-an-aging-singapore/

Ashley, R. A., & Patterson, D. M. (1989). Linear versus nonlinear macroeconomies: A statistical test. *International Economic Review*, *30*(3), 685–704. DOI: 10.2307/2526783

Aung, M. N., Koyanagi, Y., Nagamine, Y., Nam, E. W., Mulati, N., Kyaw, M. Y., Moolphate, S., Shirayama, Y., Nonaka, K., Field, M., Cheung, P., & Yuasa, M. (2022). Digitally inclusive, healthy aging communities (DIHAC): A cross-cultural study in Japan, Republic of Korea, Singapore, and Thailand. *International Journal of Environmental Research and Public Health*, *19*(12), 6976. DOI: 10.3390/ijerph19126976

Aydin, E., Cavlan, G. I., Forson, C., & Ozbilgin, M. (2019). Senior entrepreneurship, gender diversity and intersectionality. In Maâlaoui, A. (Ed.), *Handbook of research on elderly entrepreneurship* (pp. 125–138). Springer., DOI: 10.1007/978-3-030-13334-4_8

Badran, M., López, R., Valarezo, A., & Pérez-Amaral, T. (2025). E-commerce in Spain: Trends, growth, and market dynamics (2018–2021). *Telecommunications Policy, 49*(7). Advance online publication. DOI: 10.1016/j.telpol.2025.103003

Baltes, P. B. (1987). Theoretical propositions of life-span developmental psychology: On the dynamics between growth and decline. *Developmental Psychology, 23*(5), 611–626. DOI: 10.1037/0012-1649.23.5.611

Barber, S. L., Ong, P., & Han, Z. A. (2021). Long-term care in ageing populations. In *Handbook of Global Health* (pp. 1–34). Springer International Publishing.

Barney, J. (1991). Firm resources and sustained competitive advantage. *Journal of Management, 17*(1), 99–120. DOI: 10.1177/014920639101700108

Becker, G. S. (1964). *Human Capital: A Theoretical and Empirical Analysis, with Special Reference to Education.* Columbia University Press for the National Bureau of Economic Research.

Becker, G. S. (1975). *Human capital: A theoretical and empirical analysis, with special reference to education* (2nd ed.). University of Chicago Press.

Berberi, A., Beaudoin, C., McPhee, C., Guay, J., Bronson, K., & Nguyen, V. M. (2023). Enablers, barriers, and future considerations for living lab effectiveness in environmental and agricultural sustainability transitions: A review of studies evaluating living labs. *Local Environment, 28*(12), 1547–1568. DOI: 10.1080/13549839.2023.2238750

Bergvall-Kåreborn, B., Holst, M., & Ståhlbröst, A. (2009). Concept design with a living lab approach. In *42nd Hawaii International Conference on System Sciences (HICSS)* (pp. 1–10). IEEE. https://doi.org/DOI: 10.1109/HICSS.2009.123

Berman, B., Evans, J. R., & Chatterjee, P. M. (2021). *Retail management: A strategic approach* (13th ed.). Pearson.

Bermejo, R. (2014). *Sustainable Development in the Brundtland Report and Its Distortion*. 69–82. https://doi.org/DOI: 10.1007/978-94-017-8981-3_5

Bertolazzi, A., Quaglia, V., & Bongelli, R. (2024). Barriers and facilitators to health technology adoption by older adults with chronic diseases: An integrative systematic review. *BMC Public Health, 24*, 506. DOI: 10.1186/s12889-024-18036-5

Bethune, T., Grant, C., Bayer, E., & Leavitt, T. S. (2024). Designing for Lifelong Health – A Commentary on Integrating Community Design and Healthy Aging Across the Life Course. *Journal of Public Health Management and Practice, 31*, 143–144. DOI: 10.1097/phh.0000000000002081 PMID: 39808761

Bhagwat, V. R., Paikrao, P. L., & Shrawankar, U. (2020). IoT wearable sensors and devices in elderly care: A literature review. *Sensors (Basel), 20*(10), 2826. DOI: 10.3390/s20102826

Biggs, N. B., Hafner, J., Mashiri, F. E., Huntsinger, L., & Lambin, E. (2021). Payments for ecosystem services within the hybrid governance model: Evaluating policy alignment and complementarity on California rangelands. *Ecology and Society, 26*. Advance online publication. DOI: 10.5751/ES-12254-260119

Biney, E. E., Gyamfi, C., Karikari, A., & Darko, D. (2025). Reservoir ecological health assessment Methods: A systematic review. *Ecological Indicators*. Advance online publication. DOI: 10.1016/j.ecolind.2025.113130

Bisbee, J., Clinton, J. D., Dorff, C., Kenkel, B., & Larson, J. M. (2024). Synthetic replacements for human survey data? The perils of large language models. *Political Analysis, 32*(4), 401–416. DOI: 10.1017/pan.2024.5

Blasi, J. R., Freeman, R. B., & Kruse, D. L. (2010). Do workers gain by sharing? Employee outcomes under employee ownership, profit sharing, and broad-based stock options. In Kruse, D. L., Freeman, R. B., & Blasi, J. R. (Eds.), *Shared capitalism at work* (pp. 257–290). University of Chicago Press.

Blasi, J., Freeman, R. B., & Kruse, D. L. (2013). *The citizen's share: Putting ownership back into democracy*. Yale University Press.

Blasi, J., Freeman, R., & Kruse, D. (2016). Do broad-based employee ownership, profit sharing and stock options help the best firms do even better? *British Journal of Industrial Relations, 54*, 55–82. DOI: 10.1111/bjir.12135

Blasi, J., Kruse, D., & Freeman, R. B. (2018). Broad-based employee stock ownership and profit sharing: History, evidence, and policy implications. *Journal of Participation and Employee Ownership, 1*(1), 38–60. DOI: 10.1108/JPEO-02-2018-0001

Bleichrodt, H., & Quiggin, J. (2000). Life-cycle preferences over consumption and health: When is cost-effectiveness analysis equivalent to cost-benefit analysis? *Journal of Health Economics, 18*, 681–708. DOI: 10.1016/S0167-6296(99)00014-4

Bloom, D. E., Canning, D., & Fink, G. (2010). Implications of population aging for economic growth. *Oxford Review of Economic Policy, 26*(4), 583–612. DOI: 10.1093/oxrep/grq038

Bloom, D. E., Canning, D., & Lubet, A. (2015a). Global population aging: Facts, challenges, solutions & perspectives. *Daedalus, 144*(2), 80–92. DOI: 10.1162/DAED_A_00332

Bloom, D. E., Chatterji, S., Kowal, P., Lloyd-Sherlock, P., McKee, M., Rechel, B., Rosenberg, L., & Smith, J. P. (2015b). Macroeconomic implications of population aging and selected policy responses. *Lancet, 385*(9968), 694–657. DOI: 10.1016/S0140-6736(14)61464-1 PMID: 25468167

Bloom, D., Canning, D., & Sevilla, J. (2003). *The demographic dividend: A new perspective on the economic consequences of population change*. Rand Corporation.

Bocken, N. M., Short, S. W., Rana, P., & Evans, S. (2014). A literature and practice review to develop sustainable business model archetypes. *Journal of Cleaner Production, 65*, 42–56. DOI: 10.1016/j.jclepro.2013.11.039

Boersch-Supan, A. (2001). *Labor Market Effects of Population Aging*. National Bureau of Economic Research., DOI: 10.3386/w8640

Bohlmann, C., Rauch, A., & Zacher, H. (2017). A lifespan perspective on entrepreneurship: Perceived opportunities and skills explain the negative association between age and entrepreneurial activity. *Frontiers in Psychology, 8*, 2015. Advance online publication. DOI: 10.3389/fpsyg.2017.02015 PMID: 29250004

Borda, A., Schuurman, D., Pedell, S., Spagnoli, F., & Konstantinidis, E. (2024). Editorial: Living labs and open innovation approaches to scale impact for human well-being. *Frontiers in Public Health, 12*, 1378932. DOI: 10.3389/fpubh.2024.1378932

Bosworth, B., Bryant, R., & Burtless, G. T. The Impact of Aging on Financial Markets and the Economy: A Survey (July 1, 2004). Available at *SSRN*: https://ssrn.com/abstract=1147668 or http://dx.doi.org/DOI: 10.2139/ssrn.1147668

Bowen, D. E., & Ostroff, C. (2004). Understanding HRM–firm performance linkages: The role of the 'strength' of the HRM system. *Academy of Management Review, 29*(2), 203–221. DOI: 10.5465/amr.2004.12736076

Boxall, P. (2012). High-performance work systems: What, why, how and for whom? *Asia Pacific Journal of Human Resources, 50*(2), 169–186. DOI: 10.1111/j.1744-7941.2011.00012.x

Boxall, P., & Mack, K. (2009). Research and theory on high-performance work systems: Progressing the high-involvement stream. *Human Resource Management Journal, 19*(1), 3–23. DOI: 10.1111/j.1748-8583.2008.00082.x

Bratanova, B., Summers, J., Liu, S., & Vauclair, C. M. (2019). A rising tide lifts some boats, but leaves many others behind: The harms of inequality-induced status seeking and the remedial effects of employee ownership. In Jetten, J., & Peters, K. (Eds.), *The Social Psychology of Inequality*. Springer., DOI: 10.1007/978-3-030-28856-3_5

Bridi, M. E., Soliman-Junior, J., Granja, A. D., Tzortzopoulos, P., Gomes, V., & Kowaltowski, D. C. C. K. (2022). Living labs in social housing upgrades: Process, challenges and recommendations. *Sustainability*, *14*(5), 2595. DOI: 10.3390/su14052595

Brown, J. R., & Finkelstein, A. (2009). The private market for long-term care insurance in the United States: A review of the evidence. *The Journal of Risk and Insurance*, *76*(1), 5–29. DOI: 10.1111/j.1539-6975.2009.01286.x PMID: 20046809

Brown, T. (2008, June). Design thinking. *Harvard Business Review*, *86*(6), 84–92. https://hbr.org/2008/06/design-thinking

Brüchert, T., Quentin, P., Baumgart, S., & Bolte, G. (2017). Intersectoral collaboration of public health and urban planning for promotion of mobility and healthy ageing: Protocol of the AFOOT project. *Cities & Health*, *1*, 83–88. DOI: 10.1080/23748834.2017.1312086

Bryson, A., & Freeman, R. B. (2010). To join or not to join? Factors influencing employee share plan membership in a multinational corporation. In Eriksson, T., Bryson, A., & Kato, T. (Eds.), *Advances in the economic analysis of participatory and labor-managed firms* (Vol. 11, pp. 1–22). Emerald Group Publishing Limited.

Bryson, A., & Freeman, R. B. (2018). The role of employee stock purchase plans—Gift and incentive? Evidence from a multinational corporation. *British Journal of Industrial Relations*, *57*(1), 86–106. DOI: 10.1111/bjir.12420

Buchko, A. A. (1992). Effects of employee ownership on employee attitudes: A test of three theoretical perspectives. *Work and Occupations*, *19*(1), 59–78. DOI: 10.1177/0730888492019001004

Buffel, T., & Phillipson, C. (2016). Can global cities be 'age-friendly cities'? Urban development and ageing populations. *Cities (London, England)*, *55*, 94–100. DOI: 10.1016/j.cities.2016.03.016

Bunch, M. (2017). Ecosystem Approaches: Navigating Complexity. *Promoting Health*, *1*, •••. https://consensus.app/papers/ecosystem-approaches-navigating-complexity-promoting-bunch/7c4c045cb46a5fecabddc89c0dc6e860/

Butt, S. A., Elhadjamor, E. A., Pappel, I., Õunapuu, E., & Draheim, D. (2021). A knowledge map for ICT integration in the silver economy. *Procedia Computer Science, 181*, 693–701. DOI: 10.1016/j.procs.2021.01.220

Cabri, A., Rovetta, S., Masulli, F., Sharma, A., Meo, P. G., & Magliulo, M. (2023). *Remote Healthcare System Based on AIoT*. 215–221. https://doi.org/DOI: 10.1007/978-3-031-48121-5_30

Cady, S. H., & Dannemiller, K. D. (2016). Whole system transformation: The five truths of change. In Rothwell, W., Stavros, J. M., & Sullivan, R. (Eds.), *Practicing organization development: leading transformation and change* (4th ed., pp. 440–455). John Wiley & Sons, Inc.

Cai, Y., & Lattu, A. (2022). Triple helix or quadruple helix: Which model of innovation to choose for empirical studies? *Minerva, 60*, 257–280. DOI: 10.1007/s11024-021-09453-6

Camargo, C. M. L., et al. (2020). Exploring sources of uncertainty in steric sea-level change estimates. *Journal of Geophysical Research: Oceans*, 125, e2020JC016551. https://doi.org/DOI: 10.1029/2020JC016551

Camp, N., Di Nuovo, A., Hunter, K., Johnston, J., Zecca, M., Lewis, M., & Magistro, D. (2022). Perceptions of socially assistive robots among community-dwelling older adults. In F. Cavallo, J.-J. Cabibihan, L. Fiorini, A. Sorrentino, H. He, X. Liu, Y. Matsumoto, & S. S. Ge (Eds.), *Social Robotics: 14th International Conference, ICSR 2022* (pp. 540–549). Springer. https://doi.org/DOI: 10.1007/978-3-031-24670-8_48

Carayannis, E. G., & Campbell, D. F. J. (2010). Triple Helix, Quadruple Helix and Quintuple Helix and how do knowledge, innovation and the environment relate to each other? *International Journal of Social Ecology and Sustainable Development, 1*(1), 41–69. DOI: 10.4018/jsesd.2010010105

Carberry, E. J., Kim, J. O., Han, J. H., Weltmann, D., Blasi, J., & Kruse, D. (2025). Feeling like owners: The impact of high-performance work practices and psychological ownership on employee outcomes in employee-owned companies. *International Review of Applied Economics, 39(5), 595-616.* DOI: 10.1080/02692171.2024.240488

Carey, R. (2004). *Democratic capitalism: The way to a world of peace and plenty*. Authorhouse.

Caridà, A., Varrone, N., Altimari, A., & Melia, M. (2022). The transformative power of technology to turn the silver economy into a gold society: A systematic literatüre review. *Sinergie Italian Journal of Management, 40*(3), 19–49. DOI: 10.7433/s119.2022.02

Carrere, J., Reyes, A., Oliveras, L., Fernández, A., Peralta, A., Novoa, A. M., Pérez, K., & Borrell, C. (2020). The effects of cohousing model on people's health and wellbeing: A scoping review. *Public Health Reviews, 41*, 22. DOI: 10.1186/s40985-020-00138-1 PMID: 33042597

Carris Reels, (2023). *Annual Report (*distributed to Employee-Owners).

Carris Reels. (2024). *Annual Report (*distributed to Employee-Owners).

Carris, W. (1994). *The long term plan for Carris community of companies.*

Caryl, C. (2025, August 29). *Why employee ownership is a bipartisan issue*. Harvard Business School Institute for Business in Global Society. https://www.hbs.edu/bigs/corey-rosen-employee-ownership

Cau an, C. (2024). Implementation of European Public Environmental Policies in the Context of Improving Public Health. *2024 E-Health and Bioengineering Conference (EHB)*, 1–4. https://doi.org/DOI: 10.1109/EHB64556.2024.10805664

Census and Statistics Department. (2015). *Hong Kong Population Projections 2015–2064*. Government of the Hong Kong Special Administrative Region. Retrieved from https://www.statistics.gov.hk/pub/B1120015062015XXXXB0100.pdf

Chang, E. S., Kannoth, S., Levy, S., Wang, S. Y., Lee, J. E., & Levy, B. R. (2020). Global reach of ageism on older persons' health: A systematic review. *PLoS One, 15*(1), e0220857. DOI: 10.1371/journal.pone.0220857 PMID: 31940338

Charness, N., & Boot, W. R. (2016). Technology, gaming, and social networking. In *Handbook of the psychology of aging* (pp. 389–407). Academic Press., DOI: 10.1016/B978-0-12-411469-2.00020-0

Chaudhary, S., McGregor, A., Houston, D., & Chettri, N. (2018). Reprint of: Environmental justice and ecosystem services: A disaggregated analysis of community access to forest benefits in Nepal. *Ecosystem Services, 29*, 316–332. DOI: 10.1016/J.ECOSER.2018.01.009

Chauhan, S., & Jaiswal, M. P. (2022). Determinants of small business adoption of digital payment services in India: A SEM–ANN approach. *Journal of Enterprise Information Management, 35*(6), 1660–1680. DOI: 10.1108/JEIM-08-2021-0338

Cheng, E. (2020). *Theories and Interpretations of Environmental Policy.* https://consensus.app/papers/theories-and-interpretations-of-environmental-policy-cheng/8154bb700b3452209a955ec1c061e410/

Chen, S., Bao, Z., & Lou, V. (2022). Assessing the impact of the built environment on healthy aging: A gender-oriented Hong Kong study. *Environmental Impact Assessment Review*. Advance online publication. DOI: 10.1016/j.eiar.2022.106812

Chen, Y., Li, W., & Yang, H. (2024). Determinants of physical activity behavior among older adults with subjective cognitive decline based on the Capability, Opportunity, Motivation, and Behaviour (COM-B) model: Mediating and moderating effects. *Frontiers in Public Health, 11*, 1338665. DOI: 10.3389/fpubh.2023.1338665

Chesbrough, H. W. (2003). *Open innovation: The new imperative for creating and profiting from technology*. Harvard Business Press.

Chetty, R., Dobbie, W. S., Goldman, B., Porter, S., & Yang, C. (2024). Changing opportunity: Sociological mechanisms underlying growing class gaps and shrinking race gaps in economic mobility. *NBER Working Paper* 32697 https://www.nber.org/papers/w32697

Cheung, K., Chau, A. K. C., & Woo, J. (2023). The age-based digital divide in an increasingly digital world: A focus group investigation during the COVID-19 pandemic. *Archives of Gerontology and Geriatrics, 106*, 104920. DOI: 10.1016/j.archger.2022.104920

Chi, Y.-C., Wu, C.-L., & Liu, H.-T. (2021). Effect of a multi-disciplinary active aging intervention among community elders. *Medicine, 100*. Advance online publication. DOI: 10.1097/MD.0000000000028314 PMID: 34941126

Choi, N. G., Choi, B. Y., & Marti, C. N. (2025). Digital divide among homebound and semi-homebound older adults. *Journal of Applied Gerontology*. Advance online publication. DOI: 10.1177/07334648241292971

Choi, N. G., & DiNitto, D. M. (2013). The digital divide among low-income homebound older adults: Internet use patterns, eHealth literacy, and attitudes toward computer/Internet use. *Journal of Medical Internet Research, 15*(5), e93. DOI: 10.2196/jmir.2645

Choy, Y. (2015). 28 Years Into Our Common Future: Sustainable Development In The Post-Brundtland World. *WIT Transactions on the Built Environment, 168*, 1197–1211. DOI: 10.2495/sd151032

Christensen, J., Bloch, P., Møller, S. R., Søgaard, C. P., Klinker, C., Aagaard-Hansen, J., & Bentsen, P. (2018). Health in All local Policies: Lessons learned on intersectoral collaboration in a community-based health promotion network in Denmark. *The International Journal of Health Planning and Management, 34*. Advance online publication. DOI: 10.1002/hpm.2620 PMID: 30118138

Cleveland, J. N., & Shore, L. McF. (1992). Self-and Supervisory Perspectives on Age and Work Attitudes and Performance. *The Journal of Applied Psychology, 77*(4), 469–484. DOI: 10.1037//0021-9010.77.4.469

Cloutier, C., & Langley, A. (2020). What makes a process theoretical contribution? *Organization Theory, 1*(1). Advance online publication. DOI: 10.1177/2631787720902473

Cochran, F., Jackson, L., Neale, A., Lovette, J., & Tran, L. (2019). A Community EcoHealth Index from EnviroAtlas Ecosystem Services Metrics. *International Journal of Environmental Research and Public Health, 16*. Advance online publication. DOI: 10.3390/ijerph16152760 PMID: 31382383

Cohen, S. A., & Greaney, M. L. (2023). Aging in rural communities. *Current Epidemiology Reports, 10*, 1–16. DOI: 10.1007/s40471-022-00313-9

Cole, C., Laurent, G., Drolet, A., Ebert, J., Gutchess, A., Lambert-Pandraud, R., Mullet, E., Norton, M. I., & Peters, E. (2008). Decision making and brand choice by older consumers. *Marketing Letters, 19*, 355–365. DOI: 10.1007/s11002-008-9058-x

Coleman, R., Clarkson, J., & Cassim, J. (2008). *Design for inclusivity: A practical guide to accessible, innovative and user-centred design*. Routledge.

Constantinidis, C., Lebègue, T., El Abboubi, M., & Salman, N. (2019). How families shape women's entrepreneurial success in Morocco: An intersectional study. *International Journal of Entrepreneurial Behaviour & Research, 25*(8), 1786–1808. DOI: 10.1108/IJEBR-12-2017-0501

Conway Lenihan, A., & McGuirk, H. (2022). Small enterprises and the silver economy. *Small Enterprise Research, 29*(1), 1–5. DOI: 10.1080/13215906.2022.2048205

Coughlin, J. F. (2017). *The longevity economy: Unlocking the world's fastest-growing, most misunderstood market*. PublicAffairs.

Creswell, J. W., & Plano Clark, V. L. (2017). *Designing and conducting mixed methods research* (3rd ed.). SAGE Publications.

Cristea, M., Noja, G. G., Stefea, P., & Sala, A. L. (2020). The Impact of Population Aging and Public Health Support on EU Labor Markets. *International Journal of Environmental Research and Public Health, 17*(4), 1439. DOI: 10.3390/ijerph17041439 PMID: 32102277

Csoba, J., & Ladancsik, T. (2022). The silver generation in the labor market: Work and time management of the 65+ age group in North-Eastern Hungary. *Journal of Women & Aging*, *35*(4), 319–342. DOI: 10.1080/08952841.2022.2048591 PMID: 35324394

Cui, Y., He, Y., Xu, X., Zhou, L., & Nutakor, J. A. (2024). Can cultural capital, cognitive ability, and economic capacity help rural older adults bridge the digital divide? Evidence from an empirical study. *Frontiers in Public Health*, *12*, 1393651. DOI: 10.3389/fpubh.2024.1393651

Curl, A. L., & Hokenstad, M. C. "Terry. (2006). Reshaping Retirement Policies in Post-Industrial Nations: The Need for Flexibility. The Journal of Sociology &amp. *Social Welfare*, *33*(2). Advance online publication. DOI: 10.15453/0191-5096.3162

Damiyana, D., Maulina, E., Muftiadi, A., Auliana, L., & Kurniadi, K. (2024). The influence of innovation, knowledge management, and e-commerce adoption on MSME performance, and its impact on MSMEs' sustainability. Journal of Infrastructure. *Policy and Development*, *8*(11). Advance online publication. DOI: 10.24294/jipd.v8i11.7994

Dataintelo. (2024). *Silver economy market report: Global forecast from 2024 to 2032*. https://dataintelo.com/report/global-silver-economy-market

Davies, J. B., Sandström, S., Shorrocks, A., & Wolff, E. N. (2016). The level and distribution of global household wealth. *Economic Journal (London)*, *126*(593), 296–334. DOI: 10.1111/j.1468-0297.2010.02391.x

de Luca, C., Langemeyer, J., Vaňo, S., Baró, F., & Andersson, E. (2021). Adaptive resilience of and through urban ecosystem services: A transdisciplinary approach to sustainability in Barcelona. *Ecology and Society*. Advance online publication. DOI: 10.5751/es-12535-260438

De Witte, N. A. J., Adriaensen, I., Broeckx, L., Van der Auwera, V., Van Daele, T., & De Marez, L. (2021). Cross-cultural differences in user-centred research: An international living lab survey. *Health Informatics Journal*, *27*(1), 14604582211038268. DOI: 10.1177/14604582211038268

DeClerck, F., Jones, S., Attwood, S., Bossio, D., Girvetz, E., Chaplin-Kramer, B., Enfors, E., Fremier, A., Gordon, L., Kizito, F., Noriega, I., Matthews, N., McCartney, M., Meacham, M., Noble, A., Quintero, M., Remans, R., Soppe, R., Willemen, L., & Zhang, W. (2016). Agricultural ecosystems and their services: The vanguard of sustainability? *Current Opinion in Environmental Sustainability*, *23*, 92–99. DOI: 10.1016/J.COSUST.2016.11.016

Del Sordo, E., & Zattoni, A. (2025). The role of employee ownership, financial participation, and decision-making in corporate governance: A multilevel review and research agenda. *Corporate Governance, 33*, 529–549. DOI: 10.1111/corg.12614

Dell'Era, C., & Landoni, P. (2014). Living lab: A methodology between user-centred design and participatory design. *Creativity and Innovation Management, 23*(2), 137–154. DOI: 10.1111/caim.12061

Demirbilek, T., & Öktem Özgür, A. (2017). Gümüş ekonomi ve aktif yaşlanma bağlamında yaşlı istihdamı. *Yaşlı Sorunları Araştırma Dergisi,* 10(1), 14-28. https://dergipark.org.tr/tr/pub/yasad/issue/27680/291744

Dennis, M., Barker, A., Anderson, J., Ashton, J. C., Cavan, G., Cook, P. A., French, D., Gilchrist, A., James, P., Phillipson, C., Tzoulas, K., Wheater, C., Wossink, A., & Lindley, S. (2022). Integrating knowledge on green infrastructure, health and well-being in ageing populations: Principles for research and practice. *Ambio, 52*, 107–125. DOI: 10.1007/s13280-022-01765-5 PMID: 35932422

DeSoto, H. (2000). *The mystery of capital: Why capitalism triumphs in the West and fails everywhere else*. Basic Books.

Dhakal, S., & Aryal, M. M. (2022). *Ageing and Health Agenda for Nepal: Challenges and Policy Responses for Sustainable Development*. Ageing Asia and the Pacific in Changing Times., DOI: 10.1007/978-981-16-6663-6_10

Ding, X., & Ran, M. (2021). *Research on the Application of Role Theory in Active Aging Education Service System Design*. 205–222. https://doi.org/DOI: 10.1007/978-3-030-90328-2_13

Dobbs, C., Escobedo, F. J., Clerici, N., de la Barrera, F., Eleutério, A., MacGregor-Fors, I., Reyes-Paecke, S., Vásquez, A., Camaño, J. D. Z., & Hernández, H. (2018). Urban ecosystem Services in Latin America: Mismatch between global concepts and regional realities? *Urban Ecosystems, 22*, 173–187. DOI: 10.1007/s11252-018-0805-3

Dorato, E. (2020). *Participatory experiences supporting more healthy and active cities. The research-intervention Anziani&Città*. 240–244. https://doi.org/DOI: 10.1201/9781003027379-45

Doucouliagos, C. (1995). Worker participation and productivity in labor-managed and participatory capitalist firms: A meta-analysis. *Industrial & Labor Relations Review, 49*(1), 58–77. DOI: 10.1177/001979399504900104

Drucker, P. (1954). The practice of management, Harper, New York, 1954; Heinemann, London, 1955; revised edn, Butterworth-Heinemann, 2007.

Duxbury, J., & Dickinson, S. (2007). Principles for sustainable Governance of the coastal zone: In the context of coastal disasters. *Ecological Economics*, *63*, 319–330. DOI: 10.1016/j.ecolecon.2007.01.016

Dwivedi, Y. K., Hughes, L., Coombs, C., Constantiou, I., Duan, Y., Edwards, J. S., Gupta, B., Lal, B., Misra, S., Prashant, P., Raman, R., Rana, N. P., Sharma, S. K., & Upadhyay, N. (2023). Digital and social media marketing: Implications for marketing strategies. *International Journal of Information Management*, *68*, 102518. DOI: 10.1016/j.ijinfomgt.2022.102518

Dwivedi, Y. K., Ismagilova, E., Hughes, L., Carlson, J., Filieri, R., Jacobson, J., Jain, V., Karjaluoto, H., Kefi, H., Krishen, A. S., Kumar, V., Rahman, M. M., Raman, R., Rauschnabel, P. A., Rowley, J., Salo, J., Tran, G. A., & Wang, Y. (2022). Setting the future of digital and social media marketing research: Perspectives and research propositions. *International Journal of Information Management*, *59*, 102168. DOI: 10.1016/j.ijinfomgt.2020.102168

Eatock, D. (2015). *The silver economy: Opportunities from ageing* (EPRS Briefing 565.872). European Parliamentary Research Service. Retrieved from https://www.europarl.europa.eu/EPRS/EPRS-Briefing-565872-The-silver-economy-FINAL.pdf

Ehrlich, P. R. (1968). *The population bomb*. Ballantine Books.

Ellerman, D. (2025, October 11). Why fair market valuations' are inappropriate for employee-owned firms and partnerships. https://ellerman.org/wp-content/uploads/2025/10/MarketValuations.pdf

Ellerman, D. (2021). *The democratic worker-owned firm (Routledge Revivals): A new model for the East and West*. Routledge.

Ellerman, D., & Gonza, T. (2024). A critical analysis of different forms of employee ownership. *International Review of Applied Economics*, *39*(2–3), 261–276. DOI: 10.1080/02692171.2024.2435408

Employee Ownership Foundation. (n.d.). *ESOP financing*. Employee Ownership Foundation.

Empowerline. (2022, January 19). Older People & the Digital Divide 101. https://empowerline.org/older-people-the-digital-divide-101/

Engez, A., Leminen, S., & Aarikka-Stenroos, L. (2021). Urban living lab as a circular economy ecosystem: Advancing environmental sustainability through economic value, material, and knowledge flows. *Sustainability*, *13*(5), 2811. DOI: 10.3390/su13052811

Etzkowitz, H., & Leydesdorff, L. (2000). The dynamics of innovation: From national systems and "Mode 2" to a Triple Helix of university–industry–government relations. *Research Policy, 29*(2), 109–123. DOI: 10.1016/S0048-7333(99)00055-4

Eurofound. (2023). *Intergenerational inequalities: How to close the gaps?* Publications Office of the European Union. https://www.eurofound.europa.eu/en/publications/all/intergenerational-inequalities-how-close-gaps

European Commission. (2015). *The 2015 Ageing Report: Economic and budgetary projections for the 28 EU Member States (2013–2060).* Publications Office of the European Union. Retrieved from https://ec.europa.eu/economy_finance/publications/european_economy/2015/pdf/ee3_en.pdf

European Commission. (2018). *The silver economy: How to stimulate the economy by hundreds of millions of euros per year.* Publications Office of the European Union. Retrieved from https://op.europa.eu/en/publication-detail/-/publication/2dca9276-3ec5-11e8-b5fe-01aa75ed71a1/language-en

European Commission. (2018a). *The 2018 ageing report: Economic and budgetary projections for the EU member states (2016–2070).* Institutional Paper 079. https://economy-finance.ec.europa.eu/system/files/2018-05/ip079_en.pdf

European Commission. (2018b). *The Silver Economy: Final report.* Publications Office of the European Union. https://vanuseioletakistuseks.ee/sites/default/files/imce/ee/The%20Silver%20Economy.%20Final%20Report.%20European%20Union%202018.pdf

European Commission. (2020). Green paper on ageing: Fostering solidarity and responsibility between generations. Publications Office of the European Union. https://op.europa.eu/en/publication-detail/-/publication/d918b520-63a9-11eb-aeb5-01aa75ed71a1

European Commission. (2021). European Innovation Partnership on Active and Healthy Ageing (EIP-AHA). https://digital-strategy.ec.europa.eu/en/policies/eip-aha

European Commission. Directorate-General for Communications Networks, Content and Technology, Oxford Economics & Technopolis. (2018). The silver economy: final report. Publications Office. https://data.europa.eu/doi/10.2759/685036

European Network of Living Labs. (2019). *Adherent Member Application Guidelines: 13th Wave—2019.* Retrieved from https://enoll.org/wp-content/uploads/2019/01/enoll-application-guidelines-13th-wave-1-1.pdf

European Network of Living Labs. (2022). *ENoLL Membership Application Guidelines — Wave 2022 (16th): Empowering everyone to innovate*. Retrieved from https://enoll.org/wp-content/uploads/2021/12/application-guidelines-wave-2022.pdf

European Network of Living Labs. (n.d.). *About us*. Retrieved from https://enoll.org/about-us/

European Parliament. (2021, July 7). *Report on an old continent growing older – possibilities and challenges related to ageing policy post-2020* (A9-0194/2021). Retrieved from https://www.europarl.europa.eu/doceo/document/A-9-2021-0194_EN.html

European Social Fund Plus. (2025, May 28). *Living Labs for digital and innovative solutions for elderly and disabled citizens*. European Commission. Retrieved from https://european-social-fund-plus.ec.europa.eu/en/social-innovation-match/case-study/living-labs-digital-and-innovative-solutions-elderly-and-disabled-citizens

Eurostat. (2021). *Ageing Europe — 2021 interactive edition*. Publications Office of the European Union. https://ec.europa.eu/eurostat/web/products-interactive-publications/-/ks-08-21-259

Eurostat. (2024). Business demography statistics. Statistics Explained. Retrieved from https://ec.europa.eu/eurostat/statistics-explained/index.php?title=Business_demography_statistics

Evans, P. (2019). *Living lab methodology handbook*. North Wales Regional Partnership Board. Retrieved from https://www.northwalescollaborative.wales/wp-content/uploads/2020/10/Living-lab-methodology-handbook_r.pdf

Fang, E. F., Xie, C., Schenkel, J. A., Wu, C., Long, Q., Cui, H., Aman, Y., Frank, J., Liao, J., Zou, H., Wang, N. Y., Wu, J., Liu, X., Li, T., Fang, Y., Niu, Z., Yang, G., Hong, J., Wang, Q., . . . Woo, J. (2020). A research agenda for ageing in China in the 21st century (2nd edition): Focusing on basic and translational research, long term care, policy and social networks. *Aging Research Review,* 64, 1-26. https://doi.org/DOI: 10.1016/j.arr.2020.101174

Fang, Y. X., Gill, S. S., Kunasekaran, P., Rosnon, M. R., Talib, A. T., & Abd-Aziz, A. (2022). Digital divide: An inquiry on the native communities of Sabah. *Societies (Basel, Switzerland), 12*(6), 148. DOI: 10.3390/soc12060148

Federal Communications Commission. (2024, March). *Inquiry Concerning the Deployment of Advanced Telecommunications Capability to All Americans (Section 706 Report)* (FCC 24-27). Retrieved from https://docs.fcc.gov/public/attachments/FCC-24-27A1.pdf

Feng, C., Huang, J.-B., & Wang, M. (2019). The sustainability of China's metal industries: Features, challenges and future focuses. *Resources Policy, 60*, 215–224. DOI: 10.1016/j.resourpol.2018.12.006

Fernández-López, S., Rodeiro-Pazos, D., Zapata-Huamaní, G. A., & Rodríguez-Gulías, M. J. (2022). Senior and technology entrepreneurship: An analysis for OECD countries. *Strategic Change, 31*(4), 447–460. DOI: 10.1002/jsc.2514

Festa, N., Hsu, J., Hammitt, J., & Gill, T. (2022). Reappraising the public health benefits conferred by environmental policy: Considerations for an aging society. *Journal of the American Geriatrics Society, 71*, 1291–1299. DOI: 10.1111/jgs.18219 PMID: 36585900

Festinger, L. (1954). A theory of social comparison processes. *Human Relations, 7*, 117–140.

Figueiredo, T., Midão, L., Carrilho, J., Videira Henriques, D., Alves, S., Duarte, N., Bessa, M. J., Fidalgo, J. M., García, M., Facal, D., Felpete, A., Filgueira, I. R., Carlos Bernárdez, J., Rodríguez, M., Cerqueira, J. F., & Costa, E. (2024). A comprehensive analysis of digital health–focused living labs: Innovative approaches to dementia. *Frontiers in Medicine, 11*, 1418612. DOI: 10.3389/fmed.2024.1418612

Financial Conduct Authority. (2016). The ageing population and financial services. Future Horizons Research. https://www.fca.org.uk/publication/research/future-horizons-ageing-population-financial-services.pdf

Finn, K., & Johnston, H. (2024). *Living Lab integrates Indigenous perspective into ag research. Canadian Cattlemen*. Retrieved from https://www.canadiancattlemen.ca/research/living-lab-integrates-indigenous-perspective-into-ag-research/

Fisher, B., Wit, L. A., & Ricketts, T. (2021). Integrating Economics into Research on Natural Capital and Human Health. *Review of Environmental Economics and Policy, 15*, 95–114. DOI: 10.1086/713024

Fleming, W., Hallman, T. A., Hoek, J. V. D., Johnson, S. M., & Biedenweg, K. (2022). Measuring Spatial Associations between Environmental Health and Beliefs about Environmental Governance. *Environmental Management, 70*, 1038–1050. DOI: 10.1007/s00267-022-01706-8 PMID: 36167922

Fonds de recherche du Québec. (2024). *Funding Program for Intersectoral Research on Aging – Living Laboratories – 2025–2026*. Retrieved from https://frq.gouv.qc.ca/en/program/funding-program-for-intersectoral-research-on-aging-living-laboratories-2025-2026/

Formosa, M. (2019). Active Ageing Through Lifelong Learning: The University of the Third Age. In Formosa, M. (Ed.), *The University of the Third Age and Active Ageing. International Perspectives on Aging* (Vol. 23). Springer., DOI: 10.1007/978-3-030-21515-6_1

Foster, L., & Walker, A. (2015). Active and successful aging: A European policy perspective. *The Gerontologist, 55*(1), 83–90. DOI: 10.1093/geront/gnu028 PMID: 24846882

Fotis, T., Kioskli, K., Sundaralingam, A., Fasihi, A., & Mouratidis, H. (2022). Co-creation in a digital health living lab: A case study. *Frontiers in Public Health, 10*, 892930. DOI: 10.3389/fpubh.2022.892930

Friemel, T. N. (2016). The digital divide has grown old: Determinants of a digital divide among seniors. *New Media & Society, 18*(2), 313–331. DOI: 10.1177/1461444814538648

Fuellen, G., Kulaga, A., Lobentanzer, S., Unfried, M., Avelar, R. A., Palmer, D., & Kennedy, B. K. (2025). Validation requirements for AI-based intervention-evaluation in aging and longevity research and practice. *Ageing Research Reviews, 104*, 102617. DOI: 10.1016/j.arr.2024.102617

Galway, L. P., Levkoe, C. Z., Portinga, R. L. W., & Milun, K. (2021). A scoping review examining governance, co-creation, and social and ecological justice in living labs literature. *Challenges, 13*(1), 1–16. DOI: 10.3390/challe13010001

Gambo, I., Bueno-Delgado, M. V., Mooses, K., Melero Muñoz, F. J., Zviel-Girshin, R., Andrushevich, A., & Taveter, K. (2023). Technology adoption review for ageing well: Analysis of technical solutions. *Frontiers in Public Health, 11*, 1169192. DOI: 10.3389/fpubh.2023.1169192

Gao, J., Siddik, A., Abbas, S., Hamayun, M., Masukujjaman, M., & Alam, S. (2023). Impact of E-Commerce and Digital Marketing Adoption on MSMEs' Financial and Sustainability Performance during the COVID-19 Pandemic: An Empirical Study. *Sustainability (Switzerland), 15*(2). Advance online publication. DOI: 10.3390/su15021594

Gao, S., Ho, E. L.-E., Chua, V., & Feng, C.-C. (2024). More than aging in place: "Aging in networks" in Singapore. *Annals of the Association of American Geographers, 114*(9), 2132–2152. DOI: 10.1080/24694452.2024.2370922

Geissdoerfer, M., Savaget, P., Bocken, N. M., & Hultink, E. J. (2017). The Circular Economy–A new sustainability paradigm? *Journal of Cleaner Production, 143*, 757–768. DOI: 10.1016/j.jclepro.2016.12.048

Geneletti, D., Cortinovis, C., Zardo, L., & Esmail, B. A. (2019). *Towards Equity in the Distribution of Ecosystem Services in Cities*. SpringerBriefs in Environmental Science., DOI: 10.1007/978-3-030-20024-4_6

George, G., & Thomas, S. (2021). Sustainable business models for digital platforms: Lessons from India. *Strategic Entrepreneurship Journal, 15*(4), 561–580. DOI: 10.1002/sej.1407

Ghosh, S., & Ghosh, S. (2023). FEEL: FEderated LEarning Framework for ELderly Healthcare Using Edge-IoMT. *IEEE Transactions on Computational Social Systems, 10*, 1800–1809. DOI: 10.1109/TCSS.2022.3233300

Gibbs, G. (1988). *Learning by Doing, A guide to Teaching and Learning Methods*. Oxford Polytechnic.

Gilbert, S., Mathias, R., Schönfelder, A., Wekenborg, M., Steinigen-Fuchs, J., Dillenseger, A., & Ziemssen, T. (2025). A roadmap for safe, regulation-compliant living labs for AI and digital health development. *Science Advances, 11*(20), eadv7719. Advance online publication. DOI: 10.1126/sciadv.adv7719

Glass, A. P. (2013). Lessons learned from a new elder cohousing community. *Journal of Housing for the Elderly, 27*(4), 348–368. DOI: 10.1080/02763893.2013.813426

Global Entrepreneurship Monitor. (2023). *Global entrepreneurship monitor 2023/2024 global report*. GEM Consortium. https://gemconsortium.org/report

Global Entrepreneurship Monitor. (2024). *Global Entrepreneurship Monitor 2023/2024 global report: 25 years and growing*. Global Entrepreneurship Research Association. https://gemconsortium.org/report/51377

Global Entrepreneurship Monitor. (2025). *Global Entrepreneurship Monitor 2024/2025 United States report: National entrepreneurship assessment for the United States*. Global Entrepreneurship Research Association. https://gemconsortium.org/report/51640

Golant, S. M. (2017). A theoretical model to explain the smart technology adoption behaviors of elder consumers (Elderadopt). *Journal of Aging Studies, 42*, 56–73. DOI: 10.1016/j.jaging.2017.07.003 PMID: 28918822

Goldstein, B. B. (2006). *A guide to Drucker's systematic innovation*. Kauffman Foundation. https://www.entrepreneurship.org/articles/2006/05/a-guide-to-druckers-systematic-innovation

Golomski, C., Corvini, M., Kim, B. R., Wilcox, J., & Valcourt, S. (2022). Aspects of ICT connectivity among older adults living in rural subsidized housing: Reassessing the digital divide. *Journal of Enabling Technologies, 16*(1), 17–27. DOI: 10.1108/JET-12-2020-0052

Gong, C. H., & He, X. (2019). Factors Predicting Voluntary and Involuntary Workforce Transitions at Mature Ages: Evidence from HILDA in Australia. *International Journal of Environmental Research and Public Health, 16*(19), 3769. DOI: 10.3390/ijerph16193769 PMID: 31597239

Gonyea, J. G. (2013). Changing family demographics, multigenerational bonds, and care for the oldest old. *The Public Policy and Aging Report, 23*(2), 11–15.

González-Baldovinos, D. L., Sánchez-Fernández, L. P., Cano-Rosas, J. L., López-Chau, A., & Guevara-López, P. (2025). Innovations and Technological Advances in Healthcare Remote Monitoring Systems for the Elderly and Vulnerable People: A Scoping Review. *Applied Sciences (Basel, Switzerland)*. Advance online publication. DOI: 10.3390/app15063200

Goyal, N., & Arora, S. (2021). Impact of government policies on SME e-commerce adoption: A longitudinal analysis. *Government Information Quarterly, 38*(3), 101594. DOI: 10.1016/j.giq.2021.101594

Gratton, L., & Scott, A. J. (2021). *The 100-year life: Living and working in an age of longevity*. Bloomsbury Publishing.

Griva, A., Mitroulia, M., & Armakolas, S. (2024). Strategic management of the silver economy. *European Journal of Management and Marketing Studies, 9*(1), 1–17. DOI: 10.46827/ejmms.v9i1.1693

Gruss, B., & Noureldin, D. (2025, June). Sustaining growth in an aging world. *Finance & Development, 62*(2), 48–51. https://www.imf.org/en/Publications/fandd/issues/2025/06/sustaining-growth-in-an-aging-world-bertrand-gruss

Gschwendtner, P. (2020). Silver economy strategies: A comparative study of Japanese and South Korean governmental measures. *Vienna Journal of East Asian Studies, 12*(1), 62–91. DOI: 10.2478/vjeas-2020-0003

Guido, G., Ugolini, M. M., & Sestino, A. (2022). Active ageing of elderly consumers: Insights and opportunities for future business strategies. *International Journal of Consumer Studies, 46*(1), 146–162. PMID: 35018351

Guillemard, A. M. (2000). *Aging and the welfare-state crisis*. University of Delaware Press.

Guo, Y., Liu, M., Wang, J., Xia, Y., & Zhao, D. (2023). Demographic challenge: The rise of the silver economy in China. *Advances in Economics, Management, and Political Sciences, 34*, 120–125. DOI: 10.54254/2754-1169/34/20231688

Gurram, H., Trehan, A., Pradhan, C., Bhadade, D. P., Mathurkar, P. K., & Rane, D. S. R. (2025). Blockchain Integration in Information Systems: Transforming Data Security and Transaction Transparency. *Journal of Information Systems Engineering & Management*. Advance online publication. DOI: 10.52783/jisem.v10i11s.1585

Gutowski, T., Sekulic, D. P., & Bakshi, B. (2009). Preliminary thoughts on the application of thermodynamics to the development of sustainability criteria. *2009 IEEE International Symposium on Sustainable Systems and Technology*, 1–6. https://doi.org/DOI: 10.1109/issst.2009.5156699

Habiyaremye, A. (2020). Knowledge exchange and innovation co-creation in living labs projects in South Africa. *Innovation and Development, 10*(2), 207–222. DOI: 10.1080/2157930X.2019.1580940

Hare, C., Kirk, D., & Lang, T. (1999). Identifying the expectations of older food consumers - more than a ‘shopping list’ of wants. *Journal of Marketing Practice: Applied Marketing Science*, 5 (6/7/8), 213-232. https://doi.org/DOI: 10.1108/EUM0000000004575

Harms, R., Luck, F., Kraus, S., & Walsh, S. (2014). On the motivational drivers of gray entrepreneurship: An exploratory study. *Technological Forecasting and Social Change, 89*, 358–365. DOI: 10.1016/j.techfore.2014.08.001

Harper, S. (2006). *Ageing societies: Myths, challenges and opportunities*. Hodder Arnold.

Harper, S. (2014). Economic and social implications of aging societies. *Science, 346*(6209), 587–591. DOI: 10.1126/science.1254405 PMID: 25359967

Harper, S., & Hamblin, K. (Eds.). (2014). *International handbook on ageing and public policy*. Edward Elgar Publishing.

Harrington, C. N. (2020). The forgotten margins: What is community-based participatory health design telling us? *Interaction, 27*(3), 24–29. DOI: 10.1145/3386381

Hasenkamp, W. (Host). (2025, March 13). Otto Scharmer—Changing Systems [Audio Podcast Transcript]. https://podcast.mindandlife.org/otto-scharmer/

Hazell, E. (2020). Disaggregating Ecosystem Benefits: An Integrated Environmental-Deprivation Index. *Sustainability*. Advance online publication. DOI: 10.3390/su12187589

He, R. (2024). The Influence of Population Aging on China's Economy. *Advances in Economics, Management and Political Sciences*. https://doi.org/DOI: 10.54254/2754-1169/2024.ld18195

Health and Aging in Africa: Longitudinal Studies in South Africa (HAALSA). (2023). *About HAALSA*. https://haalsi.org/about/

Henning-Smith, C., Powell, M. A., & Lahr, M. (2022). Approaches to serving rural older adults in State Plans on Aging: A policy content evaluation. *Journal of Applied Gerontology*, *41*(10), 2132–2139. DOI: 10.1177/07334648221104085

Hill, A., Mellon, L., & Goddard, J. (2018). How winning organizations last 100 years. *Harvard Business Review*. https://hbr.org/2018/09/how-winning-organizations-last-100-years

Hoedemakers, M., Tsiachristas, A., & Mölken, M. R. R. (2022). Moving Beyond Quality-Adjusted Life-Years in Elderly Care: How Can Multicriteria Decision Analysis Complement Cost-Effectiveness Analysis in Local-Level Decision Making. *Value in Health : The Journal of the International Society for Pharmacoeconomics and Outcomes Research*. https://doi.org/DOI: 10.1016/j.jval.2022.04.1728

Holsman, D. K. K. (2023). *Climate Change 2022 – Impacts, Adaptation and Vulnerability*. https://doi.org/DOI: 10.1017/9781009325844

Homburg, C., & Giering, A. (2001). Personal Characteristics as Moderators of the Relationship Between Customer Satisfaction and Loyalty – An Empirical Analysis. *Psychology and Marketing*, *18*(1), 43–66. DOI: 10.1002/1520-6793(200101)18:1<43:AID-MAR3>3.0.CO;2-I

Hong, C., Sun, L., Liu, G., Guan, B., Li, C., & Luo, Y. (2023). Response of global health towards the challenges presented by population aging. *China CDC Weekly*, *5*(39), 884–887. DOI: 10.46234/ccdcw2023.168 PMID: 37814614

Hong, S., Jang, E., Cho, J., Lee, J., Rhee, J. H., Lee, H., Lee, M., Cha, S. H., Koo, C., Baik, O. M., & Heo, Y. (2024). A living lab to develop smart home services for the residential welfare of older adults. *Technology in Society*, *77*, 102577. DOI: 10.1016/j.techsoc.2024.102577

Hong, W., Liang, C., Ma, Y., & Zhu, J. (2025). Intergenerational digital feedback and digital social integration of older adults: An empirical study from personal initiative perspective. *Humanities & Social Sciences Communications*, *12*, 5518. DOI: 10.1057/s41599-025-05518-z

Huang, J. H., & Thomas, E. (2021). A review of Living Lab research and methods for user involvement. *Technology Innovation Management Review, 11*(9/10), 88–107. DOI: 10.22215/timreview/1467

Hughes G, Bennett KM, Hetherington MM.(2004). Old and alone: barriers to healthy eating in older men living on their own. *Appetite*. Dec;43(3):269-76. doi: DOI: 10.1016/j.appet.2004.06.002

Hussain, N. Y., Babalola, F. I., Kokogho, E., & Odio, P. E. (2024). Blockchain Technology Adoption Models for Emerging Financial Markets: Enhancing Transparency, Reducing Fraud, and Improving Efficiency. *International Journal of Multidisciplinary Research and Growth Evaluation*. https://doi.org/DOI: 10.54660/.ijmrge.2024.5.1.1281-1292

Hwangbo, Y. (2023). Korea's citizen-centric smart city development by adopting living labs and design thinking methodologies and their implications for ASEAN countries. In *Sustainable Development and the Digital Economy* (pp. 225–242). Routledge., DOI: 10.4324/9781003388753-14

I-CHANGE Project. (n.d.). *Living Lab of West Africa*. https://ichange-project.eu/category/living-lab/living-lab-of-west-africa/

IEEE Connecting the Unconnected. (2023, February 9). *The elderly digital divide: Age is just a number, and so is your smartphone password*. https://ctu.ieee.org/blog/2023/02/09/the-elderly-digital-divide-age-is-just-a-number-and-so-is-your-smartphone-password/

IMF. (2025). The rise of the silver economy: Global implications of population aging. *World Economic Outlook*, April 2025, Chapter 2. https://www.imf.org/-/media/Files/Publications/WEO/2025/April/English/ch2.ashx

Inter-American Development Bank. (2020). *The silver economy in Latin America and the Caribbean: Aging as an opportunity for innovation, entrepreneurship, and inclusion*. Inter-American Development Bank. https://publications.iadb.org/en/the-silver-economy-in-latin-america-and-the-caribbean-aging-as-an-opportunity-for-innovation-entrepreneurship-and-inclusion

Inter-American Development Bank. (2025, March 19). *The demographic wave drives the silver economy in Latin America and the Caribbean*. https://blogs.iadb.org/trabajo/en/the-demographic-wave-drives-the-silver-economy-in-latin-america-and-the-caribbean/

International Finance Corporation. (2024, August 27). *IFC launches Silver Economy Initiative to address growing underserved population in Latin America & the Caribbean.* https://www.ifc.org/en/pressroom/2024/ifc-launches-silver-economy-initiative-to-address-growing-underserved-population-in-latin-america-the-caribbean

International Monetary Fund. (2025). *The rise of the silver economy: Global implications of population aging.* (World Economic Outlook, April 2025, Chapter 2). IMF. https://www.imf.org/en/Publications/WEO/Issues/2025/04/10/world-economic-outlook-April-2025

International Monetary Fund. (2025, April). *World Economic Outlook, April 2025—Chapter 2: The rise of the silver economy.* https://www.imf.org/-/media/Files/Publications/WEO/2025/April/English/ch2.ashx

ISO/TC 176. (2015). *ISO 9001:2015—Quality management systems—Requirements.* International Organization for Standardization. https://www.iso.org/standard/62085.html

IST-Africa. (n.d.). *Supporting the evolution of sustainable Living Labs.* http://www.ist-africa.org/home/default.asp?page=livinglabs

Istat (2025). Demo. https://demo.istat.it/

Jafari, A., Keivan-behjou, F., & Mostafazadeh, R. (2024). Ecosystem health assessment using multicriteria approach in a forested ecotone area in northwest Iran. *Journal for Nature Conservation.* Advance online publication. DOI: 10.1016/j.jnc.2024.126589

Jain, P., & Kumar, R. (2020). Digital ecosystems and SME performance in India: The moderating role of government support. *Journal of Small Business Management, 58*(5), 923–945. DOI: 10.1080/00472778.2019.1709382

Jaušovec, M., & Gabrovec, B. (2023). Architectural Evaluation of Healthcare Facilities: A Comprehensive Review and Implications for Building Design. *Buildings (Basel, Switzerland).* Advance online publication. DOI: 10.3390/buildings13122926

Jha, A. K., & Agarwal, S. (2023). E-commerce adoption among Indian SMEs: An innovation diffusion perspective. *Journal of Business Research, 157*, 113484. DOI: 10.1016/j.jbusres.2022.113484

John T. Gorman Foundation & Federal Reserve Bank of Boston. (2023). *The importance of wealth to family well-being: Seeding innovation to address the structural roots of inequality.* https://www.jtgfoundation.org/wp-content/uploads/2023/05/Importance-of-wealth-to-family-well-being-full-report3.pdf accessed November 27, 2025

Kamberidou, I. (2020). "Distinguished" women entrepreneurs in the digital economy and the multitasking whirlpool. *Journal of Innovation and Entrepreneurship, 9*(3), 1–26. DOI: 10.1186/s13731-020-0114-y

Kanev, A., Kobyakova, O., Kurakova, N., & Shibalkov, I. (2024). *Population ageing and national healthcare systems sustainability. A review of world practices*. National Health Care., DOI: 10.47093/2713-069x.2023.4.4.5-13

Kapoor, K., Dwivedi, Y. K., Piercy, N. F., & Lal, B. (2021). Digital transformation in emerging markets: Enablers and challenges for SMEs. *Business Horizons, 64*(5), 599–611. DOI: 10.1016/j.bushor.2021.04.002

Kapuria, P. (2021). Digitising Indian Retail: Analysing Challenges and Exploring Growth Models. Observer Research Foundation. Retrieved from https://www.orfonline.org/research/digitising-indian-retail-analysing-challenges-and-exploring-growth-models

Karuga, R., Kabaria, C., Chumo, I., Okoth, L., Njoroge, I., Otiso, L., & Mberu, B. (2023). Voices and challenges of marginalized and vulnerable groups in urban informal settlements in Nairobi, Kenya: Building on a spectrum of community-based participatory research approaches. *Frontiers in Public Health, 11*, 1175326. DOI: 10.3389/fpubh.2023.1175326

Kasai, T. (2021). Preparing for population ageing in the Western Pacific Region. *The Lancet Regional Health. Western Pacific, 6*, 100069. DOI: 10.1016/j.lanwpc.2020.100069

Kaswan, M. J. (2022). Property, ownership and employee ownership: Employee control in ESOPs. *Journal of Participation and Employee Ownership, 5*(1), 14–31. DOI: 10.1108/JPEO-11-2020-0028

Katona, G. (1958). Attitude change: Instability of response and acquisition of experience. *Psychological Monographs, 72*(10), 1–38. DOI: 10.1037/h0093789

Kautonen, T. (2013). *Senior entrepreneurship* (OECD Local Economic and Employment Development [LEED] Papers No. 2013/19). OECD Publishing. https://doi.org/DOI: 10.1787/39915b50-en

Kautonen, T., Down, S., & Minniti, M. (2014). Ageing and entrepreneurial preferences. *Small Business Economics, 42*(3), 579–594. DOI: 10.1007/s11187-013-9489-5

Kautonen, T., Kibler, E., & Minniti, M. (2017). Late-career entrepreneurship and retirement. *Journal of Business Venturing, 32*(3), 432–448. DOI: 10.1016/j.jbusvent.2017.02.005

Kautonen, T., Tornikoski, E. T., & Kibler, E. (2011). Entrepreneurial intentions in the third age: The impact of perceived age norms. *Small Business Economics, 37*(2), 219–234. DOI: 10.1007/s11187-009-9238-y

Kebede, A. S., Ozolins, L. L., Holst, H., & Galvin, K. (2022). Digital engagement of older adults: Scoping review. *Journal of Medical Internet Research, 24*(12), e40192. DOI: 10.2196/40192

Kegan, R., & Lahey, L. (2016b). An everyone culture: Becoming a deliberately developmental organization. *Stanford Social Innovation Review.* https://ssir.org/books/excerpts/entry/becoming_a_deliberately_developmental_organization#

Kegan, R., & Lahey, L. (2016a). *An everyone culture: Becoming a deliberately developmental organization.* Harvard Business Review Press.

Keller, D., & Singer, R. (2025). *The state of play for employee share ownership.* Harvard Business School Institute for Business in Global Society. https://www.hbs.edu/bigs/joseph-blasi-employee-ownership

Kelly, M. (2012). *Owning our future: The emerging ownership revolution.* Berrett Koehler.

Kelso, L., & Hetter Kelso, P. (1986). *Democracy and economic power: Extending the ESOP revolution through binary economics.* University Press of America.

Kim, Y. (2024). Payments for Ecosystem Services Programs and Climate Change Adaptation in Agriculture. SSRN *Electronic Journal.* https://doi.org/DOI: 10.2139/ssrn.4746066

Kim, H. K., & Lee, S.-H. (2021). The effects of population aging on South Korea's economy: The National Transfer Accounts approach. *The Journal of the Economics of Ageing, 20*, 100340. DOI: 10.1016/j.jeoa.2021.100340

Kim, J. S., & Kim, S. K. (2024). Ageing population and green space dynamics for climate change adaptation in Southeast Asia. *Nature Climate Change.* Advance online publication. DOI: 10.1038/s41558-024-01980-w

Kim, J., Kim, Y. L., Jang, H., Cho, M., Lee, M., & Lee, S.-H. (2020). Living labs for health: An integrative literature review. *European Journal of Public Health, 30*(1), 55–63. DOI: 10.1093/eurpub/ckz105

Klimczuk, A. (2021). The silver economy as a constructive response in public policy on aging. In *Strategic approach to aging population: Experiences and challenges* (pp. 19-35). Sveučilište Josipa Jurja Strossmayera u Osijeku, Ekonomski fakultet u Osijeku.

Klimczuk, A. (2012). Supporting the development of gerontechnology as part of silver economy building. *Ad Alta: J Interdisciplinary Res*, *2*(2), 52–56.

Klimczuk, A. (2016). Comparative analysis of national and regional models of the silver economy in the European Union. *International Journal of Ageing and Later Life*, *11*, 1–29. DOI: 10.3384/ijal.1652-8670.15286

Knight-Davidson, P., Lane, P., & McVicar, A. (2020). Methods for co-creating with older adults in living laboratories: A scoping review. *Health and Technology*, *10*(5), 997–1009. DOI: 10.1007/s12553-020-00441-6

Knoefel, F., Wallace, B., Thomas, N., Sveistrup, H., Goubran, R., & Laurin, C. L. (2024). *Supportive smart homes: Their role in aging in place*. Springer., DOI: 10.1007/978-3-031-37337-4

Knowles, M. S., & Knowles, H. F. (1959) *Introduction to group dynamics*. Chicago: Association Press. Revised edition 1972 published by New York: Cambridge Books.

Knowles, M. S., & Knowles, H. F. (1955). *How to develop better leaders*. Association Press.

Kohijoki, A. M. (2011). The effect of aging on consumer disadvantage in grocery retail services among the Finnish elderly. *Journal of Retailing and Consumer Services*, *18*(4), 370–377. DOI: 10.1016/j.jretconser.2011.04.0

Kohijoki, A. M., & Marjanen, H. (2013). The effect of age on shopping orientation—Choice orientation types of the ageing shoppers. *Journal of Retailing and Consumer Services*, *20*(2), 165–172. DOI: 10.1016/j.jretconser.2012.11.004

Kohlbacher, F., & Herstatt, C. (2008). *The silver market phenomenon: Business opportunities in an era of demographic change*. Springer.

Kohli, M. (2007). The institutionalization of the life course: Looking back to look ahead. *Research in Human Development*, *4*(3-4), 253–271. DOI: 10.1080/15427600701663122

Kolb, D. A. (1984). *Experiential learning: Experience as the source of learning and development* (Vol. 1). Prentice-Hall.

Kotschy, R., & Bloom, D. E. (2023). Economic growth prospects in the face of population ageing. *VOX, CEPR Policy Portal*. https://cepr.org/voxeu/columns/economic-growth-prospects-face-population-ageing

Kovalchuk, O., Ruslan, S., & Banakh, S. (2024). Cryptocurrency Crime Risks Modeling: Environment, E-Commerce, and Cybersecurity Issues. *IEEE Access : Practical Innovations, Open Solutions, 12*, 50673–50688. DOI: 10.1109/ACCESS.2024.3386428

Krzyminiewska, G. (2019). Silver economy in rural areas in the context of (un) sustainable development. *Annals of the Polish Association of Agricultural and Agribusiness Economists, XXI*(3), 212–219. DOI: 10.5604/01.3001.0013.2858

Krzyminiewska, G. (2020). Ethical dilemmas of the silver economy. *Ekonomia i Prawo, 19*(1), 61–71. DOI: 10.12775/EiP.2020.005

Kurtulus, F. A., & Kruse, D. L. (2017). *How did employee ownership firms weather the last two recessions?: Employee ownership, employment stability, and firm survival in the United States: 1999-2011*. W.E. Upjohn Institute for Employment Research.

Lak, A., Rashidghalam, P., Amiri, S. N., Myint, P., & Baradaran, H. (2020). An ecological approach to the development of an active aging measurement in urban areas (AAMU). *BMC Public Health, 21*. Advance online publication. DOI: 10.1186/s12889-020-10036-5 PMID: 33388040

Lambert Pandraud, R., Laurent, G., & Lapersonne, E. (2005). Repeat Purchasing of New Automobiles by older consumers: Empirical Evidence and Interpretations. *Journal of Marketing, 69*(2), 97–113. DOI: 10.1509/jmkg.69.2.97.60757

Lam, L., Fadrique, L., Bin Noon, G., Shah, A., & Morita, P. P. (2022). Evaluating challenges and adoption factors for Active Assisted Living smart environments. *Frontiers in Digital Health, 4*, 891634. DOI: 10.3389/fdgth.2022.891634

Lancaster, L., & Stillman, D. (2002). *When Generations Collide: Who They Are. Why They Clash. How to Solve the Generational Puzzle at Work*. Collins Business.

Lashitew, A. (2023). When businesses go digital: The role of CEO attributes in technology adoption and utilization during the COVID-19 pandemic. *Technological Forecasting and Social Change, 189*. Advance online publication. DOI: 10.1016/j.techfore.2023.122324 PMID: 36718420

Laterra, P., Nahuelhual, L., Vallejos, M., Berrouet, L., Pérez, E. A., Enrico, L., Jiménez-Sierra, C., Mejía, K., Meli, P., Rincón-Ruíz, A., Salas, D., Špirić, J., Villegas, J. C., & Villegas-Palacio, C. (2019). Linking inequalities and ecosystem services in Latin America. *Ecosystem Services*. Advance online publication. DOI: 10.1016/j.ecoser.2018.12.001

Lazzarini, G., & Lucia, M. G. (2024). Demographic aging: Challenges and opportunities for ecological transition. *Journal of Emerging Perspectives*. https://doi.org/ DOI: 10.36253/jep-16902

Leal Filho, W., Ozuyar, P. G., Dinis, M. A. P., Azul, A. M., Will, M., & Frankenberger, F. (2023). Living labs in the context of the UN sustainable development goals: State of the art. *Sustainability Science*, *18*, 1163–1179. DOI: 10.1007/s11625-022-01240-w

Lee, S. M., & Trimi, S. (2018). Innovation for creating a smart future. *Journal of Innovation & Knowledge*, *3*(1), 1–8. DOI: 10.1016/j.jik.2016.11.001

Leighton, C., & Seaman, C. E. A. (1997). The elderly food consumer: Disadvantaged? *International Journal of Consumer Studies*, *21*(4), 363–370. DOI: 10.1111/j.1470-6431.1997.tb00294.x

Leminen, S., Westerlund, M., & Nyström, A.-G. (2012). Living labs as open-innovation networks. *Technology Innovation Management Review*, *2*(9), 6–11. https://timreview.ca/sites/default/files/article_PDF/Leminen_et_al_TIMReview_September2012.pdf

Lemon, K. N., & Verhoef, P. C. (2016). Understanding Customer Experience Throughout the Customer Journey. *Journal of Marketing*, *80*, 69–96. DOI: 10.1509/jm.15.0420

Leporati, M., Torres Marin, A. J., & Roses, S. (2021). Senior entrepreneurship in Chile: Necessity or opportunity? A GEM perspective. *European Business Review*, *33*(6), 892–917. DOI: 10.1108/EBR-11-2020-0277

Lévesque, M., & Minniti, M. (2006). The effect of aging on entrepreneurial behavior. *Journal of Business Venturing*, *21*(2), 177–194. DOI: 10.1016/j.jbusvent.2005.04.003

Lévesque, M., Stephan, U., Kautonen, T., & Bakker, R. (2026). Entrepreneurship, age, and the lifespan: Taking stock and avenues for future research. *Journal of Business Venturing*, *41*(1), 106548. Advance online publication. DOI: 10.1016/j.jbusvent.2025.106548

Levy, B. R. (2009). Stereotype embodiment: A psychosocial approach to aging. *Current Directions in Psychological Science*, *18*(6), 332–336. DOI: 10.1111/j.1467-8721.2009.01662.x PMID: 20802838

Levy, M., Weitz, B. A., & Grewal, D. (2022). *Retailing management* (11th ed.). McGraw-Hill Education.

Li, F., Su, X., & Hu, Y. (2023). Digital transformation and organizational resilience: Evidence from Chinese manufacturing firms. *Technovation*, *124*, 102711. DOI: 10.1016/j.technovation.2023.102711

Lindgren, E., & Elmqvist, T. (2017). *Ecosystem Services and Human Health*. https://doi.org/DOI: 10.1093/ACREFORE/9780199389414.013.86

Liu, L., Daum, C., Miguel Cruz, A., Neubauer, N., Perez, H., & Ríos Rincón, A. (2022, September). Ageing, technology, and health: Advancing the concepts of autonomy and independence. In *Healthcare Management Forum* (Vol. 35, No. 5, pp. 296-300). Sage CA: Los Angeles, CA: SAGE Publications. https://doi.org/DOI: 10.1177/08404704221110734

Liu, R., & Meng, X. (2023). Exploration on the Construction of a Big Data Ecosphere for the Rural Elderly Health Promotion from the Perspective of Collaborative Governance. *2023 13th International Conference on Information Technology in Medicine and Education (ITME)*, 795–799. https://doi.org/DOI: 10.1109/ITME60234.2023.00163

Liu, B.-P., Huxley, R., Schikowski, T., Hu, K.-J., Zhao, Q., & Jia, C.-X. (2024). Exposure to residential green and blue space and the natural environment is associated with a lower incidence of psychiatric disorders in middle-aged and older adults: Findings from the UK Biobank. *BMC Medicine*, *22*. Advance online publication. DOI: 10.1186/s12916-023-03239-1 PMID: 38221612

Liu, X., Chau, K.-Y., Liu, X., & Wan, Y. (2025). Synergistic evaluation system of "technology and service" in smart elderly care institutions. *Digital Health*, *11*. Advance online publication. DOI: 10.1177/205520762513266 PMID: 40290271

Li, Z., Li, F., Wang, X., Fu, Q., & Ren, W. (2024). Ethical considerations and fundamental principles of large language models in medical education: Viewpoint. *Journal of Medical Internet Research*, *26*, e60083. DOI: 10.2196/60083

Lundström, A. (Ed.). (2008). *Entrepreneurship policy in the Nordic countries: Perspectives of the development since 2003*. Nordic Council of Ministers / Swedish Foundation for Small Business Research. https://norden.diva-portal.org/smash/record.jsf?pid=diva2%3A707143&utm_source=chatgpt.com&dswid=-9615

Maâlaoui, A., Bouchard, G., & Safraou, I. (2014). Les seniorpreneurs: Motivations, profils, accompagnement. *Entreprendre & Innover*, *20*(1), 50–61. DOI: 10.3917/entin.020.0050

Maestas, N., Mullen, K. J., & Powell, D. (2023). The effect of population aging on economic growth, the labor force, and productivity. *American Economic Journal. Macroeconomics*, *15*(2), 306–332. DOI: 10.1257/mac.20190196

Mahani, A., Lyeo, J., Fung, A., Husack, K., Muhajarine, N., Diener, T., Brown, C., & Conceptualization. (2023). *At the end of the day, it is Council's decision: Integration of health and equity into urban design and urban planning decisions and policies in Regina Saskatchewan*. https://doi.org/DOI: 10.1101/2023.12.05.23299446

Maity, S., Maji, S., Sil, S., Roy, A., Sarkar, S., Dhabal, S., & Venkateswaran, P. (2024). Homecare Robotic Systems: Wearable Remote Sensing with Interactive AI Features. *2024 IEEE Applied Sensing Conference (APSCON)*, 1–4. https://doi.org/DOI: 10.1109/APSCON60364.2024.10465959

Malamas, V., Koutras, D., Dasaklis, T. K., Vassilakopouls, V., & Kotzanikolaou, P. (2024). Blockchain Revolution in the Metaverse: Challenges, Applications and Future Directions. *2024 International Conference on Artificial Intelligence, Metaverse and Cybersecurity (ICAMAC)*, 1–6. https://doi.org/DOI: 10.1109/icamac62387.2024.10829333

Malorgio, A., Teti, E., & Dallocchio, M. (2021). Green Bonds: The Evolution of a Sustainable Financial Instrument on the Cutting Edge. *International Review of Environmental and Resource Economics*. Advance online publication. DOI: 10.1561/101.00000134

Marrone, N. L., Nieman, C. L., & Coco, L. (2022). Community-based participatory research and human-centered design principles to advance hearing health equity. *Ear and Hearing*, *43*(Suppl. 1), 33S–44S. DOI: 10.1097/AUD.0000000000001183

Mason, A. (2005, August). Demographic transition and demographic dividends in developed and developing countries. In *United Nations expert group meeting on social and economic implications of changing population age structures* (Vol. 31, No. 5). New York: United Nations, Population Division.

Mason, A., & Lee, S.-H. (2019). *The economic impact of population aging: How should policymakers respond?* https://consensus.app/papers/the-economic-impact-of-population-aging-how-should-mason-lee/373ef245b7b75f84943ed085fea2a8f8/

Masunaga, Y., Jaiteh, F., Manneh, E., Balen, J., Okebe, J., D'Alessandro, U., & Muela Ribera, J. (2021). The community lab of ideas for health: Community-based transdisciplinary solutions in a malaria elimination trial in The Gambia. *Frontiers in Public Health*, *9*, 637714. DOI: 10.3389/fpubh.2021.637714

Ma, Y., Sun, Y., Guo, Q., & Li, H. (2024). Evolutionary game analysis of building a sustainable intelligent elderly care service platform. *Scientific Reports*, *14*, 28653. DOI: 10.1038/s41598-024-79976-x

Ma, Y., & Xing, T. (2024). Encourage sustainable consumption among the elderly through generativity. *Journal of Retailing and Consumer Services, 81*, 104053. DOI: 10.1016/j.jretconser.2024.104053

McIntyre, K. M., Vogler, B., Chantziaras, I., Coelho, A., Díez, J. G., Esteves, A., Igrejas, G., Lurz, P., Martins, S. B., Mastin, A., Murray, A., Parnell, S., Poeta, P., Ramos, S., Saraiva, C., Speranza, C. I., McMahon, B. J., Rüegg, S., Häsler, B., & Zinsstag, J. (2018). *Assessing the ecological dimension of One health.* 126–169. https://doi.org/DOI: 10.3920/978-90-8686-875-9

Meneely, L., Burns, A., & Strugnell, C. (2009). Age associated changes in older consumers retail behaviour. *International Journal of Retail & Distribution Management, 37*(12), 1041–1056. DOI: 10.1108/09590550911005010

Meneely, L., Strugnell, C., & Burns, A. (2009). Elderly consumers and their food store experiences. *Journal of Retailing and Consumer Services, 16*(6), 458–465. DOI: 10.1016/j.jretconser.2009.06.006

Menke., & Associates. (2011). *The origin and history of the ESOP and its future role as a business succession tool.* Menke. Retrieved December 3, 2025, from https://www.menke.com/esop-archives/the-origin-and-history-of-the-esop-and-its-future-role-as-a-business-succession-tool/

Merino-Barbancho, B., Abril Jiménez, P., Mallo, I., Lombroni, I., Cea, G., López Nebreda, C., Cabrera, M. F., Fico, G., & Arredondo, M. T. (2023). Innovation through the Quintuple Helix in living labs: Lessons learned for a transformation from lab to ecosystem. *Frontiers in Public Health, 11*, 1176598. DOI: 10.3389/fpubh.2023.1176598

Mezirow, J. (2000). Learning to think like an adult: Core concepts of transformation theory. In Mezirow, J. (Eds.), *Learning as transformation: Critical perspectives on a theory in progress* (pp. 3–33). Jossey-Bass.

Mesthrige, J. W., & Cheung, S. L. (2020). Critical evaluation of 'ageing in place' in redeveloped public rental housing estates in Hong Kong. *Ageing and Society, 40*(9), 2006–2039. DOI: 10.1017/S0144686X19000448

METI. (Ministry of Economy, Trade and Industry, Japan). (2019). *Annual report on the ageing society [Summary]* FY 2019. Government of Japan. https://www8.cao.go.jp/kourei/english/annualreport/2019/pdf/2019.pdf

Miji Africa Living Lab. (n.d.). *Home*. https://mijiafrica.com/

Mitsanas, M., & Lee, C. (2024, February 19). How South Korea is tackling its demographic crisis. *TIME*. https://time.com/6696414/south-korea-elderly-workforce/

Modigliani, F., & Brumberg, R. (1954). Utility analysis and the consumption function: An Interpretation of cross-section data. In *Post-Keynesian Economics* (pp. 388–436). Rutgers University Press., https://www.princeton.edu/~deaton/downloads/Deaton_Franco_Modigliani.pdf

Mohrman, S. A., & Lawler, E. E.III. (2011). *Useful research: Advancing theory and practice*. Berrett-Koehler Publishers.

Morand, S. (2022). *ONE HEALTH: AN ECOSYSTEM-BASED ECOLOGY OF HEALTH*. https://consensus.app/papers/one-health-an-ecosystembased-ecology-of-health-morand/5cb3ace534135d95aa9abea88ba3a026/

Moschis, G. P. (1994). Consumer Behavior in Later Life: Multidisciplinary Contributions and Implications for Research. *Journal of the Academy of Marketing Science*, *22*(3), 195–204. DOI: 10.1177/0092070394223001

Moschis, G. P. (2007). Life course perspectives on consumer behavior. *Journal of the Academy of Marketing Science*, *35*, 295–307. DOI: 10.1007/s11747-007-0027-3

Moschis, G. P. (2012). Consumer Behavior in Later Life: Current Knowledge, Issues, and New Directions for Research. *Psychology and Marketing*, *39*(2), 57–75. DOI: 10.1002/mar.20504

Moschis, G. P. (2019). *Consumer Behavior over the Life Course – Research Frontiers and New Directions*. Springer Nature Switzerland., DOI: 10.1007/978-3-030-05008-5

Moulaert, F., MacCallum, D., Mehmood, A., & Hamdouch, A. (Eds.). (2013). *The International Handbook on Social Innovation: Collective Action, Social Learning and Transdisciplinary Research*. Edward Elgar Publishing.

Mubarak, F., & Suomi, R. (2022). Elderly forgotten? Digital exclusion in the information age and the rising grey digital divide. *INQUIRY: The Journal of Health Care Organization, Provision, and Financing*, *59*, 00469580221096272. DOI: 10.1177/00469580221096272

Mulati, N., Aung, M. N., Field, M., Nam, E. W., Ma, C. H. K., Moolphate, S., Lee, H., Goto, Y., Kweun, N. H., Suda, T., Koyanagi, Y., Nagamine, Y., & Yuasa, M. (2022). Digital-based policy and health promotion policy in Japan, the Republic of Korea, Singapore, and Thailand: A scoping review of policy paths to healthy aging. *International Journal of Environmental Research and Public Health*, *19*(24), 16995. DOI: 10.3390/ijerph192416995

Nakatani, H. (2024). International promotion of Japanese aging-related health services and products: Perspective of an international agency. *Global Health & Medicine*, *6*(1), 49–62. DOI: 10.35772/ghm.2024.01004

Narayan, B., & Narayan, P. (2022). FinTech adoption by Indian MSMEs: Drivers and barriers. *International Journal of Bank Marketing, 40*(4), 783–802. DOI: 10.1108/IJBM-07-2021-0301

National Bureau of Economic Research. (2023). Examining an aging population in Sub-Saharan Africa. *National Bureau of Economic Research.* https://www.nber.org/brd/20234/examining-aging-population-sub-saharan-africa

National Center for Employee Ownership. (2018), "Employee ownership and economic well- being," accessed November 11, 2025, https://www.ownershipeconomy.org

National Research Council Canada. (2021–2022). *Aging in Place: Technology and Innovation – Program plan. National Research Council Canada.* https://nrc.canada.ca/en/research-development/research-collaboration/programs/aging-place-technology-innovation-proposed-program-plan

National Telecommunications and Information Administration. (2024, November 20). *Celebrating Native American Heritage Month: Empowering Native Communities Through Digital Equity.* U.S. Department of Commerce. https://www.ntia.gov/blog/2024/celebrating-native-american-heritage-month-empowering-native-communities-through-digital-equity

New Jersey State Policy Lab. (2022, January 13). *Bridging the digital divide in Native American communities.* Rutgers University. https://policylab.rutgers.edu/publication/bridging-the-digital-divide-in-native-american-communities/

News, M. I. T. (2020, December 3). Indigenous knowledge and technology at MIT: "Is it wise?" *MIT News.* https://news.mit.edu/2020/indigenous-knowledge-technology-mit-is-it-wise-1203

North, D. C. (1990). *Institutions, institutional change and economic performance.* Cambridge university press.

Nyström, A.-G., Leminen, S., Westerlund, M., & Kortelainen, M. (2014). Actor roles and role patterns influencing innovation in living labs. *Industrial Marketing Management, 43*(3), 483–495. DOI: 10.1016/j.indmarman.2013.12.016

O'Boyle, E. H., Patel, P. C., & Gonzalez-Mulé, E. (2016). Employee ownership and firm performance: A meta-analysis. *Human Resource Management Journal, 26*(4), 425–448. DOI: 10.1111/1748-8583.12115

OECD & European Commission. (2023). *The Missing Entrepreneurs 2023: Policies for inclusive entrepreneurship and self-employment.* OECD Publishing., DOI: 10.1787/230efc78-

OECD. (2018). *Working Better with Age*. OECD Publishing., DOI: 10.1787/9789264201996-

OECD. (2020). Who cares? Attracting and retaining care workers for the elderly. OECD Health Policy Studies. https://www.oecd.org/content/dam/oecd/en/publications/reports/2020/05/who-cares-attracting-and-retaining-care-workers-for-the-elderly_735ab920/92c0ef68-en.pdf

OECD. (2022). *OECD Reviews of Innovation Policy: Germany 2022 — Building agility for successful transitions*. OECD Publishing. https://www.oecd.org/en/publications/oecd-reviews-of-innovation-policy-germany-2022_50b32331-en.html

OECD. (2024). Addressing demographic headwinds in Japan: A long-term perspective. OECD Publishing. https://www.oecd.org/content/dam/oecd/en/publications/reports/2024/04/addressing-demographic-headwinds-in-japan-a-long-term-perspective_85b9a67f/96648955-en.pdf

OECD. (2025), The Economic Benefit of Promoting Healthy Ageing and Community Care, OECD Health Policy Studies, OECD Publishing, Paris, https://doi.org/DOI: 10.1787/0f7bc62b-en

OECD. (2025). *OECD Employment Outlook 2025*. OECD Publishing. https://www.oecd.org/en/publications/oecd-employment-outlook-2025_194a947b-en.html

Office of Disease Prevention and Health Promotion. (2025, March 17). *Social determinants of health and older adults*. https://odphp.health.gov/our-work/national-health-initiatives/healthy-aging/social-determinants-health-and-older-adults

Olamijuwon, J., & Zouo, S. J. C. (2024). The impact of health analytics on reducing healthcare costs in aging populations: A review. *International Journal of Management & Entrepreneurship Research*. https://doi.org/DOI: 10.51594/ijmer.v6i11.1690

Ollevier, A., Aguiar, G., Palomino, M., & Simpelaere, I. S. (2020). How can technology support ageing in place in healthy older adults? A systematic review. *Public Health Reviews*, *41*, 26. Advance online publication. DOI: 10.1186/s40985-020-00143-4

Oppio, A., Caprioli, C., Dell'Ovo, M., & Bottero, M. (2024). Assessing Ecosystem Services through a Multimethodological Approach Based on Multicriteria Analysis and Cost-Benefits Analysis: A case study in Turin (Italy). *Journal of Cleaner Production*. Advance online publication. DOI: 10.1016/j.jclepro.2024.143472

Oritsemolebi, A., Mayowa, A., & Munashe, N. M. (2025). The use of employee ownership structures as strategies for the resilience of smaller entities in the US. *International Journal of Science and Research Archive*, *14*(01), 1002–1018. DOI: 10.30574/ijsra.2025.14.1.0039

Orlando, L., DePinto, A. J., & Wallace, K. (2022). Ecohealth Villages: A Framework for an Ecosystem Approach to Health in Human Settlements. *Sustainability*. Advance online publication. DOI: 10.3390/su14127053

Oswald, F., & Kaspar, R. (2012). On the quantitative assessment of perceived housing in later life. *Journal of Housing for the Elderly*, *26*(1-3), 72–93. https://doi.org/10.1080/02763893.2012.673391

Pais-Magalhães, V. (2022). A commentary regarding the link between two of today's biggest global challenges: A rapidly ageing population and energy consumption. *American Journal of Aging Science and Research*, *3*(1), 27–32. https://www.probiologists.com/article/a-commentary-regarding-the-link-between-two-of-today-s-biggest-global-challenges-a-rapidly-ageing-population-and-energy-consumption

Palomino, M., Allen, R., Aider, F., Tirotto, F. A., Giorgi, I., Alexander, H., & Masala, G. (2022). The mood of the silver economy: A data science analysis of the mood states of older adults and the implications on their wellbeing. *Annals of Computer Science and Information Systems*, *32*, 251–258. DOI: 10.15439/2022F50

Park, N., & Farr, C. (2007). Retail Store Lighting for Elderly Consumers: An Experimental Approach. *Family and Consumer Sciences Research Journal*, *35*(4), 316–337. DOI: 10.1177/1077727X07300096

Parment, A. (2013). Generation Y vs. Baby Boomers: Shopping Behavior, Buyer Involvement and Implication for Retailing. *Journal of Retailing and Consumer Services*, *20*(2), 189–199. DOI: 10.1016/j.jretconser.2012.12.00

Parsons, T. (1951). *The social system*. Free Press.

Parsons, T. (1967). *Sociological theory and modern society*. Free Press.

Paterson, T. A., & Welbourne, T. M. (2019). I am therefore I own: Implications of organization-based identity for employee stock ownership. *Human Resource Management*, *59*(2), 1–9. DOI: 10.1002/hrm.21985

Pauhofova, I., & Dovalova, G. (2015). POTENTIAL OF SILVER ECONOMY IN THE EUROPEAN UNION (SELECTED VIEWS). *European Scientific Journal, ESJ*, *11*(10). Retrieved from https://eujournal.org/index.php/esj/article/view/6149

Peek, S. T., Wouters, E. J., Van Hoof, J., Luijkx, K. G., Boeije, H. R., & Vrijhoef, H. J. (2014). Factors influencing acceptance of technology for aging in place: A systematic review. *International Journal of Medical Informatics*, *83*(4), 235–248. DOI: 10.1016/j.ijmedinf.2014.01.004 PMID: 24529817

Peine, A., Marshall, B. L., Martin, W., & Neven, L. (2021). *Socio-gerontechnology: Interdisciplinary critical studies of ageing and technology*. Routledge.

Pérez Jolles, M., Willging, C. E., Stadnick, N. A., Crable, E. L., Lengnick-Hall, R., Hawkins, J., & Aarons, G. A. (2022). Understanding implementation research collaborations from a co-creation lens: Recommendations for a path forward. *Frontiers in Health Services, 2*, 942658. Advance online publication. DOI: 10.3389/frhs.2022.942658

Phillipson, C. (2013). *Ageing*. John Wiley & Sons.

Picard, R. G. (2011). *Digitization and media business models* (Mapping Digital Media Reference Series No. 5). Open Society Foundations. https://www.opensocietyfoundations.org/uploads/d7f96f08-8c77-48a0-84ad-7ac6ebdbe2f1/mapping-digital-media-digitization-media-business-models-20110721.pdf

Pillemer, K. (2021). *Older people and action on climate change: A powerful but underutilized resource.* Cornell University & United Nations ESCAP. https://www.unescap.org/sites/default/d8files/event-documents/KPillemer_paper.pdf

Pimpin, L., Pérez-Ferrer, C., Knuchel-Takano, A., Retat, L., Jaccard, A., Brown, M., & Webber, L. (2016). Modelling the long-term epidemiological and cost impact of a multicomponent lifestyle intervention and a sugar-sweetened beverage tax in the European Union: Results from the EConDA project. *Lancet, 388*. Advance online publication. DOI: 10.1016/S0140-6736(16)32324-8

Pinto, M. de M., & Pedruzzi Fonseca, L. (2013). Profundizando la comprensión de los Living Labs de Brasil. *CTS: Revista Iberoamericana de Ciencia, Tecnología y Sociedad, 8*(23), 231–247. https://ojs.revistacts.net/index.php/CTS/article/view/650

Pirzada, P., Wilde, A., Doherty, G. H., & Harris-Birtill, D. (2022). Ethics and acceptance of smart homes for older adults. *Informatics for Health & Social Care, 47*(1), 10–37. DOI: 10.1080/17538157.2021.1923500

Polasky, S., & Daily, G. (2021). An Introduction to the Economics of Natural Capital. *Review of Environmental Economics and Policy, 15*, 87–94. DOI: 10.1086/713010

Ponce, M., & Etchegoyen, J. F. (2025, July 30). *Silver opportunity: Financial innovation for an aging population in Latin America. World Bank Blogs.* https://blogs.worldbank.org/en/latinamerica/financial-innovation-aging-population-latin-america

Popper, R., & Kroll, B. (2003). Food Preference and Consumption Among the Elderly. *Food Technology*, •••, 57.

Posthuma, R. A., & Campion, M. A. (2009). Age stereotypes in the workplace: Common stereotypes, moderators, and future research directions. *Journal of Management, 35*(1), 158–188. DOI: 10.1177/0149206308318617

Prager, C., Varga, A., Olmsted, P., Ingram, J., Cattau, M., Freund, C., Wynn-Grant, R., & Naeem, S. (2016). An assessment of adherence to basic ecological principles by payments for ecosystem service projects. *Conservation Biology, 30*. Advance online publication. DOI: 10.1111/cobi.12648 PMID: 26502915

Prahalad, C. K., & Ramaswamy, V. (2004). Co-creation experiences: The next practice in value creation. *Journal of Interactive Marketing, 18*(3), 5–14. DOI: 10.1002/dir.20015

Priday, G., Pedell, S., Livingstone, A., Margelis, G., & Gould, G. (2024). Building a living lab network to support technology innovation within the Australian aged care sector. In C. P. Lim, A. Vaidya, N. Jain, M. N. Favorskaya, & L. C. Jain (Eds.), *Advances in Intelligent Healthcare Delivery and Management* (Intelligent Systems Reference Library, Vol. 258, pp. 147–169). Springer. https://doi.org/DOI: 10.1007/978-3-031-65430-5_7

Project Equity. (n.d.). *Build a loyal and motivated workforce with employee ownership*. https://project-equity.org/building-loyal-motivated-workforce-guide/

Qiu, L., Chen, Q., & Gao, T. (2021). The Effects of Urban Natural Environments on Preference and Self-Reported Psychological Restoration of the Elderly. *International Journal of Environmental Research and Public Health, 18*. Advance online publication. DOI: 10.3390/ijerph18020509 PMID: 33435508

Quigley, R., Russell, S. G., Larkins, S., Taylor, S., Sagigi, B., Strivens, E., & Redman-MacLaren, M. (2022). Aging well for Indigenous peoples: A scoping review. *Frontiers in Public Health, 10*, 780898. Advance online publication. DOI: 10.3389/fpubh.2022.780898

Racine, E., D'Anjou, B., Dallaire, C., Dumez, V., Favron-Godbout, C., Hudon, A., Montreuil, M., Olivier, C., Quintal, A., & Chenel, V. (2024). Developing a living lab in ethics: Initial issues and observations. *Bioethics, 38*(2), 153–163. DOI: 10.1111/bioe.13246

Raghavan, A., Demircioglu, M. A., & Taeihagh, A. (2021). Public health innovation through cloud adoption: A comparative analysis of drivers and barriers in Japan, South Korea, and Singapore. *International Journal of Environmental Research and Public Health, 18*(1), 334. DOI: 10.3390/ijerph18010334

Rahayu, R., Dayani, F., & Wibowo, A. (2023). Determinants of digital payment adoption in MSMEs in Indonesia: The role of financial literacy and technology acceptance. *Journal of Entrepreneurship in Emerging Economies, 15*(4), 1230–1250. DOI: 10.1108/JEEE-02-2022-0090

Rambaud, A. (2024). How Can Accounting Reformulate the Debate on Natural Capital and Help Implement Its Ecological Approach? *International Journal of Political Economy, 53*, 67–95. DOI: 10.1080/08911916.2024.2321428

Ramos, E. R. A. (2024). Economía plateada: Development in Peru and its growing perspectives. *Economía y Sociedad, 29*(65), 1–24. DOI: 10.15359/eys.29-65.1

Rana, N. P., Luthra, S., Mangla, S. K., Islam, R., Roderick, S., & Dwivedi, Y. K. (2020). Barriers to adopting e-commerce in Indian SMEs: A combined DEMATEL and AHP approach. *Technological Forecasting and Social Change, 152*, 119908. DOI: 10.1016/j.techfore.2019.119908

Ranjan, R. (2024). Creating synergies between payments for ecosystem services, green bonds, and catastrophe insurance markets for enhanced environmental resilience. *Land Use Policy*. Advance online publication. DOI: 10.1016/j.landusepol.2023.106970

Rasset, P., Mange, J., & Augustinova, M. (2024). What do we really know about age-related stereotypes and well-being of older adults? A commentary on the state of the art. *Frontiers in Psychology, 15*, 1358403. DOI: 10.3389/fpsyg.2024.1358403 PMID: 38807961

Ravasi, D., Rindova, V., & Stiglianithe, I. (2019). Stuff of legend: History, memory, and the temporality of organizational identity construction. *Academy of Management Journal, 62*(5), 1523–1555. DOI: 10.5465/amj.2016.0505

Regalado, F., Ortet, C. P., Costa, L. V., Santos, C., & Veloso, A. I. (2023). Assessing older adults' perspectives on digital game-related strategies to foster active and healthy ageing. *Media and Communication, 11*(3), 88–100. DOI: 10.17645/mac.v11i3.6796

Rhodes, A., & McNichols, C. C. (2025). Aging in Place and Healthcare Equity: Using Community Partnerships to Influence Health Outcomes. *Health Care, 13*. Advance online publication. DOI: 10.3390/healthcare13101132 PMID: 40427968

Ribeiro, A., Soares, R., Barbosa, L., Silva, A., Ferreira, R., Terroso, S., Andriolli, A. C., Silva, L., & Ribeiro, C. A. (2024). Green Environments and Healthy Aging: Analyzing the Role of Green Infrastructure in the Functional Well-Being of Seniors A Pilot Study. *International Journal of Environmental Research and Public Health, 22*. Advance online publication. DOI: 10.3390/ijerph22010035 PMID: 39857487

Rizzo, A., Habibipour, A., & Ståhlbröst, A. (2021). Transformative thinking and urban living labs in planning practice: A critical review and ongoing case studies in Europe. *European Planning Studies*, *29*(10), 1739–1757. DOI: 10.1080/09654313.2021.1911955

Rocha de Jesus Fernandes, A., & Lanza Queiroz, B. (2024). Aging, education and some other implications for the silver dividend in developing countries: Evidence from Brazil. *The Journal of the Economics of Ageing*, *27*, 100497. DOI: 10.1016/j.jeoa.2023.100497

Rogers, E. M. (2003). *Diffusion of innovations* (5th ed.). Free Press.

Rosa, G. B., & Ourique, M. (2024). Clean-up actions as catalysts for sustainability and physical activity promotion. *European Journal of Public Health*, *34*. Advance online publication. DOI: 10.1093/eurpub/ckae144.1369

Rosen, C., & Case, J. (2022). *Ownership: Reinventing companies, capitalism, and who owns what*. Berrett Koehler.

Rosen, C., Case, J., & Staubus, M. (2005). Every employee an owner. Really. *Harvard Business Review*, *83*(6), 122–130. PMID: 15938443

Roszkowska, E. (2020). Similarity of regions in terms of the elderly population-proposition of a measure. *Optimum. Economic Studies*, *2*(100), 148–162. DOI: 10.15290/oes.2020.02.100.11

Rothermund, K. (2024). Age stereotypes: Dimensions, origins, and consequences. *Current Opinion in Psychology*, *53*, 101577. DOI: 10.1016/j.copsyc.2023.101747 PMID: 38035656

Rothschild & Co. (2024). Silver economy: The age of opportunity. https://www.rothschildandco.com/en/newsroom/insights/2024/12/thematic-insights-silver-economy-the-age-of-opportunity/

Rowe, J. W., & Kahn, R. L. (1987). Human aging: Usual and successful. *Science*, *237*(4811), 143–149. PMID: 3299702

Ryder, N. B. (1985). The Cohort as a Concept in the Study of Social Change. In Mason, W. M., & Fienberg, S. E. (Eds.), *Cohort Analysis in Social Research*. Springer., DOI: 10.1007/978-1-4613-8536-3_2

Ryszawska, B., Rozwadowska, M., Ulatowska, R., Pierzchała, M., & Szymański, P. (2021). The power of co-creation in the energy transition — DART model in citizen energy communities projects. *Energies*, *14*(17), 5266. DOI: 10.3390/en14175266

Sadana, R., Soucat, A., & Beard, J. (2018). Universal health coverage must include older people. *Bulletin of the World Health Organization*, *96*, 2–2. DOI: 10.2471/BLT.17.204214 PMID: 29403091

Sánchez-González, D., & Egea-Jiménez, C. (2021). *Outdoor Green Spaces and Active Ageing from the Perspective of Environmental Gerontology*. 235–251. https://doi.org/DOI: 10.1007/978-3-030-58031-5_14

Sauer, S. (2013). *User innovativeness in living laboratories: Everyday user improvisations with ICTs as a source of innovation* (Doctoral dissertation, University of Twente). https://research.utwente.nl/files/6060272/thesis_S_Sauer.pdf

Scharmer, O. (2025) The Art of Social Innovation. https://aositoronto.weebly.com/theory-u.html accessed 03/24/25/

Scharmer, C. O. (2018). *The essentials of theory U: Core Principles and Applications*. Berrett-Koehler Publishers.

Scharmer, C. O., & Kaufer, K. (2025). *Presencing: 7 practices for transforming self, society, and business*. Berrett-Koehler Publishers.

Scheese, R. (2021). *More than a company: Leading a values-based ecosystem*. Advantage.

Schein, E. H. (2004). *Organizational culture and leadership* (3rd ed.). Jossey-Bass.

Schultz, T. W. (1961). Investment in human capital. *The American Economic Review*, *51*(1), 1–17. http://links.jstor.org/sici?sici=0002-8282%28196103%2951%3A1%3C1%3AIIHC%3E2.0.CO%3B2-4

Schulz, R., Wahl, H. W., Matthews, J. T., De Vito Dabbs, A., Beach, S. R., & Czaja, S. J. (2015). Advancing the aging and technology agenda in gerontology. *The Gerontologist*, *55*(5), 724–734. DOI: 10.1093/geront/gnu071 PMID: 25165042

Schumpeter, J. A. (1942). *Capitalism, socialism and democracy*. Harper & Brothers.

Schuurman, D. (2015). *Bridging the gap between open and user innovation? Exploring the value of living labs as a means to structure user contribution and manage distributed innovation* (Doctoral dissertation). Ghent University & Vrije Universiteit Brussel. https://biblio.ugent.be/publication/5931264

Seah, B., Espnes, G., Ang, E., Lim, J. Y., Kowitlawakul, Y., & Wang, W. (2020). Supporting the mobilization of health assets among older community dwellers residing in senior-only households in Singapore: A qualitative study. *BMC Geriatrics*, *20*. Advance online publication. DOI: 10.1186/s12877-020-01810-6 PMID: 33076833

Secretariat, A. S. E. A. N. (2024, March 18). *Old age poverty and active ageing in ASEAN: Trends and opportunities. The ASEAN Magazine*. Retrieved from https://theaseanmagazine.asean.org/article/old-age-poverty-and-active-ageing-in-asean-trends-and-opportunities/

Senior Eco-Nect Project. (2024). Horizon Europe project. https://www.senior-eco-nect.com

Sharma, R., & Sheth, J. (2023). Resurgence of e-commerce in post-pandemic India: A consumer behavior perspective. *Journal of Retailing and Consumer Services, 70*, 103113. DOI: 10.1016/j.jretconser.2022.103113

Shemshad, M., Synowiec, A., Kopyra, M., & Benedek, Z. (2025). The Community-Driven Ecosystem Resilience and Equity Framework: A Novel Approach for Social Resilience in Ecosystem Services. *Sustainability*. Advance online publication. DOI: 10.3390/su17083452

Shestakova, N. N., Djanelidze, M. G., & Skvortsova, M. B. (2022). Prospects for silver economy development in the Russian megapolis. *Advances in Gerontology, 35*(6), 948–956. PMID: 36905600

Shrestha, S. T., & Ghosh, A. (2025). Enhancing Elderly Care with AI: A Review of Artificial Intelligence and Machine Learning Applications. *SoutheastCon, 2025*, 900–905. DOI: 10.1109/SoutheastCon56624.2025.10971504

Shrivastava, P., & Ali, S. S. A. S. S. (2025). Analyzing the impact of aging populations on healthcare system sustainability. *Journal of Neonatal Surgery*. Advance online publication. DOI: 10.52783/jns.v14.1554

Silver Economy Innovation. (2024). *Silver Economy meets Innovation: Aging Better, Together*. https://silvereconomyinnovation.com/

Simon, C. (2025). *Rising birth rates no longer tied to economic prosperity*. Harvard Gazette. https://news.harvard.edu/gazette/story/2025/10/rising-birth-rates-no-longer-tied-to-economic-prosperity/

Singapore Department of Statistics. (2025). *Population and population structure — latest data*. https://www.singstat.gov.sg/find-data/search-by-theme/population/population-and-population-structure/latest-data

Singh, A., Bothra, V., Sen, A., & Chakraborty, D. (2025). Navigating the Digital Marketplace: Understanding the E-Commerce Adoption Journey of Emergent Users in India. *Proceedings of the ACM on Human-Computer Interaction, 9*(5). Advance online publication. DOI: 10.1145/3743728

Singh, S., & Hess, T. (2022). Digital transformation strategies of Indian SMEs: A resource-based view. *Information & Management, 59*(8), 103675. DOI: 10.1016/j.im.2022.103675

Sixsmith, A., & Sixsmith, J. (2008). Ageing in Place in the United Kingdom. *Ageing International, 32*, 219–235. DOI: 10.1007/s12126-008-9019-y

Siyakhula Living Lab. (n.d.). *About us.* https://www.siyakhulall.com/about-us

Slama, M. E., & Tashchian, A. (1985). Selected Socioeconomic and Demographic Characteristics Associated with Purchasing Involvement. *Journal of Marketing, 49*, 72–82. DOI: 10.1177/002224298504900107

Slowey, M., & Zubrzycki, T. (2018). *Living longer, learning longer – working longer? Implications for new workforce dynamics.* Dublin City University., https://www.dcu.ie/sites/default/files/staff/2022-02/Living%20longer%2C%20learning%20longer%20-%20working%20longer%3F%20Implications%20for%20new%20workforce%20dynamics_final%20report_0.pdf

Smallbone, D., & Welter, F. (2012). Entrepreneurship and institutional change in transition economies: The Commonwealth of Independent States, Central and Eastern Europe and China compared. *Entrepreneurship and Regional Development, 24*(3-4), 215–233. DOI: 10.1080/08985626.2012.670914

Smith, A. W. (2021). *Digital age: a study of older adults' user experiences with technology* [unpublished dissertation]. Purdue University, Indiana, USA. https://doi.org/DOI: 10.25394/PGS.15044157.v1

Socci, M., Clarke, D., & Principi, A. (2020). Active Aging: Social Entrepreneuring in Local Communities of Five European Countries. *International Journal of Environmental Research and Public Health, 17*(7), 2440. DOI: 10.3390/ijerph17072440 PMID: 32260209

Social Gifting. (2023, March 2). *Japan X Singapore — Ageing well with innovative Japanese tech (What we can learn from Japan on ageing population).* https://www.social-gifting.com/en-gb/blogs/news/what-we-can-learn-from-japan-on-ageing-population

Song, S. (2019). Challenges in Technology, Aging, and Market Transparency. *Chinese Economy, 52*(6), 423–426. DOI: 10.1080/10971475.2019.1617942

Sosa, A. L., Brucki, S. M. D., Crivelli, L., & Lopera, F. J.. (2024). Advancements in dementia research, diagnostics, and care in Latin America: Highlights from the 2023 Alzheimer's Association International Conference satellite symposium in Mexico City. *Alzheimer's & Dementia, 20*(7), 5009–5026. DOI: 10.1002/alz.13850

Souza, M. S. E., & Machado, C. (2018). [Governance, intersectoriality and social participation in public policy: The National Council on the Rights of the Elderly]. *Ciencia & Saude Coletiva, 23*(10), 3189–3200. DOI: 10.1590/1413-812320182310.14112018 PMID: 30365839

Spinelli, G., Weaver, P., Marks, M., & Victor, C. (2019). Making a case for creating living labs for aging-in-place: Enabling socially innovative models for experimentation and complementary economies. *Frontiers in Sociology, 4*, 19. DOI: 10.3389/fsoc.2019.00019

Stavros, J. M., Godwin, L. N., & Cooperrider, D. L. (2016). Appreciative inquiry: Organization development and the strengths revolution. In Rothwell, W. J., Stavros, J. M., & Sullivan, R. L. (Eds.), *Practicing organization development: Leading transformation and change* (4th ed., pp. 96–116). John Wiley and Sons., DOI: 10.1002/9781119176626.ch6

Sterman, J. D. (1989). Deterministic chaos in an experimental economic system. *Journal of Economic Behavior & Organization, 12*(1), 1–28. DOI: 10.1016/0167-2681(89)90074-7

Stichting Co-VAL. (n.d.). *ZorgLab – Ageing in Place Aalst.* https://www.co-val.eu/case-studies/blog/project/zorglab-ageing-in-place-aalst/

Stjernberg, M., Sigurjónsdóttir, H. R., & Wøien Meijer, M. (2021). *Unlocking the potential of silver economy in the Nordic Region*. Nordregio.

Storz, C., & Pascha, W. (2011). Japan's silver market: Creating a new industry under uncertainty. In C. Storz, M. Taube, & W. Pascha (Eds.), *Institutional Variety in East Asia* (pp. 222–267). Edward Elgar Publishing.

Stouten, J., Rousseau, D. M., & De Cremer, D. (2018). Successful organizational change: Integrating the management practice and scholarly literatures. *The Academy of Management Annals, 12*(2), 752–788. DOI: 10.5465/annals.2016.0095

Stutzer, M. J. (1980). Chaotic dynamics and bifurcation in a macro model. *Journal of Economic Dynamics & Control, 2*, 353–376. DOI: 10.1016/0165-1889(80)90070-6

Stypińska, J. (2018). The enterprising self: A panacea for all or a new fictitious social role for older adults? The analysis of European policies for senior entrepreneurship. *Journal of Population Ageing, 11*(1), 43–65. DOI: 10.1007/s12062-017-9214-2

Stypińska, J., Franke, A., & Myrczik, J. (2019). Senior Entrepreneurship: The Unrevealed Driver for Social Innovation. *Frontiers in Sociology, 4*. Advance online publication. DOI: 10.3389/fsoc.2019.00030 PMID: 33869354

Sudbury-Riley. Lynn, A Multivariate Segmentation Model of Senior Consumers (December 3, 2009). *Journal of Consumer Marketing*, 26/4 (2009), 251–262, Available at SSRN: https://ssrn.com/abstract=2362843

Sumner, J., Chong, L. S., Bundele, A., & Lim, Y. W. (2021). Co-designing technology for aging in place: A systematic review. *The Gerontologist, 61*(7), e395–e409. DOI: 10.1093/geront/gnaa064

Tamula, K. E., Navidad, N. C., Peregrino, T. D., Abing, M. J. J., Teves, M. R. Y., Capulong, C. M., & Laygan, R. M. C. (2024). The Effect of Green Bonds on Natural Capital Protection: Worldwide Evidence. *Journal of Economics Research and Social Sciences*. https://doi.org/DOI: 10.18196/jerss.v8i2.21604

Tan, K. (2022, July 6). Commentary: Singapore's ageing population does not only bring challenges. *CNA Lifestyle.* https://www.channelnewsasia.com/commentary/singapore-ageing-population-longevity-economy-opportunity-challenge-2790051

Teller, C., & Gittenberger, E. (2011). Patronage behaviour of elderly supermarket shoppers–antecedents and unobserved heterogeneity. *International Review of Retail, Distribution and Consumer Research, 21*(5), 483–499. DOI: 10.1080/09593969.2011.619701

Tercanli, H., & Jongbloed, B. (2022). A systematic review of the literature on living labs in higher education institutions: Potentials and constraints. *Sustainability, 14*(19), 12234. DOI: 10.3390/su141912234

Thangavel, P., & Chandra, B. (2024). Digital Immigrants Versus Digital Natives: Decoding Their E-commerce Adoption Behavior. *SAGE Open, 14*(4). Advance online publication. DOI: 10.1177/21582440241282437

The Lancet Healthy Longevity. (2021, April). Care for ageing populations globally. *The Lancet,* 2(4), e180. https://doi.org/DOI: 10.1016/s2666-7568(21)00064-7

Thompson, W. (1929). Population. *American Journal of Sociology, 34*, 959–975. DOI: 10.1086/214874

Tian, W., Cao, K., & Feng, Q. (2025). The Impact of Environmental Exposure on the Health of Older Adults: A Review From the GIScience Perspective. *Transactions in GIS, 29*. Advance online publication. DOI: 10.1111/tgis.70056

Tian, Y. J., Felber, N. A., Pageau, F., Schwab, D. R., & Wangmo, T. (2024). Benefits and barriers associated with the use of smart home health technologies in the care of older persons: A systematic review. *BMC Geriatrics, 24*, 152. DOI: 10.1186/s12877-024-04702-1

Toni, N., Goh, T., Edward, Y., & Calen. (2025). Supply Chain Sustainability And Financial Performance: The Role Of E-Commerce, Digital Banking, And Digital Marketing Of Smes. Economics - Innovative and Economics Research Journal, 13(1), 487–507. https://doi.org/DOI: 10.2478/eoik-2025-0027

Topol, E. J. (2015). *The patient will see you now: the future of medicine is in your hands* (Vol. 130). Basic Books.

Torbert, B. (2004). *Action inquiry: The secret of timely and transforming leadership.* Berrett-Koehler.

Toso, F., Brankaert, R., Hendriks, N., Lenaerts, L., & Wilkinson, A. (2023). Reflecting on Living Labs as multi-stakeholder collaborative networks to evaluate technological products for people living with dementia. *International Journal of Environmental Research and Public Health, 20*(3), 1673. DOI: 10.3390/ijerph20031673

Turkey Republic Ministry of Treasury and Finance. (2025). İstatistikler. https://www.hmb.gov.tr/kamu-finansmani-istatistikleri

U.S. Census Bureau. (2022, April 13). *Why study aging in Africa, region with world's youngest population?* https://www.census.gov/library/stories/2022/04/why-study-aging-in-africa-region-with-worlds-youngest-population.html

Udayana, A., Fatmawaty, A., Makbul, Y., Priowirjanto, E., Ani, N., Siswanto, E., Susanti, W., & Andriani, S. (2024). Investigating the role of e-commerce application and digital marketing implementation on the financial and sustainability performance: An empirical study on Indonesian SMEs. *International Journal of Data and Network Science, 8*(1), 167–178. DOI: 10.5267/j.ijdns.2023.10.007

UNFPA India & International Institute for Population Sciences. (2023, September 26). *India Ageing Report 2023: Caring for our elders — Institutional responses.* United Nations Population Fund India. https://india.unfpa.org/sites/default/files/pub-pdf/20230926_india_ageing_report_2023_web_version_.pdf

Unger, J. M., Rauch, A., Frese, M., & Rosenbusch, N. (2011). Human capital and entrepreneurial success: A meta-analytical review. *Journal of Business Venturing, 26*(3), 341–358. DOI: 10.1016/j.jbusvent.2009.09.008

United Nations Economic Commission for Europe. (2021, July). *Ageing in the digital era: Key actions to ensure digital inclusion of older persons* (Policy Brief No. 26). https://unece.org/sites/default/files/2021-07/PB26-ECE-WG.1-38_0.pdf

United Nations, Department of Economic and Social Affairs, Population Division. (2019). *World Population Ageing 2019 Highlights.* UN. https://digitallibrary.un.org/record/3846855

United Nations, Department of Economic and Social Affairs, Population Division. (2022). *World Population Prospects 2022: Summary of Results*. UN DESA/POP/2022/TR/NO. 3. Available at: https://www.un.org/development/desa/pd/sites/www.un.org.development.desa.pd/files/wpp2022_summary_of_results.pdf

University of Tokyo. (n.d.). *Creating the International Collaborative Living Laboratory: Towards an active aging society.* https://www.u-tokyo.ac.jp/adm/uci/en/projects/sdgs/projects_00112.html

Venkatesh, V., Thong, J. Y. L., & Xu, X. (2023). Unified Theory of Acceptance and Use of Technology: A decade of research. *Management Information Systems Quarterly*, *47*(2), 425–478. DOI: 10.25300/MISQ/2023/15210

Verbeek, H., Zwakhalen, S. M. G., Schols, J. M. G. A., Kempen, G. I. J. M., & Hamers, J. P. H. (2020). The Living Lab in Ageing and Long-Term Care: A sustainable model for translational research improving quality of life, quality of care and quality of work. *The Journal of Nutrition, Health & Aging*, *24*(1), 43–47. DOI: 10.1007/s12603-019-1288-5

Verloo, H., Lorette, A., Rosselet Amoussou, J., Gillès de Pélichy, E., Matos Queirós, A., von Gunten, A., & Perruchoud, E. (2021). Using living labs to explore needs and solutions for older adults with dementia: Scoping review. *JMIR Aging*, *4*(3), e29031. DOI: 10.2196/29031

Vibriyanti, D., Triyono, H., Hidayatina, A., Ikawati, D., Naviandi, U., Fasriani, A., & Yusuf, A. H. (2025). The COVID-19 pandemic and its impacts on changes in social and demographic conditions of Indigenous peoples. In Pamungkas, C., Surtiari, G. A. K., & Seftiani, S. (Eds.), *The impact of the pandemic on Indigenous People in Indonesia* (pp. 57–88). Springer., DOI: 10.1007/978-981-96-4222-9_4

Villares, L. (2020). *Blockchain and Conservation: Why Does It Matter*. 346–355. https://doi.org/DOI: 10.1007/978-3-030-55374-6_34

Villegas Plá, B. (2025). The care agenda in Latin America: Towards a new understanding of well-being? *Development and Change*, *56*(3), 426–456. DOI: 10.1111/dech.70001

Vimarlund, V., Nikula, N., & Nøhr, C. (2021). Business models and eHealth social innovations for social care services: Serving the two sides of the market. *Health Policy and Technology*, *10*(4), 100555.

Vines, J., Pritchard, G., Wright, P., Olivier, P., & Brittain, K. (2015). An age-old problem: Examining the discourses of ageing in HCI and strategies for future research. [TOCHI]. *ACM Transactions on Computer-Human Interaction, 22*(1), 1–27. DOI: 10.1145/2696867

von Hippel, E. (2005). *Democratizing innovation.* MIT Press. https://web.mit.edu/evhippel/www/democ.htm

von Hippel, E. (2011, September 21). *The user innovation revolution. MIT Sloan Management Review.* https://sloanreview.mit.edu/article/the-user-innovation-revolution/

von Hippel, E. (1988). *The sources of innovation.* Oxford University Press., https://web.mit.edu/evhippel/www-old/books/sources/SofI.pdf

Voorwinden, A., van Bueren, E., & Verhoef, L. (2023). Experimenting with collaboration in the Smart City: Legal and governance structures of Urban Living Labs. *Government Information Quarterly, 40*(4), 101875. DOI: 10.1016/j.giq.2023.101875

Wachholz, P. A., Morsch, P., Villalobos Dintrans, P., Barrientos-Calvo, I., Browne, J., Bello-Chavolla, O. Y., & Vega, E. (2024). Institutional care in four Latin American countries: The importance of fostering public information and evaluation strategies. *Pan American Journal of Public Health, 48*, e14. DOI: 10.26633/RPSP.2024.14

Walker, A. (2002). A strategy for active ageing. *International Social Security Review, 55*(1), 121–139. DOI: 10.1111/1468-246X.00118

Wang, Y., Zhao, W. & Meng, W. (2022). Bilateral effect of aging population on consumption structure: evidence from China. *Frontiers in Public Health,* 10, 01-16. https://doi.org/DOI: 10.3389/fpubh.2022.941485

Wang, H., Zhou, R., Luo, H., Liang, S., & Kong, Y. (2024). The impact of environmental protection tax on the health of middle-aged and older adults: Evidence from CHARLS data in China. *Frontiers in Public Health, 12*. Advance online publication. DOI: 10.3389/fpubh.2024.1446248 PMID: 39234086

Wang, L., Liang, J., & Wang, B. (2024). Population Aging and Sustainable Economic Development: An Analysis Based on the Role of Green Finance. *Finance Research Letters.* Advance online publication. DOI: 10.1016/j.frl.2024.106239

Wang, M., Huang, H., Xiong, J., Yuan, Z., & Zeng, K. (2023). Impact of ecological reserves on the local residents' health: Evidence from a natural experiment in China. *Social Science & Medicine, 336*. Advance online publication. DOI: 10.1016/j.socscimed.2023.116186 PMID: 37778142

Wang, P., & Zhao, T. (2024). Impact of population aging on corporate digital transformation strategies: An empirical investigation based on population census data from various provinces in China. *Finance Research Letters*, *67*, 105838. DOI: 10.1016/j.frl.2024.105838

Wang, Q., Zhang, Y., Ban, J., Zhu, H., Xu, H., & Li, T. (2021). The relationship between population heat vulnerability and urbanization levels: A county-level modeling study across China. *Environment International*, *156*. Advance online publication. DOI: 10.1016/j.envint.2021.106742 PMID: 34224997

Wang, S., Bolling, K., Mao, W., Reichstadt, J., Jeste, D., Kim, H.-C., & Nebeker, C. (2019). Technology to support aging in place: Older adults' perspectives. *Health Care*, *7*(2), 60. DOI: 10.3390/healthcare7020060

Wang, X., Li, Y., & Zhang, S. (2024). Association of social integration with cognitive function trajectories among older adults. *Frontiers in Aging Neuroscience*, *16*, 1322974. Advance online publication. DOI: 10.3389/fnagi.2023.1322974 PMID: 38274988

Wang, Z. (2025). Technological innovations in the silver economy: AI-driven financial management, smart products, and entrepreneurial support for aging populations. *Applied and Computational Engineering*, *118*, 101–106. DOI: 10.54254/2755-2721/2025.20844

Weber, M. (2019). How the City of Utrecht develops a Health and Equity in all Policies approach. *European Journal of Public Health*. Advance online publication. DOI: 10.1093/eurpub/ckz185.733

Weber, P., & Schaper, M. (2004). Understanding the grey entrepreneur. *Journal of Enterprising Culture*, *12*(2), 147–164. DOI: 10.1142/S0218495804000121

Weissbourd, J., Conway, M., & Klein, J. (2021). *Race and gender wealth equity and the role of employee share ownership*. https://www.aspeninstitute.org/wp-content/uploads/2023/05/Race-and-Gender-Wealth-Equity-and-the-Role-of-Employee-Share-Ownership.pdf accessed November 27, 2025

Wierzbicka, W., & Farelnik, E. (2024). Population aging and the potential for developing a silver economy in the Polish national cittaslow network. *Sustainability*, *16*, 1–19. DOI: 10.3390/su16166768

Wiklander, M. S. (2025). *Inner growth as a team sport: Unlocking capability to create impact and smarter organizations*. Icebug AB.

Wilckens, M. R., Wöhrmann, A. M., Deller, J., & Wang, M. (2021). Organizational practices for the aging workforce: Development and validation of the Later Life Workplace Index. *Work, Aging and Retirement*, *7*(4), 352–386. https://doi.org/10.1093/workar/waaa012

Wildman, J., McMeekin, P., Grieve, E., & Briggs, A. (2016). Economic evaluation of integrated new technologies for health and social care: Suggestions for policy makers, users and evaluators. Social Science &amp. *Medicine*, *169*, 141–148. DOI: 10.1016/j.socscimed.2016.09.033 PMID: 27721138

Wilson, L., Alexander, A., & Lumbers, M. (2004). Food Access and Dietary Variety Among Older People. *International Journal of Retail & Distribution Management*, *32*, 109–122. DOI: 10.1108/09590550410521789

Wong, A., Bayuo, J., Wong, F., Yuen, W. S., Lee, A. Y. L., Chang, P. K., & Lai, J. C. (2022). Effects of a Nurse-Led Telehealth Self-care Promotion Program on the Quality of Life of Community-Dwelling Older Adults: Systematic Review and Meta-analysis. *Journal of Medical Internet Research*, *24*. Advance online publication. DOI: 10.2196/31912 PMID: 35311680

Wood, G., Pykett, J., Daw, P., Agyapong-Badu, S., Banchoff, A., King, A., & Stathi, A. (2022). The Role of Urban Environments in Promoting Active and Healthy Aging: A Systematic Scoping Review of Citizen Science Approaches. *Journal of Urban Health*, *99*, 427–456. DOI: 10.1007/s11524-022-00622-w PMID: 35587850

World Health Organization [WHO]. (2021). Ageing and health. https://www.who.int/news-room/fact-sheets/detail/ageing-and-health

World Health Organization. (2002). *Active ageing: A policy framework* (WHO/NMH/NPH/02.8). World Health Organization. https://iris.who.int/handle/10665/67215

World Health Organization. (2025, October 1). *Ageing and health*. https://www.who.int/news-room/fact-sheets/detail/ageing-and-health

Worth, T. (2024, April 25). Are robots the solution to the crisis in older-person care? *Nature*. Advance online publication. DOI: 10.1038/d41586-024-01184-4

Wu, M., Xue, Y., & Ma, C. (2025). The association between the digital divide and health inequalities among older adults in China: Nationally representative cross-sectional survey. *Journal of Medical Internet Research*, *27*(1), e62645. DOI: 10.2196/62645

Wu, W., Ying, S., & Wu, Y. (2025). Silver economy industry market consumption characteristics research. *Journal of Modern Social Sciences*, *2*(1), 94–98. DOI: 10.71113/JMSS.v2i1.187

Yang, R., Gao, S., & Jiang, Y. (2024). Digital divide as a determinant of health in the U.S. older adults: Prevalence, trends, and risk factors. *BMC Geriatrics*, *24*, 1027. Advance online publication. DOI: 10.1186/s12877-024-05612-y

Yap, Y.-Y., Tan, S.-H., & Choon, S.-W. (2022). Elderly's intention to use technologies: A systematic literature review. *Heliyon*, *8*(1), e08765. DOI: 10.1016/j.heliyon.2022.e08765

Yasuoka, M., Akasaka, F., Kimura, A., & Ihara, M. (2018). Living labs as a methodology for service design—An analysis based on cases and discussions from a systems approach viewpoint. In D. Marjanović, M. Štorga, S. Škec, N. Bojčetić, & N. Pavković (Eds.), *DS 92: Proceedings of the DESIGN 2018 15th International Design Conference* (pp. 127–136). Design Society. https://doi.org/DOI: 10.21278/idc.2018.0350

Yin, Y., Pei, E., & Ranchhod, A. (2013). The shopping experience of older supermarket consumers. *Journal of Enterprise Information Management*, *26*(4), 444–471. DOI: 10.1108/JEIM-05-2013-0025

Yi, P. (2023). *Chinas Population Aging: Economic Problems, Solutions and Prospect*. Advances in Economics, Management and Political Sciences., DOI: 10.54254/2754-1169/32/20231570

Yoon, C., Cole, C. A., & Lee, M. P. (2009). Consumer decision making and aging: Current knowledge and future directions. *Journal of Consumer Psychology*, *19*(1), 2–16. DOI: 10.1016/j.jcps.2008.12.002

Yuan, Z., Wang, Y., Sun, T., & Xu, H. (2025). Democratizing Data Analytics Products to Drive SME Growth: A Natural Experiment. *Manufacturing & Service Operations Management*, *27*(4), 1053–1067. DOI: 10.1287/msom.2024.1138

Zaidi, A., Gasior, K., Zolyomi, E., Schmidt, A., Rodrigues, R., & Marin, B. (2017). Measuring active and healthy ageing in Europe. *Journal of European Social Policy*, *27*(2), 138–157. DOI: 10.1177/0958928716676550

Zangwill, W. I. (1966). A deterministic multi-period production scheduling model with backlogging. *Management Science*, *13*(1), 105–119. DOI: 10.1287/mnsc.13.1.105

Zhang, C., Liu, S., Chen, G., & Harper, S. (2024). Green finance and the silver economy: Catalyzing China's low-carbon development. *Frontiers in Environmental Science*, *12*, 1406812. DOI: 10.3389/fenvs.2024.1406812

Zhang, Q. (2023). An interpretable biological age. *The Lancet. Healthy Longevity*, *4*(12), e662–e663. DOI: 10.1016/S2666-7568(23)00213-3

Zhang, T., Stough, R., & Gerlowski, D. (2022). Digital exposure, age, and entrepreneurship. *The Annals of Regional Science*, *69*(3), 633–681. PMID: 35466286

Zhang, Y., Leuk, J. S. P., & Teo, W. (2022). Domains, Feasibility, Effectiveness, Cost, and Acceptability of Telehealth in Aging Care: Scoping Review of Systematic Reviews. *JMIR Aging*, *6*. Advance online publication. DOI: 10.2196/40460 PMID: 37071459

# About the Contributors

**Zyed Achour** is a Senior Lecturer at the National Institute of Labor and Social Studies, University of Carthage. He holds a Master's degree in Management Sciences from the University of Bordeaux (France) and a Ph.D. in Management Sciences from the University of Tunis. His research lies at the intersection of corporate social responsibility, labor studies, sustainable development, trade unionism, gender diversity, and strategic human resource management. He has edited and coordinated several interdisciplinary academic volumes, contributing to cross-disciplinary scholarly dialogue. His work has been published primarily in peer-reviewed international journals, as well as in scholarly book chapters, and is recognized for its analytical rigor and contribution to contemporary organizational and societal debates. He is a graduate of the Publons Academy.

**Ihsen Abid** holds a Ph.D. in Management Sciences with a specialization in Finance. She is an academic researcher and lecturer whose work focuses on finance, banking, financial management, and economic development. Her research examines financial sector dynamics, banking systems, and applied financial analysis, with particular attention to corporate finance and the role of financial institutions in supporting sustainable economic growth. Dr. Abid has published in peer-reviewed journals, and her research is characterized by a strong policy-oriented and development-focused perspective.

***

**Lawal Abdulwahab Olamilekan** has a PhD in Economics from the Universiti Brunei Darussalam, School of Business and Economics (AACSB-accredited). He holds a Master's degree in Health Economics and a Bachelor's in Economics Education from Taraba State University, Nigeria. His research interests span natural resource economics, health economics, development, and macroeconomics, particularly in Africa and emerging economies. With over six years of academic experience, he has taught and supervised students across Nigeria, Somalia, Somaliland, and Brunei. His teaching expertise covers economics, management, and public health, while his research contributions include conference papers, journal articles, and book chapters. Lawal's proficiency in quantitative and qualitative methodologies, coupled with his advanced skills in econometric modelling and using software such as Stata, SPSS, and EViews, instills confidence in his technical abilities. He is a member of the World Economics Association and the Institute of Chartered Economists of Nigeria. He continues to engage in collaborative research that bridges health policy, governance, and economic development to provide evidence-based insights for sustainable growth.

**Cecile G. Betit** (Ph.D.) is an Independent Researcher, whose two major studies involve Vermont Towns' selectboard members and the Carris Companies transition to employee ownership and governance. These studies share a focus on the roots of values and interests in social change. In addition to published articles, she has presented internationally on the Carris transition, is working on a forthcoming volume and was awarded a Louis O. Kelso Fellowship. Dr. Betit holds certifications in Leadership for Change, Appreciative Inquiry, Spiral Dynamics Integral and Strategic Planning. Professionally, she has experience as a faculty member on all levels, and as a high school principal, college administrator, VP for administration for a regional accrediting association and consulting for groups and businesses in organization development. Elected to her town's selectboard, Dr. Betit has also served on state committees and boards of directors. She lives in central Vermont.

**Vikas Garg**, PhD, has an almost 20+ years of experience and has more than 10 PhD scholars under his guidance. He has published numerous research papers in various Scopus and ABDC indexed international and national journals. He is acting as Associate Editor of the Journal of Sustainable Finance and Investment, (indexed in the WoS and Scopus). He is also acting as the Book Series Editor for Taylor and Francis for three books series: Technology Innovations: Strategies for Business Sustainability and Growth; Emerging Trends in Technology in Management and Commerce; and Electronic Commerce Management for Business. He has been working with new innovative ideas in the field of patents and copyrights. He has been the lead organizer in conducting various international conferences, workshops, and case study competitions, including those affiliated with IEEE. He has been conferred with many national and international awards for being best academician, researcher, and employee.

**Oner Gumus** graduated from Anadolu University Department of Economics in English in 2010, from Anadolu University Department of Public Finance in 2015, from Anadolu University Justice Associate Degree Program in 2018, and from Atatürk University Civil Air Transportation Management Associate Degree Program in 2024. He received a master's degree in public finance from Kutahya Dumlupinar University in 2014, a master's degree in economics from Kutahya Dumlupinar University in 2018, and a doctorate degree from the same university in 2020. The author continues his studies as an Assistant Professor at Kutahya Dumlupinar University Tavsanli Vocational School. He has authored/co-authored books and book chapters, many journal and conference papers. His research areas include public finance, economics, and taxation.

**Deepak Gupta** is a distinguished academician with over 20 years of teaching experience and expertise in Computer Science and Engineering. He holds a Ph.D. in Computer Engineering and has an extensive research portfolio, including many international journal papers, multiple conference proceedings, and several books. His research interests span machine learning, artificial intelligence, and data mining. Currently, Dr. Gupta serves as an Associate Professor and Head of Department of CSE (Emerging Branches) at ITM Gwalior, MP, India. He has also contributed significantly to the field through patents and copyrights and actively engages as a reviewer, conference chair and editor.

**Francesca Negri**, PhD, is Assistant Professor at the Catholic University of Sacred Heart (UCSC), where she studies and teaches Retail & Trade Marketing and Digital Marketing in the DISES Department (Piacenza - Italy). She also strictly works with REM Lab, a research centre focused on Trade Marketing innovation. On these topics she authored national and international contributions, also taking part in academic and managerial conferences.

**Y. Dasaratha Rami Reddy** is currently working in Chitanya Bharathi Institute of Technology, Proddatur as Professor in Computer Science and Engineering Department. He completed his M.Tech(CSE) from Acharya Nagarjuna University and was awarded with Ph.D. from Bharath University in 2016. He published more than 20 research papers in National and International journals, he published 5 patents to his credit and also participated in 15 National and International Conferences. He taught all Computer science and Machine Learning subjects for Undergraduate and Post graduate students. He has a stint of 22 years of experience in various reputed colleges and universities at various academic and administrative positions.

**Göran Roos** is a globally recognised expert in intellectual capital management, manufacturing competitiveness, industry policy, and innovation systems. With around 19,000 Google citations and more than 300 publications, he has established himself as a leading authority on strategic management, economic complexity, and sustainable industrial development. Academic Credentials and Appointments Professor Roos holds a PhD from the University of South Australia (2019), an MBA from INSEAD (1989), and an MSc in Engineering Physics from Chalmers University of Technology (1982). His current academic positions and fellowships include: Adjunct Professor at the Institute for Sustainability, Energy and Resources (ISER), The University of Adelaide (2023-2025) Fellow of the Australian Academy of Technological Sciences and Engineering (ATSE) since 2014 Fellow of the Royal Swedish Academy of Engineering Sciences (IVA) since 2015 Areas of Expertise Intellectual Capital and Knowledge Management Professor Roos is a world-renowned expert in intellectual capital, having developed theories and implemented practical solutions that have shaped the

**S. Murugesan** is presently working as an Assistant Professor in the Department of Computer Science and Engineering at Saveetha Engineering College, Chennai, India. He has around 15 years of teaching experience and 1 year of industrial experience. He received his Bachelor of Engineering in Computer Science and Engineering from Anna University, Chennai in 2007, Master of Engineering in Software Engineering from Anna University, Tiruchirappalli in 2010 and obtained Ph.D., in Information and Communication Engineering from Anna University in 2023. He has published more than 20 papers in Reputed International and National Journals. His area of expertise includes Artificial Intelligence, Mobile AdHoc Network, Computational Theory and Database Management Systems.

# Index

## A



## C



## D



## E

# P



# R



# S



# U

www.ingramcontent.com/pod-product-compliance
Lightning Source LLC
LaVergne TN
LVHW062322300926
849161LV00007B/1540